INTERNATIONAL COMPARISONS OF PRODUCTIVITY AND CAUSES OF THE SLOWDOWN

INTERNATIONAL COMPARISONS OF PRODUCTIVITY AND CAUSES OF THE SLOWDOWN

edited by
John W. Kendrick

A Joint Publication of
American Enterprise Institute / Ballinger

BALLINGER PUBLISHING COMPANY • Cambridge, Massachusetts
A Subsidiary of Harper & Row, Publishers, Inc.

iv

International Standard Book Number: 0-88410-934-8

Library of Congress Catalog Card Number: 84-3107

Printed in the United States of America

Library of Congress Cataloging in Publication Data

Main entry under title:
    International comparisons of productivity and causes of
the slowdown.

    Includes bibliographical references and index.
    1. Industrial productivity—Congresses. 2. Economic history—
1945-   —Congresses. I. Kendrick, John W. II. American
Enterprise Institute for Public Policy Research.
HC79.I52158   1984   338'.06   84-3107
ISBN 0-88410-934-8

CONTENTS

List of Figures   ix

List of Tables   xi

Introduction—*John W. Kendrick*   xvii

Chapter 1
Accounting for Slower Economic Growth:
An Update—*Edward F. Denison*   1

Comments—*Edward Wolff*   47

Chapter 2
Comparative Analysis of the Productivity Situation in
the Advanced Capitalist Countries—Angus Maddison   59

Comments—*Walter W. McMahon*   93

Chapter 3
The Diffusion of Economic Growth in the World
Economy, 1950-80—*Irving B. Kravis* and
Robert E. Lipsey   109

Comments—*Laurits R. Christensen*   153

v

Chapter 4
Trends and Cycles in Productivity, Unit Costs,
and Prices: An International Perspective—
Geoffrey H. Moore and *John P. Cullity*   157

Comments—*William H. Waldorf*   191

Chapter 5
International Comparison of Tax Rates and Their
Effects on National Income—*George S. Tolley* and
William B. Shear   197

Comments—*Charles S. Friedman*   227

Chapter 6
International Comparisons of Research and
Development Outlays and Indicators of Technological
Progress—*Rolf Piekarz, Eleanor Thomas,* and
Donna Jennings   235

Comments—*John K.L. Thompson*   275

Chapter 7
The Role of Energy in Productivity Growth—
Dale W. Jorgenson   279

Comments—*Ernst Berndt*   325

Chapter 8
The Contribution of Education to Economic Growth:
International Comparisons—*George Psacharopoulos*   335

Comments—*Theodore W. Shultz*   357

Chapter 9
U.S. and European Approaches to Improving Labor
Productivity and the Quality of Working Life—
Ted Mills   361

Comments—*Joji Arai*   393

Chapter 10
Where Are We in the Discussion? Retrospect and
Prospect—*Richard R. Nelson*   397

Index   411

About the Contributors   419

About the Editor   427

LIST OF FIGURES

3-1   Indexes of Real World GDP and of Real World GDP
       per Capita, 1950-80   124

4-1   Growth Rates in Labor Costs, Prices, Profits, and
       Productivity, Nonfarm Business—United States   158

4-2   Growth Rates in Labor Costs, Prices, Profits, and
       Productivity in Manufacturing—United Kingdom   162

4-3   Growth Rates in Labor Costs, Prices, Profits, and
       Productivity in Manufacturing—West Germany   164

4-4   Growth Rates in Labor Costs, Prices, Profits, and
       Productivity in Manufacturing—Japan   166

4-5   Recession Recovery Patterns: Productivity Costs,
       Prices, and Profits   168

4-6   Growth Rates in Productivity and in the Leading
       Indexes—Four Countries   174

4-7   International Reactions to the Productivity Slowdown   177

4-8   Growth Trends in Productivity, Compensation, Costs,
       and Prices, Nonfarm Business Section—United States,
       1948-81   182

6-1A   R&D as a Percentage of Gross Domestic Product for
           Six Large Industrial Nations, 1963–80   244

6-1B   R&D as a Percentage of Gross Domestic Product for
           Seven Small Industrial Nations, 1963–80   245

6-2   Total R&D for Thirteen Industrial Nations in Terms
           of 1975 Prices and Dollars, 1969, 1975, 1979   246

6-3   Annual R&D for Thirteen Industrial Nations in 1975
           Prices and Dollars, 1963–80   247

6-4A   Business-Funded R&D as a Percentage of
           Manufacturing Gross Domestic Product for Five
           Large Nations, 1964–78   252

6-4B   Business-Funded R&D as a Percentage of
           Manufacturing Gross Domestic Product for Five
           Small Nations, 1963–78   254

6-5   Business-Funded R&D as a Percentage of Gross Fixed
           Capital Formation in Manufacturing for Seven
           Industrial Nations, 1963–78   254

LIST OF TABLES

1-1   U.S. Nonresidential Business Sector: Growth Rates and Sources of Growth of Real National Income and National Income Per Person Employed, 1948–73 and 1973–81 (percentages)   4

1-2   Contributions to Growth Rates in Nonresidential Business: Summary of Changes from 1948–73 to 1973–81 (percentages)   7

1-3   U.S. Nonresidential Business Sector: Average Weights, Growth Rates, and Contributions of Factor Inputs, 1948–73 and 1973–81   9

1-4   Comparison of Weights on Gross and Net Bases   13

2-1   GDP Per Man-hour (annual average compound growth rates)   61

2-2   Conjuncture Indicators 1969–81 and 1929–38 (annual average compound growth rates)   63

2-3   Growth of Nonresidential Fixed Capital Stock Per Person Employed   65

2-4   Changes in the Inflation-Adjusted Industrial Share Index   65

2-5A   Energy Consumption per $1,000 of Real GDP (GDP in 1975 U.S. relative prices; energy in tons of oil equivalent)   67

2-5B   Energy "Productivity" (annual average compound growth rate)   68

2-6   The Convergence in Productivity Levels, 1950–81 (U.S. = 100.0 in specified year)   69

2-7   Research and Development Expenditure as Percentage of GDP   70

2-8   Impact of Structural Shift in Employment on Growth of GDP per Person Employed, 1950–81   71

2-9   Growth of GDP per Employee by Sector   73

2-10   Government Expenditure as Percentage of GDP at Current Prices   75

2-11   Impact of Changes in the Age/Sex Composition of Employment on Labor Productivity Growth Rates and on Productivity Levels   78

2-12   Denison and Kendrick Estimates of Sources of Labor Productivity Growth (annual average percentage point contribution to growth)   80

2-A1   A Comparison of Nominal and Real Levels of GDP and the Purchasing Power of Currencies in 1975   84

2-A2   Index of GDP in Constant Prices (1913 = 100)   84

2-A3   Employment (000s)   85

2-A4   Hours Worked per Person per Year   85

2-A5   Productivity Levels (GDP per man-hour) ($ at 1975 relative price levels and purchasing power)   86

2-A6   Midyear Nonresidential Fixed Capital Stock at Constant Prices (1950 = 100)   86

2-A7   Ratio of Trade in Goods and Services to GDP, 1950–80   87

2-A8   Employment Structure: Employment by Sector as Percentage of Total Employment, 1870–1981   87

2-A9   Government Expenditure as Percentage of GDP   88

3-1   Total Real GDP, Population and Per Capita Real
       GDP, Groups of Countries and the World, 1950 and
       1980 (GDP figures in 1975 international dollars)   113

3-2   Relative Levels of Real GDP Per Capita, 1950 and
       1980 (world = 100)   114

3-3   Comparison of PPP-Converted and Exchange-Rate-
       Converted GDPs Per Capita, 1975   115

3-4   Coefficients of Determination for 1950-80 Growth
       Rates Regressed against Real Per Capita GDP $, 1950   116

3-5   Real GDP Per Capita and Per Economically Active
       Persons, Groups of Countries, and the World, 1950
       and 1975   118

3-6   GDP in Relation to the Number of Workers and the
       Number of Adults, 1950 and 1975   119

3-7   Index of Labor Quality and Output Per Quality-
       Adjusted Member of the Labor Force, 1975   121

3-8   Annual Rates of Growth in GDP and GDP Per
       Capita, 1950-80   122

3-9   Per Annum Growth Rates, Industrial Countries,
       1900-75   125

3-10   Rates of Growth Per Decade in Total Product,
       Population, and Product Per Capita, Selected Less
       Developed Countries   125

3-11   Growth Rates for Industrial and Developing Countries   126

3-12   Comparison of Population Weighting with Results of
       Conventional Growth Rate Calculations   128

3-13   Growth Rates for Three Groups of Developing
       Market Economies, Classified by 1950 Per Capita
       GDP   128

3-14   Frequency Distribution of Countries and Population,
       According to the Rate of Growth in Real GDP Per
       Capita and Type of Country, 1950-52 to 1978-80   129

3-15   Annual Growth Rates in Total GDP, Selected Periods
       and Years, 1950-81   131

3-16   Annual Growth Rates in Per Capita GDP, Selected
       Periods and Years, 1950-81   132

3-17   Intertemporal Indexes of Real GDP Per Capita and
        Per Worker Groups of Countries and the World,
        Quinquennial Years 1950-75 (1950 = 100)   133

3A-1   Total Real GDP, Population and Per Capita Real
        GDP, Groups of Countries and the World,
        Quinquennial Years 1950-80 (GDP figures in 1975
        international dollars)   140

3A-2   World Gross Domestic Product (GDP and GDP Per
        Capita, by Country Groups, 1950-80 in 1975
        international dollars)   142

3A-3   Real GDP Per Capita and Per Economically Active
        Person, Groups of Countries, and the World,
        Quinquennial Years, 1950-75   145

4-1   Productivity Changes over Business Cycles, United
        States (percentage change at annual rate)   161

5-1   Summary of Tax Revenue, United States (in millions
        of dollars)   205

5-2   Summary of Tax Revenue, United Kingdom (in
        millions of pounds sterling)   207

5-3   Summary of Tax Revenue, France (in millions of
        French francs)   209

5-4   Summary of Tax Revenue, West Germany (in millions
        of Deutsche marks)   211

5-5   Summary of Tax Revenue, Japan (in billions of
        Japanese yen)   213

5-6   Effective Tax Rates on Physical Capital Earnings
        (percentage)   214

5-7   Effective Tax Rates on Human and R&D Investments,
        1977 (percentage)   215

5-8   Effective Tax Rates on Labor Earnings (percentage)   215

5-9   Effects of Taxation on Savings Using Growth Model
        with Physical Capital (percentage)   218

5-10   Effects of Taxation on Savings Using Growth Model
        with Physical, Human, and R&D Capital (percentage)   219

6-1   Percentage of Government Funds in National R&D
      Expenditures for Six Large Industrial Countries,
      1963-81   249

6-2   Percentage of Government Funds in National R&D
      Expenditures for Seven Small Industrial Countries,
      1970-79, Selected Years   249

6-3   Percentage of Business Funds in National R&D
      Expenditures for Six Large Industrial Countries,
      1963-81   250

6-4   Average Annual Real Growth of Business and
      Government-Funded R&D for Six Large Industrial
      Nations, 1964-72 and 1972-80 (percentage)   251

6-5   Research as a Percentage of R&D Expenditures for
      Ten Industrial Countries, Average for Available Years
      between 1967-77   255

6-6   Basic Research as a Percentage of R&D for Eight
      Industrial Nations, 1967-77, Selected Years   256

6-7   R&D in Five Industries as a Percentage of Total
      Manufacturing R&D in Nine Nations, Average for
      Available Years between 1963-64 and 1977   258

6-8   R&D in Five Industries as a Percentage of Business-
      Funded Manufacturing R&D in Nine Nations,
      Average for Available Years between 1963-64 and
      1977   259

6-9   Distribution of Government R&D Funding among
      Nine Social Objectives for Thirteen Industrial
      Nations, Average for 1975 and 1979   262

6-10 Distribution of Government R&D Funding Net of
      General University Funds among Nine Social
      Objectives for Ten Industrial Nations, Average for
      1975 and 1979   263

7-1   Industrial Sectors   286

7-2   Parameter Estimates   288

7-3   Classifications of Industries by Biases of Technical
      Change   303

8-1   The Contribution of Education to Economic Growth
      (percentage)   337

8-2   Economic Growth and Literacy (percentage)   338

8-3   Downward Bias of the Estimated Contribution of
       Education to Economic Growth Because of Omission
       of the Maintenance Component (percentage)   341

8-4   The Earnings Differential by Economic Sector   342

8-5   The Returns to Eduction by Sex (percentage)   343

8-6   Female Labor Force Participation by Level of
       Education (percentage)   343

8-7   Economic Growth and Life Expectancy   345

8-8   The Relationship between Education and Fertility:
       Results of Case Studies   346

8-9   The Effect of Literacy on Mortality, per 1,347
       population (percentage)   347

8-10   The Returns to Education by Region and Country
       Type (percentage)   349

9-A1   Industrial Democracy in Europe: Analysis by Country   386

9-A2   Selected Data on Labor in Europe: Analysis by
       Country   390

INTRODUCTION

John W. Kendrick

The causes and economic impacts of productivity growth within any given country can be understood on several levels. At the macroeconomic level, increase in productivity—defined as output per unit of all associated inputs—is the chief source of rising planes of living; it is a key variable in unit cost and price changes, both cyclically and secularly. More recently, growth accounting has been used to good effect to try to disentangle, measure, and weight the various causes of productivity change. Single-nation macroeconomic studies are facilitated by significant changes in trend rates of growth, and in recent years economists have had a field day in trying to explain the productivity slowdown that hit the United States and most other countries after 1973.

A second approach to understanding productivity growth, which can be pursued in greater or lesser detail, is the study of interindustry differences. These differences, working through relative price changes, are influential in generating changes in the industrial structure of the economy. Further, they provide a useful means of analyzing causal forces through multiple regressions with differences in levels or rates of change of those variables.

At the level of firms (or establishments) within industries, differences in levels or changes in productivity are a chief element in explaining differences or changes in profit rates. On the causal side, interfirm studies are a means of advancing the science or art of management.

At all of these levels, the results of studies confined to one country can be enhanced, and new insights obtained, by international comparisons. Because of insufficient data for most other countries, the study of com-

xvii

parative morphology relating to world productivity differences and changes has not progressed as far or as fast as studies of U.S. developments. Edward F. Denison's early study *Why Growth Rates Differ* (1967) used his pioneering growth accounting techniques to compare U.S. growth with that of eight other member countries of the Organization for Economic Cooperation and Development. He followed that work with a comparison of the growth rates of real product and productivity of the United States and Japan. The first study was based on estimates for the years 1950 through 1962, while the Japanese comparison was carried through 1966.

In 1981 I extended the Denison work through 1979, using a somewhat different framework, methodology, and group of countries. "International Comparisons of Recent Productivity Trends" (Kendrick 1981) indicated that a somewhat different set of forces accounted for the changes in productivity growth after 1960 than before—particularly the strength of international technological transfer and its role in allowing other countries to catch up with U.S. technology. It also indicated that the United States and all the other countries suffered a significant slowdown in productivity growth after 1973 for many of the same reasons. Moreover, my study convinced me that much could be learned by increasing the number of countries surveyed and by examining more deeply the causes of productivity change. It was to this end that I first began to sense a need for the conference whose papers and discussions comprise the present volume. It was a project that enjoyed at all stages of planning and organization the full support and sensible counsel of Thomas F. Johnson, director of economic policy studies at the American Enterprise Institute.

The papers and commentaries here follow the same order they did at the conference. The organizational structure is simple. The first four papers, presented the first day, describe recent productivity trends and cycles in the United States, in other industrialized nations, and in regional groupings of all countries in the world. The various causes of U.S. productivity growth and slowdown in growth, and the factors accounting for international differences in trends and cycles, are analyzed and evaluated in detail. One of the papers sets forth the interrelationships among productivity, wages, unit labor costs, and prices and their role in the business cycles in the United States and six other industrialized economies.

The five papers presented the second day examine forces affecting productivity—tangible investment, research and development, energy, education, and labor-management relations. The paper on energy focuses on energy's role in U.S. productivity trends by industry groupings, but the others employ a comparative, international approach.

In addition to the invited commentary on each paper published in this volume, a number of participants contributed written comments, and two contributed short papers. These will be available on request to me at AEI for the first year or so after publication of this volume. The comments were written by Martin Neil Baily and by Charles Taylor on the paper by Denison; by Piero Ferri and Francesco Silva on the paper by Maddison; by Gary C. Hufbauer on the paper by Tolley and Shear; by Michael F. Mohr and John A. Tatom on the paper by Jorgenson; and by John K.L. Thompson on the paper by Mills. The two contributed papers were "A Comparison of the U.S. and Japanese Productivity Slowdown," by Charles R. Hulten and Mieko Nishimizu, and "Assessing the Role of R&D Capital in U.S. Productivity Growth, 1949-1981," by Nestor E. Terleckyj. These individuals and the many others who contributed to the discussions from the floor added greatly to the intellectual stimulation derived from the conference.

It is not necessary to summarize the papers and comments in this introduction. Most of the papers contain a summary or conclusion, and in the final paper, Richard Nelson summarizes the highlights of each paper and evaluates the conference proceedings as a whole. He says that "A bit more light has been shed on the puzzle" and suggests several directions in which further advances in our understanding of productivity growth can be made. Doubtless, there will be many more volumes on the subject. But in my view this one is a milestone.

REFERENCES

Denison, Edward F. 1967. *Why Growth Rates Differ*. Washington, D.C.: The Brookings Institution.
Kendrick, John W. 1981. "International Comparisons of Recent Productivity Trends." In *Essays in Contemporary Economic Problems: Demand, Productivity, and Population, 1981-1982 Edition*, edited by William Fellner, pp. 125-170. Washington: American Enterprise Institute.

1 ACCOUNTING FOR SLOWER ECONOMIC GROWTH: AN UPDATE

Edward F. Denison[1]

The sharp retardation of productivity advance that battered all advanced economies and most industries during the last decade has been publicized in a host of articles, but its causes are not well understood. Serious research has been small compared to the costs of the setback. My own *Accounting for Slower Economic Growth: The United States in the 1970s* contributed, I hope constructively, to the discussion of American experience even though results were, in substantial part, inconclusive (Denison 1979a).

Published in 1979, that book provided some data through 1978, but detailed estimates of the sources of growth of national income and national income per person employed ended with 1976. This paper brings those estimates up-to-date for the nonresidential business sector. Many explanations of the slowdown of productivity growth have been advanced by others. *Accounting for Slower Economic Growth* reported and evaluated seventeen such explanations that, if correct, would affect the residual component of my series for output per unit of input. More recent discussions of some of these proposed explanations are examined here, as are procedures other analysts have used to assign capital a larger role in the slowdown than I do.

In the United States the pronounced slowdown of productivity growth—which in fact amounts to cessation or near-cessation of growth—dates from the 1973–74 change. I shall therefore focus on comparing changes since 1973 with earlier changes, those from 1948 to 1973. Although retardation as early as the late 1960s can be identified, it was small and easily explained as due in part to the drop in the intensity of use of employed labor and capital from a peak reached in 1965–66 and in part from developments that were

1

inevitable or even welcome. The latter included diminishing gains from the transfer of surplus farm labor to nonfarm jobs as the pool of such labor dwindled, an increased proportion of inexperienced workers among the employed as a result of changes in age distribution and entry of adult women into employment, and costs of new social regulation presumably thought to have benefits in excess of their costs.

For data, I rely on my own growth accounting series and the official national income and product accounts (NIPAs) of the Bureau of Economic Analysis. A planned update of the former series for The Brookings Institution is still a year in the future. For this paper I adopted series that have already been updated for the Brookings study and used shortcut methods to derive the rest of the series needed to complete preliminary estimates through 1981.[2]

A benchmark revision of the NIPAs was introduced in the December 1980 *Survey of Current Business* (Denison and Parker 1980:1–26). These data, including employment and capital stock estimates, are incorporated back to 1948 in the growth accounting series used here. Recent NIPA data are from the March 1982 *Survey*; revisions appearing in the July 1982 *Survey* are not used.[3] Revisions of the growth accounting estimates for reasons other than changes in the NIPAs have not, in general, been introduced prior to 1972. Some standard sources used in the growth accounting series were not available for 1981 when the estimates were made. The advantage of dealing with the longest possible post-1973 time period outweighs losses of accuracy resulting from shortcut methods and preliminary or incomplete data. Output is measured by real national income (net national product at factor cost). Definitions of series and estimating procedures are unchanged from *Accounting for Slower Economic Growth* except for the use of shortcut methods for some series in recent years.[4]

Before I turn to the sources of growth, a brief general description of economic performance is in order. In the *whole economy,* I estimate that the growth rate of potential national income fell by two-fifths, from 4.0 percent in 1948–73 to 2.4 percent in 1973–81. This drop occurred despite an increase from 1.6 percent to 2.4 percent in the growth rate of potential employment. On a potential basis, the growth rate of national income per person employed, which had been 2.3 percent in 1948–73, fell to zero.

Growth rates of employment and output were lower on an actual than on a potential basis in both periods because unemployment was higher, and employed resources were used less intensively, in 1973 than in 1948 and in 1981 than in 1973. However, changes in growth rates from the earlier to the later period on an actual basis were rather similar to those on a potential basis. That of actual national income fell from 3.7 percent in 1948–73 to 2.0 percent in 1973–81, that of actual employment rose from 1.5 to 1.9, and that of national income per person employed fell from 2.2 to 0.1. The nation's command over goods and services resulting from current production fared even worse than production itself because the terms of trade deteriorated as a result of higher oil prices. The growth rate of "command" per person employed fell from 2.2 percent to −0.2 percent.[5] The period after 1973 also featured high inflation, high unemployment, high interest rates, and frequent cyclical movements.

Changes in *nonresidential business* were even more pronounced than those in the economy as a whole. Acceleration of employment growth was from 1.2 percent a year in 1948–73 to 2.7 percent in 1973–81 for potential employment, and from 1.1 to 2.0 for actual employment. On a potential basis the growth rate of national income per person employed fell from 2.6 percent in 1948–73 to −0.2 percent in 1973–81. On an actual basis, the rates were 2.5 percent and −0.2 percent. It is this latter decline—in the growth of actual national income per person employed in nonresidential business—that the bulk of this paper will explore. During the 1973–81 period this series showed some variation, of course; it fell below its 1973 starting point from 1974 through 1976, wandered a little above it from 1977 through 1979, then fell below it again in 1980 and 1981. The growth rate of national income per labor hour was above that of national income per person employed but fell almost as much, from 3.0 percent to 0.4 percent.[6]

Within nonresidential business, the productivity slowdown was widespread. It appears in all major industry groups (i.e., mining, durable goods manufacturing, nondurable goods manufacturing, retail trade, etc.) except communication. For very detailed industries only a thin sample is available, from the Bureau of Labor Statistics, but three-fourths of the industries covered by data show retardation after 1973. The fraction is the same in manufacturing industries and nonmanufacturing industries. The productivity slowdown was, moreover, international in scope. After 1973 lower growth rates of gross domestic product per person employed in the whole economy and of output per hour in manufacturing appear in series for all industrial countries for which the Bureau of Labor Statistics reports and for per capita GNP in L.W. International Financial Research, Inc., series for all Eastern European countries.

CHANGES IN THE SOURCES OF GROWTH

Table 1–1 shows my estimates of the sources of growth in nonresidential business in 1948–73 and 1973–81. The left side refers to the sector's total output, as measured by national income, and the right to output per person employed. The right side differs from the left only because employment disappears as a source of growth and capital and land are measured per person employed. Contributions to growth made by changes in characteristics

Table 1-1. Nonresidential Business Sector: Growth Rates and Sources of Growth of Real National Income and National Income Per Person Employed, 1948–73 and 1973–81 (percentage points).

	Real National Income			Real National Income Per Person Employed		
	1948–73	1973–81	Change	1948–73	1973–81	Change
Sector national income	3.59	1.80	– 1.79	2.46	– 0.22	– 2.68
Total factor input	1.60	2.13	0.53	0.47	0.10	– 0.37
Labor	1.03	1.67	0.64	0.12	– 0.01	– 0.13
Employment	0.91	1.67	0.76	—	—	—
Hours	– 0.24	– 0.40	– 0.16	– 0.24	– 0.41	– 0.17
Average hours	– 0.41	– 0.49	– 0.08	– 0.41	– 0.49	– 0.08
Efficiency offset	0.06	0.07	0.01	0.06	0.06	0.00
Intergroup shift offset	0.11	0.02	– 0.09	0.11	0.02	– 0.09
Age-sex composition	– 0.17	– 0.21	– 0.04	– 0.17	– 0.21	– 0.04
Education	0.53	0.61	0.08	0.53	0.61	0.08
Capital	0.57	0.46	0.11	0.39	0.18	– 0.21
Inventories	0.15	0.08	– 0.07	0.10	0.01	– 0.09
Nonresidential structures and equipment	0.42	0.38	– 0.04	0.29	0.17	– 0.12
Land	0.00	0.00	0.00	– 0.04	– 0.07	– 0.03
Output per unit of input	1.99	– 0.33	– 2.32	1.99	– 0.32	– 2.31
Advances in knowledge and miscellaneous determinants	1.42	– 0.26	– 1.68	1.42	– 0.26	– 1.68
Improved resource allocation	0.37	0.04	– 0.33	0.37	0.04	– 0.33
Farm	0.26	0.06	– 0.20	0.26	0.06	– 0.20
Nonfarm self-employment	0.11	– 0.02	– 0.13	0.11	– 0.02	– 0.13
Legal and human environment	– 0.04	– 0.21	– 0.17	– 0.04	– 0.21	– 0.17
Pollution abatement	– 0.02	– 0.13	– 0.11	– 0.02	– 0.13	– 0.11
Worker safety and health	– 0.01	– 0.05	– 0.04	– 0.01	– 0.05	– 0.04

Dishonesty and crime	−0.01	−0.03	−0.02	−0.01	−0.03	−0.02
Economies of scale	0.42	0.30	−0.12	0.42	0.31	−0.11
Irregular factors	−0.18	−0.20	−0.02	−0.18	−0.20	−0.02
Weather in farming	0.00	0.02	0.02	0.00	0.02	0.02
Labor disputes	0.00	0.00	0.00	0.00	0.00	0.00
Intensity of demand	−0.18	−0.22	−0.04	−0.18	−0.22	−0.04

of labor and determinants of output per unit of input are the same on both sides of the table, except for trifling differences due to interaction terms and rounding. The contributions of all growth sources are direct estimates except for that of "advances in knowledge and miscellaneous determinants," which is obtained as a residual. Presentation in the form of contributions to growth rates makes it possible to compare periods of different length. My classification of output determinants is crucial to understanding of Table 1-1 (see Denison 1979a).

In *Accounting for Slower Economic Growth* the 1948-73 period, shown here as a unit, was subdivided into four time spans in order to separate periods of faster and slower growth of total potential national income in the whole economy. The periods and growth rates of total potential national income were:

1948-53	4.74
1953-64	3.21
1964-69	4.53
1969-73	3.79[7]

Both in the whole economy and in nonresidential business factor input was largely responsible for the changes in growth of potential output between these periods. Together with changes in the intensity of use of employed resources resulting from fluctuations in intensity of demand ("intensity of demand" in Table 1-1), factor input also largely accounted for changes in the growth rate of actual output. Directly estimated sources accounted for almost the entirety of changes in the growth rates of all output series; the residual was about the same size in all periods.

In contrast, components of output per unit of input, other than intensity of demand, were responsible for the drop in the growth rate of total nonresidential business national income after 1973 and most of the drop appears in the residual. Table 1-2 divides changes in growth rates among directly estimated sources that contributed more in the later period than in the earlier period, directly estimated sources that contributed less in the later period, and the residual. Although the residual series dominates the changes, reductions in contributions of directly estimated growth sources would, by themselves, have reduced the 1948-73 growth rate of national income per person employed by 1.10 percentage points or 45 percent.

I now examine the individual sources of growth of output per person employed, starting with the directly estimated sources that contributed most strongly to the slowdown in its growth.[8] The pattern of differences between 1948-73 and 1973-81 is broadly similar to that between 1948-73 and 1973-76 (Denison 1979a), but for many determinants extension of the post-1973 period from three years to eight has reduced the difference from 1948-73.

Table 1-2. Contributors to Growth Rates in Nonresidential Business: Summary of Changes from 1948-73 to 1973-81 (percentages).

	Change in Contributions	
	Real Sector NI	Real Sector NI Per Person Employed
Directly estimated determinants that:		
Contributed more in 1973-81	0.86	0.10
Contributed less in 1973-81	−0.97	−1.10
Residual series	−1.68	−1.68
Growth rate	−1.79	−2.68

Improved Resource Allocation

A smaller gain from improvement in resource allocation accounted for 0.33 percentage points of the decline in the growth rate, of which 0.20 points are related to farm labor and 0.13 points to nonfarm self employment. I think coverage of these two changes suffices to provide a substantially complete measure for changes in the allocation of resources in the aggregate. Misallocation in detail—the round pegs in the square holes problem—is not included.

Overallocation of labor to farming has been chronic, mainly because the demand for farm labor has been falling for many decades while the supply, though also falling, always lagged behind. Farming used about 14.2 percent of labor input in nonresidential business in 1948 and 4.3 percent in 1973. Hence the percentage of sector labor input that was misallocated to farming would have been reduced by seven-tenths (9.9 ÷ 14.2) even if the percentage of farm labor that was excessive had not declined—which it did. The farm percentage of the sector's national income in 1972 prices was smaller than its labor input percentage and declined much less: 3.0 percentage points as against 9.9 points. The gain in output per unit of input from the shift of labor out of farming (0.26 percentage points per year in 1948-73) is calculated on the premise that 1 percent more nonfarm labor at any point in time would raise nonfarm output by 0.8 percent while 1 percent less farm labor would reduce farm output by 0.33 percent. The former number (0.8) is used because it is approximately the labor share of national income. Use of the latter number (0.33) presumes that the reduction in labor would be concentrated on small farms with little output to the same extent as was the actual reduction of labor in farming, and that it would not affect land and capital input. The shift of labor from agriculture raises output per unit of input in nonresidential business both because national income per person employed is far larger in nonfarm industries than in farming and because elimination of excess labor raised productivity within farming. The contribution to the growth rate was only 0.06 percentage points from 1973 to 1981, when the drop in the farm share of labor input was from 4.3 percent to 3.4 percent, as against 0.26 points in 1948-73.

Persons who are underemployed or whose labor is very wastefully utilized are also present among nonfarm self-employed and unpaid family workers in small, inefficient enterprises. Little or no paid labor is hired, which holds down out-of-pocket expenses and enables an enterprise to survive when it could not do so if labor had to be paid in cash. Reduction in the share of such persons in total nonfarm business employment contributed 0.11 percentage points to the 1948-73 growth rate, but in 1973-81 the employment shift was reversed and the contribution was −0.02 points.

Capital

The growth rate of capital input in nonresidential business, covering both fixed capital and inventories, declined a little, from 3.7 percent in 1948-73 to 3.4 percent in 1973-81. This was entirely due to inventories, whose growth rate fell from 3.6 percent to 2.4 percent. My measure of the input of nonresidential structures and equipment grew 3.8 percent a year in both periods. Growth of the gross fixed capital stock actually accelerated, from 3.6 percent a year to 3.9 percent. Growth of the net stock slipped, from 4.2 percent a year to 3.5 percent, but net stock is a measure of the future services stored up in capital and has no direct relevance to an investigation of a contemporaneous slowdown in growth of output. In measuring fixed capital input I give changes in net stock a weight of one-fourth (as against three-fourths for gross stock), but introduction of net stock in this way is only a convenient means to construct an index that makes a reasonable allowance for deterioration in the performance or increase in the maintenance costs of capital goods as they age.

In any period, the contribution of each type of factor input to the growth rate of real national income in the nonresidential business sector is approximately equal to the product of its growth rate and the average ratio of its earnings to the sector's national income (adjusted to eliminate cyclical variations).[9] Table 1-3 shows these rates and ratios for both types of capital input, as well as for labor and land.

The contribution of capital to the growth rate of total sector national income was 0.57 percentage points in 1948-73. It fell by only 0.11 percentage points, or less than one-fifth, from 1948-73 to 1973-81. Only half of this drop was due to slower growth of capital; the rest was due to a lower weight, reflecting the reduction in capital's share of sector national income and

Table 1-3. U.S. Nonresidential Business Sector: Average Weights, Growth Rates, and Contributions of Factor Inputs, 1948–73 and 1973–81.

| Type of Input | Weight | | Total Real Sector NI | | | | Real Sector NI per Person Employed | | | |
| | | | 1948-73 | | 1973-81 | | 1948-73 | | 1973-81 | |
	1948-73	1973-81	Growth Rate	Contribution	Growth Rate	Contribution	Growth Rate	Contribution	Growth Rate	Contribution
Labor	0.809	0.830	1.25	1.03	2.01	1.67	0.14	0.12	-0.01	-0.01
Inventories	0.043	0.033	3.57	0.15	2.36	0.08	2.44	0.10	0.24	0.01
Nonresidential structures and equipment	0.110	0.100	3.76	0.42	3.76	0.38	2.63	0.29	1.70	0.17
Land	0.038	0.037	0.00	0.00	0.00	0.00	-1.09	-0.04	-1.98	-0.07

hence of total input. With accelerated employment growth the contribution of additional capital per worker to the increase in output per worker, which had been 0.39 points in 1948–73, fell by 0.21 percentage points, or more than one-half. This drop would have been only 0.02 percentage points smaller if weights had not changed. Inventories contributed 0.09 points to this drop and nonresidential structures and equipment 0.12 points.

Higher Estimates of the Contribution of Capital

Analysts have used various means to get larger amounts than I do for the contributions of capital to the slowdown, although few contend capital is the main culprit. In this section I digress from my results to explain briefly why I believe nine such ways are inappropriate. (This digression, though necessary, is long and those interested only in my results can skip to the next section.)

1. Net stock is used to measure input of nonresidential structures and equipment. Net stock per person employed grew at annual rates of 3.06 percent in 1948–73 and 1.41 percent in 1973–81. Use of these rates in Table 1–3 for input of structures and equipment (instead of 2.63 and 1.70) would raise by only 0.08 percentage points (from 0.21 to 0.29) the amount of the 2.68 percentage point slowdown in the growth rate of national income per person employed that is attributed to capital. I have already stated that net stock is a measure of stored up future services. The future services of the one-hoss shay declined annually while current services were unchanged. Net stock value declines too fast to provide an appropriate measure of current services.

2. A vintage model is used to try to capture in the capital contribution the effect of the capital stock becoming older or newer. The average age of nonresidential structures and equipment fell in 1948–73 and rose in 1973–81, even when the effects of changes in the composition of the stock are removed. *Accounting for Slower Economic Growth* describes a simple vintage model that gives the largest possible effect of changes in average age by making the extreme assumptions that, to be implemented, all advances in knowledge must be embodied in structures and equipment and that after 1973 advances in knowledge continued without retardation at the 1948–73 rate. It yields the result that the change in average age added 0.10 percentage points to the 1948–73 growth rate by bringing average production practice closer to the frontier of knowledge and subtracted 0.08 points in 1973–81 by dropping it farther behind, thus contributing 0.18 points to the slow-down.[10] But vintage models are indefensible even if one adopts the unreasonable supposition that all advances in knowledge must be embodied in structures and equipment.[11] The reason, which I have stated many times, is as follows.

During any span of time, different types of capital goods undergo very different amounts of quality improvement. The greater the quality improvement in new goods of any type, the greater the obsolescence of existing capital for which the new goods are a substitute. Other things being equal, the rate of return on replacement investment, and hence the incentive to invest, is highest for types of capital goods that have experienced the most obsolescence. Any substantial gross investment in a period permits investment opportunities created by sizable quality improvments in new capital goods to be grasped. It is only the less profitable investments, involving replacement of capital goods for which quality change has been small, that are sensitive to variations in the amount of gross investment (on which changes in average age depend). Thus, the margin of difference between two levels of investment is unlikely to include capital embodying large improvements in quality. Similarly, the advantage of improvements will be greater in some uses than others even for the same type of good, and new acquisitions will be used first where the gains are greatest. The gain in the average quality of the capital stock that vintage models imagine to be derived from additional new investment is not realized because the change in average age automatically is largely offset by a reduction in the average amount of quality improvement incorporated in new capital.[12]

3. The contribution of capital to the growth rate of potential national income per person potentially employed is computed and compared with the growth rate of actual national income per person actually employed.[13] Capital input is, by definition, the same on a potential as on an actual basis but potential employment accelerated more than actual employment after 1973. Hence the growth rate of capital input (structures, equipment, and inventories) per person employed fell more on a potential basis than on an actual basis. As compared with the 0.21 percentage points that capital contributed to the slowdown in growth of sector national income per person employed on an actual basis, it can be computed that capital contributed 0.29 percentage points to the slowdown in potential national income per person potentially employed.

This computation correctly describes the situation that would have prevailed in 1981 if employment had suddenly jumped to the potential level (and 1948 and 1973 employment had also been at potential). Use of capital per person potentially employed is also appropriate to examine the adequacy of the capital stock under conditions of high employment. But in the absence of a very special situation, the 0.29 points is not appropriate for examination of the slowdown in growth of actual output per person. This special situation, which does not prevail, would be one in which (a) each worker has a portion of structures, equipment, and inventories assigned to him so inflexibly that, if he does not work, "his" capital stands idle *and* (b) the 1981 capital stock had been allocated among worker slots on the assumption that employment would be at the potential level. Without commenting on *(a)*, I shall observe that *(b)* might possibly have been plausible if the gap between actual and potential employment had resulted from a 1981 drop in actual employment, but not in the real situation, in which the gap emerged as actual employment increased strongly for six straight years but the potential labor force grew even faster.

4. Capital diverted from the production of measured product to compliance with certain government regulations is deleted from capital input, accentuating its retardation. There are two problems with this. First, consistency requires that labor diverted to compliance with regulations be similarly deleted from labor input, but analysts deleting capital do not delete labor. This creates a mix-up. The deceleration of the rise in the capital/labor ratio is exaggerated, but the effect of regulation on output per unit of total input is only partly reassigned to input because diverted labor remains in input. Second, even if this defect were remedied, the classification is unsatisfactory since regulation, not any change in the amount of saving and investment, caused the output retardation. The classification used in my estimates is more realistic. Capital and labor input include amounts diverted to comply with regulation, and the effect of the diversion on output is isolated as a separate determinant of output per unit of input.

5. Output is measured by gross national product instead of by national income or net national product. Capital consumption allowances with capital consumption adjustment then become part of the contribution of capital. In nonresidential business such allowances, measured in 1972 prices, grew more rapidly in 1973–81 (4.70 percent a year) than in 1948–73 (4.45 percent), but per person employed they grew less rapidly than before because of the sharp acceleration of employment growth. The result is that, if gross product is analyzed instead of net product, the slowdown in the growth of output per worker is lessened while the contribution of capital to the slowdown is increased—though not a great deal.

Gross product is usually analyzed by adding capital consumption to the weight of capital input, instead of dealing with it directly as an addition to net output and the capital contribution, but the effect is similar (Denison 1969: 12–13). Weights on gross and net bases compare as in Table 1–4. Addition of capital consumption allowances raises the weight of capital but eliminates the interperiod decline in capital's weight. Substitution of these gross income weights in Table 1–3 adds only 0.04 percentage points to the amount

Table 1-4.   Comparison of Weights on Gross and Net Bases.

	National Income Basis		Gross Income Basis	
	1948-73	*1973-81*	*1948-73*	*1973-81*
Labor	0.809	0.830	0.734	0.734
Inventories	0.043	0.033	0.039	0.029
Nonresidential structures				
equipment	0.110	0.100	0.192	0.204
(Total capital)	(0.153)	(0.133)	(0.231)	(0.233)
Land	0.038	0.037	0.034	0.034

of the slowdown in output per worker that is attributable to capital and does not change the combined contribution of all inputs to the slowdown. I have often explained that gross national product is inappropriate for growth analysis because it is a duplicated measure of output and why reasons often given for its use are not valid.[14]

6. Growth of the capital stock (which BEA measures by the perpetual inventory method, using constant service lives for most components) is reduced in recent years on the rationale that economic change has accelerated and this has increased obsolescence and made service lives shorter than before. Martin N. Baily (1981: 17–50) pointed to increases in government regulation, foreign competition, and changes in relative prices, especially that of oil, as causes. Others stress mainly the price of oil. Baily attempted to appraise the effect by introducing James Tobin's q, the ratio of the market value of corporate securities to the replacement value of corporate assets. He argued that overstatement of the increase in replacement value because of unexpected obsolescence was the common cause of at least part of the decline in q and the retardation of output per unit of input: A correct capital stock series would reduce or eliminate both.[15]

Baily does not claim that values of securities measure the value of the corporate capital stock better than perpetual inventory series, for he recognizes that q is affected by many influences. Instead, he calculates what the results would be if one were to use for structures and equipment input the weighted geometric mean of indexes of the BEA net capital stock series, weighted two, and a series derived from security values, weighted one.[16] (This weighting is offered only for illustration.) The effect, according to calculations by Robert J. Gordon, is to reduce the 1978 stock relative to the 1973 stock by 14 percent. Baily's results indicate that use of such a series would eliminate most of the drop from 1948–73 to 1973–78 in the growth rates of total factor productivity in nonfinancial corporations and in manufacturing, and convert the drop in the growth rate in nonfarm business to an increase. Baily's calculations are based on gross output, a 25 percent weight for nonresidential structures and equipment, and use of a Cobb-Douglas type production function.

These results require comment. Use of what I consider a more realistic 20 percent weight (see above) instead of 25 would increase by one-fourth the percentage by which it would be necessary to reduce BEA's estimates of the stock of structures and equipment at the start of his earlier period and the end of his later period in order to eliminate the slowdown in output per unit of input. The latter amount would be further, and greatly, raised if the end of the later period were moved from 1978 to 1981 or 1982. To eliminate the retardation in the growth rate of *net* output per unit of input a huge reduction in the end-of-the-period stock would be needed. Indeed, it can be calculated from the sources-of-growth estimates in Table 1-1 and from the 10 percent share weight for structures and equipment shown in Table 1-3 that, if a Cobb-Douglas type production function is used, my 1981 estimate of structures and equipment input that is derived from BEA capital stock data would have to be reduced by more than three-fourths, 1948 and 1973 being unchanged, to eliminate the decline in even my residual series from 1948–73 to 1973–81. It would have to be reduced by more than nine-tenths to eliminate the decline in the growth rate of national income per person employed.

When Baily's paper was presented, Robert J. Gordon, Robert M. Solow, and others who commented on it complimented Baily for calling attention to the possibility of unusually rapid obsolescence but did not find convincing the evidence adduced to show that obsolescence actually was greater than in previous decades. Baily's reason for the decline in q was strongly questioned by Franco Modigliani and others. My own view is that a persuasive case has not been made for introduction after 1973 of service lives shorter than those used in 1948–73, when economic change was commonly considered to be occurring at an unprecedented pace. Examples of premature discarding can be cited, of course, but autos, the one important asset for which real service lives can be obtained (from registrations), appear to have remained in service *longer* after pollution, safety, and fuel consumption controls were introduced and gasoline prices raised. In any case, after reviewing the composition of the stock, by type of structure and equipment, I find it hard to believe that regulation, oil prices, and foreign competition changed service lives enough in either direction to have a major effect on the calculation of output per unit of input in nonresidential business as a whole. Those who think otherwise might fruitfully set down their own conjectures as to the change in the service life of each component they think was affected, and recompute the stock with these changing lives to see how much its growth from, say, 1973 to 1981 would be altered.

7. The scope of the sector analyzed may differ from my nonresidential business sector in a way that magnifies the role of capital in the slowdown. Thus the Bureau of Labor Statistics business sector, which Norsworthy, Harper, and Kunze analyzed (1979: 387–421; Denison 1979b: 436–40), includes tenant-occupied dwellings. Christensen and Jorgenson not only include dwellings but also impute a return to durable goods owned by consumers; however, this series seems not to have entered the productivity slowdown debate.[17] Since all the value added by houses and consumer durables is a contribution of capital, and both studies measure value-added gross of capital consumption, these additions are important. Indeed, they completely change the scope of the contribution of capital.

I consider the addition of the gross services of consumer durables to output especially undesirable (Denison 1972: 99, 1982a). However, I confine myself here to noting that the additions described are irrelevant to analysis of the productivity slowdown in nonresidential business, my subject here, and the slowdown that has people concerned.

8. Capital input is adjusted for changes in capital utilization, usually by use of a capacity utilization series prepared by the Department of Commerce, Federal Reserve Board, or Wharton School. Depending on the series used and exact dates compared, this may or may not increase the contribution to the slowdown that is ascribed to capital.

This is mainly a matter of classification. I classify as a separate source of growth—a component of output per unit of input—changes in the intensity of utilization of employed labor, land, and capital that result from fluctuations in the strength of demand.[18] To derive this series is hard enough, and it seems to me unnecessary to take what I consider the much more difficult step of estimating utilization for each input separately. In addition, I want to keep the contribution of capital closely identified with saving and investment.

9. Elasticities that are larger than capital's share of national income or GNP at factor cost are used to represent the effect on output of an increase in capital input. These higher elasticities are sometimes obtained by correlating time series for output with time series for capital input, labor input, and time (or some other variable or variables). One recent example (of many) is a study by Richard W. Kopcke (1980: 26–59; Denison 1980b) that implies that a 1 percent increase in fixed capital alone would raise gross product by 0.26 percent, much more than is indicated by fixed capital's share of total gross earnings (around 0.20 percent). Even higher elasticities are obtained by correlating across countries the growth rate of output per unit of labor with that of capital per unit of labor, or by some similar international correlation (such as correlation of output growth rates and investment ratios). Results of the international correlations are then applied to domestic time series to estimate the contribution of capital to growth. Assar Lindbeck (1983) has used this method to derive estimates that a 1 percent increase in capital alone raises output by 0.7 to 0.9 percent.[19] John Kendrick reports that such a calculation yields the result that a 1 percent increase in capital input raises output by 0.88 percent.[20] However, Kendrick does not endorse this result which, he says results from the fact that changes in the capital/labor ratio are positively correlated with other variables promoting productivity growth. "In my opinion," he concludes, "a growth-accounting approach, by which variables are weighted by their estimated marginal productivities, yields more reliable results."

The case for the use of income shares as weights, which rests on the principle of proportionality and requires only that firms seek to minimize costs or yield to firms that do, is very powerful. It requires no assumption as to how the factor prices that face firms are determined but only that business enterprises combine labor, structures and equipment, inventories, and land in such a way as to minimize costs when factor prices are given. If enterprises do minimize costs, they will use factors in such proportions that the marginal products of the several factors, per unit of input, are proportional to their prices, or earnings per unit. Unless this condition is satisfied, enterprises could reduce costs by substituting one factor for another. Departures from this situation are assumed to be small or offsetting so that total earnings of the four inputs are proportional to the number of units of each times its marginal product. There is, of course, a range of uncertainty in measuring the earnings of the factors and also in their cyclical adjustments (Denison 1974: 51–52, 260–72, esp. 268–72; 1979a: 49–50, 170–73). But the range of uncertainty is not large. Moreover, results are stable; weights are similar in different advanced countries and in different time periods.

Attempts to derive weights by correlation of time series is, in practice, much less satisfactory because it is extremely difficult to cyclically adjust output, fixed capital, inventories, and labor, taking proper account of leads and lags, and, simultaneously, to correctly introduce all output determinants into the analysis. In practice no one even attempts this. There are also a variety of possible statistical procedures. Not surprisingly, coefficients for capital obtained from correlation vary greatly. The more careful analysts who use correlation, such as Robert M. Solow, take care that elasticities are close to those that income shares provide. In such cases, one wonders why they do not use income shares directly (Denison 1964: 720–25).[21]

Use of coefficients obtained by correlations of international data such as I have described has no ascertainable theoretical basis. Moreover, if investment behavior is such that capital output ratios are constant (as economic folklore has long held), this practice must yield the nonsensical result that a 1 percent increase in capital alone yields a 1 percent increase in output; this would mean that the amounts of labor and land used in production do not affect output at all.[22] The figures of "0.7 to 0.9" obtained by Lindbeck and 0.88 reported by Kendrick are close to this.

It should be noted that my estimates of the contributions of labor, capital, and land are calculated as if a simultaneous 1 percent increase in *all* inputs would raise output by 1 percent even though my estimate is 1 1/8 percent. In Table 1-1 the difference is classified in a separate source of growth, gains from economies of scale. In a different classification the elasticities I use for all inputs, and the contributions made to growth by all sources except economies of scale, would be raised by one-eighth.

It is not always clear whether coefficients obtained by correlation are meant to include economies of scale. Time series studies often constrain the sum of elasticities to one, but the international correlations apparently have no corresponding constraint. However, little of the gap between my capital elasticity and that from international correlations would be eliminated if my classification were changed. This concludes the "detour," and I return to the contributions of the sources shown in Table 1-1.

Legal and Human Environment

In the last fifteen years the institutional and human environment within which business must operate has changed in several ways. Among them are (1) new requirements to protect the physical environment against pollution; (2) increased requirements to protect the safety and health of employed persons, including those driving vehicles for business purposes; and (3) a rise in dishonesty and crime against business. I have estimated the adverse effects on output per unit of input in nonresidential business of diversion of labor and property input from the production of measured output to other uses in response to these three changes.

My initial study of these effects ended with estimates for 1975. It showed that output per unit of input in nonresidential business was 1.8 percent smaller in 1975 than it would have been if business had operated under 1967 conditions. Of this amount, 1.0 percent was ascribable to pollution abatement and 0.4 percent each to employee safety and health programs and to the increase in crime. The annual increases in these reductions had been small in 1968–70 but were rising rapidly in the early 1970s. They cut the annual change in output per unit of input from 1972 to 1973 by 0.2 percentage points, the change from 1973 to 1974 by 0.4 percentage points, and the change from 1974 to 1975 by 0.5 percentage points. This was an important contributor to the productivity slowdown from 1948–73 to 1973–75 (Denison 1978: 21–44).

A subsequent study showed that, although pollution abatement requirements continued to cut productivity growth in 1975-78, they did so by much smaller amounts than in 1973-75 (Denison 1979c: 58-59). With the caution that the estimates to be cited are particularly tentative, I note that since 1978 impairment of the growth rate of output per unit of input by pollution abatement programs has not been much above the reduced 1975-78 rate, while after 1976 only minimal additional impairment of output per unit of input was caused by safety and health programs and costs of crime against business. Of the reduction in the growth rate from 1948-73 to 1973-81 as a whole, 0.17 percentage points can be ascribed to these three determinants—a substantial amount but much less than in the first years of the period.

Hours of Work

Another 0.17 percentage points of the decline in the growth rate of output per person employed is ascribed to changes in working hours. Average hours actually declined only 0.09 percent a year faster in 1973-81 than in 1948-73. This would have lowered the growth rate of output by only 0.08 percentage points (the amount shown as the contribution of "average hours" in Table 1-1) if a reduction in average hours for any reason lowered labor input proportionally. My estimates imply that to assume a proportional reduction is reasonable if a change in average hours results from a change in the relative numbers of full-time workers and part-time workers, from a change in the average hours of part-time workers, or from a change in the relative numbers of male and female workers, but not if it results from two other changes.

A reduction in sector average hours resulting from shorter hours for full-time nonfarm wage and salary workers of either sex reduces labor input less than proportionally because its effect is diminished by lessened fatigue and reduced costs of absenteeism. A change in the extremely long hours of full-time farm workers or full-time nonfarm self-employed and unpaid family workers of either sex is judged to have no effect on labor input. (These hours actually fluctuate erratically, with little trend.) Inclusion in Table 1-1 of the line "efficiency offset" implements these judgments.

Average hours have been reduced by a shift in the distribution of full-time workers from employment on farms or as nonfarm self-employed and unpaid family workers to nonfarm wage and salary work, in which hours are much shorter. Such shifts are not considered to change labor input because otherwise similar individuals in these different categories are considered to represent the same amount of labor input if they work the average hours of full-time workers of their sex in their own category.[23] The effects of such shifts upon the contribution of "average hours" are offset in Table 1-1 by inclusion of the line labeled "intergroup shift offset."

Less of the reduction in average hours stemmed from such shifts in 1973-81 than in 1948-73 and more from an increase in part-time employment and other changes, and this is why "hours" contributed more to the productivity slowdown than the simple change in average hours would suggest.

Age/Sex Composition

Entrance into employment of many millions of relatively inexperienced women and young people figures prominently in nearly everyone's litany of the causes of the productivity slowdown, but quantitatively it was not a big factor in a comparison of the periods considered here. (The amount would be larger on a potential output basis.) Although shifts in the age/sex composition of total hours worked reduced the 1973-81 growth rate by a substantial 0.21 percentage points, such shifts had been under way since 1954-55 and had subtracted 0.17 points from the 1948-73 growth rate. Hence, only 0.04 percentage points of the drop in the growth rate from 1948-73 to 1973-81 is ascribable to age/sex composition, and that stems from the beginning of the latter period—before 1977, when the share of teenagers peaked.

Land

With the quantity of land (including natural resources) estimated to be unchanged, accelerated employment growth meant an accelerated decline in land per worker. This is credited with 0.03 percentage points of the decline from 1948-73 to 1973-81 in the growth rate of output per worker.

Irregular Factors

Output per unit of input is greatly influenced by the intensity with which labor, capital, and land are used. Fluctuations in the intensity of use resulting from fluctuations in the strength of demand introduce cyclical movements into output per unit of input. It is difficult to estimate the effect of this influence, but I believe the procedure, based on the nonlabor share of national income originating in nonfinancial corporations, that I used for 1948-73 is satisfactory in that period. After 1973 changes in the economy necessitated modifications of this method, results are less dependable, and for 1981 the data needed were available only in the crudest form. Consequently, the estimate of the effect upon the 1973-81 growth rate shown in the "intensity of demand" line of Table 1-1, −0.22 percentage points, is subject to substantial error. This estimate implies that changes in intensity of demand contributed 0.04 percentage points to the lowering of the growth rate from 1948-73 to 1973-81. From the standpoint of the productivity slowdown the main interest in this figure stems from its effect on the residual series. Although the estimate for this irregular factor could be changed with an offsetting change in the residual, no conceivable change would alter the finding that the drop in determinants of the residual series dominated the productivity slowdown. Irregularities in work stoppages did not affect the growth rate of output per unit of input while the effect of weather on farm output was the only output determinant except education that was more favorable (by 0.02 percentage points) to growth in 1973-81 than in 1948-73.

Economies of Scale

The retardation of growth of both actual and potential output meant smaller gains from the economies of scale that accompany growth in the local, regional, and national markets that business is organized to serve. Had growth of total factor input (especially employment) not accelerated, there would have been even greater retardation in the expansion of markets, in gains from economies of scale, and in growth of output per worker and output per unit of input.

My procedures indicate that 0.11 percentage points of the drop in the growth rate of national income per person employed stemmed from smaller gains from economies of scale. This is a very rough estimate, but I have no doubt that there was an appreciable reduction.

Education

Increased education of employed persons was a major source of growth of national income per person employed in nonresidential business in 1948-73 and its contribution increased by 0.08 percentage points in 1973-81. Changes in the distribution of employment between nonresidential business, on the one hand, and government, nonprofit institutions, and private households, on the other, more than account for the increase. From 1948 to 1973 a disproportionate number of the highly educated who newly entered employment had entered teaching and other jobs outside of business, and the educational distribution rose less in nonresidential business than in the economy as a whole; this differential movement was reversed in 1973-81. (The reversal began a few years earlier.) Changes in unemployment, which hits hardest at the less educated, and changes in the age distribution also favored a faster rise in the educational distribution in the recent period.

The increase in education's contribution would have been greater in the absence of a change in weights introduced in *Accounting for Slower Economic Growth*. The range of the weights assigned different education groups was narrowed a little as of 1969, reflecting slightly narrowed earnings differentials in nonresidential business. Data from the Current Population Survey indicate no subsequent narrowing of differentials. (Data for 1979 from the decennial Census of Population, the best source, are not yet available.) The striking fact is not that differentials have changed but that they have changed very little, an indication that percentage differences between marginal products of persons at different educational levels has not diminished much in response to the increase in education.

Scores on achievement tests given pupils at various grade levels and college aptitude tests given to high school seniors have been falling for nearly twenty years. The Advisory Panel on the Scholastic Aptitude Test Score Decline found that after 1970 declines in scores on that test did not result from compositional shifts in the group taking it.

Test scores have not been used in measuring education of employed persons for Table 1-1; distributions of employed persons by highest school grade completed, with an adjustment for changes in days of school per year for persons leaving school before college, are used. In *Accounting for Slower Economic Growth* I explained that up to 1976, when the estimates presented there ended, omission of test scores from the procedure was unimportant because scores have moved in cycles, rather than following a steady trend. This "assures that changes in a series for the average test scores received by employed persons when they were students would be small and gradual—very muted in comparison with movements in students scores." The point is still valid, but its force diminishes as the period of low scores is extended.

Advances in Knowledge and Miscellaneous Determinants

The combined contribution of all other output determinants is measured as a residual but this need not introduce ambiguity as to its conceptual content. The contribution of advances in knowledge is the gain in measured output that results from the incorporation into production of new knowledge of any type—managerial and organizational as well as technological—regardless of the source of that knowledge, the way it is transmitted to those who can make use of it, or the way it is incorporated into production. In principal, one can distinguish between advances in knowledge as such and changes in the lag of actual average practice behind the best known. Miscellaneous determinants fall into seven main groups:

1. Changes in personal characteristics of workers that I have not measured, especially how hard they work;
2. Changes in the extent to which the allocation of individual workers among individual jobs and of capital among individual types of capital departs from that which would maximize national income;
3. Changes in the gap between actual production technique and best technique that results from obstacles imposed by governments, labor unions, and others outside the firm;
4. Changes in the cost of "business services to government," such as collecting taxes or providing statistics;
5. Changes in the adequacy of "government services to business," such as police protection, courts, and roads for business use;
6. Changes in aspects of the legal and human environment within which business must operate that affect costs of production by business, other than the three for which I made specific estimates; and
7. Changes in productive efficiency that take place independently of changes in any of the other determinants identified. Efficiency, so defined, rather clearly differs among countries and I surmise that it may vary over time within a country. One plausible explanation is that efficiency actually achieved is affected by the strength of competitive pressures upon firms to minimize costs.

The main problem that the presence of the residual series presents is neither conceptual ambiguity nor statistical inaccuracy (though it does pick up the net error in other series) but inability to allocate the combined contribution of these several disparate influences among them, or to allocate the contribution of advances in knowledge by type or source of new knowledge.

The residual, at 1.42 percentage points, probably provides a tolerable measure of the contribution of advances in knowledge alone to the growth rate from 1948 to 1973, but advances in knowledge cannot plausibly be charged with most of the abrupt 1.68 percentage point drop in the residual from 1948-73 to 1973-81. The cause of the decline must center in the miscellaneous determinants.

REASONS SUGGESTED FOR THE DECLINE IN THE RESIDUAL

The contribution of advances in knowledge and miscellaneous determinants to the growth rate of nonresidential business national income fell from 1.4

percentage points in 1948-73 to -0.3 points in 1973-81, or by 1.7 percentage points. The decline in the growth rate of this residual series starts with the 1973-74 change; no retardation at all appears until then. In *Accounting for Slower Economic Growth*, I described as a "mystery" the cause of the similar, but even larger, decline that I reported as occurring from 1948-73 to 1973-76. By this I did not mean that no one had a hypothesis as to the cause. Quite the opposite! There was a surfeit of alleged causes, not a scarcity: I stated, analyzed, and evaluated seventeen different causes that had been advanced by various observers as the cause of the slowdown. None, in my opinion, were *demonstrably* able to explain more than a small part—if any—of the slowdown. The remainder of this paper capsulizes these seventeen explanations and my earlier evaluation of them; for six of the last seven it also comments on some more recent literature.

The cause of the slowdown in the residual remains a mystery to me although others do not hesitate to state it.[24] Most—not all—of the supporting argument falls into one or more of the following categories.[25]

a. A situation that is considered adverse to productivity is described as present now and the cause of the slowdown. The describer overlooks the fact that observations for at least two dates are needed to obtain a trend and at least three to obtain a change in trend, as is necessary to explain a slowdown. In most such cases the description even of the present is based on casual empiricism with no quantification. Much of the people-don't-want-to-work-anymore and underground economy literature is of type *a*.

b. A change that, if it occurred, could impair productivity is described but the describer, more sophisticated than those in the first category, claims only that it *might* have occurred and thus is a *possible* cause of the slowdown. Leibenstein's article about setting of plant work standards and Leijonhufvud's on inflation, both cited below, are examples.[26]

c. Correlation between some other time series and a productivity series is used to show that the former series caused some or all of the productivity slowdown, and to quantify the amount of the slowdown for which it was responsible. Robert R. Ling of Clemson University starts a recent book review in the *Journal of the American Statistical Association* as follows (1982: 489-90): "The author of this book holds the view, apparently shared by many social scientists and economists, that causal inference from correlational data (in the absence of controlled experiments) is a valid form of statistical and scientific inference. My view has been that the methods and techniques, developed and applied under that premise, for causal inference (e.g., path analyses) are at best a form of statistical fantasy." One could be far more tolerant than Ling and still regard as absurd most of the studies in this third category since they show no more than that two time series tend to move together or apart in some systematic way. This characteristic is shared by countless pairs of economic time series and, in itself, can tell nothing about causation. Moreover, the claim is often made that if r^2 is 0.98, then 98 percent of the change in productivity is explained by the behavior of the other series—even though it is not r^2 but the slope of the regression line that describes the effect of one variable on the other if there is an effect. I suspect one could explain the productivity slowdown fifteen times over by correlating productivity with each of twenty other economic time series chosen almost at random. Since commodity prices, employment, unemployment, variability of exchange rates, productivity, and many other economic series have behaved much differently since 1973 or thereabouts than they did before, it is especially easy, by the correlation technique, to ascribe the behavioral change since 1973 in almost any series to any one of a wide variety of others.

d. The most useful analyses establish a solid case that there is or is not a causal connection between some determinant and residual productivity and show that there has or has not been a change in the trend of that determinant. They are usually unable, however, to quantify the effect of that change upon productivity. This is not surprising because output determinants whose effects can be even tolerably well quantified on an annual basis are shown separately in Table 1–1 (unless their contributions appear to be consistently zero). Hence they are not among the determinants that affect the residual. Nevertheless, it is sometimes possible to reach a judgment as to the order of magnitude of such effects, and thus to decide whether they are likely to be an important part of the slowdown story.

The first four of the seventeen suggestions reviewed below concern advances in knowledge and their application, the next seven taxation and government regulation, and the last six other subjects. Advances in knowledge could scarcely turn negative, and it is not plausible to suppose that they are responsible for the entire change in the path of the residual, but they could have contributed to it. The magnitude of this change can be illustrated by noting that by 1981, national income per person employed in nonresidential business was 12.5 percent or $3,200 lower than it would have been had the 1948–73 trend of the residual continued after 1973, contributions of other sources having declined as they did.

1. Curtailment of expenditures on research and development. The main trouble with this explanation is that little or no reduction actually occurred in constant-dollar expenditures for types of organized R&D that contribute to the growth of measured productivity (those for improvement of intermediate products and capital goods, and for process improvements). Also, 0.3 percentage points at most of the growth rate of measured productivity before 1973 can be ascribed to organized R&D in the United States. Hence a decline of even one-third in such spending would be expected to impair the growth rate by only one-tenth of a percentage point.

2. Decline in the opportunity for major new technical advances. The period since World War II has witnessed exceptional technological progress. Some observers believe this was made possible by science-based technology, the so-called second industrial revolution; that the major possibilities made available by the scientific advances of the last century have now been exploited; and that we may have to wait decades for the reservoir to be replenished. It is indeed possible that opportunities have dwindled, but the diversity of the economy should ensure that the resulting retardation of growth would be gradual. Receding opportunities for technological advances seem unlikely to explain much of the sudden retardation of productivity growth after 1973.

3. Decline in Yankee ingenuity and deterioration of American technology. Perhaps Americans have become less ingenious, but this is undocumented. The allegation sometimes made that there has been long-run deterioration of American engineering refers to too early a period to explain the recent productivity slowdown.

4. Increased lag in the application of knowledge due to the aging of capital. For reasons explained earlier, this cannot be significant except as a byproduct of government regulation (point 8).

5. Diversion of labor and capital from the production of measured output to activities required to comply with government regulations other than those related to pollution abatement and worker safety and health. This is certainly a factor but probably not a big one because all other programs together appear to impose smaller costs of this type than the two for which estimates were made.

6. Government-imposed paperwork. Analysis of the available data indicates that paperwork can be eliminated as a significant source of productivity decline after 1973, although it may have been a factor—not a major one—if one goes back to the mid-1960s.

7. Diversion of business executives from ordinary business affairs (including cost reduction) to dealing with government; top management characteristics altered to favor "soft" types good at dealing with government and unions and at public relations rather than production and innovation; management's emphasis of short-term profits to the near-exclusion of long-term growth (because of uncertainty introduced by regulation but also because of incentives provided by the system of rewards to top management and of fears of corporate takeovers). The importance of these points defies quantification but could have been considerable. They have been receiving increasing acceptance.

8. Delay of new projects by government regulation. This unquestionably contributed to the retardation of productivity growth, partly by slowing the introduction of new technology. The amount is unknown.

9. Misallocation of total labor and capital among uses as a result of regulation and taxation. This effect is widespread. Nevertheless, I doubt that it can account for a substantial part of the productivity slowdown. *Various regulations, especially those limiting the use of tests in hiring, are said also to cause misallocation in detail—that is, getting the right people in the right jobs.*

10. Effects of high tax rates on incentives and efficiency. Evidence documenting these effects is absent. Herbert Stein found that from 1956 to 1973 the effects of government spending and taxes on economic growth were "at least uncertain and probably small." The period after 1973 was not one in which the government share shot up abruptly.

11. Increase in the tax rate on capital gains contained in the Revenue Act of 1969. This was said to reduce growth by curtailing investment (which would reduce the contribution of capital, not my residual series), by curtailing R&D (which would have affected the contribution of the advances in knowledge component of the residual), already rejected as the dominant cause of the slowdown, or by biasing the distribution of investment and R&D away from the more risky undertakings (which, by accentuating misallocation, would reduce the "miscellaneous determinants" component of the residual). The small size of the extra tax burden that the 1969 law imposed on capital gains (less than $1 billion at 1978 income levels) "suggests that the misallocation resulting from it, though doubtless present, was not large" (Denison 1979a: 133). The Revenue Act of 1978 had eliminated the 1969 increase so, if it was the reason for the productivity slowdown, it was now gone.

The Wall Street Journal questioned that conclusion, as follows, in an editorial ("Accounting for Slower Growth" 1979: 20): "The small amount of extra revenues collected convinces Mr. Denison that the higher capital gains tax rate added only slightly to the tax burden. But one could just as well see the small yield in revenues as evidence that an awful lot of activities were discouraged by the sharp increase in the tax rate."[27] The *Journal* view had some background in a 1978 paper by Martin S. Feldstein, Joel Slemrod, and S. Yitzhaki (1978), which indicated that a cut in capital gains tax rates much like that which became law in 1978 would triple realizations of capital gains, and in the case of corporate stock even increase tax revenues from capital gains.[28] That paper's conclusions were promptly attacked by John Yinger as gross overestimates (1978: 428), defended by Feldstein (1978:

507–08) and further attacked by William D. Nordhaus (1978: 652, 659), all in what was, to say the least, a vigorous exchange.[29] In October 1979 Joseph J. Minarik examined the question (1981: 241–81); his 'preferred' equation indicated that each 1 percent decrease in capital gains tax rates (for example, from 20.0 to 19.8 percent) would increase realizations by 0.79 percent. This implied, according to Minarik, that the rate changes in the 1978 act would raise realizations by 15.8 percent, as against the Feldstein-Slemrod-Yitzhaki estimate of 200 percent. In the event, as Minarik subsequently has pointed out (1982: 5), realizations reported on the returns increased only 15.4 percent in 1978 and less than 1 percent more in 1979. Thus, my original use of the extra tax burden imposed by the 1969 act as an indication that its economic impact could not have been massive was evidently correct. The absence of any improvement in productivity performance after the 1978 act also is an indication that the 1969 act was not the cause of the productivity problem.

12. "People don't want to work any more" and its variant, "young people don't work like we did at their age." I earlier reported that most of the public and some economists believe this to be the cause of the productivity setback but that evidence cited is impressionistic and inconclusive (Denison 1979a); to explain a slowdown in the residual, intensity of work while at work rather than time at work would have to drop—and more rapidly than in the past.

Subsequently, Randall K. Filer (1980: 109–27) has reported information from the 1969, 1972, and 1977 Quality of Employment Surveys conducted by the Survey Research Center at the University of Michigan. Workers were asked to consider the statement, "I am not asked to do excessive amounts of work," with respect to their primary job, and to respond "very true," "somewhat true," "not too true," or "not at all true." If scores of 4, 3, 2, and 1 are assigned these answers, the average score declined from 3.07 in 1969 to 2.93 in 1972 and 2.80 in 1977. Filer states, "This pattern is consistent with one of two explanations. Either jobs have been getting harder . . . or else people are perceiving the jobs as becoming harder. . . . If the amount of work people regard as being excessive has fallen, there is every reason to believe that they would be willing to put less effort in any given job, and therefore that output per man hour of labor input would fall." Filer speculates that "the effort component of labor supply may have fallen since 1970 in a way that it did not do prior to that date," but also cites other attitudinal data that show no such change or even an opposite change. It may be noted that the average score fell more per year (0.05 points) from 1969 to 1972, before the slowdown in residual productivity, than from 1972 to 1977 (0.03 points), so the explanation does not match the timing of the slowdown. Also to be noted is that the interpretation is reversed if jobs really were getting harder.

Harvey Leibenstein has explained that the level of effort that prevails in a firm need not be as high as would be advantageous to both the firm and its employees if they could separate decisions about the size of output from decisions about its distribution (1982: 92–97).[30] The actual prevailing effort may be some lower peer group standard that gives both firm and workers less satisfaction. "Entrants to the firm observe the average effort level, and set their own effort approximately at or fairly close to the observed average. If the observed level were higher, many would simply shift their own level to a higher level, and similarly if it were somewhat lower." The convention is stable within the bounds of an "inert area"; only if the values of certain variables get beyond the inert area bounds is the convention destabilized. Thus, a change requires "a necessary 'shock' in order to destabilize the operating effort convention; and a movement towards a new convention."

Leibenstein does not suggest any "shock" that could have lowered peer standards in many firms since 1973 and thus adversely affected the nation's productivity. I have suggested that "programs to hire the 'hard core' unemployed that do not require them to meet as stringent performance standards. . . as the ordinary work force pose a possible danger: acceptance of lower standards for a special group in an establishment may reduce performance standards for the rest of the work force . . . ," and that "hiring to meet objectives of legislation to promote equal employment opportunities has a similar potential" (Denison 1979a: 135). However, it is far from having been established that such a lowering of standards actually occurred.

In an article titled "The Work Ethic That Never Was," Paul Bernstein (1980: 19–25), after arguing that the Protestant work ethic has not been widespread for centuries and that "there is no clear evidence that the passage of time has created a work force that is less motivated than its predecessors," nevertheless asserts that

> as the seventies progressed . . . new meanings were sought from work. These different demands tend to transcend age and sex. Workers increasingly expected employment to maximize their individual potentials, provide meaningful tasks on the job, and allow them to participate in decision-making. Far fewer members of this "new breed" accepted the maxim that "hard work really paid," and many were unwilling to subordinate personal interests to those of the organization.

Whether this means Bernstein thinks effort has declined is unclear in view of the earlier quotation.

Martin N. Baily addressed the "young people don't work like we did" variant (1981: 11–14). Could the productivity slowdown be explained by deterioration in the labor provided by each successive age cohort of workers after those born in 1942—whether the deterioration was provided by increasing aversion to work, deteriorating education, television, or what not? His conclusion that the deterioration would have had to be implausibly sharp to explain more than a small fraction of the slowdown is convincing. My summation is that no important new evidence supporting either the hypothesis or its variant has appeared.

13. Impairment of efficiency by inflation. Inflation has had powerful adverse effects on the economy, but most of the effects did not directly affect the residual series. Most visibly, and perhaps most importantly, inflation made necessary macroeconomic policies that held output well below the economy's productive potential. Restraint has been exercised predominantly through high interest rates. These, in turn, contributed to overvaluation of the dollar in foreign exchange markets. Inflation hampered investment by forcing a low ratio of actual output to high employment output, by high interest rates, and perhaps through other channels. Inflation distorted the tax system and provided an excuse to legislate additional distortions in a futile effort to compensate for those that inflation introduced. The effect on output of these consequences of inflation is captured in the contributions to growth of labor and capital input, economies of scale, and intensity of utilization of employed resources, which were separately estimated.

Inflation also affects the residual series. It increases costs of information, prediction, and transactions. Information and forecasts needed for decisionmaking worsen despite costly efforts to prevent deterioration, so misallocation of labor and property resources increases. One aspect is misallocation of capital among components with different turnover periods. Management attention is diverted from production and sales to problems of raising and investing funds and to anticipating and responding to price changes. "That inflation impairs productivity seems certain. But I have no idea how much it may have done so from 1973 to 1976" (Denison 1979a: 136).

Although new advocates of inflation as the cause of productivity retardation have appeared since I wrote those words, they have not uncovered valid new evidence as to its actual importance in the post-1973 retardation. Following is a sampling of recent literature:

A. Leijonhufvud (1977: 265-312) has produced a paper powerfully advancing the thesis that inflation *can* seriously impair productivity. For the most part, the routes that he considers would affect the contribution of the residual. Leijonhufvud emphasizes possible adverse effects of inflation on the very framework of economic and political institutions, and on incentives. Anyone who is confident that the costs of inflation are necessarily minor, or that there are adequate substitutes for stable money, would do well to read him. However, Leijonhufvud does not show that the *possible* consequences of inflation that he fears *actually* affected U.S. productivity after 1973; he hardly could have done so since (he says) he wrote in the spring of 1975, when the slowdown had just begun. Vernon W. Ruttan (1979: 896–902) has also stressed *possible* effects of inflation.

Peter K. Clark (1982: 149–54), in addition to restating ways in which inflation could impair productivity, stresses the temporal association of high inflation and low productivity in the postwar United States. Impressed by the correlations between deviations from their 1948–65 trends of annual changes in labor productivity and in the price level, Clark explores the way the causation runs. However, he finds productivity and prices change simultaneously so causation can't be inferred from timing. He seems, nonetheless, to favor the hypothesis that causation runs from inflation to productivity. To me, it seems much more likely that the reason for correlation between short period changes runs from productivity to inflation, whatever the long-run connection may be. If wages are set in anticipation of a continuation of past productivity trends this is almost inevitable (Denison 1979a: 16–18). Clark also considers with favor the possibility that the observed negative correlation is introduced by errors in price data rather than anything real; I consider this argument later. Clark ignores the possibility that third causes affecting both productivity and inflation were responsible for the correlation between them.

J. Peter Jarrett and Jack G. Selody (1981) concluded, also from correlation analysis, that in Canada "the increased inflation rates of the 1970s are sufficient to explain virtually the entire recent slowdown in productivity growth." (They attribute 83 percent of the inflation effect to anticipated inflation, and the remaining 17 percent to unanticipated inflation, which suggests interesting ideas for policy!) They also report that, conversely, their estimates "indicate clearly" that the recent productivity slowdown has "contributed to rising inflation." (They suggest that it is not "the sole cause of the current high levels of inflation"; if it is the main cause we have the interesting situation that changes in productivity and inflation are each the cause of changes in the other.)

Art Pine (1981: F1–3) documented the diversion of management attention to "beating the inflation game" in a recent article. Leijonhufvud's article describes the same process colorfully.

Against all this, one may cite William D. Nordhaus (1980: 147–72) and Robert M. Solow. Commenting on a paper by Nordhaus, Solow (1980: 176) says: "The third cliche Nordhaus attacks is the one that blames the productivity slowdown, like everything else from the high divorce rate to the failure of Red Sox pitching, on the recent inflation, and concludes that, if only we could stop the inflation, productivity would revive and Mike Torrez would be able to get the side out. Nordhaus doesn't believe it, and neither do I."

14. Reduced efficiency caused by lessening of the pressure of competition and resulting deterioration in the quality of business management. That there actually has been a decline in competition is not well established (Denison 1979a: 136–38), and I discount the possibility that this is an important factor in the slowdown. Spreading foreign competition, especially from Japan, is currently a spur to American management but results are as yet uncertain.

15. Rise in energy prices. The rise in energy prices had major adverse consequences, but the question is whether they contributed much to the setback in residual productivity. Robert H. Rasche and John A. Tatom assigned energy prices full responsibility for the slowdown and some others considered them important. However, most analysts regard the weight of energy in the value of output and the size of the reduction in energy use as too small for energy to have played a major role. Pending more research, an estimate that the energy price increase reduced the growth rate of my residual by 0.1 percentage point from 1973 to 1976 is reasonable (Denison 1979a: 138–42).

Subsequently, Tatom (1982) and Rasche and Tatom (1981a, 1981b) have extended their view that energy prices were responsible for the energy slowdown to the entire 1973–81 period and to other countries, and Robert J. Gordon (1981) has rejected their analysis. Ernst R. Berndt (1980) and Paul P. Gregory (1980)—as well as many others—have concluded that oil prices were not a major influence in the United States. Meanwhile, Jack Alterman has been developing better series for energy use that should aid future analysis. Berndt reviewed the literature at a September 21 meeting of the Aspen Institute, and later in this volume he comments on Dale Jorgenson's chapter on energy, so I shall not discuss energy at greater length.

16. Shift to services and other structural changes. "Whenever productivity is discussed at any length, someone will assert that opportunities to raise productivity are less for services than for commodities, that the service share of the economy is rising rapidly, and that the overall rate of productivity advance must therefore decline (Denison 1979a: 142). I have dismissed this allegation, as it pertains to nonfarm business, as having "no substance." (Gains from movement of labor out of farming, as well as from nonfarm self-employment, have been removed from the residual series.)

Two subsequent studies reach the same conclusion. George Sadler studied the subject at the American Productivity Center (Grossman and Sadler 1982) and reported (Malabre 1981): "Economics is a social science plagued by many myths—and one of the larger ones, it now appears, is that service jobs bear much of the blame for the country's lackluster productivity gains. In fact, the true situation seems to be precisely the opposite." Irving Leveson's findings from a nonstatistical approach are similar. After citing "preposterous" writings such as a December 19, 1979, *New York Times* editorial, "To Make America Productive," that listed "to slow the growth of service industries" as second only to fighting inflation among the ways Washington could help most to improve productivity, Leveson stated (1980: 765–803): "The service industries are rapidly emerging as a leading sector in the forefront of innovation and economic growth. Yet the rhetoric continues to treat services as if they were a drag on the economy. . . . Volumes of trade literature, descriptive materials, industry studies and proprietary research document the explosive pace of change. . . ."

17. Possible errors in the data. I have examined suggestions that some development might have introduced a sudden bias into the output measure such that the observed productivity slowdown was a statistical error rather than anything real and found no such development that was likely to be important (Denison 1979a). Subsequently, inflation and the underground economy have again been proposed as sources of error creating an artificial slowdown.

Inflation

In an article already cited, Peter Clark (1982: 152) asserts that "even a cursory examination of the way aggregate labor productivity is estimated suggests that part *or all* [italics mine] of the observed decline in productivity growth may be a statistical artifact [of overdeflation resulting from inflation]. . . . Clark gives four reasons that this might be so. None are persuasive.

First, Clark argues, inflation heightens the probability that price controls will be imposed. To guard against this contingency firms could raise list prices above transactions prices prior to controls, hoping that under controls only their list prices would be effectively controlled and they could then raise transaction prices to list prices. During a period when controls were increasingly feared but not yet imposed, list prices would increase more than transactions prices. Clark considers list prices pertinent because some components of producers' durable goods in the NIPAs are deflated by components of the producers' price index that are list prices. If the list prices of these components rose more than transactions prices, growth of real ouput would be understated.

Besides noting that the process described is highly speculative, and that it isn't clear why its timing need conform to that of the productivity slowdown, I have two comments.[31] First, producers' durables are only 3 percent of the net national product of nonresidential business, and deflation of only a fraction of this amount is tainted by list prices. These list prices would have to diverge from corresponding transaction prices by incredibly large amounts to account for any noticeable part of the 12.5 percent shortfall of residual productivity from its past trend. Second, growth of the capital stock as well as output would be understated if producers' durables were overdeflated. Increases in output growth would not carry over to the residual because the contribution of capital would also be raised.[32] Second, Clark says that increases in output of nonresidential structures are probably understated because of use of input price indexes "unlikely to account fully for labor savings generated by high construction wages" (p. 152). But Clark gives no reason for the size of the bias to be related to the rate of inflation, or greater after 1973 than before. Also, as with producers' durables, if the increase in nonresidential structures were understated, so would be the contribution of capital.

Clark's third point is puzzling. If the following attempt to summarize and sharpen it is inaccurate, I apologize in advance. Clark says "errors in the measurement of the price deflator for nominal output may . . . explain a part of the negative correlation [that he observes] between [quarterly changes in] inflation and productivity" and generate an erroneous "negative relationship between [quarterly changes in] real output and the price level. . . . Because the 'linkage' procedure used to construct many price series allows errors to persist over time, unbiased errors cannot be ruled out as a cause of the observed reduction in productivity growth" (p. 152). I am compelled to ask, What are these linked price series that understate quarterly price increases when the increase in real output is above average but do not overstate them when it is below average? If such indexes exist, why is the size of the cumulative bias they generate related to the rate of inflation? Why is the bias more likely to increase than to decrease when inflation intensifies? I can answer none of these questions.

Fourth, Clark says "it is possible that an increasing fraction of improvements in the quality of output may have been overlooked since the mid-1960's " (p. 152). What this has to do with inflation eludes me. Also, while such a "rising fraction" is possible, a falling fraction is just as possible. Albert Rees (1980: 342), the chairman of the recent National Academy of Sciences Task Force on Productivity Measurement, observes that

> I know of nothing that suggests that [downward-biasing errors related to quality changes, or to errors in measurement of hours worked have been] getting larger through time . . . , and a good deal that suggests the opposite. . . . Ten years ago we used more input proxies to measure output, and had poorer adjustments for quality change than we do now. . . . In short, the lag in measured productivity growth seems to me to be entirely a real phenomenon and in no part attributable to measurement error. Indeed, if anything the deceleration has been understated.

Actually, it is not clear whether Clark has in mind the type of quality change that, in general, is measured in output series or the type that is not. Where two products existing simultaneously, such as an expensive car and an inexpensive one, sell at different prices, they are counted as different quantities of product, the quantities differing in the ratio of their selling prices. Where different commodities do not exist simultaneously, they are counted as different products in the ratio of what their cost (used as a substitute for price) would be if both were known and produced at the same time. No account is or can be taken of the fact that some or even all consumers may have a subjective evaluation of the relative merits of products that differs from the ratio of their prices or costs. The quality differences measured by this procedure are "measured" or "economic" quality differences. If Clark refers to "measured" quality differences, it seems fair to state (as Rees implies) that, over time, the Bureau of Labor Statistics and other agencies have become more rather than less sensitive to the need to prevent such changes from appearing as price increases, and better equipped to do so. But perhaps Clark refers to "unmeasured" quality change. I do not know whether unmeasured quality change has increased or decreased.[33] But even an increase would not slow the growth of measured productivity unless it resulted from division of R&D to research on new and improved final products from research that could have raised measured productivity (i.e., research on processes and on new and improved intermediate products, including capital goods).

Underground Economy

In *Accounting for Slower Economic Growth* I stated that I had not been able to visualize how growth of an illegal or barter economy could have instilled a sudden sharp downward bias in my series for output per unit of input (Denison 1979a). Subsequently, there has been explosive growth of what I can only describe as the *cult* of the underground economy because its doctrine is based on faith instead of pertinent evidence. Its doctrine is that official data show a slackening of output and productivity growth only or mainly because expansion of the underground economy has biased the numbers.[34] Stemming from brief articles by a handful of economists, this doctrine has been uncritically accepted by a coterie of newsmen who have reported the doctrine as if it were fact. Peter M. Gutmann and Edgar L. Feige are the authors usually cited by newspaper and magazine writers. The following statement of Paul W. MacAvoy is exceptional only because its writer is a respected economist rather than a full-time news commentator (1982: F3): "The underground economy has grown impressively over the last decade. . . . Averaging the illegal with the legal economy, this country has probably had a percent more growth in the 1970s than official statistics show." Many statements are even stronger.

The case rests in part on anecdotes, often fictional, most of which were already stale in 1931 when Al Capone was convicted of income tax evasion, in 1941 when I began to estimate the proprietors' income component of national income, and in 1955 when Nero Wolfe uttered his immortal truth:

"The requisitions of the income tax have added greatly to the attractions of mercenary crime" (Stout 1955: 122).[35] Its proponents never seem to face up to the obstacle that the 1970s and 1980s were not the periods of large increases in tax rates; the major rate increases came much earlier. If growth of the underground economy were a function of changes in tax rates, and bias in national income were a function of growth of the underground economy, then growth of national income would be correctly measured or overstated in recent years and understated in earlier periods so that recent growth would be *over*stated relative to the past and the mystery of productivity change magnified. Carl P. Simon and Ann D. Witte (1982: xiv, 5) actually present such a pattern.[36]

Devotees of the underground economy doctrine usually write as if it were so obvious that understatement of taxed income causes equal understatement of national income or product that it needs no explanation or proof, and they offer none.[37] In fact, however, there is so little statistical connection between taxed income and the movement of output measures that a showing of increased tax evasion would, in itself, be no evidence whatsoever of significant bias in the output measures. Robert Parker (1980) and I (1983: 1-16, esp. 2-8) have separately explained why this is so.

Attempts by exponents of the doctrine to measure the size of the downward bias that they suppose the underground economy introduces into output measures are devoid of substance. Whereas other economists debate how to measure the money supply, underground economists believe they can do so with such precision, and they have such faith in the stability of velocity (even though they count only current transactions and by no means all of them) that they confidently ascribe any fluctuation in velocity to errors in data for transactions.[38] In contrast to the underground economists, monetarists find no change in velocity in the 1970s or 1980s that requires them to resort to the underground economy for an explanation. Thus, Mac Ott (1982: 29) writes:

> In chart 2 [not reproduced here] the velocities of M_1 and M_2 are displayed. The approximate constancy of the M_2 is clearly evident here, as well as the persistent rise of M_1 velocity. Not so evident, however, is the relatively *constant rate* of M_1 velocity growth. Over the 1959-81 period, M_1 velocity grew at around 3.2 percent. Indeed, except for a noticeable slowing in the later '60s the velocity growth rate of both old M_1 and new M_1 has been between 3 percent and 4 percent since 1950.

The self-confidence of the underground economists does not end with their belief that they can measure errors in data for transactions by examining velocity. In addition, they can somehow be sure that among all possible causes of error in data for transactions, the actual cause is omission of the underground economy. Consequently, we are asked to believe, differences between actual transactions and values calculated for the case of constant velocity measure the value of underground transactions.[39]

Underground economists logically must, but often do not, distinguish between transactions entering into production or sale of products that are legal and belong in national income and product and transactions related to the underground economy that are not related to output as defined. The latter include, among others, transactions incurred in connection with the domestic production or distribution of illegal products—notably, drugs—that are excluded from national income and product by definition; with smuggling of legal or illegal products produced abroad; with illegal gambling (which not only is illegal but would be included in output only on a net basis even if it were legal); and with illegal transactions such as thefts and payment of interest to loan sharks, that would be excluded from output measures as transfer payments or consumer interest even if output were redefined to include illegal products (Denison 1983: 2–4). Proponents of the underground economy doctrine often seem unaware that by producing large estimates of underground transactions in the second category they are destroying the case they seek to make.

For reasons I provided in detail in another article (Denison 1983) and shall not repeat here, the ratio of employment to population is more pertinent to an evaluation of the output data than the ratio of transactions to money or large bills. The underground economy scenario calls for increasing understatement of employment. Indeed, any perceptible downward bias in growth of output, relative to an earlier period, as a result of growth of the underground economy, is scarcely plausible without a corresponding increase in the understatement of employment. Throughout the postwar period the ratio of total employment to adult population remained in a relatively narrow band, until in 1979 it shot *above* the band that had long prevailed. This counts heavily against a hypothesis that employment has been increasingly understated.

Advocates of the view that in the 1970s and 1980s the underground economy has introduced a new sharp downward bias in output measures have wholly failed to present a logical case that is consistent with procedures actually used to measure national income and product.[40] Until they provide something serious to refute, there is no way to refute them seriously.

Even if an increased downward bias in the growth of output that resulted from statistical errors caused by the underground economy could be established, to show that a series for productivity was similarly biased would require a demonstration that the bias was not shared by input series. For labor, absence of such a shared bias is possible in some cases but would not be present in what are presumably the more important cases, where an activity or a person is simply omitted.

Obviously, I do not mean to deny that measurement of output is subject to statistical errors that could have caused the observed productivity slowdown to be overstated or understated, although I consider it unlikely that such errors were large relative to the observed change. What I do insist is that the studies of inflation and the underground economy I have cited establish no presumption of an appreciable bias.

CONCLUSION

There is a possibility that everything has gone wrong at once among the determinants that affect the residual series, just as it did among the determinants whose effects were separately estimated. "Several developments may have combined to slow the advance in knowledge itself, and others to retard the incorporation of new knowledge into production. Similarly, inflation, regulation, soaring energy prices, high taxes, and changing attitudes may have conspired to exert the large adverse impact on the miscellaneous determinants of output that forced the residual series into an actual decline" (Denison 1979a: 145).

The Los Angeles Times proposed a new Murphy's Law to cover the situation ("The Sky Should Fall on Murphy" 1979: 18A, pt. 2), editorializing ". . . it seems time to revise Murphy's Law to read: Everything that can go wrong will go wrong at the same time. . . . We are inclined to go along with Denison's view that the problem is the revised Murphy's Law, partly because we have never held with magic answers."

With absence of any growth in the residual having now extended to 1981, this seems even more likely. As stated, national income per person employed in nonresidential business was 12.5 percent less than it would have been in 1981 if the residual had increased at its 1948–73 rate after 1973. Nevertheless, it is possible that one development was responsible for so big a gap, even though it is hard for me to visualize what it could be.

To leave much of the productivity slowdown unallocated is, of course, less than satisfactory. Richard Stone has recommended that statistical discrepancies be eliminated by distributing them among known factors not only in the national income and product accounts—which he recommended long ago—but also in growth accounting (1980: 1539–43). In other words, he suggests distributing the change in the residual among determinants in accordance with one's best guesses. So long as the possibilities remain that the slowdown problem is either a little of everything or a great deal of some one unspecified thing, I do not feel able to do this. Stone is, of course, right in saying that direct estimates should replace residuals whenever possible, even where a large element of judgment is required.

NOTES

1. The writer is Senior Fellow Emeritus of The Brookings Institution. Views expressed are those of the author and should not be ascribed to the officers, trustees, or other staff members of The Brookings Institution.

2. The same estimates are used in an article that I prepared for a conference of the Royal Economic Society (Denison 1983). To a considerable extent, of course, descriptions of the series in the two articles also overlap.
3. Their adoption would leave unchanged the 1948–73 growth rates of 3.72 percent per annum for national income in the whole economy and 3.60 percent for non-residential business national income that are used here, reduce from 2.04 to 2.02 the 1973–81 growth rate for the whole economy, and raise from 1.79 to 1.85 the 1973–81 growth rate for nonresidential business. These changes are minor.
4. An exception affecting national income in the whole economy but not in nonresidential business is the addition of the net inflow from abroad of reinvested earnings of incorporated foreign affiliates, a change introduced by the Bureau of Economic Analysis.
5. I have discussed elsewhere the concept of "command" which is now published quarterly by the Bureau of Economic Analysis (Denison 1979a: 11–12 and 1981: 17–22 and 27–28).
6. The growth rates of the official Bureau of Labor Statistics series for "output per hour in the business sector" were 2.9 percent and 0.7 percent in the same periods, both before and after the July 1982 revisions. This concept differs from mine in that output is measured by gross national product instead of national income, tenant-occupied dwellings are included, and elimination of hours for which a worker is paid when he is not at work is not attempted. There are also minor statistical differences.
7. The growth rate of actual national income in 1969–73, based on the latest (July 1982) data is 0.37 percentage points above the rate when these estimates were prepared. Incorporation of this revision will raise growth of potential output, but there will also be other changes.
8. Rounding to two decimal points is not, of course, meant to indicate precision; it is adopted because, with many small numbers, further rounding would distort changes and prevent regrouping of sources.
9. *Accounting for Slower Economic Growth* (Denison 1979a) gives an exact description of my procedures and, together with my earlier books, explains their rationale.
10. See Denison (1979a: 57–58) for the method of calculation. The 1973–81 result happens to be the same as the 1973–76 result shown there in Table 4–4.
11. I ignore here the points that it is essentially meaningless to classify advances into two groups on an either/or basis, as if it didn't matter whether a ten-cent modification of a capital good or a billion dollar investment is needed, and that, even if it were not, there is no way to meet the vintage models' need to establish the fraction of advances that must be embodied.
12. See Denison and Poullier (1967: 144–50) for earlier discussion and references. The preceding paragraph is shortened from pages 145–46.

I have pointed out cases in which the reasoning described above is not applicable, and one such case is pertinent here (Denison 1980c: 1024–25):

> This reasoning does not apply when investment is eliminated by the fiat of regulating authorities rather than because it appears insufficiently profitable. If the investment blocked departs at all from the average rate of technological improvement, it is likely to incorporate an above-average amount. This is because regulators are likely to be most cautious, and public interest groups most vociferous in their opposition, when major changes, such as the use of nuclear energy, are proposed.

Retardation of the growth of output per unit of input by regulatory fiat is a consequence of regulation and can be removed only by a change in regulation, not by changing incentives to save and invest. This effect, if its size were known, would be classified as an effect of regulation but is actually included in my residual series because it has not been estimated.

13. Capital per person in the labor force rather than per person potentially employed is sometimes used, with similar results. I have elsewhere defined potential output and employment (Denison 1979a: 12–15, 1980a).

14. The most recent statement is in Denison (1982a: 60–61).

15. Not directly pertinent to Baily's argument because he analyzes output gross of capital consumption but relevant to estimates of net output is the fact that shortening service lives would change not only the amount of the production decline explained by capital but also the amount of the production decline to be explained.

16. To derive a series for structures and equipment from security values requires elimination of the value of corporate assets other than structures and equipment, and the current-dollar series obtained in this way must be deflated for use as structure and equipment input (for which Baily uses net stock).

17. Christensen and Jorgenson's work (1970: 19–50, and numerous other publications, some with D. Cummings) presents and describes estimates with this scope.

18. Adjustment for changes in capital utilization that result from other causes are not, in general, appropriate. See Denison (1969: 18–21).

19. Lindbeck (1983) says that such coefficients are "probably upward biased" but uses them. He gives no details about the calculation or scope of output or capital; he cites a forthcoming seminar paper.

20. Kendrick's actual statement is that the relationship indicated that a 1 percent increase in capital per unit of labor increases output per unit of labor by 0.88 percent, but dropping "per unit of labor," as in the text above, does not change the meaning of the result.

21. Despite all problems and the wide range of results in different studies, including some that find no significant effect from capital, almost all studies obtaining elasticities by correlation obtain high values for r, as is customary when economic time series are correlated. For an amusing case in which thirty-nine of forty alternate production functions calculated by correlation had values of r above 0.95 and twenty had values of 0.99 (ranging up to 0.9964) even though an entirely inappropriate employment series was used to calculate them, see Denison (1968: 291).

22. Perhaps I should say only that this seems to me to be nonsense. Partly on the grounds that capital/output ratios are constant, so output is a simple multiple of capital and nothing but capital can affect output, the German research institutes once advised the German government that a general reduction in working hours would not affect the nation's output.

    Chapter 10 of Denison and Poullier (1967) explains (if any explanation is still needed) why contributions of capital to growth cannot be inferred from international correlations of GNP and investment ratios. So do numerous other books and articles.

23. If the convention were not followed, hours reduction would be shown as accounting for less of the productivity slowdown, and resource reallocation for more. See Denison (1974: 35–43, 64, 105–06) for fuller explanation of the treatment of hours.

24. For example, Tatom, who blames energy prices, states explicitly (1982: 11 n.15): "In contrast to Edward F. Denison, . . . the analysis here of post-1973 productivity developments fully explains the productivity 'puzzle.' . . ."

25. The following discussion does not apply to general analyses such as those by Kendrick, Nordhaus, and Jorgenson, whose approach to growth analysis is more comprehensive. In discussing individual causes of the slowdown I cite these authors only in those cases where it is necessary to provide a balanced discussion.

26. Most of the literature concerning determinants of differences in the productivity of individuals or groups at a point in time is implicitly of this type, since it is conceivable that a change could occur over time in the average situation prevailing nationally although it is not asserted that a change actually has occurred. An article by Arnold, Evans, and House (1980) is a particularly good example since it appears in a volume titled *Lagging Productivity Growth* (Maital and Meltz 1980), was presented at a conference devoted to the productivity slowdown, and is, besides, a first-rate paper.

27. Eisner ably disputed the editorial (1980). The same editorial misunderstands me in regard to point 10 above, stating that: "He [Denison] reasons that the rise in government tax receipts from 26.1% of GNP in 1956 to 31% in 1973 and 32.4% in 1978 is not sufficiently great to adversely affect productivity. . . ." My reason for quoting such figures (and expenditure ratios, which supported the point more strongly) was to compare the large increase in the tax ratio from 1956 to 1973, when productivity rose smartly, with "the period after 1973, [which] was one of poor growth and productivity performance but not one in which the government share shot up abruptly."

28. Even if correct, these results would not provide a *positive* demonstration of the adverse effect of the higher tax rates on growth; that would require tracing and quantifying the effect on the amount and allocation of structures, equipment, inventories, and R&D, and then the effect of these changes on growth. The results refer only to the amount of capital gains of all types that are realized.

29. Earlier, Evans (1978: 93–94) had argued for very large effects, which Bristol (1978: 531–33) denied.

30. See also sources he cites.

31. I have suggested a different relation to price controls (Denison 1979a): The post-1973 productivity slowdown could be exaggerated (but not much) because limited price controls were in force in 1973 but not after 1974 and prices are likely to be understated under controls.

32. The errors in output growth and the capital contribution, though in the same direction, need not be the same size. The difference can't be computed without specifying the size of the error in the price index *in every year*. (The 1973–81 growth rate of gross output is affected only by price indexes for 1973 and 1981, but the growth rates of net output and capital stock are affected by errors in all the intervening years and in earlier years as well. To assume a constant bias would be inappropriate for the situation Clark postulates.)

33. Clark discusses the computer under the quality change heading, but the computer is not a case where a price index that misses quality change is used but, rather, a case where there is no price series. The producer's price index omits the computer and thus assumes, in effect, that computer prices have risen like other prices. However, the NIPAs assume nominal computer prices do not change at all, so the *greater* the rate of inflation the larger is the decline implied for the real price of computers and the *smaller* is the upward bias in the index of computer prices used in the NIPAs. Computers are included in the 3 percent of nonresidential business product that consists of producers' durables. The point that the capital contribution as well as growth of net output would change if the price index were changed applies to them.

34. My critical comments in this section are directed only at this doctrine and its exponents. The extent, effects, and diminution of tax evasion and other crimes can usefully be studied, and have been.

     Following is a sample of cult literature: Gutmann (1977: 26–27, 34; 1978: 9–13; 1979: 14–17); Feige (1979: 5–13; 1980); Haulk (1980: 23–27); Knight (1981); "The Underground Economy's Hidden Force" (1982: 64–70). Books by Simon and Witte (1982) and by Bartlett (1981) give additional references.

35. This sentence does not appear in the original publication of the story (Stout 1952).

36. Simon and Witte put the growth rate of the national income of the underground economy from 1974 to 1980 at 10 percent in current prices, less than the 10.6 percent rate they report for the regular economy. Reuter (1980: 65–71) is another who had discussed the possible effect of the underground economy on statistics.

     I should perhaps mention that results for 1969, 1973, and 1976 from the Tax Compliance Measurement Program do suggest an increase in personal income tax underreporting from 1969 to 1976, but the national income and product series allow for this.

37. The implication of their writings is inescapable: Economists engaged in national accounting, despite devoting full time to national income and product estimation, use procedures containing errors that are obvious to the underground economists and that they know how to correct. My appraisal is very different.

38. Gutmann, Feige, and Haulk all have different formulas and get different answers. (Gutmann in effect measures the money supply by currency, assuming that in the absence of the underground economy the ratio of M_1 to currency would be constant.) For time series, fits actually are not good, and relationships are highly sensitive to the period analyzed. Annual output indexes adjusted to include the underground economy show wildly improbable differences from unadjusted output, as is shown by a comparison of the annual percentage changes in the "official" and "underground" GNP when the latter is computed (by the Congressional Research Service) by Gutmann's methodology. (Data appear in Bartlett (1981): 20).)

39. However, reporters do not hesitate to cite with approval estimates of the amount by which output is understated because of underground transactions that differ among themselves by more than the total size of the less extreme estimates.

40. The most detailed attempt to support the doctrine is a widely circulated paper by Feige (unpublished). A critique of it by Parker (unpublished) finds Feige's case to be unfounded.

     In addition to papers by Parker and me, critical evaluations of the underground economy literature, as it pertains to NIPAs, have been provided by Blades (1982) and Leveson (1980). Kurtz (former commissioner of Internal Revenue Service) and Pechman (director of economic studies of The Brookings Institution) (1982: A15) criticize as grossly exaggerated estimates of tax losses that were circulated by the Internal Revenue Service.

REFERENCES

"Accounting for Slower Growth." 1979. *The Wall Street Journal* (December 18): 20.
Arnold, Hugh J.; Martin G. Evans; and Robert J. House. 1980. "Productivity: A

Psychological Perspective." In *Lagging Productivity Growth,* edited by Shlomo Maital and Noah M. Meltz, pp. 13–34. Cambridge, Mass.: Ballinger Publishing Company.

Baily, Martin N. 1981. "Productivity and the Services of Capital and Labor." *Brookings Papers on Economic Activity* 1: 1–50.

Bartlett, Bruce. 1981. *Reaganomics: Supply Side Economics in Action.* Westport, Conn.: Arlington House Publishers.

Berndt, Ernst R. 1980. "Energy Price Increases and the Productivity Slowdown in United States Manufacturing." In *The Decline in Productivity Growth,* proceedings of a conference held by the Federal Reserve Bank of Boston at Edgartown, Massachusetts, June, pp. 60–89.

Bernstein, Paul. 1980. "The Work Ethic That Never Was." *The Wharton Magazine* 4, no. 3 (spring): 19–25.

Blades, Derek. 1982. "The Hidden Economy and the National Accounts—OECD Economic Outlook." *Occasional Studies.* Washington, D.C.: Organization for Economic Cooperation and Development.

Bristol, Ralph B., Jr. 1978. "Pitfalls in Using Econometric Models: The Chase and DRI Capital Gains Estimates." *Tax Notes* 6 (May 15): 531–33.

Christensen, Laurits R., and Dale W. Jorgenson. 1970. "U.S. Real Product and Real Factor Input, 1929–1967." *Review of Income and Wealth,* series 16 (March): 19–50.

Clark, Peter K. 1982. "Inflation and the Productivity Decline." *The American Economic Review* 72, no. 2 (May): 149–54.

Denison, Edward F., and Robert Parker. 1980. "The National Income and Product Accounts of the United States: An Introduction to the Revised Estimates for 1929–80." *Survey of Current Business* 60, no. 12 (December): 1–26.

Denison, Edward F., and Jean-Pierre Poullier. 1967. *Why Growth Rates Differ: Postwar Experience in Nine Western Countries.* Washington, D.C.: The Brookings Institution.

Denison, Edward F. 1964. "Capital Theory and the Rate of Return: A Review Article." *The American Economic Review* 54, no. 5 (September): 720–25.

———. 1968. " 'Embodied Technical Change and Productivity in the United States, 1929–1958'—A Comment." *The Review of Economics and Statistics* 50 (May): 291.

———. 1969. "Some Major Issues in Productivity Analysis: Examination of Estimates by Jorgenson and Griliches." *Survey of Current Business* 49, no. 5, pt. II (May): 1–27.

———. 1972. "Final Comments on Estimates by Jorgenson and Griliches." *Survey of Current Business* 52, no. 5, pt. II (May): 95–110.

———. 1974. *Accounting for United States Economic Growth, 1929–1969.* Washington, D.C.: The Brookings Institution.

———. 1978. "Effects of Selected Changes in the Institutional and Human Environment upon Output Per Unit of Input." *Survey of Current Business* 58 (January): 21–44.

———. 1979a. *Accounting for Slower Economic Growth: The United States in the 1970s.* Washington, D.C.: The Brookings Institution.

———. 1979b. "Comment on Norsworthy, Harper, and Kunze, 'The Slowdown in Productivity Growth: Analysis of Some Contributing Factors.' " *Brookings Papers on Economic Activity* 2: 436–440.

———. 1979c. "Pollution Abatement Programs: Estimates of Their Effect upon Output per Unit of Input, 1975–78." *Survey of Current Business* 59 (August): 58–59.

———. 1980a. "Changes in the Concept and Measurement of Potential Output in the United States of America." In *Empirische Wirtschaftsforschung: Konzep-*

tionen, Verfahren und Ergebnisse, edited by Joachim Frohn and Reiner Staglin. Berlin: Duncker & Humblot. (Also in General Series Reprint 367, Washington, D.C.: The Brookings Institution.)

_____ . 1980b. "Discussion of Kopcke, 'Capital Accumulation and Potential Growth.' " In *The Decline in Productivity Growth*, proceedings of a conference held by the Federal Reserve Bank of Boston at Edgartown, Massachusetts, June, pp. 6-59.

_____ . 1980c. "Research Concerning the Effect of Regulation on Productivity." In *Dimensions of Productivity Research*, vol. 2, edited by John D. Hogan, pp. 1015-25. Houston, Tex.: American Productivity Center.

_____ . 1981. "International Transactions in Measures of the Nation's Production." *Survey of Current Business* 61, no. 5 (May): 17-28.

_____ . 1982a. "Comment on Richard Ruggles and Nancy D. Ruggles, 'Integrated Economic Accounts for the United States, 1947-80.' " *Survey of Current Business* 62, no. 5 (May): 59, 65.

_____ . 1982b. "Is U.S. Growth Understated Because of the Underground Economy? Employment Ratios Suggest Not." *The Review of Income and Wealth* (March): 1-16.

_____ . 1983. "The Interruption of Productivity Growth in the United States." *The Economic Journal* 93 (March): 56-77.

Eisner, Robert. 1980. "Productivity and Taxes." *The Wall Street Journal* (January 14): 19.

Evans, Michael K. 1978. "Capital Gains Taxes and Econometric Models." *Tax Notes* 6 (May 29): 593-94.

Feige, Edgar L. 1979. "How Big Is the Irregular Economy?" *Challenge* 22 (November/December): 5-13.

_____ . 1980. "The Theory and Measurement of the Unobserved Sector of the U.S. Economy: Causes, Consequences, and Implications." Paper delivered at the 93rd annual meeting of the American Economic Association, September 6.

_____ . Unpublished. "A New Perspective on Macroeconomic Phenomena: The Theory and Measurement of the Unobserved Sector of the United States Economy—Causes, Consequences, and Implications."

Feldstein, Martin S. 1978. "The Appropriate Taxation of Capital Gains." *Tax Notes* 7 (October 30): 507-08.

Feldstein, Martin S.; Joel Slemrod; and S. Yitzhaki. 1978. "The Effects of Taxation on the Selling of Corporate Stock and the Realization of Capital Gains." New York: National Bureau of Economic Research.

Filer, Randall K. 1980. "The Downturn in Productivity Growth: A New Look at Its Nature and Causes." In *Lagging Productivity Growth: Causes and Remedies*, pp. 108-27. Cambridge, Mass.: Ballinger Publishing Company.

Gordon, Robert J. 1981. "Comment on Rasche and Tatom, 'Energy Price Shocks, Aggregate Supply and Monetary Policy: The Theory and the International Evidence. ' " In *Supply Shocks, Incentives and National Wealth*, Carnegie-Rochester Conference Series on Public Policy, vol. 14, pp. 95-101. Amsterdam: North-Holland Publishing Company.

Gregory, Paul R. 1980. "Discussion of Berndt, 'Energy Price Increases and the Productivity Slowdown in United States Manufacturing.' " In *The Decline in Productivity Growth*, proceedings of a conference held by the Federal Reserve Bank of Boston at Edgartown, Massachusetts, June, pp. 90-92.

Grossman, Elliot S., and George E. Sadler. 1982. "Establishment Data and Productivity Measurements." National Council on Employment Policy. Mimeo.

Gutmann, Peter M. 1977. "The Subterranean Economy." *Financial Analysts Journal* 33 (November/December): 26-27, 34.
_____ . 1978. "Off the Books." *Across the Board* 15 (August):9-13.
_____ . 1979. "Statistical Illusions, Mistaken Policies." *Challenge* 22 (November/December): 14-17.
Haulk, Charles, J. 1980. "Thoughts on the Underground Economy." *Economic Review of the Federal Reserve Bank of Atlanta* (March/April): 23-27.
Jarrett, J. Peter, and Jack G. Selody. 1981. "The Productivity-Inflation Nexus in Canada 1963-1979." *Bank of Canada Technical Report 23* (March).
Kendrick, John. 1981. "International Comparison of Recent Productivity Trends." In *Essays in Contemporary Economic Problems: Demand, Productivity, and Population—1981-82 edition,* edited by William Fellner, pp. 125-70. Washington, D.C.: American Enterprise Institute.
Knight, Jerry. 1981. "The Underground Economy." *The Washington Post* (July 21 to July 26, 5 pts.).
Kopcke, Richard W. 1980. "Capital Accumulation and Potential Growth." In *The Decline in Productivity Growth,* proceedings of a conference held by the Federal Reserve Bank of Boston at Edgartown, Massachusetts, June, pp. 26-53.
Kurtz, Jerome, and Joseph A. Pechman. 1982. "Tax Fraud Hyperbole." *The New York Times* (July 12): A 15.
Leibenstein, Harvey. 1982. "The Prisoners' Dilemma in the Invisible Hand: An Analysis of Intrafirm Productivity." *The American Economic Review* 72 (May): 92-97.
Leijonhufvud, A. 1977. "Costs and Consequences of Inflation." In *The Microeconomic Foundations of Macroeconomics,* edited by G.C. Harcourt, pp. 265-312. Boulder, Colo.: Westview Press.
Leveson, Irving. 1980. "Productivity in Services: Issues for Analysis." In *Dimensions of Productivity Research,* vol. 2, edited by John D. Hogan, pp. 765-803. Houston, Tex.: The American Productivity Center.
Lindbeck, Assar. 1983. "The Recent Slowdown of Productivity Growth." *The Economic Journal* 369, 93 (March): 13-34.
Ling, Robert R. 1982. "Correlation and Causation." *Journal of the American Statistical Association* (June): 489-91.
MacAvoy, Paul W. 1982. "The Underground—No Recession There." *The New York Times* (July 4): F3.
Malabre, Jr., Alfred L. 1981. "Study Disputes View That Growth of Service Jobs Crimps Productivity." *The Wall Street Journal* (June 19):?
Minarik, Joseph J. 1981. "Capital Gains." In *How Taxes Affect Economic Behavior,* edited by Henry J. Aaron and Joseph A. Pechman, pp. 241-81. Washington, D.C.: The Brookings Institution.
_____ . 1982. "Minarik Confesses." *Brookings Staff Newsletter,* no. 7 (April 9, 1982): 4-5.
Nordhaus, William D. 1978. "Claimed Effects of Gains Tax Cuts: A Mirage?" *Tax Notes* 7 (December 4): 652, 659.
_____ . 1980. "Policy Responses to the Productivity Slowdown." In *The Decline in Productivity Growth,* proceedings of a conference held by the Federal Reserve Bank of Boston at Edgartown, Massachusetts, June, pp. 147-72.
Norsworthy, J.R.; Michael J. Harper; and Kent Kunze. 1979. "The Slowdown in Productivity Growth: Analysis of Some Contributing Factors." *Brookings Papers on Economic Activity* 2: 387-421.
Ott, Mac. 1982. "Money, Credit and Velocity." *Economic Review of the Federal Reserve Bank of St. Louis* 64, no. 5 (May): 21-34.

Parker, Robert P. 1980. "The Understatement of GNP and of Charges against GNP in 1976 Due to Legal-Source Income Not Reported on Individual Income Tax Returns." Bureau of Economic Analysis. Photocopy. (Earlier version appeared in hearings on the underground economy held before the House Subcommittee on Oversight, 1979.)

Pine, Art. 1981. "Corporations React and Learn to Alter Strategy Permanently." *The Washington Post* (January 28): F1-3.

Rasche, Robert H., and John A. Tatom. 1981a. "Energy Price Shocks, Aggregate Supply and Monetary Policy: The Theory and the International Evidence." In *Supply, Shocks, Incentives and National Wealth,* Carnegie-Rochester Conference Series on Public Policy, vol. 14, edited by Karl Brunner and Allan H. Meltzer, pp. 9-93. Amsterdam: North-Holland Publishing Company.

_____ . 1981b. "Reply to Gordon." In *Supply Shocks, Incentives and National Wealth,* Carnegie-Rochester Conference Series, vol. 14, pp. 103-107. Amsterdam: North-Holland Publishing Company.

Rees, Albert. 1980. "Improving Productivity Measurement." *The American Economic Review* 70 (May): 340-42.

Reuter, Peter. 1980. "A Reading on the Irregular Economy." *Taxing and Spending* (Spring): 65-71.

_____ . 1982. "The Irregular Economy and the Quality of Macroeconomic Statistics." In *The Underground Economy in the U.S. and Other Countries.* Lexington, Mass.: D.C. Heath.

Ruttan, Vernon W. 1979. "Inflation and Productivity." *American Journal of Agricultural Economics* 61 (December): 896-902.

Simon, Carl P., and Ann D. Witte. 1982. *Beating the System: The Underground Economy.* Boston: Auburn House.

"The Sky Should Fall on Murphy." 1979. *The Los Angeles Times* (December 28): 18A, pt. 2.

Solow, Robert M. 1980. "Discussion of Nordhaus, 'Policy Responses to the Productivity Slowdown.' " In *The Decline in Productivity Growth,* proceedings of a conference held by the Federal Reserve Bank of Boston at Edgartown, Massachusetts, June, pp. 173-77.

Stone, Richard. 1980. "Whittling Away at the Residual: Some Thoughts on Denison's Growth Accounting—A Review Article." *Journal of Economic Literature* 18, no. 4 (December): 1539-43.

Stout, Rex. 1955. "This Won't Kill You." In *Three Men Out.* New York: Bantam Books. (Appeared originally in 1952 as "This Will Kill You," *American Magazine* 154 (September): 131-43.)

Tatom, John A. 1982. "Potential Output and the Recent Productivity Decline." *Economic Review of the Federal Reserve Bank of St. Louis* 64, no. 1 (January): 3-15.

"To Make America Productive." 1979. *The New York Times* (December 19): A30.

"The Underground Economy's Hidden Force." 1982. *Business Week* (April 5): 64-70.

Yinger, John. 1978. "Feldstein on Capital Gains Realizations." Council of Economic Advisers Staff Paper. Excerpts in *Tax Notes* 7 (October 9): 428.

COMMENT

Edward N. Wolff

My comments are organized in four parts. First, I will present a brief summary of Dr. Denison's major results and present a comparison of these with his earlier results in the 1979 book, *Accounting for Slower Economic Growth: The United States in the 1970s*. Second, I will make some brief remarks on the statistical concepts he uses. Third, I will compare his findings with those of some other researchers in the field. Finally, I have some comments on the mystery of the Denison "residual."

SUMMARY OF RESULTS

Denison's paper extends results reported in his 1979 book through 1981 (his earlier results went up through 1976). Here Denison finds that the rate of growth of actual NIPPE (national income per person employed) in the whole economy fell from 2.2 percent per annum in 1948–73 to 0.1 percent in 1973–81, for a change of − 2.0 percentage points (see Table 1). The rate of growth of potential NIPPE (that is, national income per person *potentially* employed) in the full economy fell from 2.3 percent to 0.0, for a change of − 2.3 percentage points. The fall in the growth rate was somewhat greater for potential NIPPE because resources were used less intensively in 1981 than in 1973. (Resources were also utilized less intensively in 1973 than in 1948, but the difference was smaller.) Another measure Denison uses is the "command over goods and services," which reflects, in part, the purchasing power of the American dollar vis-à-vis other currencies. Because of the

47

Table 1. Various Estimates of the Change in the Overall Rate of Productivity Growth over the Postwar Period.

Source	Concept	Period	Rate of Productivity Growth Per Annum (percentage)
1. Denison (1979)	National income per person employed in nonresidential business	1948-73	2.43
		1973-76	-0.54
2. Kendrick (1980)	Real product per unit of labor in the business economy	1948-66	3.5
		1966-73	2.1
		1973-78	1.1
3. Kendrick (1980)	Total factor productivity in the business economy	1948-66	2.7
		1966-73	1.6
		1973-78	0.8
4. Norsworthy, Harper, and Kunze (1979)	Gross domestic product per hour of labor input	1948-65	3.32
		1965-73	2.32
		1973-78	1.20
5. Thurow	GNP per manhour in private sector	1948-65	3.3
		1965-72	2.3
		1973-78	1.2
6. Denison (1982)	a. Actual national income per person employed in the whole economy	1948-73	2.2
		1973-81	0.1
	b. Potential national income per person potentially employed in the whole economy	1948-73	2.3
		1973-81	0.0
	c. Actual national income per person employed in nonresidential business	1948-73	2.5
		1973-81	-0.2
	d. Potential national income per person potentially employed in nonresidential business	1948-73	2.6
		1973-81	-0.2

deterioration in the terms of trade over the 1973-81 period, the change in the growth rate of the command measure per person employed was -2.3 percentage points, greater than that of actual NIPPE.

Because the productivity analysis is made for the nonresidential business economy, which accounts for over three-quarters of national income, Denison introduces comparable statistics for this sector. The growth in actual NIPPE fell by 2.7 percentage points from 1948-73 to 1973-81. This is a smaller retardation than he found in comparing the 1948-73 and 1973-76 periods, for which the drop was 3.0 percentage points. The difference reflects the slight improvement of the economy after 1976.[1] Finally the growth in potential NIPPE fell by 2.8 percentage points between 1948-73 and 1973-81. As far as overall productivity performance is concerned, there is only a small difference between the 1973-81 and 1973-76 periods.

Denison next turns to an analysis of the sources of the productivity slowdown, results of which are summarized in Table 2. The productivity measure used is actual NIPPE in the nonresidential business economy. The basic technique used in the analysis is called growth accounting, whereby the overall growth rate in productivity can be decomposed as the weighted sum of growth rates of inputs plus a residual. (One can most easily think of this from the point of view of a Cobb-Douglas production function, for which the rate of growth of output is equal to a value share weighted sum of inputs plus the rate of disembodied technical change). In Denison's analysis, the residual (which resembles the measure of disembodied technical change) dominates the slowdown, accounting for 63 percent of the retardation. I shall return to this point later.

Perhaps Denison's most controversial finding is that the change in the extent of capital formation accounts for only 8 percent of the productivity slowdown. The input of capital in the form of structures and equipment actually grew at the same rate in 1948-73 as in 1973-81, namely 3.8 percent per year. The growth in the input of capital in the form of inventories fell considerably, from 3.6 percent to 2.4 percent. Since inventories are a small part of total capital, total capital input grew at 3.7 percent in 1948-73 and 3.4 percent in 1973-81. However, because of the acceleration in employment growth between the two periods from 1.1 percent to 2.0 percent, the rate of growth of total capital input per person employed fell from 2.6 percent to 1.4 percent or by 1.2 percentage points. In growth accounting, the contribution of this decline in the growth of the capital/labor ratio depends on the share of capital income in nonresidential business national income, which Denison estimates to be between 0.13 and 0.15. Separately weighting inventories and fixed capital, Denison estimates that the capital "slowdown" explains only -0.21 percentage points, or 8 percent of the productivity slowdown (see Table 2). In Denison's 1979 work, he found that the capital "slowdown" accounted for -0.12 points of the 1973-76 productivity

Table 2   Estimates of the Percentage Importance of Selected Factors in the Productivity Slowdown.

Source	Period	Percentage of Slowdown Attributable to Factor
I. Capital formation		
A. Capital/labor ratio growth		
1. Denison (1979)	1948–73/1973–76	4
2. Kendrick	1948–66/1973–78	21
3. Clark	1948–65/1965–73	35
4. Nadiri	1948–74/1974–78	38
5. Tatom	1950–72/1972–79	39
6. Norsworthy and	1948–65/1965–73	—
Harper	1965–73/1973–77	49
7. Norsworthy, Harper,	1948–65/1965–73	—
and Kunze	1965–73/1973–78	71
8. Denison (1982)	1948–73/1973–81	8
B. Vintage effect		
1. Kendrick	1948–66/1973–78	10
2. Clark	1948–65/1965–73	14
	1965–73/1973–78	9
C. Pollution and regulation		
1. Denison (1979)	1948–73/1973–76	13
2. Kendrick	1948–66/1973–78	16
3. Denison (1982)	1948–73/1973–81	6
D. Energy price effect		
1. Denison (1979)	1948–72/1972–76	3
2. Norsworthy, Harper,		
and Kunze	1965–73/1973–78	16
3. Hudson and Jorgenson	1948–72/1972–76	approx. 20[a]
II. Labor quality		
A. Hours worked (efficiency-adjusted)		
1. Denison (1979)	1948–73/1973–76	10
2. Denison (1982)	1948–73/1973–81	6
B. Age-sex composition		
1. Denison (1979)	1948–73/1973–76	3
2. Denison (1982)	1948–73/1973–81	1
C. Education		
1. Denison (1979)	1948–73/1973–76	−12
2. Denison (1982)	1948–73/1973–81	−3
III. Research and development		
1. Denison (1979)	1948–72/1972–76	3
2. Griliches	1965–73/1973–77	10
3. Kendrick	1948–66/1973–78	13
4. Nadiri (whole economy)	1948–74/1974–78	17
5. Nadiri (private economy)	1948–74/1974–78	37
IV. Output composition (resource allocation)		
1. Denison (1979)	1948–73/1973–76	13

Source	Period	Attributable to Factor
2. Kutcher, Mark, and Norsworthy	1947-66/1966-73	23
3. Norsworthy, Harper, and Kunze	1948-65/1976-73	—
	1965-73/1973-78	24
4. Thurow	1948-65/1965-72	—
	1965-72/1972-77	45-50
5. Wolff	1947-67/1967-76	48
6. Nordhaus	1948-65/1965-71	77
7. Denison (1982)	1948-73/1973-81	12

[a]Percentage contribution based on Denison's estimate of 2.97 percentage point decline in overall productivity growth.

decline or only 4 percent. But broadly speaking, the results are comparable between the newer and earlier study.

In regard to the other major input, labor, the results are again comparable between the two studies. Changes in hours of work, adjusted for efficiency considerations (from a change between part-time and full-time work and from a shortening of excessively long hours for farm workers) contributed −0.41 points to 1973–81 productivity growth, compared to −0.54 in 1973–76. Changes in age/sex composition, which affects the average experience level of workers, contributed −0.21 points in 1973–81, compared to −0.25 in 1973–76. Finally, increases in education contributed 0.61 in 1973–81, compared to 0.88 in 1973–76. The net effect was −0.01 in 1973–81, compared to 0.09 in 1973–76—again, a small difference.

In summary, with land included as an input, Denison finds that "output per unit of input" (which others call "total factor productivity" or TFP) grew at 1.99 percent per annum in 1948–73 and −0.32 percent per annum in 1973–81, for a decline of 2.31 percentage points. In his earlier work, Denison estimated a −0.66 annual growth rate for output per unit of input in 1973–76. Thus, as in his earlier analysis, the non-input-related factors dominate the productivity retardation.

The factors not directly related to inputs can be divided into two parts: (1) those that can be directly estimated and (2) the residual. The former can be divided into four groups. The first is improved resource allocation, which is essentially the movement of labor out of low-paid farming and nonfarm self-employment jobs. With regard to farming, the argument is that the marginal product of farm labor, as measured by the wage, is substantially lower than labor in other sectors. Therefore, a shift of labor out of farming to the nonfarm sector will increase the value added generated per worker and hence NIPPE. The same argument holds for self-employed and unpaid workers in small, inefficient enterprises. The fact that the shift out of farming and nonfarm self-employment slowed down after 1973 causes the rate of productivity growth to fall. Such a slowdown in this shift accounted for 12 percent of the 1973–81 productivity slowdown, compared to 13 percent of the 1973–76 productivity slowdown.

The second factor is called changes in "legal and human environment" and refers mainly to government regulations concerning pollution and worker safety and health. This factor accounted for 6 percent of the 1973–81 productivity slowdown, compared to 13 percent of the 1973–76 slowdown. The differences is largely due to the decreased importance of pollution abatement programs in diverting capital stock from productive uses after 1975. (This effect is classified under capital formation in Table 2 because the impact of such government regulations are viewed as affecting productive capital formation.) The third factor, economies of scale, and the fourth factor, consisting of weather irregularities, labor disputes, and demand intensity, were of minor importance in explaining the 1973–81 slowdown. In conclusion, with the possible exception of government regulation, there were no major changes in the quantitative importance of the various factors accounting for the 1973–76 and the 1973–81 productivity slowdowns.

STATISTICAL CONCEPTS

There are two issues I would like to raise in regard to the choice of concepts Denison uses. The first concerns the measure of output, which is national income. National income can be defined more fully as net national product at factor cost. The major difference between national income or NI and GNP is the exclusion of depreciation and indirect business taxes. As shown in Table 1, Denison's estimates of labor productivity growth for the 1948–73 period or so are comparable to those of the other researchers cited. However, for the 1973 and after period, the discrepancy is quite large. Denison estimates a growth rate of NIPPE in nonresidential business of −0.54 in 1973–76 and −0.2 in 1973–81. In comparison, Kendrick's (1980) estimate was 1.1 for real product per unit of labor in the business economy in 1973–78; Norsworthy, Harper, and Kunze (1979) estimated 1.2 for gross domestic product per hour of labor input in 1973–78; and Thurow's (1979) estimate was the same for GDP per manhour in the private sector in 1972–77.

Why is Denison's estimate of the productivity growth rate during the slowdown period so much lower? The main factor appears to be the rapid increase in the ratio of depreciation/GNP after 1973. Depreciation (technically, capital consumption allowances, with capital consumption adjustment) increased as a percentage of GNP for the *full economy* from 7.8 in 1948 to 8.8 in 1973, 10.2 in 1976, and 11.0 in 1980. This increase subtracted about 0.4 percentage points from productivity growth, at least for the full economy. For the business economy, it was probably even more important since the excluded portion, the nonbusiness government sector, does not record depreciation.[2]

I think that from a welfare point of view, NNP is superior to GNP since the depreciation of fixed capital is an intermediate cost just like the consumption of raw materials and semifinished goods, which is also netted out as the measure of final output. However, from a statistical point of view, I am not sure what to make of the increase in the ratio of depreciation/GNP, except for a change in business accounting techniques.[3]

The second issue is the exclusion of the nonenterprise and residential sectors from the growth analysis. From the point of view of data availability for growth analysis, this is perhaps a wise decision. But from the point of view of measuring welfare, excluding the nonenterprise government sector seems unwise since the government does provide useful services such as sanitation and education. It also accounted for between 13 and 18 percent of total nonagricultural employment in 1948–80. Moreover, in terms of productivity analysis, the nonbusiness government sector is probably the most stagnant sector of the economy in terms of the growth of *physical product* per employee, I would urge that the government sector be treated as an integral part of the economy.[4]

In regard to the so-called residential sector, which is largely imputed rent to owner-occupied housing, I agree with Denison that it should be excluded from the definition of total production. The reason is that the production of housing is recorded in current product (as part of investment). Including "housing services" in the definition of output would require one to abandon a production concept of output in favor of service flows from existing wealth. Also, since most of housing services is provided by unpaid household labor, one would also have to include all unpaid household activity in the definition of output.[5]

A COMPARISON WITH OTHER STUDIES

Table 2 shows estimates made by different researchers of the contributions of various factors to the productivity slowdown. As one can see, there is such a wide variation in such estimates that it would be hard to establish a consensus on the importance of many factors. Since Denison has focused on the relation between the capital slowdown and the productivity slowdown in this paper, let me make a few comments about this.

The first is the choice of periods. Most analysts divide the productivity slowdown into two periods: 1966–73 and post-1973. Norsworthy and Harper (1979) and Norsworthy, Harper, and Kunze (1979) found the capital slowdown much more important in the second slowdown period. I looked at Denison's book to see whether this may account for the discrepancy in results but found that the contribution of capital was estimated at 0.27 in 1964–69, 0.39 in 1969–73, and 0.35 in 1973–76 (Denison 1979: 100).

The second issue is the proper choice of capital weights. As mentioned above, the contribution of capital to productivity growth is the product of its value weight and the rate of growth of capital. If we add together fixed capital and inventories, the rate of growth of capital input per person employed declined by 0.93 percentage points between 1948–73 and 1973–81. If, for example, the capital weight were as high as 40 percent, this capital slowdown would account for −0.37 of the productivity slowdown, instead of the −0.21 that Denison estimates. I agree with Denison that national income is the appropriate concept to use for measuring economic welfare. On the other side of the ledger, however, I am not sure that the capital share should exclude depreciation when measuring the contribution of capital stock to output. If one adopts a production function framework, which Denison implicitly does in growth accounting, then it is probably sensible to include depreciation as part of the services provided by capital. Most other researchers have estimated capital shares (including depreciation) between one-quarter and one-third. (Hudson and Jorgenson (1978) have estimated a capital share as high as 40 percent.) Using a weight of 0.29 (midway between 0.25 and 0.33), the contribution of capital to the slowdown using Denison's measure of capital input would be −0.27.

The third issue is the use of gross capital stocks instead of net capital stocks. I agree with Denison that we want a measure of the contemporaneous services provided by capital, not its future services. In the case of the "one hoss shay" approach that Denison uses, the value of capital input would remain unchanged until the capital good completely deteriorated, at which point its value would fall to zero. If one hoss shays lasted ten years, then in the steady state, one out of ten would cease functioning each year. This would be correctly captured by a measure of net stocks with a depreciation rate of 10 percent. I am not sure why Denison weights net stock by one-fourth (and hence gross stocks by three-fourths) in his measure of capital input. It should be noted that if net stocks are used and a capital share of 0.29 the capital slowdown would have explained about −0.48 (−1.65 × 0.29) or 18 percent of the productivity slowdown. This is somewhat closer to the results of other researchers reported in Table 2.

THE MYSTERY OF THE DENISON "RESIDUAL"

The unattributed residual still dominates the sources of the productivity slowdown in the 1973–81 period, as it did for the 1973–76 period. Denison offers seventeen possible explanations of the residual, all of which he carefully dismisses. From the menu of seventeen, I would like to take up two that happen to be my leading candidates.

The first is Denison's number 16, the shift to services and other structural changes. In this regard, I think there is a basic conceptual difficulty in using sectoral NIPPE to evaluate this factor. In a recent paper I prepared with Baumol (Baumol and Wolff 1982), we argued that in a perfectly competitive environment, the ratio of the *value* of output to the *value* of inputs would tend toward equality across sectors. Sectoral NIPPE would then tend to equal the inverse of the labor share in a sector. In the case where wage levels also differ between sectors, sectoral *levels* of NIPPE would also differ across sectors. Denison's analysis of the shift effect in this paper essentially focuses on the cases where wage levels differ between sectors. In particular, as discussed above, he concentrates on the movement of labor out of low-wage small farms and nonfarm self-employment. His interpretation of this movement is, quite correctly, one of increasing the efficiency of resource allocation.

However, there is another way of analyzing "shift effects," which is to decompose overall productivity growth into a weighted average of sectoral *rates* of productivity growth. For this analysis, one could use value measures of output, such as sectoral national income, deflated by a common price index, but such measures of sectoral productivity growth tend toward equality in equilibrium. Preferably, one could use a measure of sectoral physical productivity whose rate of growth over time will, in general, differ from value productivity. Physical productivity is the ratio of physical output (grain as opposed to the value of grain) to real inputs. In input/output terms, sectoral physical output is sectoral gross output in real terms—that is, deflated by a *sectoral* price deflator. Whereas for theoretical reasons, sectoral rates of *value* productivity growth can be expected to tend toward equality over time, sectoral rates of physical productivity growth will, in general, vary considerably across sectors. It can then be shown that if employment shifts toward sectors with low rates of physical productivity growth, overall productivity growth will decline.

This is what I believed happened after 1973 (actually starting in about 1967). Labor shifted out of agriculture, which was one of the sectors with the highest rates of physical productivity growth and which as a result depressed overall productivity growth. (This analysis is quite different than Denison's, for whom the movement of labor out of low-wage farming *added* to overall productivity growth). Services with the exception of communications and trade with the inclusion of the government were the most stagnant sector, and they absorbed most of the new employment after 1967. I estimated that such sectoral shifts in employment accounted for about half of the productivity slowdown (see Table 2). The other half was the decrease in the average rate of sectoral physical productivity growth. Almost all other researchers, with the exception of Denison, found that employment shifts were a significant contributory factor to the overall productivity slowdown.

The second is Denison's point number 1, the curtailment of expenditures on R&D. As Denison argues here and in his 1979 book, constant-dollar expenditures on nonspace or defense-related R&D showed very little reduction after 1973. I think, as most would agree, the more appropriate measure is the ratio of R&D to GNP,[6] though even this ratio did not show much decline after 1973. However, even this measure is not sufficient, since the effect of R&D on productivity growth can itself change over time. This relation is often referred to as the "rate of return to R&D." In this regard, the standard evidence is somewhat mixed. Griliches (1980), for example, estimated that the rate of return to R&D fell by over 60 percent between 1959–68 and 1969–77. Agnew and Wise (1978), Scherer (1981), and Terleckyj (1980) also found declining returns to R&D during the 1970s. On the other hand, Griliches and Lichtenberg (1981) found that there was a fairly substantial increase in the return to R&D between 1959–68 and 1969–76. A similar finding was reported by Scherer (1981). Finally Clark and Griliches (1982) found no significant change in the return to R&D after 1969.

Though these results do conflict, there are some speculative reasons why we might expect a secular decline in the return to R&D. The speculation rests on the notion that the R&D activity is itself basically stagnant in terms of its own (physical) productivity. Over time, therefore, one might expect that its cost will increase relative to the industries that use R&D. Such a relative increase in the cost of R&D is not usually captured in standard measures of constant-dollar R&D, since these series are usually deflated using the investment or GNP deflator. Such a relative increase in the cost of R&D would mean that, in real terms the actual volume of R&D activity is being overstated at a rate that increases over time. Using standard measures of R&D expenditure, one would then expect a return to R&D that decreases secularly over time (see Baumol and Wolff (1983) for a fuller exposition of this argument).

NOTES

1. The differences in results reported here between Denison's earlier work and his most recent piece also reflects, in part, the latest revision of the National Income and Product Accounts. These new data are incorporated in the present paper but not in the earlier results.
2. The remaining difference is equal to the sum of indirect business tax and nontax liability plus business transfer payments plus the current surplus less subsidies of government enterprises plus the statistical discrepancy. The ratio of this to GNP was 7.7 percent in 1948, 9.3 percent in 1973, 9.5 percent in 1976, and 8.3 percent in 1980.

3. Another possible explanation is the increased obsolescence of structures and equipment due to the rapid rise in energy prices after 1973, but this view is not widely held.

4. Another reason for its exclusion is that policy recommendations are usually couched in terms of how best to stimulate private productivity.

5. The exclusion of the residential sector may also be thought to account, in part, for the difference in productivity growth rates reported by Denison and the others cited in Table 1. Excluding the residential sector will lower both the measure of national income and that of depreciation. In regard to national income, the ratio of personal housing services (including imputed rent to owner-occupied housing) to national income grew slightly faster after 1973 than before—at approximately 1.7 percent per annum in 1973–81 and 1.4 percent per annum in 1948–73. This small difference, however, is not sufficient to explain the large difference in estimates of productivity growth rates in the post-1973 period between Denison and others.

6. Denison in his 1979 book argues that the volume of R&D may really be the appropriate concern because an increase in the volume of production does not necessarily mean a proportional increase in the number of separate products or techniques. The same amount of R&D can induce the same efficiency gains in the products of 1 million cars as in 5 million. This argument seems compelling on the surface, yet it seems to conflict with the evidence of a fairly stable proportional increase in R&D expenditures with sales in many companies without a phenomenal increase in their productivity. I'm not sure whether the reason is an expansion of processes and products with output or increasing complexity over time in inducing technical change in mass production.

REFERENCES

Agnew, C.E., and D.E. Wise. 1978. "The Impact of R&D on Productivity: A Preliminary Report," paper presented at the Southern Economic Association Meetings. Princeton: Mathtech, Inc.

Baumol, William J., and Edward N. Wolff. 1982. "A Paradox in the Measurement of Interindustry Differences in Productivity." New York University. Mimeo.

————. 1983. "Feedback from Productivity Growth to R&D." *Scandinavian Journal of Economics* 85, mp½ 2, 147–57.

Clark, Kim, and Zvi Griliches. 1982. "Productivity Growth and R&D at the Business Level: Results from the PIMS Database." Cambridge, Mass.: National Bureau of Economic Research Working Paper No. 916.

Clark, Peter K. 1977. "Capital Formation and the Recent Productivity Slowdown." Paper presented at a conference of the American Economic Association and the American Finance Association, New York, December 30.

————. 1979. "Issues in the Analysis of Capital Formation and Productivity Growth." *Brookings Papers on Economic Activity,* no. 2: 423–31.

Denison, Edward F. 1979. *Accounting for Slower Economic Growth: The United States in the 1970s.* Washington, D.C.: The Brookings Institution.

Griliches, Zvi. 1980. "R&D and the Productivity Slowdown." *American Economic Review* 70, no. 2 (May): 343–47.

Griliches, Zvi, and Frank Lichtenberg. 1981. "R&D and Productivity Growth at the Industry Level: Is There Still a Relationship?" Cambridge, Mass.: National Bureau of Economic Research.

Hudson, E.A., and Dale W. Jorgenson. 1978. "Energy Prices and the U.S. Economy, 1972–76." *Natural Resources Journal* 18, no. 4 (October): 877–97.

Kendrick, John W. 1980. "Productivity Trends in the United States." In *Lagging Productivity Growth*, edited by Shlomo Maital and Noah M. Meltz, pp. 9–30. Cambridge, Mass.: Ballinger.

Kutscher, R.E.; J.A. Mark; and J.R. Norsworthy. 1977. "The Productivity Slowdown and Outlook to 1985." *Monthly Labor Review* 100 (May): 3–8.

Nadiri, M. Ishaq. 1980. "Sectoral Productivity Slowdown." *American Economic Review* 70, no. 2 (May): 349–52.

Nordhaus, W.D. 1972. "The Recent Productivity Slowdown." *Brookings Papers on Economic Activity,* no. 3, 493–536.

Norsworthy, J.R., and Michael Harper. 1979. "The Role of Capital Formation in the Recent Slowdown in Productivity Growth." BLS Working Paper No. 87, January.

Norsworthy, J.R.; M.J. Harper; and K. Kunze. 1979. "The Slowdown in Productivity Growth: Analysis of Some Contributing Factors." *Brookings Papers on Economic Activity,* no. 2, 387–421.

Scherer, F.M. 1981. "Research and Development, Patenting, and the Microstructure of Productivity Growth," unpublished paper, Northwestern University, June.

Tatom, John A. 1979. "The Productivity Problem." *Economic Review of the Federal Reserve Bank of St. Louis* (September): 3–16.

Terleckyj, Nestor E. 1981. *R&D and U.S. Industrial Productivity in the 1970s,* Washington, D.C. National Planning Association.

Thurow, Lester. 1979. "The U.S. Productivity Problem." *Data Resources Review* (August).

Wolff, Edward. 1981. "The Composition of Output and the Productivity Growth Slowdown of 1967–76." New York University. Mimeo.

2 COMPARATIVE ANALYSIS OF THE PRODUCTIVITY SITUATION IN THE ADVANCED CAPITALIST COUNTRIES

Angus Maddison

This paper presents estimates of labor productivity (GDP per man-hour) for the United States and five other advanced countries (France, Germany, Japan, Netherlands, and the United Kingdom) and analyzes the productivity slowdown in historical and comparative perspective. All six countries have had a marked productivity slowdown since 1973. The U.S. slowdown has been second largest in proportionate terms (behind Japan) but only fifth largest in terms of percentage points deceleration because the United States already had a slow productivity growth by international standards before the deceleration occurred. By historical standards, 1973–81 U.S. productivity growth is very low, but it has a precedent in the 1929–38 period. European and Japanese productivity growth, by contrast, is still well above the 1870–1950 record. The explanation of the slowdown is divided into conjunctural and nonconjunctural forces.

All these countries have followed cautious macroeconomic policy since 1973 in order to avoid balance of payments problems arising from the OPEC-imposed price rises for energy and to try to break inflationary expectations. As a result, investment has shown virtually no rise for the past nine years, and resource allocation has become less efficient.

The decleration in the growth of capital stock per worker has been significant in all the countries since 1973. Furthermore it seems probable, as Baily has recently suggested, that a portion of the 1973 capital stock was made prematurely obsolete by the two oil shocks and the consequent change in relative prices.

It is clear that the capital slowdown is a significant factor in productivity slowdown, but its relative importance depends on (1) the weight given to capital in the "production function" and (2) how big the "Baily factor" is. Here it is argued that Baily probably exaggerated the Baily factor.

The adverse effects of the conjuncture on resource allocation have probably been bigger in Europe and Japan than in the United States because (1) Europe and Japan have experienced a sharper break from conditions of sustained prosperity, which the United States did not enjoy to the same degree in the postwar "golden age"; (2) government "industrial" and "labor market" policies have tried harder to promote labor hoarding and mitigate the employment consequences of macrocaution; and (3) the new uncertainties connected with international trade under floating rates have impacted more severely outside the United States.

On the nonconjunctural side, the paper endorses Denison's suggestion that government regulatory activity made a modest contribution to the post-1973 slowdown in the United States but suggests that such intervention probably had less important productivity effects in Europe. The author rejects the idea that growth in government size has otherwise been a major drag that can explain unmeasured elements of the productivity slowdown. The paper also rejects the view that deterioration in the quality of labor input can contribute to explaining the post-1973 productivity slowdown, though it does make some modest contribution to explaining why U.S. productivity grew more slowly than that of other countries over the past two decades.

The most fundamental nonconjunctural reason for the slowdown in productivity growth in Europe and Japan is that these countries are ceasing to enjoy the "opportunities of backwardness" because they have now drawn close to U.S. productivity levels. Operating closer to the frontier of technology makes it less profitable to sustain such high levels of investment as in the past, and these countries have to spend more than they did on R&D. The catching-up process also means smaller productivity gains from increased resource allocation because both the abnormal gains from structural shifts away from low-productivity agriculture and also the improved allocation of resources through reopening of channels for international trade specialization are now waning as sources of growth.

The waning of the U.S. leadership margin in productivity levels ought to be favorable for future U.S. productivity growth because it means that the burdens of leadership in product and process innovation can be more widely shared. On these grounds the underlying trend of U.S. labor productivity (which has averaged 2.3 percent a year since 1890) ought to improve.

However, there is a strongly held view that in the long run, productivity growth in the lead country must slacken off because the stock of knowledge cannot be expected to grow indefinitely at a steady pace. The long-run productivity curve will be S-shaped. In 1941 Kuznets suggested that this point of inflection was near. This proved to be premature, but one cannot exclude the possibility that such a point may now have arrived. After all, the present U.S. productivity level is about twelve times that of 1870, and twenty-five times that of the United Kingdom at the end of the eighteenth century.

The most obvious evidence that things may be moving this way is the predominant role of services in the output and employment structure of advanced countries, particularly in the United States. Measured productivity in services has consistently grown more slowly than in commodity production for the past century, and this sector certainly seems to be one that is more resistant to technical improvement than commodity production. Furthermore, structural shifts have had a negative impact on productivity growth since 1973.

The evidence is as yet too poor to conclude that such a fundamental slowdown is operative because it is difficult to disentangle the conjunctural and nonconjunctural elements in the recent structural shifts, and the impact of a slowdown in technical progress would be slow. After all, if all technical progress came to an abrupt halt, aggregate U.S. productivity could still be doubled, as worst-practice firms caught up with best-practice.

THE SLOWDOWN SINCE 1973

Since 1973, productivity (GDP per man hour) growth has slowed down markedly in all the countries considered here (see Table 2-1).[1] In the European countries the proportionate slowdown has been smaller than in the United States and Japan, but all countries have had a very significant productivity deceleration. Nevertheless, all the European countries and Japan

Table 2-1. GDP Per Man-hour (annual average compound growth rates).

	1870-1950	1950-60	1960-73	1973-81	Percentage Point Deceleration
France	1.9	4.4	5.5	3	−2.2
Germany	1.5	6.9	5.4	3.7	−1.7
Japan	1.6	5.7	9.3	3.1	−6.2
Netherlands	1.4	3.4	5.4	2.6	−2.8
United Kingdom	1.4	2.2	3.9	2.9	−1.0
United States	2.3	2.3	2.6	1.1	−1.5
Average	1.7	4.2	5.4	2.8	−2.6

Source: See Appendix Tables A-1 to A-5.

have remained on a growth path that is high by any historical standards except those of their postwar "golden age" (1950–73). The fastest productivity growth since 1973 has been in Germany, and not in Japan, which had grown fastest in 1960–73.

American productivity growth has been much steadier than in the other countries over the long pull. It was not adversely affected by the two world wars and did not have the great postwar acceleration that other countries enjoyed. Nevertheless there has been some degree of fluctuation in U.S. productivity history, and the present slowdown is not without precedent. In 1929–38, a slowdown of similar proportions and duration occurred and was then followed by the twelve best years of productivity growth the United States had previously experienced.

"CONJUNCTURAL" FORCES

Since 1973 there has been a prolonged situation of below-capacity resource use in these countries. There were two widespread recessions in 1974–75 and 1980–81 when the OPEC shocks set off spontaneous recessionary forces. In between there was a period of incomplete recovery. As a result, the growth of output suffered a bigger retardation than that of productivity, and unemployment has risen to a degree not seen since the 1930s.

The conjunctural element in the productivity slowdown cannot be neatly separated from other forces, but must have been substantial because of the sudden and sharp deceleration in capital formation and the dramatic character of the two energy shocks. 1973 also marked a clear and sharp turning point in the pace of productivity growth in all the countries. Most of the nonconjunctural forces described in the next section are of a type that would impact more slowly on productivity growth.

The present conjunctural difficulties in fact reflect a major crisis in methods of managing the advanced capitalist economies. The malaise is chronic rather than cyclical, so the "conjunctural" epithet may not be very apt.

The present macroeconomic posture of all these countries is remarkably similar. Because of fears of inflation and of reactivating OPEC, all the governments have followed rather deflationary macroeconomic policies, which have nevertheless not been strong enough to break inflationary expectations. From time to time individual countries have attempted to be more expansionary than the rest (e.g., Germany in 1979 or France in 1981), but they have been checked well before the full employment point by balance-of-payments fears.

One striking feature of the conjunctural situation that is different from the 1930s is that there have not been massive trade restrictions that would have adversely affected productivity (see Table 2-2). The liberal international

Table 2-2. Conjuncture Indicators 1960-81 and 1929-38 (annual average compound growth rates).

	Gross Fixed Capital Formation			Private Final Consumption		
	1960-73	1973-81	1929-38	1960-73	1973-81	1929-38
France	7.6	0.6	-3.2	5.6	3.4	0.5
Germany	4.4	0.9	1.4a	4.7	2.3	1.4a
Japan	14.2	1.2	8.9	9.2	2.8	2.0
Netherlands	5.6	-1.6	-3.0	5.6	2.4	2.0
United Kingdom	4.6	-1.3	2.8	2.8	0.9	1.7
United States	4.5	-0.1	-9.0	4.2	2.8	-0.3
Average	6.5	-0.1	-3.5	5.4	2.4	1.2

	Export of Goods and Services			Government Consumption		
	1960-73	1973-81	1929-38	1960-73	1973-81	1929-38
France	9.4	6.3	-5.0	3.9	2.8	4.2
Germany	7.9	5.6	-6.1a	4.7	2.9	11.9a
Japan	14.0	10.6	8.2	6.1	4.2	7.9
Netherlands	9.1	2.5	-3.6	2.8	2.7	2.5
United Kingdom	5.1	2.7	-2.9	2.5	1.6	6.0
United States	6.7	5.9	-1.9	2.8	1.9	4.6
Average	8.9	5.6	-1.9	3.8	2.7	6.2

	GDP			Consumer Prices		
	1960-73	1973-81	1929-38	1960-73	1973-81	1929-38
France	5.6	2.5	-0.4	4.5	11.4	1.4
Germany	4.5	2.0	3.8	3.4	5.0	-2.2
Japan	9.8	3.7	4.7	6.2	9.1	1.2
Netherlands	5.0	1.7	0.3	4.9	7.1	-2.1
United Kingdom	3.1	0.5	1.9	5.1	15.2	-0.7
United States	4.1	2.3	-0.7	3.2	8.8	-2.1
Average	5.4	2.1	1.6	4.6	9.4	-0.8

	Employment		
	1960-73	1973-81	1929-38
France	0.7	0.0	-0.9
Germany	0.2	-0.5	1.2
Japan	1.3	0.7	1.0
Netherlands	1.1	0.6	0.5
United Kingdom	0.2	-0.9	1.1
United States	1.9	1.9	-0.2
Average	0.9	0.3	0.5

a1928-38.

Note: GDP and its components are at constant prices.

Sources: GDP components 1960-81—from OECD, *National Accounts of OECD Countries* (various issues). France 1929-38—estimates for public expenditure, investment, and exports from Carre, Dubois, and Malinvaud (1972: 316); consumption derived as a residual using the GDP growth figure on p. 35 and the 1938 weights for GNP from OEEC (1967: 59). Germany 1928-8—from Erbe (1958: 100), deflated by consumer price index. Japan 1929-38—from Ohkawa and Shinohara (1979: 258). Netherlands 1929-38—from *Tachtig Jaren Statistiek in Tijdreeksen* (1979: 144-45) and from Vorstman (1974). United Kingdom 1929-38—from Feinstein (1972: T16). United States 1929-38—from U.S. Department of Commerce (1977: 324). GDP—from Table 2-A2. Employment—from Table 2-A3. Consumer prices—from Maddison (1982).

economic order has held remarkably firm, and exports have been better sustained than home demand. However, the present high degree of international integration with capital markets even more open than those for goods is also the reason for the similarity of the policy situation in the different countries. In the 1930s, governments were freer to pursue expansionist policies behind the trade barriers they had erected.

The conjunctural malaise has had three types of adverse effects on productivity:

1.   The rate of investment and the growth of capital stock has fallen;
2.   The drop in resource use has worsened resource allocation; and
3.   The very large rise in the relative price of energy has produced sharp problems of structural adjustment, requiring new factor combinations and some abnormal obsolescence of capital stock.

The Capital Stock

Since 1973, faltering demand, excess capacity, and the squeeze on profits have lowered investment rates generally, and the capital stock has grown more slowly than before (though some of the decline may be due to longer-term, nonconjunctural reasons). Table A-6 shows the movement of the aggregate nonresidential fixed capital stock, measured both gross and net. The net stock figure is more sensitive to changes in the pace of capital formation and generally shows a bigger deceleration in 1973-80 compared with 1960-73 rates of growth than does the gross stock. For the present purpose I have averaged the gross and net figures per employee (see Table 2-3). If one compares growth in 1960-73 with column A for 1973-80, it is clear that there was a significant deceleration in the growth of capital per employee in all the countries.

Furthermore, it seems desirable to make some allowance for the effect that the very large rise in real energy prices has had in rendering some kinds of capital obsolete more quickly than would otherwise have occurred.

In a recent study (1981), M.N. Baily concluded that structural changes and in particular the big increase in relative energy prices caused a 20 percent loss of effective capital in the United States from 1968 to 1978. He derived this result by using a composite measure of capital stock that gives one-third weight to Tobin's q (the ratio of the deflated market value of assets to the constant price capital stock values in the NIPA) and two-thirds to the more conventional NIPA figures (which is what I used in column A).

If the Baily method were used for other countries, it would also produce a notable deceleration of their capital stock growth because their market values had also fallen substantially and their capital stock conventionally

Table 2-3. Growth of Nonresidential Fixed Capital Stock Per Person Employed.

	Annual Average Compound Growth Rates of Capital Stock Per Employee on Different Assumptions			Percentage Point in Growth Rate on Different Assumptions	
	1960-73	*A* *1973-80*	*B* *1973-80* *5 percent* *adjustment*	*A*	*B*
France	4.8	4.5	3.9	−0.3	−0.9
Germany	6.2	4.7	4.1	−1.5	−2.1
Japan	10.6	5.8ᵃ	5.2ᵃ	−4.8ᵃ	−5.4ᵃ
Netherlands	5.9	3.4	2.9	−2.5	−3.0
United Kingdom	4.2	3.4	2.8	−0.8	−1.4
United States	2.1	1.0	0.4	−1.1	−1.7
Average	5.6	3.8	3.2	−1.8	−2.4

ᵃ1973-79.

Note: The figures are an average of gross and net stocks except for Japan and the Netherlands when they refer to the gross stock. Column *B* assumes that 5 percent of the 1973 stock has been rendered useless by the energy price rise.

measured grew faster than in the United States (see Table 2-4). I think there was in fact a "Baily effect" because of the sharp change in energy prices and that it is worthwhile to adjust for it. However, Baily's own assumptions appear to be too extreme because market valuations are not only influenced by assessments of induced obsolescence but by other factors affecting demand, capacity use, profit expectations, interest rate policies, and so forth. Furthermore, normal depreciation or retirements would have removed a significant part of the 1973 capital stock by 1980. I have therefore assumed that the Baily effect rendered only 5 percent of the 1973 stock prematurely obsolete.

Table 2-4. Changes in the Inflation Adjusted Industrial Share Index (annual average compound growth rate).

	1960-73	*1973-80*
France	−2.8	−7.3
Germany	−3.0	−5.3
Japan	4.2	−5.3
Netherlands	−3.0	−10.9
United Kingdom	−0.2	−8.1
United States	2.3	−6.7

Source: Industrial share prices from IMF, *International Financial Statistics* (various issues), deflated by consumer price indexes from OECD sources.

The importance of the capital slowdown for the productivity slowdown is a matter on which opinions differ even within the neoclassical analytical framework. Denison gives nonresidential fixed investment a weight of only 10 percent for the nonresidential business sector and about 7 percent for the economy as a whole.[2] Norsworthy and associates give a bigger weight to capital because they include depreciation in their estimates for nonresidential business (Norsworthy, Harper, and Kunze, 1979).

Baily gives capital an input weight of 25 percent against Denison's 10 percent. If one gives the capital inputs of Table 2-3 a 25 percent weight,[3] then the average contribution of these types of capital to the productivity slowdown in 1973–80 would be 0.6 percentage points a year (including my estimate of the Baily effect).

Worsened Resource Allocation

In periods of slack demand, firms are generally slow to dismiss workers and will hoard labor voluntarily for some time. This has an adverse effect on productivity in most recessions but would not normally be expected to last for a period of seven or eight years, by which time bankruptcy of less efficient firms might be expected to have the opposite effect on productivity. However, governments have tried in many ways to mitigate the impact of recession on employment by job protection legislation, job subsidies, public job creation, or takeovers and extensive help to big firms that might otherwise have gone bankrupt. Employment in the government sector, where productivity considerations are never very strong, continued to expand in the 1970s. All these job protection efforts tend to curb productivity growth in ways that are difficult to quantify. These practices are probably most important in the Netherlands, an extreme case of the welfare state, and in Japan, where labor hoarding in times of slack demand is facilitated by the flexible wage structure and other institutional habits.

In the United Kingdom, where government policy since early 1979 has been more extremely deflationary than elsewhere, the shake-out effects of recession seem to have predominated, and rather high productivity gains were seen in 1980 and 1981.

Apart from the normal impact of cyclical slack, the efficiency of resource allocation has been affected by new types of uncertainty. The volatility of exchange rates makes it more difficult to make decisions involving export markets or imported materials. The uncertainty about whether the two OPEC price rises would really be permanent also tended to cloud important business decisions, as did the variations in the pace of inflation, uncertainties about interest rates, and changes in government policy trade-offs.

These various types of loss in allocative efficiency were probably less important for the United States than for European countries and Japan, where firms are less free to fire workers than are American employers and where government has tried to mitigate the consequences of unemployment by encouraging labor hoarding. Moreover, European and Japanese firms had enjoyed more than two decades of virtually uninterrupted growth, whereas this was not true in the United States.

Another type of allocation loss is the deterioration in economies of scale. This is a very difficult area to quantify for the economy as a whole. Denison usually assumes that economies of scale are roughly 10 percent of output growth, and Kendrick's recent study (1981) follows the same practice. As output growth slackened a good deal in all the countries this means that both of these authors give a significant explanatory role to the scale factor in the productivity slowdown.

In the past I have felt that Denison has exaggerated the role of scale economies and that in the postwar golden age their importance may have been no more than half of what he suggested (Maddison 1972). However, the sharp and prolonged slowdown in growth momentum (particularly in the industrial sector) suggests that the setback to scale economies may be more than proportionate to the deceleration of output.[4] Hence I agree with the Denison-Kendrick conclusion about the importance of this effect. I also agree that it was probably greater in Europe and Japan than in the United States.

The Impact of Changed Energy Prices

As a result of the OPEC price rises, energy costs probably represent around 8 percent of GDP at factor cost in these countries instead of 2 percent in 1973. This has led to substantial changes in resource allocation requiring increases in "energy productivity," as compared with the situation from 1960–73 when energy was cheap and energy productivity fell (see Table 2-5a and b). The suddenness of the need for energy economy in 1973–81 was

Table 2-5a. Energy Consumption Per $1,000 of Real GDP (GDP in 1975 U.S. relative prices; energy in tons of oil equivalent).

	1950	1960	1973	1981
France	0.62	0.57	0.56	0.49
Germany	0.90	0.65	0.72	0.56
Japan	0.60	0.53	0.54	0.46
Netherlands	0.54	0.54	0.80	0.70
United Kingdom	1.04	0.84	0.75	0.62
United States	1.27	1.11	1.12	0.94
Average	0.83	0.71	0.75	0.63

Source: 1950 from Woytinsky (1953: 941). For 1960 and later years from International Energy Agency (1979) and subsequent IEA publications.

Table 2-5b. Energy "Productivity" (annual average compound growth rate).

	1950-60	1960-73	1973-81
France	0.8	0.1	1.7
Germany	3.2	−1.1	3.1
Japan	1.3	−0.1	2.0
Netherlands	0.0	−3.1	1.7
United Kingdom	2.1	0.9	2.4
United States	1.3	−0.1	2.2
Average	1.5	−0.4	2.2

unprecedented. Nevertheless, in historical perspective, it should be recognized that the 1960–73 experience was unusual because the long-term trend has been toward increased energy productivity (Maddison 1982: 48).

There is considerable controversy about the size of the adverse effect of the energy problem on productivity. Denison (1979) estimated the productivity loss at about 0.1 percentage points a year from 1973 to 1976 before the second OPEC shock. Kendrick (1981) has suggested that it contributed 0.3 percentage points a year to the 1973–79 productivity slowdown. Much higher estimates have been produced by Hudson and Jorgenson (1978) and by Rasche and Tatom (1977; Tatom 1981). The latter attribute almost all of the U.S. productivity slowdown since 1973 to the direct impact of the energy problem. My own view is that the direct productivity impact of the energy shocks is probably of the order that Kendrick suggests but that these losses are mostly covered by the Baily effect for which I have already allowed.

In fact the energy problem has had very complex repercussions and a full accounting of the productivity impact of the OPEC actions would undoubtedly give them major weight because these were a major cause of policies of cautious demand management, which reduced capital formation and the efficiency of resource allocation in ways already discussed. The sudden rise in oil prices and the temporary oil embargo contributed to inflation and inflationary expectations at a critical point in 1973–74. It reopened inflationary fires in 1979. It created large payments deficits and added greatly to uncertainties about the financing mechanism to cover these deficits. These factors were decisive in inducing cautious macroeconomic policies. In this sense, the energy problem is the ultimate cause of most of the "conjunctural" losses. In addition, the rise in relative energy prices worsened the terms of trade and reduced the real income of most of the countries. This income loss is not reflected in our productivity measure, whose numerator is real product and not real income.

NONCONJUNCTURAL CONSIDERATIONS

Although "conjunctural" influences probably explain a significant amount of the productivity slowdown since 1973, other, mostly longer-term influences have been at work.

The End of the Catching Up Process

In the postwar period, growth of productivity was more rapid in Europe and Japan than in the United States, due in large part to exploitation of the opportunities of backwardness. Productivity growth outside the United States had been held back by two world wars and the contraction of trade opportunities between the wars. In 1950 therefore their productivity levels were very depressed relative to those in the United States (see Table 2-6). High postwar demand induced high investment, trade channels were reopened, there was an outpouring of labor from low productivity activity in agriculture into higher productivity work in industry and services.

As these countries drew closer to U.S. productivity levels (see Table 2-6) productivity growth was more difficult to achieve because they were closer to the frontiers of technology and faced greater uncertainties in both process and product innovation. For this reason, they had to make a bigger R&D effort and rely less on borrowing from the leader (a process reflected in Table 2-7). A gradual slowdown in the rate of investment and capital stock growth was therefore to be expected at this stage, and the opportunities for productivity improvement through the efficiency effects of increased trade and structural change could not continue at the same pace as in the "golden age" (see Table 2-8 on trade and structural change). In fact, in Europe and

Table 2-6. The Convergence in Productivity Levels, 1950–81 (U.S. = 100.0 in specified year).

	GDP Per Man-hour		GDP Per Person Employed	
	1950	1981	1950	1981
France	45.9	95.5	48.8	102.7
Germany	35.9	95.5	44.4	101.4
Japan	16.1	58.5	19.3	79.1
Netherlands	56.0	97.0	66.1	100.8
United Kingdom	58.9	78.2	61.8	74.4
Average for 5 Countries	42.6	84.9	48.1	91.7

Source: Derived from appendix tables A1–A5.

Table 2-7.   Research and Development Expenditure as Percentage of GDP.

	1964	1973	1979
France	1.84	1.78	1.82
Germany	1.41	2.09	2.27
Japan	1.47	1.87	2.04
Netherlands	2.03	2.01	1.98
United Kingdom	2.32	2.13[a]	2.20[b]
United States	3.14	2.50	2.41

[a]1972.
[b]1978.
Source: OECD *Science and Technology Indicators, vol. B* (1981).

Japan the productivity slowdown after 1973, though hastened by conjunctural factors, had an element of inevitability.

Present rates of growth are still much higher than historial experience in prewar years, even in the United States. Once these countries catch up with U.S. productivity levels, it remains to be seen whether they can sustain their productivity growth at rates much above the long-run average of 2.3 percent a year attained by the United States.

For the United States, the ending of the catching-up phenomenon has implications the obverse of those for Europe and Japan. As other countries catch up with the United States, the burden of pioneering in technology will be eased, and if anything, the underlying pace of productivity growth should quicken. But it may be that the United States (and the world as a whole) has reached a stage where the frontiers of known technology will advance more slowly because new knowledge is inherently harder to gain (i.e., the Wolf's Law effect).

Fulfillment of Wolf's First Law?

Wolf (1912)[5] suggested that technical progress will ultimately be retarded because we will have exploited the easier innovations, there will be less left to discover, and the unknown will be harder to penetrate.

His position as translated by Kuznets (1930: 11) reads, "Every technical improvement, by lowering costs and by perfecting the utilization of raw materials and of power, bars the way to further progress. There is less left to improve, and this narrowing of possibilities results in a slackening or complete cessation of technical development in a number of fields."

In the 1930s, Kuznets (1930) and Burns (1934) found that the long-run history of particular industries was one of initial slow development, followed

Table 2-8. Impact of Structural Shift in Employment on Growth of GDP Per Person Employed, 1950-81.

	Actual Rate of Growth of GDP Per Person Employed		Rate of Growth of GDP Per Person Employed Assuming Employment Structure Unchanged and with Actual In-Sector Productivity Growth		Impact of Proportionate Sectoral Shift in Employment on Growth of GDP Per Person Employed	
	1950-73	1973-81	1950-73	1973-81	1950-73	1973-81
France	4.6	2.4	4.1	2.4	0.5	0.0
Germany	4.9	2.8	4.5	2.8	0.4	0.0
Japan	7.3	3.3[a]	6.0	3.2[a]	1.3	0.1[a]
Netherlands	3.9	1.8[a]	3.9	2.1[a]	0.0	0.3[a]
United Kingdom	2.2	0.9	2.2	1.3	0.0	−0.4
United States	2.4	0.0[a]	2.2	0.2[a]	0.2	−0.2[a]
Average	4.2	1.9	3.8	2.0	0.4	−0.1

[a]Preliminary, based on 1973-80 data.
Source: OECD Labour Force Statistics, National Accounts, and Quarterly National Accounts Bulletin (various issues).

by an acceleration of growth and then by retardation. Kuznets (1953: 281) suggested in 1941 that this S-shaped curve is what we might expect to be the ultimate pattern of productivity experience for the economy as a whole:

> In the industrialized countries of the world, the cumulative effect of technical progress in a number of important industries has brought about a situation where further progress of similar scope cannot be reasonably expected. The industries that have matured technologically account for a progressively increasing ratio of the total production of the economy. Their maturity does not imply a complete cessation of further technological improvements, but it does imply that economic effects of further improvements will necessarily be more limited than in the past.

This conclusion of Kuznets turned out to be premature, because the United States found other industries to take over the previous dynamic role of waning sectors and productivity growth in agriculture accelerated considerably.

Herman Kahn (1979: ch. 2) has speculated on where the turning point of the S-shaped curve might occur, and it is of course just possible that such a point of inflection may have taken place in the 1970s, exaggerated to some extent by conjunctural factors. I am rather skeptical as to whether human knowledge has yet entered the zone where Wolf's Law may start to operate, but one must at least contemplate the possibility and look at the evidence available.

To some degree the slackening in technical progress possibilities may be due to slower growth of the R&D stock. Kendrick (1976 and 1981) has made some ingenious estimates of this cumulated source of technical knowledge for individual countries and if we make a crude aggregation of the stocks of the five biggest countries, we find a growth rate of 6.3 percent a year from 1960 to 1973, reduced to 4.7 percent for 1973–79. This does not suggest a dramatic deceleration of technical progress, and in any case, the slowdown in R&D growth is not obviously due to any greater problem in producing innovation but rather in the incentives for finding it.

The economist who comes closest to endorsing the Wolf's Law position is probably Dale Jorgenson. He notes (1981) that productivity growth has slackened in all sectors of the economy (clear from Table 2-9), attributes most of the U.S. productivity slowdown to retardation in the pace of technical progress, and is rather gloomy about future prospects. However, his conclusions about the causes of the slowdown differ from mine and from those of Denison and Kendrick, and are as yet not available beyond 1976.

A neo- Schumpeterian explanation of the apparent Wolf's Law situation is that of Gerhard Mensch (1977). He suggests that we may have run into a period in which the scope for profitable exploitation of new innovations has temporarily flagged because the rapidity of growth in the 1960s reduced the normal lag between invention and innovation. However, I think the evidence he adduces for this is weak (Maddison 1982).[6]

Some of those who argue for a Wolf's Law effect would cite the growing importance of services as the major pillar of their argument. As is clear

Table 2-9. Growth of GDP Per Employee by Sector.

	1870-1950			1950-73			1973-81		
	Agriculture	Industry	Services	Agriculture	Industry	Services	Agriculture	Industry	Services
France	1.4	1.4	0.7	5.6	5.2	3.0	3.5	3.2	1.6
Germany	0.2	1.3	0.7	6.3	5.6	3.0	3.9	2.6	1.6
Japan[a]	0.7	1.7	0.5	7.3	9.5	3.6	1.1	4.7	1.9
Netherlands[a]	n.a.	n.a.	n.a.	5.5	5.8	2.4	5.2	2.5	1.3
United Kingdom[a]	1.4	1.2	0.2	4.7	2.9	1.6	2.8	1.8	0.7
United States[a]	1.3	1.6	1.1	5.5	2.4	1.8	1.6	-0.2	0.1
Average	0.9	1.4	0.6	5.8	5.2	2.6	3.0	2.4	1.2

[a]Last three columns refer to 1973-80.
Source: Maddison (1982).

from Table 2-8, productivity in services has consistently grown more slowly than in commodity production in all the countries for more than a century. It is also clear from Table 2-A8 that services account for a growing share of employment—highest in the United States where it is now two-thirds of the total. All of the advanced capitalist countries have undergone a process of deindustrialization in the course of the past two decades, and this seems likely to continue. Furthermore, the service sector is not one where the absolute level of productivity is superior to that in industry.

It seems clear therefore that the likely sectoral shifts in demand patterns are apt to produce unfavorable effects on productivity growth compared with past experience. Although this seems probable, one must remain skeptical about the locus of technical change and its pace of advance. Until the 1940s, the Ricardian view that technical change in agriculture would lag behind industry seemed to be valid, and then proved to be wrong. The same might happen in services.

Depletion of U.S. Natural Resources

In the past an important reason for U.S. productivity leadership was its rich endowment in natural resources compared with Europe and Japan. It has been clear for some time that this lead is fading and that productivity growth in some natural resource sectors has been adversely affected by depletion. Partly for this reason, and partly because of safety regulation, U.S. mining productivity has fallen considerably, whereas in some other countries (e.g., the Netherlands and United Kingdom) new natural resource developments have boosted aggregative productivity growth.

Oversized and Overactive Government?

Aggregate government spending has increased substantially in all six countries over the past three decades, but there is no clear relationship between the size of government and economic performance. Government spending absorbs a similar proportion of resources in Japan and the United States, which have had very different productivity histories. Government size is a good deal higher in the West European countries than in the United States, and again there is no apparent relationship between this phenomenon and comparative growth rates (see Tables 2-10 and 2-A9). Nevertheless it is often alleged that oversized and overactive government now impedes productivity in the following ways:

1.   High taxes reduce the incentive to work and save;
2.   High social transfers discourage work effort;

Table 2-10.   Government Expenditure as Percentage of GDP at Current Prices.

	1950	1973	1980
France	27.6	38.8	46.0
Germany	30.4	41.2	45.1
Japan	19.8	22.9	32.4
Netherlands	26.8	49.1	57.9
United Kingdom	34.2	41.5	44.7
United States	22.5	32.0	35.0
Average	26.9	37.6	43.5

Source: OECD, *National Accounts of OECD Countries* (various issues). 1950 Japan calendar year estimated from fiscal year figures in Ohkawa and Shinohara (1979: 254, 372).

3. Tax morality has weakened, so that there are rapidly growing do-it-yourself, barter, and underground economies, which reduce overall efficiency and measured output;

4. Government provision of "merit goods" is inefficient and overmanned because of pressures from the professional interests involved in a sector where "market" pressures are absent;

5. Regulation increases costs and distorts resource allocation; and

6. Tax "expenditures" have mushroomed so that the tax system distorts incentives and resource allocation.

The first two arguments are not new but have received greater prominence recently with the advent of conservative administrations in the United Kingdom and United States that stress "supply side" economics.[7] Some of the alleged impact under these headings is already reflected in the measures we have used. For instance, loss of working time for sickness is undoubtedly larger in Europe than in the United States because sickness benefits are more generous. Hence, our measure of labor input for 1980 allows for 20 days sickness absence in the United Kingdom, 18.8 in the Netherlands, 12.5 in France, 12.3 in Germany, and only 6 for the United States.[8] We have almost no evidence on changes in work effort that may have occurred during working time, but I am doubtful that any significant negative changes have occurred in a time when most people have been increasingly anxious to retain their jobs.

The third argument raises problems of measurement that are not new, as those who remember Al Capone, Mme. Claude, and the *Dreigroschenoper* will recall. But it has recently been alleged that the underground economy has grown enormously as a result of new tax and social security motives. The biggest claims for the underground economy have been made by Feige, who has suggested that it might be as much as a quarter of U.S. GDP, basing his arguments on financial ratios (Feige 1979). However, this view is regarded as a wild exaggeration by national accounts statisticians (Denison 1982), and Derek Blades has recently suggested a GDP understatement of around 3 percent for the countries considered here (Blades 1982).

My own conclusion is that Feige is wrong and that Blades and Denison are right about the likely magnitude of GDP understatement in the countries considered here, but recent revisions of national accounts (e.g., in the United States and the Netherlands) are generally upward, so that underground or not easily identified activity is probably growing proportionately. However, this will not bias our productivity measure significantly if such activity is carried out mainly outside recorded working hours or by people not recorded as employed. And this is probably the situation.

The fourth point about government and productivity has been made strongly by two British authors who have used it as an explanation of slow British growth (Bacon and Eltis 1978). Their argument is that high British government claims have distorted the structure of the economy away from industry toward services and that government is overmanned because of antiproductivity pressures from the highly unionized professionals who work for government. They also allege that "the shift in employment from industry to services, and public services in particular, had no equal in any other large Western developed economy" (1978: 11–12) and that the problem arises mainly because the public sector does not have to market its services. They therefore advocate a reduction in the public employment in teaching, health, and the social services.

The substance of the productivity problem to which Bacon and Eltis refer is already covered by Table 2–8, which shows the impact of structural employment changes on aggregate productivity. It would be interesting to disaggregate such analysis to compare productivity trends for publicly supplied services that have a market analog, such as education and health. Unfortunately the statistical information on public employment and output is not yet adequate to permit valid comparison,[9] and therefore most of the specific Bacon-Eltis conclusions about the unique character of the U.K. problem remain dubious.

In the United States, considerable stress has been given to the distorting impact of regulatory activity.[10] Here the problems of international comparison are very big because the borderline between the basic legal framework and regulation is not clear. Regulatory activity grew rapidly in the United States in the 1960s. This reflected consumerist and environmentalist activism, which was successful in modifying automobile specifications and enforcing new environmental constraints on business activity. Stiffer health and safety regulations also reduced productivity in mining, and various kinds of antidiscriminatory labor legislation may have had similar side effects. More recently the tide has turned with deregulation of airlines and of natural gas and oil. Denison (1984) now estimates that regulatory activities reduced U.S. output per unit of input by 0.2 percent a year in the 1970s, which is somewhat less adverse than his previous estimate.

Kendrick has used the earlier Denison estimates as a benchmark for judging the productivity impact of regulatory activity in other countries (using government environmental spending as an adjustment coefficient). He therefore infers a bigger adverse impact than Denison and one that is bigger outside the United States. I think Kendrick probably exaggerates the adverse impact of regulation. My impression is that the long-run trend in Europe since the war has been away from detailed governmental regulation of economic activity. Legislation on car safety features and environmental protection did have some impact in the 1970s but probably less than in the United States. Regulatory impact is greater in the United States, which usually creates specialized governmental agencies to implement new regulatory legislation. These agencies are more activist than the equivalent authority would be in Europe, and they tend to adopt an abrasive adversary posture in administering new rules, involving more litigation and less regard to business costs than in Europe.[11] However, it may well be that regulatory activity in Japan has had bigger adverse productivity effects than in the United States and Europe, as Kendrick suggests, because Japan is more highly regulated and has been more concerned with pollution.

Another "off-budget" item that now receives closer scrutiny is tax expenditures. The basic notion is one of taxes foregone or postponed—that is, derogations from levies on income that would normally be taxed, that are not inadvertent loopholes, but that are deliberately built into the tax system as a form of encouragement or implicit subsidy for certain types of behavior. There is difficulty in getting internationally comparable definitions of (1) the "normal" tax structure from which derogation is granted and (2) "normal" income as distinct from expenses incurred in producing it.

In France, on an incomplete accounting for 1975, tax expenditures amounted to 1.5 percent of GDP; in Germany in 1980 to 1.9 percent; and in the United States the federal component was 5.7 percent of GDP in 1979 (Conseil des Impôts 1979: 119-24; Deutscher Bundestag 1981: 24). Here again, the covert role of government appears to be bigger in the United States than in Europe, but I have seen no estimates of the productivity impact of this type of selective government aid.

Quality of the Employed Population

In this study all employed persons have been treated as equal. Other productivity analysts have made adjustments for differences in the quality of labor because of changes in the structure of employment by age and sex, and have generally used relative earnings as an adjustment factor (Perry 1978; Denison 1979a: 32–36).

Earnings differentials are influenced by legislative and institutional factors that vary considerably from country to country for reasons independent of the productivity contribution of different types of employee. It does not therefore seem worthwhile to make a very sophisticated earnings adjustment for purposes of international comparison, but Table 2–11 gives a crude idea of the effect of changes in the age/sex composition of employment. It shows the productivity impact when females and young males are given a weight of 0.6 compared with 1 for prime-age males.

This adjustment does not help to explain the slowdown after 1973, since the structural changes after that date were generally more favorable or less unfavorable to productivity than those in the 1960–73 period. However, it does help to explain some of the productivity growth differential between countries, particularly when one contrasts Japan and the United States. The United States had a rapid increase in the female and youth proportions, and in Japan the reverse situation occurred.

The differences in *level* of productivity between countries may also be affected by intercountry variations in the proportion of females and young males in employment. This proportion is higher in the United States than in the other five countries, and if labor input is adjusted to compare pro-

Table 2-11. Impact of Changes in the Age/Sex Composition of Employment on Labor Productivity Growth Rates and on Productivity Levels.

| | Percentage Point Impact on Growth Rate | | Level of GDP per Employee in 1981 | |
			Using Conventional Measure of Employment	Using Prime Male Equivalent to Measure Employment
	1960–73	1973–81		
France	−0.2	+0.1	102.7	98.0
Germany	−0.1	0.0	101.4	97.0
Japan	+0.2	+0.2	79.1	74.8
Netherlands	−0.1	0.0[a]	100.6[b]	93.0[b]
United Kingdom	+0.1	+0.2	74.4	72.6
United States	−0.3	−0.2	100.0	100.0

[a] 1973–80.
[b] 1980.

Source: Employment by Sex from OECD, *Labour Force Statistics,* by Age, from OECD *Demographic Trends 1950-1990,* (1979). The calculations show the difference between weighted labor inputs (males aged 25 and over = 1, others 0.6) and unweighted inputs.

ductivity levels, the U.S. standing improves (as can be seen by comparing the last two columns of Table 2-11).

One should not exaggerate the importance of these structural phenomena because the lower productivity of women and young workers is partly due to the fact that they work shorter hours than do prime-age males. This is already reflected in the hours-worked figures, so there is some degree of double counting when age/sex composition is given as a separate component of productivity. Female participation in the labor force also affects sectoral productivity performance differentially because female employment is heavily concentrated in the service sector. Here again some of the impact of the changes in sex structure is already embedded in the measures of the impact of sectoral change in Table 2-8.

Another dimension of labor quality that may affect productivity performance is the education level of the employed population, though its economic impact is not easy to diagnose. However, I conclude from evidence in an earlier study that the slowdown in productivity growth since 1973 is unlikely to have been influenced by this consideration because the educational quality of the labor force has continued to improve at a pace at least as fast as before 1973 (Maddison 1979).

CONCLUSIONS

In productivity growth accounting, it is usual to concentrate on the supply side, looking first at factor input, then at influences on the efficiency of resource allocation, and terminating with the residual, which mainly reflects technical progress. Because I wanted to stress the interactive and complex nature of the causality that includes the state of demand, expectations, and policy, as well as more technocratic factors, my paper has been a bit discursive. The imprecision is heightened by my coyness toward the total factor productivity approach and by the fact that in some respects the analysis is incomplete—I have not looked at all types of capital input.

Perhaps the best way of summarizing my position is by comment on the judgments of Denison and Kendrick, who have both produced updated and careful interpretations of recent developments. Their results are quantified in Table 2-12, which compares their viewpoints on the United States and summarizes the Kendrick analysis for France, Germany, Japan, and the United Kingdom. The periods covered are not quite the same and the two authors differ somewhat from each other and from me in their coverage of the economy (I use the whole of GDP, Kendrick excludes government, and Denison excludes government and private residential activity), but I do not think this invalidates a rough comparison.

1. In the first place, neither Denison nor Kendrick nor I would attribute any significant productivity decline to a worsening of labor quality.

Table 2-12. Denison and Kendrick Estimates of Sources of Labor Productivity Growth (annual average percentage point contribution to growth).

	Denison (U.S.) Nonresidential Business Economy		Kendrick (U.S.) Whole Business Economy		Kendrick (Four-Country Average)[a]	
	1948-73	1973-81	1960-73	1973-79	1960-73	1973-79
Output per man-hour	2.87	0.27	3.1	1.1	6.4	3.6
Factor input	0.88	0.59	1.3	1.0	2.7	2.4
Labor quality	0.53	0.48	0.1	0.5	0.3	0.4
Capital	0.35	0.11	1.2	0.5	2.4	2.0
Factor productivity	0.57	-0.06	0.6	-0.4	0.9	-0.6
Efficiency of resource allocation	0.37	0.04	0.2	-0.1	0.5	0.0
Economies of scale	0.42	0.31	0.4	0.3	0.6	0.3
Intensity of demand and weather variation	-0.18	-0.20	0.1	-0.2	-0.1	-0.4
Regulation	-0.03	-0.18	-0.1	-0.4	-0.1	-0.5
Dishonesty and crime	-0.01	-0.03				
Residual	1.42	-0.26	1.2	0.5	2.6	1.7

[a] France, Germany, Japan, and United Kingdom.

Source: Denison, (1984) and Kendrick (1981).

2. Kendrick gives bigger weight to capital than Denison does (37.1 percent for the United States in 1970 against Denison's 18.2), and the slowdown in capital growth therefore plays a bigger explanatory role in Kendrick's schema. I would give capital a slightly bigger explanatory role in the slowdown than Kendrick. For the European countries and Japan my figures for capital stock growth (Table 2–3) show bigger deceleration than his do (when the Baily effect is included), but my capital stock has a somewhat smaller weight than Kendrick, since I exclude housing, inventories, and land.

3. Denison and Kendrick both show a sizable slowdown due to worsened resource allocation. Denison shows a U.S. productivity deceleration of 0.63 percentage points a year from this cause, Kendrick a full 1.0 percent for the United States and 1.5 percentage points for the other four countries. I tend, once again, to agree with Kendrick's higher figures, but I think he overstates the impact of regulation in the slowdown, and I would stress that the decline in efficiency gains in Europe and Japan reflects both longer-term and conjunctural elements.

4. A good deal of Denison's slowdown is unexplained. 1.68 percentage points of his 2.60 percentage point slowdown is left in the mystery residual. Kendrick "explains" more—1.3 points of his 2.0-point U.S. slowdown and 1.9 points of his 2.8-point non-U.S. slowdown. The slowdown I was mainly concerned with in my six countries was the deterioration from their 1960–73 performance of 5.3 percentage points annual growth to the 2.8 points annual growth for 1973–81 (see Table 2–1)—that is, a 2.5-point shortfall. If pressed (and John Kendrick has pressed me), I should diffidently suggest a 1.3-point loss from worsened resource allocation (which is Kendrick's five-country average), a 0.6-point loss from lower capital inputs (including the Baily effect), and 0.6 points of mystery.

APPENDIX TABLES

Table 2-A1.   A Comparison of Nominal and Real Levels of GDP and the Purchasing Power of Currencies in 1975.

	GDP at Purchaser's Values Converted at Official Exchange Rates 1975 ($ million)	Ratio of Purchasing Power of Currency to Exchange Rate (U.S.A. = 1.0000)	Real GDP at U.S. Relative Prices ($ million)
France	338,820	0.9982	338,220
Germany	420,290	0.9324	391,861
Japan	498,770	1.2109	603,961
Netherlands	87,090	0.9149	79,679
United Kingdom	231,480	1.2740	294,903
United States	1,538,600	1.0000	1,538,600

Source: In order to compare levels of output in different countries it is useful to find a unit that expresses the comparative value of their currencies more accurately than the official exchange rate. Fortunately, careful estimates of purchasing power are available that make it possible to convert the different countries' GDP into comparable units. The source used for column 1 was OECD *National Accounts of OECD Countries 1951-1980*, and for column 2 Kravis, Heston (1982). These authors themselves prefer to convert output of different countries in terms of "international dollars," using purchasing power parities derived by weighting prices by a complicated Geary-Khamis technique, which provides an approximation to world prices. I have not done this but have used the purchasing powers derived by using each country's own quantity weights. When these are applied to adjust the country's GDP expressed in dollars at the official exchange rate, one obtains an estimate of the relative quantities of output valued at 1975 U.S. relative prices.

I prefer to measure output in U.S. relative prices, first because this is the price structure to which these countries are converging as their productivity and demand patterns approach U.S. levels, and second because the concept of U.S. relative prices corresponds to an identifiable reality. The compromise "international dollar" concept is a device intended for comparisons over the wider income range covered by Kravis and associates (who include Kenya and India in their comparison), but I am not keen on it in the present context, where the purpose of the level comparison is to illuminate the leader/follower dichotomy between the United States and the other countries.

Table 2-A2.   Index of GDP in Constant Prices (1913 = 100).

	France	Germany	Japan	Netherlands	United Kingdom	United States
1870	49.4	30.4	35.2	40.6	44.6	17.3
1913	100.0	100.0	100.0	100.0	100.0	100.0
1929	125.8	121.1	178.9	166.5	111.9	163.0
1938	120.8	169.1	270,0	171.6	132.5	153.6
1950	144.6	161.0	194.8	243.0	160.8	276.8
1960	225.9	346.5	453.9	378.8	211.6	375.7
1973	456.7	615.7	1,530.3	714.2	315.3	635.3
1974	471.5	619.0	1,514.4	739.5	312.2	631.6
1975	472.3	607.6	1,549.9	731.8	310.3	625.8
1976	496.8	638.9	1,632.1	770.8	321.5	659.5
1977	511.9	658.3	1,717.9	789.1	325.6	695.2
1978	530.9	679.5	1,804.3	810.3	336.3	725.6
1979	549.3	709.8	1,903.2	824.6	341.0	746.0
1980	555.6	723.4	1,987.0	829.3	336.2	745.2
1981	557.3	721.3	2,044.6	818.5	328.8	760.1
1982	569.8	728.5	2,085.5	818.5	332.9	748.7

Source: 1870-1952 from Maddison (1982); 1952-80 from OECD, *National Accounts of OECD Countries*; 1980-81 from OECD, *Economic Outlook* (July 1982).

Table 2-A3.   Employment (000s).

	France	Germany	Japan	Netherlands	United Kingdom	United States
1870	19,395	10,260	17,685	1,382	12,285	14,669
1913	21,013	17,303	26,046	2,330	18,566	40,681
1929	20,488	19,037	29,171	3,023	18,936	51,060
1938	18,948	21,204	31,855	3,169	20,818	50,142
1950	19,218	21,164	35,683	3,625	22,400	61,651
1960	19,624	26,080	44,670	4,101	24,225	69,195
1973	21,394	26,648	52,590	4,670	24,993	88,868
1974	21,539	26,155	52,370	4,700	25,068	90,496
1975	21,303	25,266	52,230	4,670	24,903	89,414
1976	21,448.	25,033	52,700	4,730	24,782	92,255
1977	21,624	24,993	53,420	4,800	24,858	95,624
1978	21,712	25,181	54,080	4,850	24,966	99,645
1979	21,695	25,519	54,790	4,940	25,045	102,285
1980	21,696	25,741	55,360	4,960	24,459	102,583
1981	21,542	25,441	55,810	4,900	23,297	103,602

Source: 1870-1950—from Maddison (1982). For 1960 onward the sources were as follows: France 1960 kindly supplied by INSEE; France 1973-81—from OECD, *Labour Force Statistics* (various issues); Germany 1960-81—from IAB (1982); Japan 1960-81—from OECD, *Labour Force Statistics* (various issues); Netherlands 1960 from Maddison and Wilpstra (1982); Netherlands 1973-81 kindly supplied by U.S. Bureau of Labor Statistics; United Kingdom 1960-81—from *Department of Employment Gazette*; United States 1960-81—from OECD, *Labour Force Statistics* (various issues), augmented by figures for fourteen- to fifteen-year-olds supplied by the U.S. Bureau of Labor Statistics. All figures are adjusted to refer to the geographic area of 1981.

Table 2-A4.   Hours Worked Per Person Per Year.

	France	Germany	Japan	Netherlands	United Kingdom	United States
1870	2,945	2,941	2,945	2,964	2,984	2,964
1913	2,588	2,584	2,588	2,605	2,624	2,605
1929	2,297	2,284	2,364	2,260	2,286	2,342
1938	1,848	2,316	2,391	2,244	2,267	2,062
1950	1,989	2,316	2,289	2,208	1,958	1,867
1960	1,983	2,083	2,450	2,177	1,913	1,795
1973	1,825	1,827	2,213	1,825	1,688	1,687
1974	1,804	1,793	2,137	1,760	1,654	1,665
1975	1,767	1,753	2,105	1,695	n.a.	1,644
1976	1,768	1,786	2,132	1,710	1,635	1,640
1977	1,739	1,758	2,136	1,681	1,618	1,632
1978	1,726	1,733	2,141	1,671	1,600	1,620
1979	1,727	1,724	2,147	1,658	1,593	1,612
1980	1,734	1,708	2,147	1,653	1,553	1,594
1981	1,701	1,681	2,140	1,644	1,503	1,582

Sources: 1870-1960—from Maddison (1982). France 1973-80—from Granier and Maddison (1981). Germany 1960 onward—from IAB (1982). Japan 1973—monthly hours worked in all industries and services in firms with five or more employees from *Yearbook of Labour Statistics* (various issues); Japan 1950-73—movement for hours of workers in industries of thirty or more employees from *50 Years of Labour Statistics* (1974). Netherlands 1960 onward—from Maddison and Wilpstra (1982). United Kingdom 19 - —revised version of procedure from "Monitoring the Labour Market" (1980). United States 1973-81—from U.S. Bureau of Labor Statistics *Employment and Earnings*, various issues; estimates refer to gross weekly hours of "production or non-supervisory workers on private non-agricultural payrolls." These figures were adjusted for vacation and sickness absence as described in Maddison (1982).

Table 2-A5. Productivity Levels (GDP per man-hour) ($ at 1975 relative price levels and purchasing power).

	France	Germany	Japan	Netherlands	United Kingdom	United States
1870	0.62	0.65	0.27	1.08	1.16	0.96
1913	1.32	1.44	0.59	1.79	1.97	2.30
1929	1.92	1.80	1.02	2.65	2.48	3.37
1938	2.48	2.23	1.39	2.62	2.68	3.60
1950	2.71	2.12	0.95	3.31	3.48	5.91
1960	4.16	4.12	1.65	4.63	4.33	7.43
1973	8.38	8.16	5.24	9.14	7.10	10.42
1981	10.89	10.89	6.67	11.06	8.93	11.40

Source: Derived by linking Table 2-A1 and 2-A2 to produce a time series for GDP at 1975 U.S relative prices, and dividing by Table 2-A4 multiplied by 2-A3.

Table 2-A6. Midyear Nonresidential Fixed Capital Stock at Constant Prices (1950 = 100).

	France	Germany	Japan	Netherlands	United Kingdom	United State
Net Stock						
1870	n.a.	18.58	n.a.	n.a.	49.55	6.94
1913	68.50	68.71	n.a.	n.a.	84.03	49.40
1929	n.a.	77.85	n.a.	n.a.	86.76	73.30
1938	n.a.	89.65	n.a.	n.a.	91.86	76.21
1950	100.00	100.00	100.00	n.a.	100.00	100.00
1960	133.60	189.30	183.40	n.a.	140.80	146.44
1973	280.70	430.10	800.40	n.a.	259.80	252.28
1980	381.10	564.98	(1,093.00)[a]	n.a.	318.20	308.77
1981	n.a.	n.a.	n.a.	n.a.	n.a.	316.66
Gross Stock						
1870	n.a.	n.a.	n.a.	n.a.	36.16	6.20
1913	n.a.	n.a.	29.94	n.a.	72.04	44.61
1929	n.a.	n.a.	60.30	n.a.	81.01	70.63
1938	n.a.	n.a.	82.51	n.a.	90.15	77.22
1950	100.00	100.00	100.00	100.00	100.00	100.00
1960	127.00	163.60	164.80	186.82	128.50	140.32
1973	242.10	358.60	727.00	445.64	214.80	230.40
1980	336.80	480.40	1,130.10[a]	598.58	267.15	289.74
1981	n.a.	n.a.	n.a.	n.a.	n.a.	298.91

n.a. = not available.
[a]1979.
Source: Generally from official sources as described in Maddison (1982). For the Netherlands, th estimate was derived as described in Maddison and Wilpstra (1982). For the United States, the figures f 1929 onward are from U.S. Department of Commerce (1982), with revisions and updating kindly supplie by John C. Musgrave.

Table 2-A7. Ratio of Trade in Goods and Services to GDP, 1950-80.

	1950 (at 1950 prices)	1980 (at 1980 prices)	1980 (at 1950 prices)
Exports			
France	14.4	22.4	35.4
Germany	11.3	27.5	42.7
Japan	10.0	14.0	51.7
Netherlands	41.2	53.1	114.4
United Kingdom	25.4	28.4	36.7
United States	4.4	10.1	9.3
Average	17.8	25.9	48.4
Imports			
France	14.0	24.1	38.8
Germany	12.7	27.9	64.0
Japan	9.3	14.9	34.9
Netherlands	48.4	53.4	110.2
United Kingdom	24.4	25.9	37.0
United States	4.0	11.1	7.9
Average	18.8	26.2	48.8

Source: OECD, *National Accounts*, 1950-78, 1951-79, and 1951-80 editions, except United Kingdom where 1950-52 movements are from the 1950-68 edition, and Japan where they are from Ohkawa and Rosovsky (1973): 278-89 (adjusted to calendar year basis).

Table 2-A8. Employment Structure: Employment by Sector as Percentage of Total Employment, 1870-1981.

		1870	1960	1973	1981
France	Agriculture	49.2	21.4	11.0	8.3
	Industry	27.8	36.2	38.6	34.3
	Services	23.0	42.4	50.3	57.4
Germany	Agriculture	49.5	13.8	7.3	5.8
	Industry	28.7	48.2	46.6	43.4
	Services	21.8	38.0	46.1	50.8
Japan	Agriculture	72.6	30.2	13.4	10.0
	Industry	n.a.	28.5	37.2	35.3
	Services	n.a.	41.3	49.3	54.7
Netherlands	Agriculture	37.0	11.1	6.6	4.9
	Industry	29.0	39.1	35.3	29.5
	Services	3.40	49.8	58.1	65.6
United Kingdom	Agriculture	22.7	4.1	2.9	2.8
	Industry	42.3	47.8	42.0	35.8
	Services	35.0	48.1	55.1	61.4
United States	Agriculture	50.0	8.0	4.1	3.4
	Industry	24.4	32.3	32.3	29.5
	Services	25.6	59.7	62.4	67.1

Source: 1870 from Maddison (1982). Later years from OECD, *Labour Force Statistics*.

Table 2-A9. Government Expenditure as Percentage of GDP.

	France 1977	Germany 1978	Japan 1979	Netherlands 1978	United Kingdom 1979	United States 1978
Total Expenditure	44.5	46.7	32.1	57.7	43.4	33.7
The Traditional Domain						
1. "Public" wants	7.3	8.2	4.2	10.3	8.7	8.5
Defense	3.2	2.9	0.9	3.0	4.8	4.7
Other general government	4.1	5.3	3.3	(7.3)	3.9	3.8
The Welfare State						
2A. "Merit" wants	14.2	13.1	12.3	(20.3)	14.2	9.2
Education	5.9	4.9	5.0	(8.2)	5.5	5.8
Health	5.6	6.3	4.5	(6.2)	4.8	2.6
Housing	2.0	1.2	2.4	(4.0)	3.4	0.4
Other	0.7	0.7	0.4	(1.9)	0.5	0.4
B. Income Maintenance	17.1	18.8	6.9	(19.4)	12.0	10.0
Pensions	10.3	10.6	4.5	7.2	6.7	6.9
Sickness	1.9	1.0	0.3	6.2	0.4	0.1
Family allocations	1.9	1.2	1.6	1.8	1.4	0.5
Unemployment compensation	1.0	1.3	0.4	0.4	0.7	0.4
Other	2.0	4.7	0.0	1.7	2.8	2.1
The Mixed Economy						
3. Publicly provided economic services	4.6	4.9	6.0	(4.6)	3.8	3.3
Capital	1.6	1.6	3.7	—	1.2	0.7
Subsidies	1.6	2.2	1.2	—	1.0	0.2
Other (R&D, etc.)	1.4	1.1	1.1	—	1.6	2.4
4. Public Debt Interest	1.4	1.7	2.7	3.1	4.7	2.8
5. Net Borrowing	0.8	2.8	4.3	2.2	3.3	0.5

Source: *National Accounts of OECD Countries 1962–1979*, Vol. II, Annex 1 for items I, IIi, III. Public debt interest and net borrowing from country tables (No. 9) and detal of IIii from national sources and OECD Statistics Division.

NOTES

1. The present paper is confined to six countries. For an analysis covering sixteen countries through 1979, see Maddison (1982), which yields similar conclusions.

2. See Denison (1979: 49, 171) for weights in the nonresidential business sector and page 87 for the weight of the latter in national income.

3. The figures in Table 2–3 refer to nonresidential fixed investment for the whole economy including government capital. If one includes depreciation and imputes a rental value for government-owned capital, its weight in GDP is around 25 percent. See Maddison (1972: Table 9). If one were to include all capital including inventories, residential property, and land, the weight for capital would be bigger.

4. See the interesting report on recent research on scale economies by Gollop (1980).

5. See Wolf (1912: 236–37), who expected the pace of technical advance in the twenty-first century to be below that in the nineteenth and twentieth.

6. See Mensch (1977). See also Maddison (1982) for a critique of long-wave theories.

7. I am not suggesting that this concern is limited to conservatives. See the gloomy assessment of Lindbeck (1981, 1983), who advances the thesis that a fundamental cause of productivity slowdown is an "arteriosclerosis" of the Western economies with a long-term deterioration in the efficiency of their "basic mechanisms."

8. For France, Germany, and the United Kingdom, see sources cited in Maddison (1980); for the Netherlands, see Maddison and Wilpstra (1982). For the United States, it was assumed that work absence was the same as in 1976; see Hedges (1977).

9. Some progress is being made; see OECD (1982), and the annexes to OECD *National Accounts* which first appeared in 1981. Some of the problems of measuring output are dealt with by Hill (1975).

10. See Stigler (1975) for some historical perspective from the viewpoint of one who believes strongly in the superiority of market forces in decisionmaking, and Weidenbaum (1980), who estimates the compliance costs of regulation in 1980 at 4.6 percent of GDP.

11. As an example of the difference in European and American attitudes, one may quote Sampson (1982: 126), who explains why bankers in London could take advantage of business opportunities in the eurodollar market, which regulation closed off in the United States: "The Bank of England for all its autocratic appearance, was much more lenient and pragmatic in its regulation than the Fed in Washington; and American bankers found that they would obtain permission for new activities in a few minutes which could take months of negotiations with armies of lawyers in Washington."

REFERENCES

Bacon, R., and W. Eltis. 1978. *Britain's Economic Problem: Too Few Producers.* 2d ed. London: Macmillan.

Baily, M.N. 1981. "Productivity and the Services of Capital and Labor." *Brookings Papers on Economic Activity* 1.

Blades, D. 1982. "The Hidden Economy and the National Accounts." *Economic Outlook: Occasional Studies.* Paris: OECD.

Burns, A.F. 1934. *Production Trends in the United States since 1870.* New York: NBER.

Carre, J-J.; P. DuBois; and E. Malinvaud. 1972. *La Croissance Française.* Paris: Seuil.

Conseil des Impôts. 1979. *Quatrième rapport au président de la république relatif à l'impôt sur le revenu.* Paris: Journaux Officiels, pp. 119-24.

Denison, E.F. 1979a. *Accounting for Slower Growth: The United States in the 1970s.* Washington, D.C.: The Brookings Institution.

_____. 1979b. "Comment on Norsworthy, Harper, and Kunze, 'The Slowdown in Productivity Growth: An Analysis of Some Contributing Factors.'" *Brookings Papers on Economic Activity* 2.

_____. 1982. "Is U.S. Growth Understated Because of the Underground Economy? Employment Ratios Suggest Not." *Review of Income and Wealth* (March).

_____. 1984. "Accounting for Slower Economic Growth: An Update." *International Comparisons of Productivity and Causes of the Slowdown.* Cambridge, Mass.: Ballinger.

Deutscher Bundestag. 1981. *Achter Subventionsbericht.* Bonn: Deutscher Bundestag (November 6), p. 24.

Erbe, R. 1958. *Die nationalsozialistische Wirtschaftspolitik 1933-1939 im Lichte der modernen Theorie.* Zurich: Polygraphischer Verlag.

Feige, E.L. 1979. "How Big Is the Irregular Economy?" *Challenge* (November/December).

Feinstein, C.H. 1972. *National Income, Expenditure and Output of the United Kingdom 1855-1965.* Cambridge: Cambridge University Press.

Gollop, F.M. 1980. "Scale Effects and Technical Change as Sources of Productivity Growth." *Dimensions of Productivity Research.* Houston, Tex.: American Productivity Center.

Granier, R., and A. Maddison. 1981. "Politiques de l'emploi et emploi." Aix-en-Procence. Mimeo.

Hedges, J.N. 1977. "Absence from Work—Measuring the Hours Lost." *Monthly Labour Review* (October).

Hill, T.P. 1975. "Price and Volume Measures for Non-Market Services." Brussels: Eurostat (OS/5/15-E, April).

Hudson, E.A., and D.W. Jorgenson. 1978. "Energy Prices and the U.S. Economy, 1972-1976." *Natural Resources Journal* (October).

IAB. 1982. *Mitteilungen,* Nuremberg: IAB.

International Energy Agency. 1979. *Energy Policies and Programmes of IEA Countries, 1978 Review.* Paris. IEA.

International Monetary Fund. Various years. *International Financial Statistics.* Washington, D.C.: IMF.

Jorgenson, D.W. 1981. "Taxation and Technical Change." In *Technology in Society,* vol. 3, pp. 151-71. London: Pergamon Press.

Kahn, H. 1979. *World Economic Development.* New York: Morrow Quill, ch. 2.

Kendrick, J.W. 1976. *The Formation of Stocks of Total Capital.* New York: NBER.

_____. 1981. "International Comparisons of Recent Productivity Trends. In *Essays in Contemporary Economic Problems,* edited by William Fellner. Washington, D.C.: American Enterprise Institute, pp. 125-70. Washington, D.C.: American Enterprise Institute.

Kravis, I.B.; A. Heston; and R. Summers. 1982. *World Product and Income.* Baltimore, Md.: Johns Hopkins University Press.

Kuznets, S. 1930. *Secular Movements in Production and Prices.* Boston: Houghton Mifflin.

———. 1953. *Economic Change.* New York: Norton.

Lindbeck, Assar. 1981. "Work Incentives in the Welfare State." Stockholm: Institute for International Economic Studies, reprint 176.

———. 1983. "The Recent Slowdown of Productivity Growth," *Economic Journal* (March).

Maddison, A. 1972. "Explaining Economic Growth." *Banca Nazionale del Lavoro Quarterly Review* (September):211–61.

———. 1979. "Long Run Dynamics of Productivity Growth." *Banca Nazionale del Lavoro Quarterly Review* (March): 3–43.

———. 80. "Monitoring the Labour Market." *Review of Income and Wealth* (June): 175–217.

———. 1982. *Phases of Capitalist Development.* Oxford: Oxford University Press.

Maddison, A., and B. Wilpstra. 1982. *Unemployment: The European Perspective.* London: Croom Helm.

Mensch, G. 1977. *Das technologische Patt.* Frankfurt: Fischer.

Norsworthy, J.R.; M.J. Harper; and K. Kunze. 1979. "The Slowdown in Productivity Growth: An Analysis of Some Contributing Factors." *Brookings Papers on Economic Activity*, no. 2. Washington, D.C.: The Brookings Institution.

Ohkawa, K., and H. Rosovsky. 1973. *Japanese Economic Growth.* Stanford, Calif.: Stanford University Press.

Ohkawa, K., and M. Shinohara. 1979. *Patterns of Japanese Economic Development.* New Haven, Conn.: Yale University Press.

OECD. 1979. *Demographic Trends 1950–1990.* Paris: OECD.

———. 1981. *Science and Technology Indicators*, vol. B. Paris: OECD.

———. 1982. *Employment in the Public Sector.* Paris: OECD.

———. 1982. *Economic Outlook.* Paris: OECD.

———. Various years. *Labour Force Statistics.* Paris: OECD.

———. Various years. *National Accounts of OECD Countries.* Paris: OECD.

———. Various years. *Quarterly National Accounts Bulletin.* Paris: OECD.

OEEC. 1957. *Statistics of National Product and Expenditure 1938 and 1947 to 1955.* Paris: OEEC.

Perry, G.L. 1978. "Potential Output: Recent Issues and Present Trends." *Brookings Reprint.* Washington, D.C.: The Brookings Institution.

Rasche, R.H., and J.A. Tatom. 1977. *Economic Review of the Federal Reserve Bank of St. Louis* (June).

Sampson, A. 1982. *The Money Lenders.* London: Coronet.

Stigler, G.J. 1975. *The Citizen and the State: Essays on Regulation.* Chicago: University of Chicago Press.

Tachtig Jaren Statistiek in Tijdreeksen. 1979. The Hague: CBS.

Tatom, J.A. 1981. *Economic Review of the Federal Reserve Bank of St. Louis.* (January).

———. Various issues. *Employment and Earnings.* Washington, D.C.: U.S. Government Printing Office.

U.S. Department of Commerce. 1977. *The National Income and Product Accounts of the United States, 1929–74, Statistical Tables.* Washington, D.C.: U.S. Government Printing Office.

———. 1982. *Fixed Reproducible Tangible Wealth in the United States, 1925–79.* Washington, D.C.: U.S. Government Printing Office.

Vorstman, G.J.T. 1974. "Een econometrische analyse van de nederlandse volkshuishouding." The Hague: CPB. Mimeo (March 21).

Weidenbaum, M.L. 1980. *Costs of Regulation and Benefits of Reform*. St. Louis: Center for the Study of American Business.
Wolf, J. 1912. *Die Volkswirtschaft der Gegenwart und Zukunft*. Leipzig: Deichert.
Woytinsky, W.S. and E.S. 1953. *World Population and Production*. New York: Twentieth Century Fund.
Yearbook of Labour Statistics. 1974. Tokyo: Ministry of Labour.

COMMENT

Walter W. McMahon

This paper by Angus Maddison is an important contribution to the analysis of the sources of the productivity slowdown. It draws upon and extends his recent works, "Long-Run Dynamics of Productivity Growth" (1979) and *Phases of Capitalist Development* (1982), as well as his earlier classic, *Economic Growth in the West* (1964), developing relative emphases on key sources of the slowdown that deserve serious attention.

By way of providing a framework for evaluating Maddison's contribution, I propose to present a structural interpretation that encompasses his useful grouping of "conjunctural" and "nonconjunctural" sources of the slowdown in productivity growth. That is, a more explicit simultaneous equation model is needed that incorporates those sources related to slack demand and low investment following the 1973 and 1979 energy price shocks, and those longer-run sources related to the "loss of the advantages of backwardness."

Both of these are important sources of the slowdown and consistent with some independent evidence, which I will present. But I am very concerned about the overly narrow view that Maddison takes of capital formation. A broader concept of total capital is needed—one that includes investment in human capital primarily via formal education and on-the-job training, as well as including investment in new knowledge capital primarily through the technical change and improvements in efficiency associated with some types of investment in R&D. Some empirical evidence consistent with these points will also be presented. It is my hope that a structural interpretation of Maddison's two key sources augmented with this concept of total capital will help

93

to provide an increasingly adequate explanation of the sources of the slowdown as well as of some of the possibilities for resumed labor productivity growth.

SOURCES OF THE SLOWDOWN—A STRUCTURAL INTERPRETATION

Maddison's two key sources, as well as the sources developed by Denison (1979, and Chapter 2 of this book) above, to whose work we owe much of what is known about this subject, are reflected through a production function. Some such production function whether implicit or explicit is the common structural frame of reference and must be the centerpiece of any structural model dealing with productivity growth.

The derivative of the production function presented below as well as the rest of the model presented later refer to the medium term, which allows capital deepening to occur and its rate to have some effect on productivity growth. The medium term, however, also permits under-utilization of human capital (Maddison's labor hoarding) and of physical capital (excess capacity) due to slack stock demand. These have adverse effects on productivity that can be incorporated in a disequilibrium model in the sense that conservative demand management policies give rise to stock disequilibrium (e.g., excess capacity of human and physical capital) and reduced capital deepening, with flow equilibrium in the products and money markets, in contrast to a focus on long-run steady-state growth solutions.

Starting with a Cobb-Douglas production function that includes human capital and also (disembodied) stocks of knowledge capital consistent with work by Denison (1983), Schultz (1982: 37), and Kendrick (1976), taking the natural logs, and differentiating with respect to time gives the growth rate of real gross domestic product (y) as a function of the rate of growth of the various inputs. The rate of growth of the number of persons employed (n) may then be subtracted from both sides under the simplifying assumption implicit in Maddison's paper of constant returns to scale to determine the rate of growth of output per worker. The result is the determinants of labor productivity growth as shown below in equation (1). (The production function from which it can be derived is shown in the appendix.)

$$(y - n) = \gamma_1 U_{H,K} + \gamma_2 (Y/N)_{-1} + \gamma_3(k - n) + \gamma_4(h - n) + \gamma_5 a + \gamma_6(e - n) \quad (1)$$

In the empirical estimates below, each variable is measured as the average for five-year periods (the medium term) between 1955 and 1980, where:

$(y - n)$ = *labor productivity growth*, measured for Table 1 below as the percentage of rate of growth in real GDP per person employed for the OECD nations,

$U_{H,K}$ = *percentage of under-utilization of human and physical capital*, measured below by assuming that slack demand and hence under-utilization of both is measured by the percent unemployed, for which data exists,

$(Y/N)_{60}$ = *the initial level of output per worker*, measured for Table 1 as GDP in 1960 in each country in constant U.S. dollars (exchange rate and prices of 1975) divided by employment in 1960 in that country—Maddison's "advantages of backwardness,"

$(k - n)$ = *the rate of physical capital formation* (k) *per worker* (n), measured in Table 1 as gross private domestic investment as a percentage of base year GDP, per person employed (gross investment allows for the embodiment of new technology through replacement investment and is consistent with the use of GDP for y rather than NIPPE; base-year GDP in the denominator substitutes for capital stock data, which does not exist),

$(h - n)$ = *the rate of human capital formation per worker*, measured for Table 1 as the increase in the average educational attainment of the working age population,

a = *the rate of increase in disembodied technical knowledge*, measured for Table 2 as nondefense public and private R&D investment at the beginning of each new five-year period as a percentage of GDP in that year, and

$(e - n)$ = *the rate of change in petroleum-energy use per worker*, measured in Table 1 as the percentage of change in net oil imports plus domestically produced and consumed oil per person employed.

This offers a framework for considering and independently evaluating the relative importance of Maddison's "conjunctural" and "nonconjunctural forces," as well as of human capital formation and R&D. I will discuss below the results of the various estimates of equation (1) and comment on Maddison's conjunctural and nonconjunctural forces, starting with the former, which are associated with the effects of under-utilization.

THE EFFECTS ON PRODUCTIVITY GROWTH OF UNDER-UTILIZATION

It is significant that the slowdown in productivity growth has been experienced in all of the major OECD countries since 1973 because it focuses attention on factors that are not unique to the United States. The restrictive demand management policies used in all of these nations following the 1973 and 1979 oil price shocks—with their adverse effects on capital formation per worker $((k-n)$ above) and on under-utilization of human and physical capital ($U_{H,K}$ which includes Maddison's labor hoarding)—fill this bill, whereas suddenly changing patterns of union strength, management efficiency, or government size do not.

To appraise the considerable importance that Maddison assigns to these conjunctural forces, consider equation (1) and the regressions shown in Table 1, which seek to explain productivity growth in the OECD nations. Notice that the effect of slack demand or under-utilization as measured by the percentage of unemployment (U) and by changes in unemployment, both of which are adjusted for differences in measurement among countries, have coefficients with the expected sign in all five instances where they are significant or very nearly significant. This is consistent with Maddison's proposition that low utilization rates slow productivity growth. The rate of physical capital formation per worker, ($k-n$), also has the expected important effect on productivity growth, increasing it prior to 1973 and slowing it since then as investment fell. This result is also consistent with Maddison's stress on the conjunctural forces related to conservative demand management policies following the two energy price shocks.

I must add, however, an important refinement. The lower rates of physical capital formation per worker—and it is capital formation *per worker* that is relevant to productivity growth—were also the result in the United States of a large wave of new workers entering the labor force in the 1970s picked up by ($k-n$) in the regressions. This can be seen in the data on increasing employment in Maddison's Table 2-A3. The big wave of postwar births entering the labor force in the United States was not matched by comparable increases in France, Germany, Japan, or the United Kingdom, where total employment remained stable in this period, with the result that the dilution of the amount of capital per worker would contribute to relatively slower productivity growth in the United States.

LOSS OF THE "ADVANTAGES OF BACKWARDNESS"

The second major source of the slowdown stressed in Maddison's paper—the longer-run loss of "technological backwardness" as Europe and Japan catch up to the United States—is reflected in the initial productivity level term in equation (1) and Table 1. It involves an ingenious use of the Rosenberg (1976) effect. Rosenberg's basic idea is a reasonable one: that the process of research, and of trial and error in innovation, imposes constraints on the pace of development of knowledge in the lead country. This is a burden borne by the United States that is now spreading to Germany and Japan.

Table 1. Growth in Labor Productivity (dependent variable: productivity change over five-year period $(y - n)$ for each country).

dependent Variables	1955-70 Coefficient	1955-70 t-statistic	1955-80 Coefficient	1955-80 t-statistic
ifteen OECD Nations				
Under-utilization (average U)	-1.23	-1.52	-1.50	-2.60
Initial productivity $(Y/N)_{60}$	-11.23	-2.62	-10.70	-3.10
Physical capital deepening (average $I/Y_{-1} - n$)	0.81	3.38	0.67	3.63
Human capital deepening $(h - n)$	0.05	2.02	0.02	1.22
Energy charge per worker $(e - n)$	0.00	0.38	0.01	1.17
Constant (e.g., stocks of knowledge)	0.14	1.70	0.16	2.32
Number of observations =	45		75	
R^2 =	0.57		0.54	
ive largest OECD nations				
Under-utilization (average U)	-3.21	-1.70	1.37	0.37
Change in under-utilization (μ)	-3.67	-3.68	-3.67	-2.18
Initial productivity (Y/N)	-6.76	-1.35	-5.01	$-.49$
Physical capital deepening $(k - n) = $ (average $I/Y_{-1} - n$)	1.01	3.45	1.67	2.29
Human capital deepening $(h - n)$	0.32	6.41	0.04	0.50
R&D knowledge formation $(a = (R\&D)_{-1}/Y_{-1})$	$-.05$	-1.23	-0.10	-1.09
Energy charge per worker $(e - n)$	0.002	0.46	0.002	0.25
Number of observations =	15		25	
R^2 =	0.97		0.68	
Simple correlation $(y - n)$ with $(R\&D)_{-1}/Y_{-1}$	0.16		-0.12	

The "advantages of technological backwardness" factor does help to explain a somewhat faster growth outside the United States—as in Japan, where the level of productivity was far behind in 1960—and a somewhat slower growth in the United States, where many of the costs of technological leadership and innovation are borne. In Table 1 the initial productivity level representing this effect does have the expected negative sign, and higher initial levels are associated with relatively slower productivity growth in all regressions. This result is consistent with Maddison's conclusion that backwardness is a factor in productivity growth and that its loss can slow a leading nation's growth rate.

HUMAN CAPITAL FORMATION

In this paper, as well as in other work that he cites on this point (Maddison 1979), Maddison tends to seriously understate and almost overlook the significance of human capital formation to the growth process. When human capital formation per worker as measured by increased average educational attainment of the working age population is introduced as shown in equation (1), it always has the expected positive sign. It is a significant factor in explaining productivity growth in the relatively stable-growth period from 1955 to 1970 and continues to have a positive relation to productivity growth in the unstable period from 1970 to 1980. Of course there is some joint dependence between human capital formation and per capita income growth. But if on further investigation the simultaneous bias should turn out to be small, this result would be consistent with the relatively high rates of return on investment in education computed from microeconomic data (see McMahon and Wagner 1982: 161–177 and 181–182 for detailed estimates for the United States and for a summary of many studies of earnings functions) and with the hypothesis that the measure of human capital formation used in Table 1 accounts for a significant fraction of the productivity growth in the postwar period in the developed nations.

When this measure of basic literacy in mathematics and language is augmented with a measure of the number of trained scientists and engineers as a percentage of the labor force in each industry, it explains how it is possible for the follower-country to adapt and use effectively the new technologies. This step is essential to be able to capitalize on the "advantages of backwardness." There are many LDCs that have not equaled the growth record of Japan and Israel, for example. The large initial stocks of human capital and higher rates of growth in education and health levels in Japan and Israel have undoubtedly made it easier for them to adapt and use western technology. The level of educational attainment in Japan was not only high initially, but the rate of increase has been considerably higher than that in the United States or the United Kingdom since 1950. This seems to me to be an essential supplement to Maddison's (1979) mention of trade as the main transmission mechanism. Although importing high technology capital goods undoubtedly transmits some kinds of new technology, there are still significant steps before these items—and perhaps even more important, the more intangible kinds of scientific findings (e.g., uses of hybrids in agriculture)—can be made effective in production.

This is consistent with regressions that have been run by the author since Table 1 was prepared, as well as with what is being found in an increasing number of studies of productivity growth in the less developed countries. To cite only one example, an interesting recent study by Yamada and Ruttan (1980: 559) of the sources of productivity growth in agriculture in forty-one developed and developing countries finds that the number of graduates of agricultural colleges per person employed in agriculture, supplemented by the average educational attainment of persons in agriculture, accounts for 30 to 32 percent of the productivity differences in agriculture among developed as well as among less developed countries.

This is not to suggest that reduced human capital formation has as yet been a major source of the slowdown in productivity growth—in this respect I agree with Maddison. But this is largely because it is not as sensitive to restrictive monetary policies as is physical capital investment, which in turn is due to the fact that relatively less human capital is financed with credit or sensitive to changes in credit terms. Nevertheless, there is some evidence that there may have been a greater reduction n the rate of effective human capital formation than is revealed by the figures. For example, the quality of education has fallen in the United States in some respects since the late 1960s as evidenced by the reduced requirements in high schools for courses in math and science and by the falling math and science scores on college admission and graduate record examinations. A weakening in college curricular requirements occurred in the United States as well as in Japan and elsewhere at the time of the campus unrest of the late 1960s. Furthermore, human capital formation in the form of on-the-job training has been sharply reduced for those unemployed during the 1975 and 1982 recessions. Since 1981 public support for education has been cut severely by U.S. federal and state governments. All of this is likely to reduce the rate that new technology is assimilated by new human capital, with effects that may have been modest prior to 1981 but are likely to be more important as growth rates are computed that link 1970 levels to 1985 levels and beyond.

It is of further significance that some of the key sources of the slowdown—such as the sharp reductions in energy-intensive investment associated with the Baily effect—are not strictly reversible since the same kinds of energy-intensive investment cannot merely be resumed. This suggests that more attention should be paid to less energy-intensive sources of productivity growth, such as human capital formation—especially improvements in the quality of management and assimilation of the new technology through math and science courses at all levels in the schools.

ADVANCES IN KNOWLEDGE THROUGH R&D

Some of the new data on the composition of public and private investment in R&D are summarized in Table 2. Certain types of this R&D may reasonably be viewed as more relevant to productivity growth than other types. For example, Japan's much larger investment as a percentage of its GDP for support of adaptation of western technology relevant to agricultural productivity, industrial productivity, and energy shown in Table 2, as well as its much smaller total public defense R&D effort relative to that in the United States and United Kingdom, could help to partially explain slower U.S. and U.K. growth as well as the shift of technological leadership to Japan in an increasing number of product lines. Maddison's exclusive reliance on the Rosenberg (1976) effect has the potential of helping to explain the slower growth in the United States but not the assumption of new leadership by Japan. His explanation therefore needs to be augmented, in my opinion, with the effects of investment in some types of advances in knowledge, a second aspect of total investment and total capital. Germany's nondefense R&D effort has even more dramatically exceeded that in the United States and the United Kingdom since 1965 (see Table 2).

Some will argue that new weapons systems and space exploration have spillover effects on productivity growth—perhaps this is Maddison's implicit assumption in looking at total R&D where the United States clearly leads. But surely those components of R&D directly oriented to improving economic efficiency and productivity or to expanding basic knowledge are likely to have a larger impact on productivity growth than those that are not—see Gilpin (1975) and National Science Foundation (1981: 9). Defense research also competes for scarce scientific research personnel. Beyond this, the United States devotes a larger fraction of its nondefense research dollars to health R&D than other countries do. There are many nonmonetary returns to health research in the form of a longer and better quality of life for which no imputations are made in the measures of GDP used in calculating productivity growth.

With respect to empirical evidence, both Germany and Japan's total public and private nondefense R&D—the only measure available for the 1960-80 period, and then only for the five largest OECD countries—has exceeded U.S. nondefense R&D since 1968, as can be seen in Table 1. When it is introduced into the regression as shown at the bottom of Table 1, its coefficient somewhat surprisingly is negative, but it is not significant at the 0.05 level. The simple correlation is positive until 1970, however, as shown

Table 2. Growth Rates and Composition of R&D Expenditure (percentage) (Countries ranked from fastest (left) to slowest (right) pre-energy-shock growth).

	Japan	Germany	France	Sweden	United States	United Kingdom
Growth rate per capita						
1966-73	9.5	3.9	4.9	3.2	2.9	2.5
1974-80	1.9	2.1	2.3	0.9	1.3	0.7
Nondefense government R&D plus private R&D as a percentage of GDP						
1965	1.53	1.53	2.01	n.a.	1.33	1.49
1975	1.89	2.19	1.80	n.a.	1.50	1.39
Government R&D by major objective						
Defense	5	19	36	33	49	61
Industrial productivity	13	15	14	3	0.4	10
Agricultural productivity	30	3	4	3	2	5
Energy	19	21	9	12	10	8
Health	7	6	5	11	12	3
Advancement of knowledge	0	9	15	5	4	4
Other (e.g., space, telecommnication environment)	25	27	17	26	23	9.2

Sources: Nondefense R&D from National Science Foundation: 212; government R&D by objective is net of general university funding from Piekarz, Thomas, and Jennings (1984: Table 10).

in the bottom line of Table 1, after which the more dramatic slowdown that occurred in the high-growth countries (see the top of Table 2) is negatively correlated with their higher R&D efforts. This all suggests that it is likely that there are longer lags involved than those introduced into this particular regression and that better controls are needed for the effects of under-utilization. It also is likely to be fruitful to extend Piekarz's data to measure those types of R&D expected to be more relevant to productivity growth over the entire 1955–80 period so they could be used in the regressions.

There is some empirical evidence of shifts in technological leadership away from the United States. The increasing number of U.S. patents secured by foreign inventors, for example, and the decline since about 1967 in the number of patents secured by American inventors (NSF 1981: 110), may also be related to the smaller nondefense R&D effort in the United States. This smaller effort has been due largely to the decline in federal sup-port for nondefense R&D, since R&D by industry has continued to grow slowly in real terms, in spite of the lower profits during the 1975 and 1982 recessions (NSF 1981: 75).

NEEDED IMPUTATIONS FOR ENVIRONMENTAL IMPROVEMENTS

Turning to Maddison's (and Denison's) point that increased governmental regulation related to better air, water, and industrial health causes some of the slowdown in productivity growth, I would like to suggest that this is largely because the National Income Accounts fail to make imputations for the returns to better health, for example, as the result of improved air and water quality (via EPA regulations) and improved health and safety in the mines and other industries (via OSHA regulations). Surely these add to utility and satisfaction as do many other final consumer services. We count the costs of cleaning up the environment that are added within firms by the regulations but then treat it as an intermediate good and fail to count the final product. If the product price is increased as the result of these added costs, it adds to the inflation rate but (except for some consumer product safety gadgets) not to the quantity of final output that is measured. Of course one must agree with Maddison, and with Denison, that measured productivity thereby is lower. It is true by definition.

When I attempted some imputations for the improvement to the en-vironment and health brought about by these regulations, based simply on factor cost, plus imputations for the services of housewives that include the dramatic improvement in their education that, as George Psacharopoulis points out, contributes among other things to better health in the family, I found no decline in growth of measured plus imputed GNP per person employed in the period from 1965 to 1973 (see McMahon 1981: 9). Making imputations for the imputed rental value of household capital, as well as the services of housewives, Kendrick (1979: 357) found much the same pattern of increasing imputed values from 1966 to 1973. Eisner and Nebhut's (1981) analysis of larger capital formation by government comes to much the same conclusion—that is, the imputed rental values for government-created capital did grow after 1966.

As Maddison points out, it is extremely desirable to increase the cost effectiveness of these regulations. But since most of us have by now had experiences such as breathing cleaner air, swimming in cleaner lakes, and observing strip miners replacing the top soil, perhaps it is now time to leave the burden of the proof that these regulations are *totally cost-ineffective* to those who use data where they have made no imputations for health or environment improvements, thereby valuing them at zero. But even including some imputations for much of this imperfectly measured final product, there is still a sharp slowdown in productivity growth beginning not in 1966 but in 1973, as Maddison stresses.

OVERSIZED AND OVERACTIVE GOVERNMENT

Maddison rejects the hypothesis that an oversized and overactive government is significantly impeding productivity growth. When one investigates this hypothesis, one finds that total taxes as a percentage of GNP are larger in France, Austria, Greece, Belgium, and especially in Germany than they are in the United States, and that all of these countries have grown faster than the United States, both postwar and since 1973. Among OECD countries where the government sector is smaller, only one, Japan, has grown faster, and several, such as Spain, Australia, and Portugal, are growing more slowly. I therefore must agree with Angus Maddison that there is no apparent relationship between government size and growth in production or in labor productivity.

The *structure* of government expenditure and taxes can have an impact, however. Some government expenditure is really investment, such as the investment in nondefense R&D and investment in physical and human capital—areas where significant cuts can have an adverse effect on the technological leadership of the nation and on productivity growth in the longer run. Conversely, some types of government expenditure support only consumption, such as the operation of large unfunded retirement systems or ADC-type welfare systems, which probably operate in the other direction to reduce personal savings rates, physical capital formation, human capital formation, and measured growth.

A MORE EXPLICIT MODEL NEEDED

A more explicit and more comprehensive model is needed—one that captures the major effects developed by Maddison, augmented with the effects suggested by the concept of investment in total capital studied above as well as by Denison, Schultz, and Kendrick. The productivity/growth function (derived from the production function) in equation (1) needs to be augmented with a more complete specification of the demand side, since the simultaneity implicit in Maddison's and Nelson's discussions in this book of the effects of cautious demand management policies is also implicit in most discussions of productivity growth. But except for a few purely theoretical long-term growth models, it is seldom taken explicitly into account.

Such a model is presented in Table 3. Its theme is that energy price shocks adversely affect the inflation rate, that higher inflation leads to tighter macroeconomic policies (particularly monetary policy), and that the resulting higher interest rates in turn restrict investment demand, capital formation, and the level of utilization of human and physical capital—all of which retard productivity growth.

The discussion in Maddison's paper is in terms of rates of change, which is typical of most discussions of this subject. So in Table 3 I have derived from a more familiar model expressed in terms of levels a structural model reexpressed in rate of change terms. After the productivity growth equation (1), which was discussed above, the inflation rate is determined through a relatively standard Phillips-type reduced form price equation that is shifted adversely by the slowdown in productivity growth. Simultaneous equation estimates of the underlying wage and price equations have been completed for U.S. annual data for 1949–1982 that include a productivity growth term in the wage equation. They cannot be reported here in detail. But they do confirm that $\beta_2 < 0$ in Table 3 is a reasonable assumption. Equation (3) determines the rate of growth of the money supply through a reaction function within which this inflation rate appears. Together with the rate of growth in the demand for money in equation (4), the slowed growth of the money supply has the net effect of tightening credit terms, r, which in turn restricts gross investment in physical capital stocks in equation (6). This in turn slows the rate of growth of aggregate demand through its effect in equation (9), with feedback effects reducing consumption demand in equation (10) and the growth of employment in equation (12). The resulting slack demand and unemployment shown in equations (13) through (14), slow the inflation rate directly via equation (2) as well as indirectly as price expectations (π) eventually readjust. But the lower income growth and slack demand also slow total capital formation as shown in equations (6) through (8) and, together with the attendant under-utilization, adversely affect productivity growth through equation (1). The result is slowed productivity growth and can be stagflation, as especially in the case of Britain.

Table 3.   A Structural Interpretation of Medium-Term Productivity Growth and of Sources of the Slowdown.

Summary of the model, incorporating Maddison's sources and total capital

Productivity growth:

(1) $(y_s - n) = \gamma_1 U + \gamma_2(Y/N)_{60} + \gamma_3(k-n) + \gamma_4(h-n) + \gamma_5 a + \gamma_6(e-n)$, $\gamma_1 < 0$, $\gamma_2 < 0$

Inflation rate:

(2) $p = \beta_1 U + \beta_2(y-n) + \beta_3 \pi + \beta_4 p_e$, $\beta_1 < 0$, $\beta_2 < 0$

Monetary policy (demand management reactions to inflation):

(3) $m_s = x_1^* y_p + x_2^* p + x_3^* u$ $x_2 < 0$

(4) $m_d = \mu_1 y + \mu_2 \dot{r} + \mu_3 \dot{\pi}$ $\mu_2 < 0$

(5) $m = m_s = m_d$

Total investment:

(6) $k = \Theta_1 y + \Theta_2 r + \Theta_3 U_K$ $k = (I - I_A)/Y_{-1}, \Theta_2 = (\Theta_2'/Y_{-1}) < 0$

(7) $h = \delta_1 y + \delta_2 g_H^*$ $h = (I_H + G_H)/Y_{-1}, g_H = G_H/Y_{-1}$

(8) $a = \epsilon_1 y + \epsilon_2 r + \epsilon_3 g_A^*$ $a = (I_A + G_A)/Y_{-1}, g_A = G_A/Y_{-1}$

Aggregate demand (flow equilibrium) and fiscal policy:

(9) $y = c + k + h + a + g + \bar{f} - 1$ $g = (G - G_H - G_A)/Y_{-1}, \bar{f} = F/Y_{-1}$

(10) $c = \lambda_0 + \lambda_1(y - t + \bar{r})$ $c = (C - I_H)/Y_{-1}$

(11) $y = y_s = y_d$ $t = T/Y_{-1}, \bar{r} = \bar{R}/Y_{-1}$

Labor requirements, underemployment equilibrium, and under-utilization:

(12) $n = (1/\gamma)y - (\gamma_7/\gamma)k$ $n = (N - N_{-1})/N_{-1}$

(13) $U = (N_p - N)/N_p$ by definition of U,

(14) $U_{H,K} = U_H = U_K = U$,   a simplifying assumption.

Variables are defined in the text under Eqs. (2-1 through 2-5), except for:

G_H = government investment in human capital and in R&D (G_A), which are netted from government purchases of goods and services ($G = (1+g)G_{-1}$)

I_H = household investment in human capital, which is netted from personal consumption expenditure (C) for inclusion in h

I_A = business investment in R&D, which is netted from gross private domestic investment (I) for inclusion in a

y = percentage rate of change in real gross domestic product (Y) demanded (y_D) and supplied (y_S) during the medium term, (5-year) period, with $y = (Y - Y_{-1})/Y_{-1}$

r = the real rate of interest, so that $r = (1 + \dot{r})r_{-1}$

p = percentage rate of change in the expected inflation rate

n = percentage rate of change in employment of labor demanded (n_D) and supplied (n_s) during the medium term (five-year) period

T = total tax receipts, R = transfer payments

U = percentage under-utilization of human capital (labor hoarding by firms, U_H), physical capital (percentage excess capacity) (U_K), raw labor unemployed (U), so that $U = (1 + u)U_{-1}$

Greek letters = all constant-term coefficients
* = policy-determined parameters and variables
Overbar = exogenous variables, and for purposes of an instantaneous (medium-term) equilibrium, all lagged endogenous variables can be regarded as predetermined.

Each of these equations expressed in terms of medium-term (five-year) rates of growth has been derived (and can be derived by the reader) from its corresponding function expressed in terms of absolute levels. The derivations will not be shown here because of the space that would be required (except for the derivation of the productivity growth equation shown in the appendix). The only exception to such a derivation is the reduced-form Phillips equation, equation (2), which has become quite standard. The rates of change (which must be expressed in different form of ratio, such as $c = C/Y_{-1}$, to be consistent in equations (6) through (11) because the aggregate demand components are additive) all are defined here to relate to medium-term (five-year) periods. Since the model is linear, it can be solved simultaneously for a medium-term (or intermediate-term) equilibrium by treating the lagged endogenous variables as parameters, which then determines a solution for each of the sixteen endogenous variables including these rates of change. This includes a solution for the rate of productivity growth in any given five-year period.

Looked at from an estimation point of view, its behavioral coefficients, expressed in Table 3 in Greek symbols, can be estimated by simultaneous equation methods, regarding the lagged endogenous varibles (as well as the exogenous variables) as predetermined for estimation purposes. The simultaneous equation bias that results, for example, from the simultaneous affects of R&D on income growth, and of income growth in turn on support for R&D, would thereby be eliminated. The result should be a more precise measure of each effect on productivity growth in the medium term.

Much more could be said about this structural model and its properties. But enough has been said above and in Table 3 to give a clear view of the more explicit simultaneous equation model that has been used for a structural interpretation of the sources of the slowdown in productivity growth discussed by Maddison.

CONCLUSION

In conclusion, let me reemphasize that I think this analysis of the sources of the slowdown focuses on the most important two groups of sources and is well-balanced. Under-utilization and reduced physical capital investment following the oil price shocks in 1973 and the loss of the "advantages of backwardness" appear independently to me to be very important. Numerous other possible sources are examined by Maddison, and many are laid to rest. To restore growth, rather than limiting human capital formation, R&D, and scientific and social scientific interchange, I would only hope that the possibilities of applying a broader concept of total capital and hence of total investment in education and in R&D, irrespective of which sector does it, would not be overlooked.

APPENDIX

The sources of productivity growth given by equation (1) in the text may be derived from the following production function:

$$Y = e^{\gamma_1 U_{HK} t} e^{\gamma_2 (Y/N) t} N^{\gamma} (A_K K)^{\gamma_3} (A_H H)^{\gamma_4} A^{\gamma_5} E^{\gamma_6} \qquad (1a)$$

Terms not already defined above under equation (1) are:

Y = real GDP, e = base of natural logs
N = employment of raw labor
A = the stock of knowledge, embodied in physical capital through replacement (and net new) investment (A_K), in human capital through education and on-the-job training (A_H), and disembodied new research discoveries or patents (A)
E = petroleum-energy inputs

Since we are concerned with capital deepening in the medium term, and not with long-run steady-state solutions, the stock of knowledge need not be assumed to change at the constant proportional rate e^{at} as is customarily done to facilitate integration and aggregation over vintages. Instead, equation (1a) is interpreted as relating to the most recent vintages of physical capital, human capital, knowledge capital (e.g., patents), and the output that this new capital produces. It also is *gross* investment in new machines, new graduates and/or continuing education, and in patents that is relevant to the analysis rather than *net* investment as in the case where all capital is homogeneous.

Taking the logs:

$$\ell n Y = \gamma_1 U t + \gamma_2 (Y/N) t + \gamma \ell n N + \gamma_3 (\ell n A_K + \ell n K) \qquad (1b)$$
$$+ \gamma_4 (\ell n A_H + \ell n H) + \gamma_5 \ell n A + \gamma_6 \ell n E.$$

Differentiating with respect to time, and using simpler lower case notation for percentage rates of change gives:

$$y = \gamma_1 U + \gamma_2 (Y/N) + \gamma n + \gamma_3 (a_K + k_K) \qquad (1c)$$
$$+ \gamma_4 (a_H + h_H) + \gamma_5 a + \gamma_6 e.$$

Assuming constant returns to scale among the inputs,

$$\gamma = 1 - \gamma_3 - \gamma_4 - \gamma_6, \ n \text{ can be subtracted from both sides.} \qquad (1d)$$

Letting gross investment represent net investment plus the embodiment of new technology occurs through replacement investment so that $(a_K + k_K) = (I/K) = k$, for example, with Y_{-1} used as a proxy to measure K, then gives

$$(y-n) = \gamma_1 U + \gamma_2 (Y/N) + \gamma_3 (k-n) + \gamma_4 (h-n) + \gamma_5 a + \gamma_6 (e-n), \quad (1)$$

the same determinants of the rate of growth in labor productivity shown in equation (1) in the text.

REFERENCES

Denison, Edward F. 1979. *Accounting for Slower Growth*. Washington, D.C.: The Brookings Institution.

Eisner, Robert, and David Nebhut. 1981. "An Extended Measure of Government Product: Preliminary Results for the United States, 1946–1976." *Review of Income and Wealth* 27, no. 1 (March): 33–64.

Gilpin, Robert, 1975. *Technology, Economic Growth, and International Competitiveness*. Washington, D.C.: Joint Economic Committee of the Congress.

Kendrick, John. 1976. *The Formation and Stocks of Total Capital*. New York: Columbia University Press.

_____ . 1979. "Expanding Imputed Values in the National Income and Product Accounts." *Review of Income and Wealth* (December): 349–63.

Maddison, Angus. 1964. *Economic Growth in the West*. New York: W.W. Norton.

_____ . 1979. "Long Run Dynamics of Productivity Growth." *Banca Nazionale del Laboro Quarterly Review*, no. 128 (March): 3–43.

_____ . 1982. *Phases of Capitalist Development*. Oxford: Oxford University Press.

McMahon, Walter W. 1981. "The Slowdown in Productivity Growth: A Macroeconomic Model of Investment in Human and Physical Capital with Energy Shocks." Faculty Working Paper No. 752. Urbana: University of Illinois.

McMahon, Walter W. and Alan P. Wagner. 1982. "The Monetary Return to Education as Partial Social Efficiency Criteria" in *Financing Education: Overcoming Inefficiency and Inequity*, edited by Walter W. McMahon and Terry Geske, pp. 150–187. Urbana, Chicago, and London: University of Illinois Press.

National Science Foundation. 1981. *Science Indicators: Report of the National Science Board, 1981*. Washington, D.C.: U.S. Government Printing Office.

Rosenberg, N. 1976. *Perspectives on Technology*. Cambridge: Cambridge University Press.

Schultz, Theodore W. 1982. "Human Capital Approaches in Organizing and Paying for Education" in *Financing Education; Overcoming Inefficiency and Inequity*, edited by Walter M. McMahon and Terry Geske, pp. 36–51. Urbana, Chicago, and London: University of Illinois Press.

Yamada, Saburo, and Vernon W. Ruttan. 1980. "International Comparisons of Productivity in Agriculture." In *New Developments in Productivity Measurement and Analysis*, edited by John W. Kendrick and B. Vaccara, pp. 509–94. Chicago: University of Chicago Press.

3 THE DIFFUSION OF ECONOMIC GROWTH IN THE WORLD ECONOMY, 1950-80

Irving B. Kravis and
Robert E. Lipsey[1]

In his early pioneering studies of economic growth, Simon Kuznets often had occasion to point out that the application of modern technology to economic activity could be observed only in a small number of European countries, a few of their overseas offshoots, and Japan. Now, from the vantage point of three decades later, it is evident that the process of economic growth has become a worldwide phenomenon. There are still some countries that have not been brought into the process, but for most of the countries with low incomes at the end of World War II, the ensuing three decades have been years of growth in per capita income that can be considered rapid by any reasonable historical standard.

New light can be shed on the diffusion of economic growth because the results of the U.N. International Comparison Project (ICP) make it possible to estimate the levels of real per capita output that each country has reached and the level at which it began the 30-year period, 1950-80. The real levels of output provide proper weights, not available before, for combining countries into relatively homogeneous groups and the groups into a world total, so that both average levels and growth rates for groups and the world can be compared. The real per capita output levels are estimated by converting the per capita GDPs of the individual countries to a common currency through the use of purchasing power parities rather than, as has been hitherto necessary, through the use of exchange rates (Kravis, Heston, and Summers 1982).[2] Because the exchange rate conversions customarily used have systematically understated the real incomes of low-income countries, a new and more accurate assessment of relative output levels is now desirable and presents a different picture of the world.

THE DATA

The nature of the data used in this survey of world output and its growth is discussed in an appendix, but a few words are in order here. The starting points for all the figures were the 1975 estimates of real per capita GDP for thirty-four benchmark countries produced in Phase III of the ICP (Kravis, Heston, and Summers 1982: 12). ("Real" GDP refers here to GDP converted to a common currency by means of purchasing power parities.) First, 1975 real per capita GDPs for ninety-two nonbenchmark countries were estimated by use of the relationship found for the benchmark countries between real per capita GDP and certain widely available variables of which the most important was exchange-rate-converted GDP per capita (Kravis, Heston, and Summers 1982:332–33). For each country the 1975 real GDP per capita was adjusted to a total GDP basis by multiplying by population and the total real GDP was extrapolated to other years in the period 1950 to 1980 by the country's own GDP series in constant prices. Compilations prepared by international agencies of the GDPs of the different countries (or sometimes of growth rates, where the GDP series themselves were not available) were used in the extrapolations. Then, the total GDPs for each year were summed across the countries in each of the country groups described below and across all 126 countries comprising the "world" for purposes of this study.

The caveats about the limitations of national accounts as measures of welfare, the defects and country-to-country incomparabilities in their measurement of what they seek to measure, the uncertainties of population estimates in a number of countries, and the doubts that must attend the constant price series even for advanced countries all apply here, some more strongly than usual. Some of the special problems encountered in the present exercise are pointed out in the data appendix.[3] It seems doubtful, however, that the errors in the data could be so consistent across groups of countries as to throw into question the main features of the story that unfolds.

The 126 countries covered by the data included nearly 98 percent of the world's population in 1980. The countries are divided first into the three major groups often distinguished in U.N. statistics and in literature dealing with the world economy:

1. The industrial countries (United States, Canada; Australia, New Zealand, South Africa; Japan; Austria, Belgium, Denmark, Finland, France, Germany, Iceland, Ireland, Italy, Luxembourg, Netherlands, Norway, Spain, Sweden, Switzerland, and the United Kingdom);

2.   The centrally planned economies (Bulgaria, People's Republic of China, Czechoslovakia, German Democratic Republic, Hungary, Poland, Romania, and the Soviet Union); and
3.   The developing market economies.

Each of the three groups contains economies that are diverse in important respects—size, endowment of natural resources, education and skills of the labor force, and so forth. The developing market economies are even more varied than the other two groups, and they are in addition quite numerous (ninety-seven countries). Consequently, they have been subdivided into four subgroups:

1.   Extremely low-income countries were singled out by taking the twenty-five countries with the lowest real GDPs per capita in 1980 (Benin, Burundi, Central African Republic, Chad, Ethiopia, Gambia, Guinea, Lesotho, Madagascar, Malawi, Mali, Niger, Rwanda, Sierra Leone, Somalia, Togo, Uganda, United Republic of Tanzania, Upper Volta, Zaire; Afghanistan, Bangladesh, Burma, Nepal; and Haiti);
2.   A separate classification was provided for the oil exporting countries (Algeria, Indonesia, Iran, Iraq, Kuwait, Libya, Nigeria, Saudi Arabia, Venezuela);
3.   A group of relatively industrialized countries was identified by selecting those that derived at least twenty percent of their 1975 GDP from manufacturing (that is, these were selected from the set that remained after the industrial countries, the centrally planned economies, and the oil exporters were identified: Hong Kong, Korea, Philippines, Rhodesia, Swaziland, Singapore; Syria; Malta, Portugal, Yugoslavia; Argentina, Brazil, Chile, Dominican Republic, Mexico, Nicaragua, Peru, Puerto Rico, and Uruguay); and
4.   The remaining developing market countries were placed in a group of "other" middle-income countries. (The term "middle-income" countries is used to cover all the developing market countries other than the twenty-five with the lowest incomes, even though some high per capita income oil exporters are included.)

This classification, based partly on structural characteristics and partly on income levels, has its arbitrary aspects. There are borderline countries that could be classified with either the industrial or the developing countries, and among the developing countries small changes in the criteria used to define oil exporters and relatively industrialized countries would shift some countries from one class to another.[4] Also, some countries underwent significant changes during the period so that their assignment depends on the reference date selected. (Since our focus is on explaining today's world we favored recent years.) Despite these unavoidable ambiguities, there is no doubt that the classification does subdivide the countries into groups that have on average the distinctiveness sought with respect to the desired characteristics. For example, Mexico was grouped with relatively industrialized countries though it satisfied some of the criteria that might be used for oil exporters, but this and other close calls do not negate the fact that the two classifications are on average very different in the degree of their reliance on oil exports and in the extent of their industrialization.

The most reliable figures are for 1975 and the least reliable for 1950 and 1955. The figures for the developing countries are more questionable than the others, especially for the early years. It should be mentioned also that the extrapolations from 1975 to the other years for the centrally planned economies are based on constant price GDP series constructed by U.S. statisticians from the countries' material product system of accounts and other data. Finally, the extrapolations involving the oil exporters, both to their 1975 real GDP levels and across time for each country are far from firmly based.

LEVELS OF REAL GDP AND
REAL GDP PER CAPITA

Table 3–1 provides internationally and intertemporally comparable estimates of levels of GDP and GDP per capita for the world as a whole and the groups of countries for the terminal years of the period 1950–80. (Data for intermediate quinquennial dates are in Table 3–A1, and annual data, in a different format, are in Table 3–A2.)

Aggregate world output was multiplied four times over the thirty years.[5] The most rapid gains were in the oil-producing countries despite the fact that we do not count their direct gains from improvements in their terms of trade.[6] The smallest gains—still almost a tripling of output—were in the group of countries still poor in 1980, a fact that points to slow growth, as well as a low starting level, as determinants of their position. The relatively industrialized middle-income countries as a group (including those sometimes referred to as "newly industrialized countries") ranked next after the oil producers in total output growth, followed by the centrally planned economies, while the industrialized countries' output grew comparatively slowly.

Among the groups of developing market economies separately shown here the range of population expansion was fairly narrow, only from a 1980/50 ratio of 1.99 to 2.15, so that the growth of aggregate output determined the relative standings of the groups with respect to the growth of output per capita. The low-income and residual ("other") middle-income groups

Table 3-1. Total Real GDP, Population and Per Capita Real GDP, Groups of Countries[a] and the World, 1950 and 1980 (GDP figures in 1975 international dollars[b]).

	1950	1980	1980/1950
Developing market economies			
Total GDP[c]	530	2399	4.53
Population[d]	1070	2177	2.03
Per capita GDP	495	1102	2.23
Low-income countries			
GDP	42	118	2.81
Population	1609	325	2.02
Per capita GDP	261	361	1.38
Middle-income countries			
Total GDP	488	2282	4.68
Population	909	1852	2.04
Per capita GDP	537	1232	2.29
Oil exporters			
Total GDP	77	467	6.06
Population	150	323	2.15
Per capita GDP	513	1448	2.82
Relatively industrialized			
Total GDP	168	933	5.55
Population	194	404	2.08
Per capita GDP	870	2310	2.66
Other			
Total GDP	243	882	3.63
Population	566	1125	1.99
Per capita GDP	429	783	1.83
Industrial countries			
Total GDP	1413	4795	3.39
Population	543	743	1.37
Per capita GDP	2602	6450	2.48
Centrally planned economies			
Total GDP	536	2628	4.90
Population	816	1392	1.71
Per capita GDP	657	1887	2.87
World			
Total GDP	2479	9822	3.96
Population	2429	4313	1.78
Per capita GDP	1020	2277	2.23

[a]See text for explanation of the country classification.

[b]An international dollar has the same purchasing power as the U.S. dollar for GDP as a whole. Its purchasing power over any particular kind of goods differs from that of a U.S. dollar because the structure of average international prices differs from the structure of U.S. prices. (See Kravis, Heston, Summers 1982: 90-92.)

[c]Billion 1975 dollars.

[d]Millions.

were losers in the growth race, especially the former, whose index of real GDP per capita declined steadily from 26 to 16 percent of the world average (see Table 3-2 and Table 3-A1). With slower population growth, the per capita GDP relative standings of the centrally planned economies improved substantially, and those of the industrialized countries slightly.

Changes in shares of world production included a decline for the industrial countries and gains for the oil exporters, the centrally planned economies, and the relatively industrialized middle-income countries. The 1980 distribution of production was a little less than half of the world total for the industrialized countries, a little more than a quarter for the centrally planned economies, and a little less than a quarter for the developing market economies.[7]

One way of describing how these figures change our picture of the world is by comparing them with the exchange-rate-converted GDPs per capita (Table 3-3). The figures in column (2) representing real per capita GDPs are similar in concept to those in Table 3-1. Column (3) shows the relative income standings of the groups of countries by the conventional pre-ICP method of comparison. (The centrally planned economies are excluded because the exchange-rate conversions are difficult to determine owing to the problems of identifying a market exchange rate.) The systematic tendency of exchange-rate conversions to understate real incomes for low-income countries is evident in the figures; the rankings of the exchange-rate deviation indexes from high to low are, except for the oil exporters, the same as the rankings of the real (PPP-converted) per capita GDPs (R's) from low to high. This is in one sense a mechanical consequence of the basic method of extrapolation from the thirty-four benchmark countries to the others, but the underlying economic reality is the correlation that has been found for benchmark countries in the three ICP studies. In 1975, for example, the adjusted coefficient of determination (R^{-2}) for the correlation of the exchange

Table 3-2.   Relative Levels of Real GDP Per Capita, 1950 and 1980 (world = 100).

	1950	1980
Developing market economies	49	48
Low-income countries	26	16
Middle-income countries	53	54
Oil exporters	50	64
Relatively industrialized	85	101
Other	42	34
Industrial countries	255	283
Centrally planned economies	64	83
World	100	100

Table 3-3. Comparison of PPP-Converted and Exchange-Rate-Converted GDPs Per Capita, 1975.

		1975 Per Capita GDP		
	Number of Countries (1)	PPP-Converted (2)	Exchange-Rate Converted (3)	Exchange Rate Deviation Index (4)=(2) ÷ (3)
Developing market economies	97	* 968	$ 631	1.53
Low-income countries	25	343	134	2.56
Middle-income countries	72	1076	717	1.50
Relatively industrialized	20	1955	1329	1.47
Oil exporters	8	1278	1017	1.26
Others	44	702	411	1.71
Industrial countries	21	5651	6393	.88
All market economies	118	2231	2184	1.02

rate deviation index and r was 0.80 for the thirty-four benchmark countries. The reasons for this association have been treated elsewhere (Kravis, Heston, and Summers 1981, 1983; Kravis and Lipsey 1983) and will not be set forth here. The important consequence in the present context is that the dispersion of real per capita incomes is and has been much smaller than pre-ICP calculations indicated. The industrial/developing country ratios for exchange-rate-converted per capita GDP, for example, is 10.1 for 1975, while the true ratio is 5.8. This gap in real terms widened from 5.3 in 1950 to 6.0 in 1970, after which it declined slightly. The low-income countries are still very poor countries and the hunger that is found in them is still very real, but these figures cast a different light on catch-up possibilities for low- and middle-income countries, particularly if the target for catch-up is thought of in terms of present income levels in the industrial countries with the lowest incomes. But this is an avenue that cannot be explored here.

Another way of assessing the real levels of per capita GDP is to follow Kuznets in inquiring into the comparable figures for the industrial countries at the beginnings of their periods of modern economic growth. Kuznets was able in one of his major works to assemble long-term data on economic growth for fourteen industrial countries for this purpose (Kuznets 1971: 24). For each of these countries, we take Kuznets' dating of the starting period of modern economic growth and the rates of growth of real per capita product he estimates between the beginning date and his terminal date, 1965. However, we substitute our estimates of 1965 real GDP per capita in 1975 prices for Kuznets's exchange-rate-converted GNP per capita in 1965 prices. The per capita GDPs in 1975 international dollars (I$) as of the beginning of growth that come out of this calculation were $210 for Japan (in 1874-79) and from $424 (Sweden in 1861-69) to $2,052 (Australia in 1900-04) for other industrial countries, with the median under $700. The lowest-income country in 1980, Upper Volta, had a real per capita GDP of $212, approximately the starting figure for Japan, but

Table 3-4.   Coefficients of Determination for 1950-80
Growth Rates and Real Per Capita GDPs, 1950.

	Number of Countries	R^{-2}
Low-income countries	25	0.58
Middle-income countries	72	0.0
Industrial countries	21	0.52
CPEs	8	0.39
World	126	0.29

each of the twenty lowest-income countries had per capitas below $424, the other-than-Japan minimum beginning point. On the other hand, sixty-three of the ninety-seven developing market economies had 1980 per capitas above $700, the median starting income of the industrial countries, and more than a score of developing countries had per capita real GDPs in excess of $2,052, the highest starting point. Most of the developing world is working its way up to and beyond the level from which today's industrial countries started their periods of rapid growth.

This is not, however, to claim that there has been a pervasive tendency for countries with low incomes to grow faster and to narrow the gap between them and countries with higher incomes. For the world as a whole there is a rather weak catch-up effect observable when 1950–80 growth rates for individual countries are regressed against 1950 real per capita GDPs ($R^{-2} = 0.29$). Within some groups of countries, including the industrial countries and the low-income countries, the catch-up tendency is more marked. In the former group, for example, Canada and the United States had high starting incomes and slow growth while the opposite was true for Japan and to a lesser degree for France and Germany. The relationships were all positive when R^{-2} was above zero (Table 3-4).

PRODUCTIVITY GROWTH AND LEVELS

The improvement in the per capita GDPs of the world economy and of the various groups of countries over the period 1950–80 could be attributable to more per capita inputs of labor and capital or to more output per unit of input—that is, either to a growth of inputs or to an increase in productivity. To move from these data on GDP per capita to productivity measures we should replace the denominator, consisting of population in Table 3-1, with a measure of total factor inputs. Of course, if we were able to take account of every factor that could influence output—not only capital, labor, and natural resources of given qualities but also, for example, the quality of management, the extent of knowledge about production techniques, and the scale of operations—output per unit of input would be the same everywhere. This is a standard assumption in trade theory, but no one has been able to measure all these influences, and the most common practice has been to limit the inputs to labor or to labor and capital.

The shift from output per capita to output per economically active person (used here interchangeably with "worker," "engaged person," or "member of the labor force") is the easiest to make conceptually and statistically. It will tell us to what extent the high outputs per capita observed for some countries are due to high per capita inputs of labor and the low outputs to low labor inputs, but it still leaves unanswered the questions of how much of the difference in output per engaged person is due to differences in the quality of the labor inputs or to the differences in the amount of capital.

Relatively comparable data on labor force participation rates (measured by the ratio of labor force to population rather than the ratio of labor force to population over sixteen years old, as is the U.S. practice) are available for quinquennial years from 1950 to 1975.[8] Table 3-5 gives the per capita GDP figures and shows the average participation rates (including both employed and unemployed persons) and real GDP per engaged person in 1950 and 1975. (Table 3-A3 shows the data for all the quinquennial years in the period 1950-75.) In principle, output per engaged person could also be obtained by dividing output per capita by the participation ratio, but rounding errors would make the numbers slightly different.

Participation rates declined over the twenty-five-year period in the developing countries—from 42 percent in 1950 to 37 percent in 1975—while in the industrial countries the rate remained stable at 43 or 44 percent and in the centrally planned economies varied between 46 and 49 percent. The relatively low participation ratios of the developing countries and their decline over time against the stability of the participation rates of the industrial and centrally planned economies produce smaller differences in productivity than in income. The difference is greatest at the end of the period; the industrial/developing country per capita income ratio is 5.8 in 1975, but the corresponding ratio for output per person engaged is 4.9. The industrial country/centrally planned economy ratios for GDP per capita and per worker both show declining tendencies, although the trend is not a smooth one in either case; the per capita ratio is near 4.0 in 1950 and 3.4 in 1975, while the per worker ratio is 4.2 and 3.7 at the two terminal dates.

The differences in participation rates are related to the age distribution of the various groups of countries, the extent of participation among those of working age, and the age at which labor force participation usually begins. The developing countries have younger populations than the industrial economies and the centrally planned economies, but higher ratios of working to adult populations. Output comparisons are thus least unfavorable

Table 3-5.   Real GDP Per Capita and Per Economically Active
Person, Groups of Countries, and the World, 1950 and 1975.

	1950	*1975*	*1975/1950*
Developing market economies			
Per capita GDP	495	968	1.96
Participation rate	42	37	0.88
GDP per active person	1176	2639	2.24
Low-income countries			
Per capita GDP	261	343	1.31
Participation rate	46	41	0.89
GDP per active person	566	836	1.48
Middle-income countries			
Per capita GDP	537	1076	2.06
Participation rate	41	36	0.88
GDP per active person	1296	2997	2.31
Oil exporters			
Per capita GDP	513	1278	2.49
Participation rate	38	33	0.87
GDP per active person	1338	3831	2.96
Relatively industrialized			
Per capita GDP	870	1955	2.25
Participation rate	37	34	0.92
GDP per active person	2347	5788	2.47
Other			
Per capita GDP	429	702	1.64
Participation rate	44	37	0.84
GDP per active person	981	1877	1.91
Industrial countries			
Per capita GDP	2602	5651	2.17
Participation Rate	44	44	1.00
GDP per active person	5951	12881	2.16
Centrally planned economies			
Per capita GDP	657	1646	2.50
Participation rate	46	47	1.02
GDP per active person	1422	3488	2.45
World			
Per capita GDP	1020	2038	2.00
Participation rate	44	41	0.93
GDP per active person	2327	4916	2.11

to the developing countries when related to persons of working age (fifteen
years and older) and most unfavorable when related to the entire population. These points are brought out in Table 3-6. The 1975 in-
dustrial/developing country GDP per adult ratio, for example, is 4.5 as
compared to a per worker ratio of 4.9 and a per capita ratio of 5.8.

Table 3-6. GDP in Relation to the Number of Workers and the Number of Adults, 1950 and 1975.

	1950		1975	
	Absolute	Relative to Industrial Countries	Absolute	Relative to Industrial Countries
Developing market economies				
Participation rate	42	95	37	84
Percentage 15 years and older	60	82	57	76
Working population as percentage of adult population	70	117	65	110
GDP per				
capita	495	19	968	17
worker	1176	20	2639	20
adult	831	23	1691	22
Industrial countries				
Participation rate	44	100	44	100
Percentage 15 years and older	73	100	75	100
Working population as percentage of adult population	60	100	59	100
GDP per				
capita	2602	100	5651	100
worker	5951	100	12881	100
adult	3579	100	7561	100
Centrally planned economies				
Participation rate	46	105	47	107
Percentage 15 years and older	68	93	69	92
Working population as percentage of adult population	68	113	68	115
GDP per				
capita	657	25	1646	29
worker	1422	24	3488	27
adult	944	27	2398	32

It is difficult to go very much beyond this rough and incomplete treatment of the denominator of the output/input ratio that defines productivity. The effort to adjust on any systematic basis for the quality of labor or for the amount of capital encounters formidable data problems even for the developed countries. For the developing countries and the world as a whole any serious attempt to carry out such an exercise is beyond the scope of this paper.[9] We can, however, point to the probable effects of the inclusion of these input factors on the undifferentiated labor productivity indexes of Table 3-5. In addition, we offer some rough calculations for the year 1975 to provide some notion of the possible size of the labor quality effects on the Table 3-5 productivity ratios.

Since international differences in the quality of labor, judged in terms of skills appropriate for production, are presumably positively correlated with national per capita incomes, adjusting the labor inputs for quality would increase the inputs in standardized terms for high-income countries relative to low-income ones and thus narrow the productivity differences. The addition of capital would have the same impact if, as seems very possible, capital per worker, and even capital per standardized worker, rises across countries with per capita incomes. (At least we could count on this effect on productivity if we assigned equal weights to the indexes of labor and capital inputs in all countries.) The impact of rising amounts of capital also depends on the effect on the capital/output ratio. If the capital/output ratio rises faster than capital per worker, the addition of capital would again diminish the range of productivity differences.[10]

Our method of adjusting the labor inputs for 1975 was to multiply them by a quality index based on Denison's evaluation of labor quality for nine different levels of education on the basis of 1959 earnings of U.S. males cross classified by age, region, race, and farm vs. nonfarm occupation. We extended the Denison index from the eleven countries covered by Denison to thirty-seven other countries.[11] (All forty-eight countries are in our present industrial or middle groups.) The quality index and output per quality-adjusted member of the labor force (i.e., output per adjusted unit of labor input) for 1975 are shown in Table 3-7. Since a number of countries included in Tables 3-1 and 3-2 are omitted here for lack of data, the outputs per capita and per unadjusted worker are also shown for the present set of countries.

If credence could be placed in this quality adjustment in productivity differentials, the spread in overall productivity among countries now attributable to factors other than the quantity and quality of labor would be much smaller. The ratio of the industrial to the middle-income developing countries would be 3.7 instead of 4.6 for GDP per unit of unadjusted labor input and 5.5 for GDP per capita.[12] The output per unit of quality-adjusted labor for the oil exporters would be notably higher than that of any other group of countries, reflecting, of course, the high prices of oil and the small effort required to produce it in these countries—or, in other words, the high resource endowment per worker, not counted here as an input.

The omission of natural resource wealth affects not only the oil exporters. It is likely that it biases upward the productivity measures of all or most low-income countries since land and other natural resources probably represent a higher share of wealth in such countries than in rich countries.

Since no time series on capital stock are available for most countries of the world, there was no possiblity of including capital input in our measures of productivity growth. Also, as there are no comprehensive measures of capital stock even for a single year for most countries, we were precluded

Table 3-7. Index of Labor Quality and Output Per Quality-Adjusted Member of the Labor Force, 1975.

	Number of Countries	Index of Labor Quality	Index of Labor Inputs Per Capita		Index of GDP Per Worker		
			Unadjusted	Adjusted	Capita	Unadjusted	Adjusted
Middle-income countries	29	92	93	85	39	41	45
Relative industrialized	10	94	83	77	76	91	98
Oil exporters	5	79	89	69	41	46	60
Other	14	95	98	92	26	26	28
Industrial countries	19	116	113	129	216	192	167
Market economies	48	100	100	100	100	100	100

from taking capital input into account even in a single time cross-sectional productivity comparison.[13]

The highly tentative inference that can be drawn from this experiment, especially if the further impact of the inclusion of capital is considered, is that a substantial part of the difference in output per capita may well be attributable to larger per capita inputs in the richer countries. Sensitivity analysis based on alternative ways of adjusting for the quality of labor and of estimating relative amounts of capital should help clarify this point.

THE GROWTH OF REAL GDP

Table 3-1 already tells us the essential overall story of world economic growth in the 1950-80 period. With population less than doubling, the quadrupling of world GDP in real terms meant that world GDP per capita more than doubled. Growth in per capita production at such a rate, approximately doubling in a quarter of a century, is in itself a rather remarkable record, especially during a period in which world population also rose notably. A fuller assessment requires, of course, comparisons with previous periods in modern economic history and an analysis of some of the features of the recent record, especially the contributions of various countries to the overall result.

For the further analysis of growth rates we shift away from the use of individual terminal years to rates of change calculated for periods. These are set out in Table 3-8, both for total GDP and per capita GDP. Each of the 1950-80 growth rates for total GDP (or for per capita GDP) is derived

Table 3-8. Annual Rates of Growth in GDP and GDP per Capita, 1950-80.[a]

	Total GDP	GDP per Capita
Developing market economies	5.30	2.79
Low-income countries	3.20	0.80
Middle-income countries	5.44	2.91
Oil exporters	6.69	3.93
Relatively industrialized	5.98	3.38
Other	4.48	2.05
Industrial countries	4.30	3.20
Centrally planned economies	5.31	3.38
All except China	5.23	3.70
World	4.77	2.75

[a]Each growth rate represents the (antilog of b) − 1 with b estimated from the equation $\ln GDP = a + bT$. GDP is total or per capita *GDP* for the group of countries indicated in the stubs, *T* stands for time and the observations cover the years in the column headings.

from the coefficient of a variable representing time in a regression in which the logarithm of total GDP (or of per capita GDP) for the group of countries or the world is the dependent variable and time is the independent variable.[14] Figure 3-1 shows the total and per capita GDP series for the world economy. The index numbers of total and per capita GDP and base period international dollar values are in Table 3-A2.

For the world as a whole, for example, the annual growth rate in total GDP of 4.77 percent represents a more than fourfold increase in thirty years, while the 2.75 percent rate for GDP per capita provides a multiple of 2.25 in the same period. Relatively comprehensive records that make possible the addition of world GDP or the calculation of worldwide growth rates are not available for earlier periods, but there are reasonably adequate bases for two major inferences about growth in the 1950-80 period relative to earlier experiences: Growth was very rapid, and it was widely diffused.

The Rapidity of Growth

For the developed countries, for which reasonably well-based comparisons with earlier periods can be made, growth rates of total GDP and per capita GDP substantially exceeded those of the first two quarters of the twentieth century. None of the thirteen industrial countries for which Kuznets (1971: 38-39) offers growth rates for these earlier periods exceeded the 4.30 percent per annum growth in total product of the twenty-one industrial countries in the 1950-80 period.[15] If comparisons are confined to Kuznets's thirteen countries, which accounted for 83 percent of the 1975 total real GDP of the twenty-one countries classified here as industrial, we have per annum growth rates for the first three quarters of this century as shown in Table 3-9.[16]

Historical data for the other groups of countries are very scarce. Table 3-10 reproduces some growth rates for periods prior to the 1950s for seven developing countries assembled by Kuznets (1971:30-31) and adds growth rates for 1950-80 computed in a similar way. Two kinds of comparisons are in order.

First, still following Kuznets, the evidence suggests lower growth rates in both total and per capita GDP in developing countries than in the industrial countries for the fifty or one hundred years preceding 1950. This is supported by comparisons of the Kuznets data in Table 3-10 with growth rates he provides for industrial countries (for the latter, see Kuznets 1971: 39-39) (Table 3-11).

The sample of developing countries is, however, small, and Kuznets rests the case for lower developing country growth also on the argument that growth in the developing countries in the century or century and a half

Figure 3-1.   Indexes of Real World GDP and of Real
World GDP per-capita, 1950-1980 (1975 = 100).

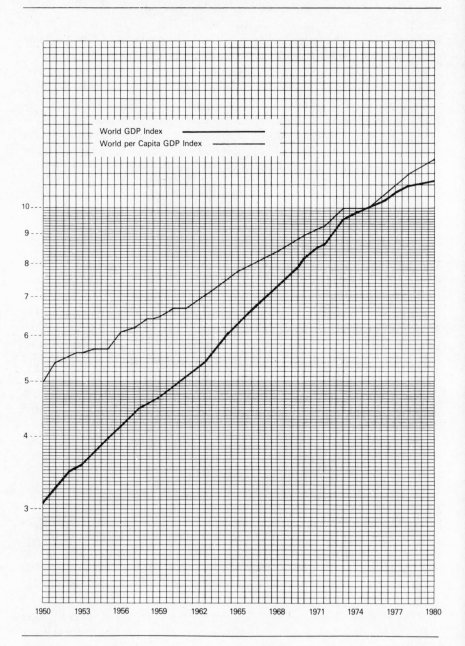

Table 3-9.   Per Annum Growth Rates, Industrial Countries[a]
1900-75.

	Total GDP	Population	GDP per Capita
1900-09 to 1925-29	3.05	1.52	1.95
1925-29 to 1950-54	2.43	.64	1.78
1950-54 to 1976-80	4.12	1.02	3.07

[a]See text.

Table 3-10.   Rates of Growth per Decade in Total Product, Population, and Product per Capita, Selected Less Developed Countries.

	Duration of Period (Years) (1)	Rates of Growth per Decade (percentage)		
		Total Product (2)	Population (3)	Product per Capita (4)
Argentina				
1900-04 to 1925-29	25	57.0	40.2	12.0
1950-54 to 1976-80	26	41.1	16.5	21.1
Mexico				
1895-99 to 1925-29	30	20.7	6.5	13.3
1950-54 to 1976-80	26	185.4	37.6	34.8
Jamaica				
1832 to 1930	98	10.9	10.9	0
1929-31 to 1950-52	21	27.6	17.2	8.9
1950-54 to 1976-80	26	71.5	15.6	48.4
Ghana				
1891 to 1911	20	32.1	10.1	20.0
1911 to 1950-54	41	45.2	27.5	13.9
1950 to 1976-80	28	71.8	34.7	27.5
Philippines				
1902 to 1938	36	34.2	22.5	9.6
1938 to 1950-54	14	19.8	24.7	−3.9
1950-54 to 1976-80	26	82.8	34.0	36.4
Egypt				
1895-99 to 1945-49	50	11.9	14.4	−2.2
1950-54 to 1976-80	26	62.0	26.4	28.2
India				
1861-69 to 1881-89	20	19.1	5.3	13.1
1881-89 to 1901-09	20	1.4	4.6	−31.1
1901-09 to 1952-58	50	16.8	9.9	6.3
1950-54 to 1976-80	26	40.1	24.2	12.8

Source: 1950-54 to 1976-80: present authors. Other data: Kuznets (1971: 30ff).

Table 3-11. Growth Rates for Industrial and Developing Countries.

	Number of Countries	Number of Intervals	Median Growth Per Decade[a]	
			Total GDP	GDP Per Capita
Industrial	14	53	30	16
Developing	7	16	20	10

[a]The unit of observation here is an interval which varies in timing and number from country to country. This is not a very satisfactory substitute for the use of countries as the observations, each with the same number and dating of intervals, and it should be clear that this method of summarizing the statistics is ours and not Kuznets's.

preceding the 1950s must have been slow relative to that of the industrial countries, since considering very low 1950 per capita incomes, rapid growth rates would have implied incredibly low incomes fifty or one hundred years earlier.

Secondly, the developing countries have been growing faster since 1950 than before. For total GDP (sometimes GNP or NNP in the Kuznets data), the Table 3-6 data show that the recent growth rates in total GDP are, with the exception of those for Argentina, higher, and by very substantial margins, than those relating to the pre-1950 periods. Population growth is also higher though with two exceptions and not by such wide margins. The upshot is, again with a single exception, more rapid growth in per capita product since 1950 than before by margins that are not as large as those for total product but are still substantial.

The Diffusion of Growth

This evidence rests, however, on a small number of countries, and a return to the data of Table 3-8 enables us to strengthen and broaden the point. Briefly put, (1) the growth of the developing market economies in total GDP during the period 1950-80 was faster than that of the industrialized countries (5.30 percent per annum against 4.30 percent); (2) the industrial countries expanded their GDP more rapidly after 1950 than before; (3) prior to 1950 growth in the industrial countries was at a higher rate than that in developing countries; and, therefore, (4) the developing countries' growth after 1950 must have been much accelerated relative to growth before 1950. For per capita GDP in the 1950-80 period, higher population growth reduced the growth in developing countries to a level below that of the industrial countries but still high by historical standards.

Growth in total GDP in the centrally planned economies also outstripped that of the industrial countries, about matching that of the developing countries. When growth in population is taken into account and per capita growth rates calculated, the per annum rate for the CPEs is 3.38 percent as compared to 3.20 percent for the industrial countries and 2.79 percent for the developing market economies.

But these overall comparisons of the three major groups lump together countries within each with very different growth records in the recent period, and for each group the high average growth rate may reflect extremely high rates in relatively few countries. The possibility of such diversity is of particular interest among the developing countries, with the lowest average incomes of the three sets. It is indeed true that there are some developing countries that grew slowly. The total GDP of the twenty-five lowest-income countries grew at a rate of 3.20 percent per annum, but with high rates of population increase, their growth in per capita GDP was only 0.80 percent per annum. However, all the other groups of developing countries (oil exporters, relatively industrialized, and other middle income) did better. In total GDP, each exceeded the growth of the industrial countries. Each of the three groups had faster population growth than the industrial countries, and thus their per capita growth rates compare less favorably. Even so, the per capita rates for the oil exporters and the industrialized middle-income countries were above that of the industrial countries. The rate for other middle-income countries fell below that of the industrial countries but was still over 2 percent per annum, a very respectable rate by the historical record of fast-growing countries.

Our method of calculation of the growth rates in per capita GDP for each group of countries implicitly weights each country's per capita growth rate by its share in total product and its relative population growth over the period. Kuznets (1972: 193) has raised the question whether more insightful welfare-oriented results might not be obtained by weighting each country's growth in per capita GDP by population alone. The results of population weighting is compared in Table 3–12 with the results of the conventional method of calculating the growth rate after aggregating the initial and terminal period GDPs. The alternative method of calculation raises the growth rate among industrial countries (by reducing the weight of slow-growing United States and Canada) and lowers the growth rate of the developing countries (by raising the weights of slow-growing Bangladesh, India, and Pakistan). The differences are similar to those obtained by Kuznets with data for 1954–58 to 1964–68.

Even on this basis, however, the conclusion seems clear that rapid economic growth has become a much more diffused phenomenon than was the case in the first half of the twentieth century or in the preceding periods.[17] In terms of the grouped data we have been using, rapid growth

Table 3-12. Comparison of Population Weighting with Results of Conventional Growth Rate Calculations.

| | Growth Rate in GDP per Capita, 1950-52 to 1978-80, based on | |
	Aggregation of Countries' GDP	Weighting Each Country's Growth Rate by Its Initial-Period Population
Developing market economies	2.22	1.95
Low-income countries	1.22	1.45
Middle-income countries	2.34	2.03
Industrial countries	2.27	2.83
Centrally planned economies	2.73	2.82
World	2.28	2.44

has bypassed only a fifth of the nations of the world containing less than 10 percent of the world's population.

To what extent are these proportions dependent on the classification employed? There are two ways of checking on this. One is to experiment with a different classification. The other is to examine the distribution of countries with respect to growth rates.

Growth rates are given in Table 3-13 for three groups of developing market economies (excluding the oil exporters) arrayed according to their 1950 real per capita GDPs, the first consisting of the twenty-five lowest-income countries (in 1950) and the other two of the remaining countries divided evenly between them. The growth rates in the twenty-five lowest-income non-oil exporting developing market economies are—as one might anticipate from the substitution of beginning-of-period for end-of-period income levels as the selection criterion—higher than those of the low-income countries in Table 3-8. The main reason the difference is so small is

Table 3-13. Growth Rates for Three Groups of Developing Market Economies, Classified by 1950 per Capita GDP.

| Income Groups | Number of Countries | Per Annum Growth In | |
		Total GDP	GDP per Capita
Lowest[a]	25	4.26	1.20
Middle	32	5.91	2.89
Highest	32	6.93	3.23

[a]Twenty-five lowest income countries in 1950: Benin, Botswana, Burundi, Ethiopia, The Gambia, Kenya, Lesotho, Liberia, Malawi, Mali, Niger, Rwanda, Sierra Leone, United Republic of Tanzania, Togo, Upper Volta, Zaire; Afghanistan, Bangladesh, Burma, India, Jordan, Nepal, Pakistan, Sri Lanka.

the substantial overlap between the countries in the two lists: Eighteen of the twenty-five lowest-income countries as of 1980 are also among the twenty-five lowest non-oil exporting developing countries as of 1950. Both lists are characterized by a predominance of African countries. In the 1980 list eighteen of the twenty-five are African countries; in the 1950 list seventeen out of twenty-five; and fourteen out of the eighteen on both lists are African.

Most of the non-African countries found on the low-income lists are on the Indian subcontinent, very broadly defined to include Afghanistan and Nepal in the north to Sri Lanka in the south. India, by far the most populous of these countries, is on the 1950 list but narrowly misses the 1980 list.[18]

The unavoidable arbitrariness of any classification of which this reminds us suggests the frequency distribution analysis presented in Table 3-14. Here individual countries and their populations are distributed according to rates of growth in real per capita GDP. About 1 percent of the world population lived in countries in which real per capita GDP actually

Table 3-14. Frequency Distribution of Countries and Population, According to the Rate of Growth in Real GDP per Capita and Type of Country, 1950-52 to 1978-80.[a]

Rate of growth Per Annum (percentage)	Low	Middle	Industrial	CPE	World
A. *Number of Countries*					
Negative	5	2	—	—	7
0-0.99	9	8	—	—	17
1-1.99	5	18	3	—	26
2-2.99	4	16	8	3	31
3-3.99	1	14	7	2	24
>4	1	14	3	3	21
Total	25	72	21	8	126
B. *Percentage of World Population*					
Negative	0.5	0.4	—	—	0.9
0-0.99	3.5	0.6	—	—	4.1
1-1.99	1.0	17.7	8.4	—	27.1
2-2.99	1.5	7.5	2.3	1.9	13.2
2-3.99	0.0	7.7	6.8	30.0	44.5
>4	0.1	3.5	4.9	1.7	10.2
Total	6.6	37.4	22.4	33.6	100.0

[a]The growth rates in this table are calculated as annual rates of growth for the twenty-eight year interval between the midyears of the two terminal periods.

declined, and 4 percent where the increases in real per capita product were under 1 percent per annum. For this 5 percent of the world's population, there has been no alleviation of the problems stemming from low income levels and from the slow or nil growth rates in per capita GDP that characterized pre-modern societies. Another 27 percent of the world's population lived in countries that experienced growth rates in per capita GDP of 1 to 2 percent per annum, clearly above the pre-modern growth rates estimated by Kuznets (1971:68) for Europe but perhaps starting at (1950) per capita levels that may have been lower. This third of the world's population with pre-modern or only moderately above pre-modern growth rates is concentrated in sub-Sahara Africa and Southeast Asia.

But the story for the other two-thirds of the world is different. These two-thirds live in countries that enjoyed per capita GDP growth rates of 2 percent per annum or more in the three decades 1950–80. By historical standards these growth rates are high; 2 percent is a little above the rate enjoyed by the industrial countries in the first half of the twentieth century. Thus, very rapid growth has come not just to the European sliver of the world population plus Japan but also to countries with over 45 percent of the people living in developing market economies and about 70 percent of those outside of the industrial countries.[19]

The Variability of Growth

In addition to variations in individual country experience, fluctuations in growth rates within the 1950–80 period may be concealed by our concentration to this point on the period as a whole. Was growth sustained throughout the period, or was the remarkable growth record achieved in large spurts after World War II followed by lagging growth in later years? This question requires more careful analysis than we can give it here, but the answer based on superficial impressions is one of rather continuously high though not uniform growth for the world economy and indeed for most of the country groups in Table 3–8. An inspection of Figure 3–1 suggests that a straightline trend fits the world GDP series pretty closely. The equation is

$$n\ GDP = 7.789 + 0.0466\ T \quad \bar{R}^2 = 0.998$$
$$SEE = 0.0192^{\cdot}$$

In pressing this inquiry a little further, our first inclination was to separate growth rates for each of the three decades—the 1950s, the 1960s, and the 1970s,[20] but an examination of Figure 3–1 suggests a hint of an upward tilt in the world series around 1962 or 1963 and a slackening of growth around 1973. The latter was of course a year of important real and monetary changes in the world economy and is clearly a strong candidate for selection as a year of demarcation. However, it is also the demarcation that produces the most pessimistic picture of the direction of the change, since the last period includes two major oil price increases and two recessions, one early in the period and the other at the end. 1963 was also taken though with less clear cut justification. We are thus left with three subperiods—1950-63, 1963-73, and 1973-80 (see Tables 3-15 and 3-16).

The best subperiod for the world and for all three major groups of countries in terms of growth was 1963-73. This was a period of remarkably high growth in real per capita GDP—over 3 percent per annum—which was widely shared by all groups of countries except the low-income countries.

In the years from 1973 to 1980 average growth rates declined for each group but still remained high by historical standards—near the 2 percent level for world per capita GDP. There was a marginal absolute decline in world per capita GDP in 1974-75, followed by three years of high growth. In the final years, 1978-80, growth was between 1 and 2 percent, and preliminary figures reflect the worsening of the world recession after 1980. Note, however, that the growth rates of the developing market economies and of the CPEs tended to be more sustained in the 1973-80 period than those of the industrial countries. Taken by and large, the period 1973-80, for all its troubles, was a period of rapid and widely diffused growth.[21] However, it was clear near the end of 1982 that the long period of substantial growth in the world economy has been at least interrupted. Whatever lies ahead, however, the case for the feasibility of economic progress in a diversity of institutional settings has been greatly strengthened.

The impression of the maintenance of high though somewhat variable growth rates during the entire thirty-year period for most groups of countries

Table 3-15.   Annual Growth Rates in Total GDP, Selected Periods and Years, 1950-81.

	Developing Market Economies (1)	Industrial Countries (2)	Centrally Planned Economies (3)	World (4)
1950-63	4.7	4.1	5.5	4.5
1963-73	5.8	4.8	6.0	5.3
1973-80	5.0	2.9	4.2	3.7
1974/73	5.1	0.7	3.6	2.4
1975/74	4.0	-0.5	4.6	1.8
1976/75	6.2	5.2	2.2	4.6
1977/76	5.7	3.7	5.2	4.6
1978/77	5.3	4.0	5.5	4.7
1979/78	3.5	3.2	3.7	3.4
1980/79	4.7	1.4	3.8	2.8

Table 3-16.   Annual Growth Rates in per Capita GDP, Selected Periods and Years, 1950–81.

	Developing Market Economies (1)	Industrial Countries (2)	CPE (3)	World (4)
1950–63	2.4	2.8	3.5	2.6
1963–73	3.2	3.8	3.7	3.1
1973–80	2.5	2.1	2.8	1.9
1974/73	2.5	−0.1	1.8	0.5
1975/74	1.2	−1.3	3.0	−0.2
1976/75	3.7	4.4	0.8	2.8
1977/76	3.3	3.0	3.9	2.8
1978/77	2.9	3.1	4.3	2.9
1979/78	1.1	2.4	2.4	1.6
1980/79	2.2	0.5	2.6	1.1

and for the world has not been checked against the experience of earlier periods. Such an effort would be difficult in view of the data problems and would probably have to be limited to the industrial countries, but it would not be impossible. However, just a recollection of the broad history of the twentieth century suggests that growth might have been less variable in the third quarter than in the first two. Each of the earlier quarters included a world war and the second one the Great Depression also. It cannot be claimed that the third quarter was unmarked by important conflicts, but none was so cataclysmic or so embracing as the events of the earlier quarters. A relatively peaceful and stable world was a favorable background for rather continuous growth in the world economy. This does not mean that growth rates for individual countries were relatively constant during the period. An examination would doubtless show a great deal of temporal variability in the growth experience of particular countries.

TRENDS IN PRODUCTIVITY

Some comments about changes in labor productivity were already made in connection with the discussion of levels in Table 3–8. In Table 3–17 the productivity indexes based on undifferentiated labor are presented in the form of intertemporal indexes so that any notable trends in the productivity relationships will be easier to see.

Output per member of the labor force rose by nearly 50 percent even in the slow-growing low-income countries, and nearly tripled in the fastest growing group, the oil exporters. For the world as a whole output per worker more than doubled.

Table 3-17. Intertemporal Indexes of Real GDP Per Capita and Per Worker Groups of Countries and the World, Quinquennial Years 1950-75 (1950 = 100).

	1950	1955	1960	1965	1970	1975
A. *Indexes of GDP Per Capita*						
Developing market economies	100	113	128	145	170	196
Low-income countries	100	116	120	128	131	131
Middle-income countries	100	113	128	146	173	200
Oil exporters	100	114	141	166	208	249
Relatively industrialized	100	116	133	153	184	225
Other	100	110	121	133	151	164
Industrial countries	100	120	134	163	195	217
Centrally planned economies	100	130	154	179	214	251
World	100	119	133	155	180	200
B. *Indexes of GDP Per Worker*						
Developing market economies	100	116	137	159	191	224
Low-income countries	100	119	126	137	144	148
Middle-income countries	100	117	138	162	196	231
Oil exporters	100	118	150	183	233	286
Relatively industrialized	100	119	142	167	203	247
Other	100	115	129	147	172	191
Industrial countries	100	122	138	167	198	216
Centrally planned economies	100	125	145	171	206	245
World	100	119	134	160	188	211

The differences between the series on output per capita and output per worker are not large and were noted earlier: The chief difference, it will be recalled, was a larger increase in the productivity index relative to output per capita for the developing countries than for the others owing to a tendency over time for labor force participation rates to diminish in the developing countries.

How would these productivity trends be altered were we able to introduce trends in quality adjusted labor and in capital? If as seems possible the upgrading of the working force in terms of skills and education has proceeded more rapidly in developing countries, for which there was much more room for improvement in 1950, then the quality-adjusted labor productivity indexes for the developing countries would show slower growth relative to the two other sets of countries than the indexes based on labor inputs without quality adjustments.

The effect of the addition of capital on the productivity indexes depends on the rate of increase in capital per worker in the various sets of countries. The generally lower proportions of GDP devoted to capital formation, especially in real terms (Kravis, Heston, and Summers 1982:18–19) and the faster rate of population increase in developing countries operate to produce a slower growth of capital per worker than in the industrial and centrally planned economies. On the other hand, the low initial level of capital per worker in low-income countries might nevertheless produce a higher rate of growth in the capital labor ratio. If the net result is a more rapid increase in capital per worker in the developing countries, the index of total factor productivity would rise less than the labor productivity index, relative to the behavior of the two sets of productivity indexes in each of the other groups of countries.

CONCLUSION

The three decades from 1950 to 80 were unique in economic history in two important respects. First, the industrial countries, which had enjoyed rapid economic growth in previous eras, experienced unprecedented rates of expansion. What is more remarkable is the diffusion of growth, and rapid growth, to almost the entire world. Indeed, for countries including a large fraction of the people of the developing world, it can be said for the first time that three recent decades have seen a great deal of progress. The two-thirds of the world's population living in countries that have enjoyed very rapid growth (i.e., growth over 2 percent per annum in real per capita GDP) include over 45 percent of the people living in developing market economies and about 70 percent of those outside of the industrial countries. It must quickly be added that for substantial numbers, concentrated in Africa between the Mahgreb and South Africa and in the Indian subcontinent, rapid growth has not reached them; 5 percent of the world's population living in countries with abysmally low per capita income levels have experienced slow growth (below 1 percent per annum in real per capita GDP) or even (for countries including 1 percent of the world's population) a decline in per capita income. But what is new is the demonstration that rapid economic growth is not purely a European or European-linked phenomenon and that Japan, although still unique in the timing and speed of its growth, does not provide the sole non-European soil for rapid growth. For many other countries of the world, living standards like those of the United States or Germany may still be distant if attainable at all, but in many countries that were growth laggards in the century or century and a half preceding 1950, living standards like those of Spain or Italy are within reach of persons living today. None of this is to claim that the complex and poorly understood web of social, political, and economic conditions that produce rapid growth will in fact be present; present trends in the world economy make favorable outcomes less likely, at least in the near future. It is simply to say that the statistical gaps often used to assess such possibilities do not seem to rule them out.

The widely used approach to the assessment of the economic performance of developing countries in terms of the gap in per capita incomes between the developing and the industrial countries has directed attention away from the great gains of most developing countries and of most of the world's population living outside of the small number of industrial countries. In any case, the actual gaps as measured by the ratio of real GDP per capita of the industrial to the developing countries is of the order of 6 to 1 rather than 10 or 12 to 1. (The former is based on PPP conversions and the latter on the misleading conversions via exchange rates.) This gap in real (PPP) terms widened between 1950 and 1970 (from 5.3 to 6.0) and then narrowed slightly (to 5.8 in 1980). But what the gap analysis tends to overlook is that with extremely rapid growth in the rich countries, a relatively stable gap means rapid growth in poor countries.

The gap in productivity between rich and poor countries is almost surely smaller than the gap in per capita incomes. Inputs of labor per capita (i.e., labor force participation rates) are higher in the rich countries, and if allowance is made for the higher quality of the labor force in rich countries in terms of skills and education, the gap in labor productivity becomes smaller still. In a crude and mainly illustrative calculation, we found that the 1975 ratio of industrial to middle-income developing country output per undifferentiated worker of 4.6 shrank to 3.7 when allowance was made for the higher rich-country labor input per worker represented by superior education. The productivity ratio would shrink still again if capital could be taken into account. It seems possible that a substantial part of the differences in output per capita between rich and poor countries is due to the quantity and quality of inputs rather than to productivity—that is, to superior utilization of given inputs in the rich countries.

It is clear that this period of rapid and widespread economic growth has been at least interrupted. But it can no longer be doubted that rapid economic progress is within the reach of the political, social, and economic institutions of all or almost all of the peoples of the world.

APPENDIX

Our knowledge of the growth of output and productivity of the world economy is sharply limited now not so much by the availability of data as by its uncertain and uneven quality. When Simon Kuznets began his great series on the "Quantitative Aspects of the Economic Growth of Nations" (1956) in the mid-1950s, he had available long (forty years or more) time series on national product and population for less than a score of countries and estimates for a shorter time span (1938 and 1949) for about seventy based on compilations by W.S. and E.S. Wyotinsky and the United Nations. A quarter of a century later, we have compilations of national accounts covering as many as 180 countries with over 100 of them available as early as 1950 produced by four important international agencies: the United Nations, the World Bank, the IMF, and the OECD. The latter organization produces detailed compilations of the national accounts statistics in standard tables for its (mainly developed) member countries, while its Development Center publishes less detailed materials for developing countries. The United Nations Conference on Trade and Development (UNCTAD) has also published statistical compilations, which include GDP and population data for many countries.

Unfortunately, the data reported by these various sources are often conflicting. For example, an internal document of the World Bank recently reported that even for a relatively current year (1975), the U.N.-reported GDP differed by 10 percent or more from that reported by the IMF for 15 percent of the countries; the corresponding percentages for U.N.-World Bank differences were 18 percent and for IMF-World Bank differences 9 percent (Ahmad undated). An analysis of the causes for the differences between IMF and World Bank figures revealed that about two-thirds were due to adjustments of the country data made mainly by the World Bank for reasons such as conforming the data to an SNA basis, the fuller inclusion of subsistence sectors, and estimating gaps in the data (Ahmad and Kwon 1981). Another important cause of differences (28 percent) was the different vintage of the data, with neither organization being consistent in incorporating the latest version. The advantage of the World Bank in having country specialists to adjust the data may be offset by the lack of systemization and recordkeeping in this work, with possible unfavorable consequences for the continuity of the series.

The World Bank and U.N. data were available to the authors in the form of machine readable tapes that gave constant price GDP series for more countries than are published in the former's *World Tables* or the latter's *Yearbook of National Accounts Statistics.* It is to be expected that differences will be more numerous for the unpublished series, but even so it seems worthwhile to include these uncertain figures for the sake of comprehensiveness. Since our interest is in data for groups of countries, some of the differences may be expected to offset one another.

Unfortunately, there are notable differences even in average growth rates for groups of countries. Table 3–A2 compares annual growth rates for the period 1960–70 as derived from World Bank and U.N. sources. In the upper half of the table the comparisons are based on data for an overlapping set of countries for which data are found in both sources. Comparisons are made both for the common set of countries for which data are published in the World Bank's *1980 World Tables* and in the United Nation's *Yearbook of National Accounts Statistics, 1979,* and for the larger set of countries found on both tapes. In general, the average growth rates based on published materials are very similar. Even where the average refers only to two countries the difference is only 5 percent.

When the comparisons are extended to include all countries found on both tapes, larger differences emerge. This is to be expected since such materials presumably leave more scope for or even require adjustments and choices among alternative sources and estimates. The most glaring difference, for middle-income countries, is attributable mainly to different estimates for Libya. The U.N. tape shows a forty-five-fold increase in Libya's real per capita GDP in contrast to a five-fold increase on the World Bank tape. The figures in parentheses show how much closer the growth rates from the two sources are, when Libya is excluded from both. Since the IMF publishes series on GDP in constant prices and population figures that produce per capita changes close to the World Bank rate of increase (*International Monetary Fund* 1981), the World Bank figures were used in the present paper.

The other notable discrepancy was the higher World Bank tape average for the low-income countries. The two sets of data for countries with differences as large as 10 percent in the per capita growth rate were examined. It was found that the differences were much more frequent in the rate of growth in total GDP rather than in population, but without research into each country there was little basis for choosing one source over the other. There were a few cases in which published IMF data were available, which sometimes supported one source and sometimes the other. Aside from the

Libyan case, using IMF data on the basis of choice would not have affected the group averages very much. Insofar as the 1960–70 data can be relied upon to tell the story about data reliability for the entire period, the broad conclusions of this paper would not be affected by the choice of sources.

Actually, the data for market economies used in this study were taken from three sources. The U.N. tape, which contained data for the years 1950 to 1977, was used for the 1950–75 period. The 1975–80 data were obtained by extrapolating the 1975 U.N. tape figures to 1980 on the basis of annual percentage changes obtained from the World Bank tape, which contained data for the period 1960–80.[22]

For the period 1950 to 1960 the U.N. tape had at least some missing data for fifty-five of the 118 market economies covered in the study. For this period and for these countries, growth rates in total and per capita GDP were taken from an UNCTAD (1976) source. This left us with total GDP and GDP estimates per capita for 1950 and 1960 for all of our countries, but with data for individual years in the 1950–60 period only for sixty-three of the market economies. All the countries including the fifty-five with missing data for intermediate years were classified into the groups described in the main part of the paper, and for each group the average year-to-year changes in GDP and population of the available set of countries were used to interpolate annual indexes of total GDP and of population between 1950 and 1960, the values for 1950 and 1960 being determined by averages for the full set of countries.

The data for the centrally planned economies were taken mainly from work by U.S. statisticians based on the sources of each country.[23] All of the centrally planned economies use the material product system of accounts, and a major task was to find supporting materials for making the additions and subtractions necessary to convert net material product into gross domestic product.

APPENDIX TABLES

Table 3-A1. Total Real GDP, Population and Per Capita Real GDP, Groups of Countries[a] and the World, Quinquennial Years 1950–80 (GDP figures in 1975 international dollars[b]).

	1950	1955	1960	1965	1970	1975	1980
Developing market economies							
Total GDP[c]	530	664	844	1080	1436	1874	2399
Population[d]	1070	1158	1331	1506	1708	1936	2177
Per capita[e]	495	560	634	717	841	968	1102
Low-income countries							
Total GDP	42	54	62	74	86	98	118
Population	161	178	198	223	253	286	325
Per capita GDP	261	302	314	333	341	343	361
Middle-income countries							
Total GDP	488	612	782	1006	1350	1776	2282
Population	909	1007	1133	1283	1455	1650	1852
Per capita GDP	537	608	690	784	928	1076	1232
Oil exporters							
Total GDP	77	97	136	182	262	361	467
Population	150	166	188	214	246	283	323
Per capita GDP	513	585	721	850	1065	1278	1448
Relatively industrialized							
Total GDP	168	220	287	377	513	709	933
Population	194	219	249	283	320	363	404
Per capita GDP	870	1006	1154	1332	1601	1955	2310
Other							
Total GDP	243	294	360	447	575	705	882
Population	566	622	697	786	889	1004	1125
Per capita GDP	429	472	517	569	647	702	783

Industrial countries						
Total GDP	1413	1799	2142	2761	3474	4040	4795
Population	543	577	613	652	684	715	743
Per capita GDP	2602	3120	3493	4237	5083	5651	6450
Centrally planned economies						
Total GDP	536	766	1002	1254	1670	2152	2628
Population	816	897	991	1065	1189	1307	1392
Per capita GDP	657	854	1011	1177	1405	1646	1887
World						
Total GDP	2479	3230	3988	5095	6581	8065	9822
Population	2429	2632	2935	3223	3581	3958	4313
Per capita GDP	1020	1227	1359	1581	1838	2038	2277
Indexes of real GDP per capita (world = 100)						
Developing market economies	49	46	47	45	46	48	48
Low-income countries	26	25	23	21	19	17	16
Middle-income countries	53	50	51	50	50	53	54
Oil exporters	50	48	53	54	58	63	64
Relatively industrialized	85	83	85	84	87	96	101
Other	42	38	38	36	35	34	34
Industrial countries	255	257	257	268	277	277	283
Centrally planned economies	64	70	74	74	76	81	83
World	100	100	100	100	100	100	100

a See text and text footnoted for explanation of the country classification.

b An international dollar has the same purchasing power as the U.S. dollar for GDP as a whole. Its purchasing power over particular kind of goods differs from that of a U.S. dollar because the structure of average international prices differs from the structure of U.S. prices. (See Kravis, Heston, Summers 1982a: 90–92.)

c Billions international dollars.

d Millions.

e International dollars.

Table 3-A2. World Gross Domestic Product (GDP) and GDP Per Capita, by Country Groups, 1950-80 (in 1975 international dollars).

| | | Middle-Income Countries | | | | | | Centrally Planned | |
	Low-Income Countries	Oil Exporters	Relatively Industrialized	Other	All Middle	All Developing	Industrial	Economies	World
A. Index Numbers of GDP, 1975 = 100									
1950	43	21	24	34	27	28	35	25	31
1951	48	21	25	36	29	30	38	27	33
1952	50	23	26	37	30	31	39	30	35
1953	52	24	27	39	31	32	41	31	36
1954	52	26	29	40	33	34	42	33	38
1955	55	27	31	42	34	35	45	36	40
1956	57	29	33	43	36	37	46	38	42
1957	59	30	35	45	38	39	47	41	44
1958	59	32	36	47	40	41	48	45	46
1959	61	34	37	48	41	42	50	46	47
1960	63	38	40	51	44	45	53	47	49
1961	66	40	43	52	46	47	55	45	51
1962	68	40	45	54	48	49	58	47	53
1963	73	43	47	58	51	52	61	50	56
1964	73	47	51	62	55	56	65	54	60
1965	76	50	53	63	57	58	68	58	63
1966	78	52	56	65	59	60	72	63	67
1967	82	54	58	69	62	63	75	65	69
1968	84	60	62	73	66	67	79	67	73
1969	88	65	68	77	71	72	83	71	77
1970	88	72	72	82	76	77	86	78	82
1971	86	77	78	85	81	81	89	82	85
1972	89	83	83	88	85	85	94	84	88
1973	93	92	90	92	91	92	100	92	96
1974	96	98	97	95	96	96	101	96	98
1975	100	100	100	100	100	100	100	100	100
1976	106	110	106	105	106	106	105	102	105
1977	109	118	111	111	112	112	109	108	109
1978	113	121	117	118	119	118	113	114	115
1979	116	126	125	119	123	122	117	118	118
1980	120	129	131	125	129	128	119	122	122

B. Index Number of GDP Per Capita, 1975 = 100

Year									
1950	70	40	45	61	50	51	46	40	50
1951	83	39	46	63	51	53	49	44	54
1952	85	42	47	64	52	54	50	46	55
1953	87	42	47	66	54	55	52	47	56
1954	85	45	50	67	55	57	52	49	57
1955	88	46	51	67	56	58	55	52	57
1956	90	47	53	68	58	59	56	54	61
1957	91	48	55	69	59	60	57	56	62
1958	89	51	56	71	61	62	57	62	64
1959	90	53	56	71	61	63	60	61	65
1960	91	56	59	74	64	66	62	61	67
1961	94	58	61	73	65	67	64	59	67
1962	94	58	63	75	66	68	66	62	70
1963	98	60	64	78	68	70	69	64	72
1964	96	63	67	82	72	73	72	68	75
1965	97	66	68	81	73	74	75	72	78
1966	98	67	70	81	74	75	78	76	80
1967	100	67	71	84	75	77	81	76	82
1968	100	72	74	87	79	80	84	77	84
1969	102	77	79	89	82	83	88	79	87
1970	99	83	82	92	86	87	90	85	90
1971	95	87	86	94	89	89	92	88	92
1972	97	91	90	94	92	92	96	89	95
1973	99	98	95	97	96	96	101	95	100
1974	99	101	99	97	99	99	101	97	100
1975	100	100	100	100	100	100	100	100	100
1976	103	107	103	102	104	104	104	101	103
1977	103	112	106	106	107	107	108	105	106
1978	105	112	110	110	111	110	111	109	109
1979	105	113	115	108	112	111	114	112	111
1980	105	113	118	112	114	114	114	115	112

Table 3-A2 (continued).

| | Developing Market Economies | | | | | | | |
| | Low-Income Countries | Middle-Income Countries | | | | | Industrial | Centrally Planned Economies | World |
		Oil Exporters	Relatively Industrialized	Other	All Middle	All Developing			
C. Base Year (1975) Values for GDP and Per Capita GDP (in international dollars)									
GDP (bil $I)	98.3	361.2	709.3	705.0	1775.6	1873.8	4040.0	2151.6	8065.4
Per capita GDP ($I)	343	1278	1955	702	1076	968	5651	1646	2038

TABLE 5-A3. Real GDP Per Capita and Per Economically Active Person, Groups of Countries, and the World, Quinquennial Years, 1950–75.

	1950	1955	1960	1965	1970	1975
Developing market economies						
Per capita GDP	495	561	634	717	841	968
Participation rate	42	41	39	38	37	37
GDP per active person	1176	1368	1606	1875	2252	2639
Low-income countries						
Per capita GDP	261	302	314	333	341	343
Participation rate	46	45	44	43	42	41
GDP per active person	566	671	713	776	813	836
Middle-income countries						
Per capita GDP	537	608	690	784	928	1076
Participation rate	41	40	39	37	37	36
GDP per active person	1296	1520	1783	2094	2539	2997
Oil exporters						
Per capita GDP	513	585	721	850	1065	1278
Participation rate	38	37	36	35	34	33
GDP per active person	1338	1581	2112	2445	3120	3831
Relative industrialized						
Per capita GDP	870	1006	1154	1332	1601	1955
Participation rate	37	36	35	34	34	34
GDP per active person	2347	2794	3331	3919	4765	5788
Other						
Per capita GDP	429	472	517	569	647	702
Participation rate	44	42	41	39	38	37
GDP per active person	981	1124	1262	1444	1691	1877
Industrial countries						
Per capita GDP	2602	3120	3493	4237	5083	5651
Participation rate	46	48	49	48	48	47
GDP per active person	1422	1779	2055	2437	2935	3488
Centrally planned economies						
Per capita GDP	657	854	1011	1177	1405	1646
Participation rate	46	48	49	48	48	47
GDP per active person	1422	1779	2055	2437	2935	3488
World						
Per capita GDP	1020	1216	1359	1581	1838	2038
Participation rate	44	44	43	42	42	41
GDP per active person	2327	2764	3129	3723	4383	4916

NOTES

1. The statistical work involved in preparing this paper was performed by Martin Shanin, and the typing was done by Kathleen Conway. This version of the paper has benefited from coments made at the conference by L. Christensen and others.

2. Growth rates, it should be noted, are from widely available sources. See the following section, The Data. For some problems with respect to these growth rates, see the appendix.

3. In particular, the different growth rates for individual countries reported in a number of cases by different international agencies. On the same point, see Kuznets (1972).

4. The list of oil exporters was based on an IMF classification. See *International Monetary Fund* (1982: 53). This classification has the same list of industrial countries as our list except that we added Luxembourg (probably omitted from the IMF tabulation because of its economic union with Belgium) and South Africa.

5. The rapid growth of the years following World War II has hardly gone unnoticed. See, for example, Kuznets (1972) and Morawetz (1977).

6. If constant prices for an earlier year had been used—say, 1960—the whole series of dollar figures shown for the oil exporters would have been lower, but the trend relative to the world would not have been very different. See the discussion of the distinction between gross domestic income and gross domestic product in Kravis, Heston, and Summers (1982: 328–29).

7. For an analysis of the distribution of world gross domestic income among countries and persons, see Summers, Kravis, and Heston (1981).

8. The ILO made an effort to reduce the inherent incomparabilities of labor force data for these dates. Among major definitional differences in the data reported by different countries are the treatment of unpaid family workers, particularly females, and the age ranges of persons included. See International Labor Organization (1977). This source contains data for the quinquennial years in the period 1950–70; comparable 1975 data were published in International Labor Organization (1979: 15–16).

9. There have been several investigations for small numbers of mainly developed countries, for which data could be obtained. See, for example, Maddison's paper for this conference (Chapter 2 above) and Christensen, Cummings, and Jorgenson (1981), Kendrick (1981), and Denison and Poullier (1967).

10. This is easily seen for labor productivity: $Y = K \div K / L = L \div Y$, where Y is output, L the labor force, and K the amount of capital.

11. Mainly on the basis of second- and third-level enrollment ratios (Kravis and Lipsey 1982). Denison labor quality indexes based on 1969 and later data do not differ very much from those based on 1959 data (Denison 1979: 168).

12. An alternative labor quality index constructed directly out of 1970 enrollment ratios with weights of 3, 5, and 10 assigned to the three levels of education narrowed the gap still further. When this index was applied to the labor inputs of 118 market economies the industrial-to-developing-country ratio was 2.2, and the industrial-to-middle-income-country ratio 2.1. In preparing this index, weights were based on mean 1969 incomes of persons eighteen-years-old and over by years of school completed as calculated from U.S. Bureau of the Census (1970: Table 249). The incomes were in the ratio 3:4.4.:6.3 both for males and for females who completed the three levels of education. Some

evidence suggests that the U.S. third- to second-level ratio is not unusual for industrial countries and also that the ratio has declined in the 1970s (Freeman 1981). However, the weights were rounded to 3, 5, and 10 to make allowance for a presumed wider differentiation of incomes according to educational level in developing countries. These weights are not very different from those suggested by data presented by Psacharopolous (1973: 185) on ratios of annual wages of persons having completed different levels of schooling: The unweighted average ratios for all countries point to weights of 1, 2, and 4:

	Number of Countries	Secondary/Primary	Higher/Secondary
Developing	14	2.2	2.4
Developed	8	1.4	1.6
All	22	1.9	2.2

For a brief discussion of the problems posed by the education approach to labor quality, see Kravis and Lipsey (1982).

13. We experimented with the calculation of estimates of capital stock in 1975 for a large number of countries by cumulating capital expenditure data. These are available for many countries back as far as 1950, and we assumed that the pre-1950 stock had disappeared by 1975. Data were cumulated and depreciated in constant own-currency prices, put in 1975 own-currency prices, translated into U.S. dollars with 1975 exchange rates, and then translated into international prices for 1975 using estimates of the price levels and capital formation derived from Kravis, Heston, and Summers (1982).

As would be expected, the introduction of capital stock into the measure of factor inputs reduced the range of variation in productivity, mainly by raising the estimate for the poorest countries relative to the more affluent ones. However, some of the individual country results seemed strange, and the capital stock figures did not accord well with more adequate estimates available for a few countries. For example, many European countries appeared more capital abundant than the United States. Also, total factor productivity in Guatamala and Brazil appeared higher than in the United States. The main lesson was that this method of estimating capital stock was too crude to be relied on.

14. The growth rates in Table 3–8 are, however, consistent with those that can be calculated from Table 3–1, in that they are based on the same underlying series. The method used in Table 3–8 avoids giving undue importance in measures of rates of change to the choice of particular terminal years.

15. Calculated for the twenty-one-year period from 1950–59 to 1971–80 to match Kuznets' method, the decade growth rate for the industrial countries was 52 percent. The Japanese decadal growth rate for 1905–14 to 1925–29 (51 percent) virtually matched the recent rate. The next closest was Sweden with 46 percent for 1925–29 to 1950–54. For the nineteenth century, U.S. decadal growth rates exceeded 50 percent for the period prior to the Civil War.

16. Our 1950–54 figures on real GDP and population were extrapolated to 1925–29 and to 1900–09 using Kuznets' growth rates for each country (Kuznets 1971: 3840). Kuznets' growth rates did not always apply precisely to the terminal dates in the text table, but these differences can hardly affect the result. If this exercise had been pushed back into the nineteenth century, the average growth rates might have been slightly higher for 1860 to 1900 than the

text table shows for the first quarter of the twentieth century. Kuznets himself concludes that there was "no significant acceleration or deceleration" of growth in per capita product "after modern economic growth began" (1971: 41).

17.   However, a still less favorable assessment might ensue if the growth rates in per capita GDP of very low-income countries were assigned weights larger than their population weights. Kuznets suggests as an example the possibility of weights inversely proportional to per capita incomes. For an application of this idea of weighting income increments accruing to low-income people more heavily, see Chenery et al. (1974: ch. 2). Kuznets also offers other reasons for a possible tendency for the growth rates of developing countries to be overstated relative to those of developed countries.

18.   The inclusion of China in the 1950 list of the twenty-five lowest-income countries, rather than its assignment to the centrally planned economies (CPE), would have raised the growth rates of the 1950 low-income countries substantially because of China's large size and high growth rates (6.01 in total GDP and 3.74 in per capita GDP). It would have had a lesser but still notable impact on the per annum CPE growth rates, too, as follows:

| | Total GDP | | GDP Per Capita | |
	Without China	With China	Without China	With China
1950–80	5.23	5.31	3.70	3.38
1950–63	6.28	5.47	4.10	3.54
1963–73	5.08	6.00	4.14	3.70
1973–80	2.66	4.17	1.84	2.77

For a skeptical appraisal of China's growth record, see Malenbaum (1982).

19.   Table 3–14 makes it clear that the conclusion regarding the wide diffusion of growth is based, as it should be, on the experience of individual countries. It is not dependent on the use of purchasing power parities in lieu of exchange rates, the practice followed elsewhere in this paper where countries are aggregated into groups.

20.   For the world economy these dates produce a lesser differentiation in growth rates among the three subperiods than those found for the subperiods used in Table 3–5:

| | Growth Rates Per Annum in | |
	Total GDP	GDP Per Capita
1950–60	4.73	2.70
1960–70	5.29	3.17
1970–80	4.08	2.17

21.   The countries for which 1973–80 was the period of poorest growth tended to be the richer ones—the industrial countries and the centrally planned economies—rather than the poorer ones.

22.   For 1975 all the nominal and real GDP figures for the thirty-four ICP benchmark countries are those reported in the Phase III ICP report (Kravis,

Heston, and Summers 1982); it is these data that are extrapolated to the other years by the United Nations and World Bank series.

23. These data were assembled jointly with Robert Summers. Population figures for Bulgaria, Czechoslavakia, East Germany, Hungary, Poland, Romania, and the Soviet Union and Yugoslavia were basically from Shoup (1981). The population figures for China were basically those given by Aird (1982). Slightly revised and updated versions of the Shoup and Aird data were actually used; they were provided by Gottfried Baldwin of the Foreign Demographic Analysis Division of the U.S. Bureau of the Census.

Each country's 1975 GDP in international dollars (I$) was estimated and extrapolated to other years, except in the case of the Soviet Union, for which a 1976 estimate was the starting point. The Soviet/U.S. GNP Fisher index given by Edwards, Hughes, and Noren (1979: 369-401) was converted to a per capita basis and adjusted for the difference between multilateral and binary indexes. Soviet GNP was extrapolated to other years on the basis of a series given by Edwards, Hughes, and Noren with interpolations for a number of years on the basis of an earlier series by Greenslade (1976). For Hungary, Poland, and Romania 1975 ICP estimates were used. The 1975 per capita GDP of the People's Republic of China was taken from Kravis (1979). The 1975 per capita GDPs in I$ for Bulgaria, Czechoslavakia, and East Germany were based on 1973 estimates, derived by the physical indicator method reported in United Nations (1980: 15). These 1973 estimates were extrapolated to 1975 on the basis of per capita GNPs in 1978 dollars given by Alton et al. (1979) and then raised by 4 percent to convert them to an ICP basis; this was based on the average ratio between 1975 ICP estimates and Alton-extrapolated U.N. estimates for Hungary, Poland, and Romania. The extrapolation from 1973 to 1975 for Yugoslavia was based on data in World Bank (1980).

All these 1975 per capita estimates were converted to total GDP with the aid of the poulation data described above. The GDPs of Bulgaria, Czechoslvakia, East Germany, Hungary, Poland, and Romania were extrapolated to other years on the basis of annual GDP estimates in Alton (1982), and that for Yugoslavia on the basis of data in World Bank (1980). The GDP of the People's Republic of China was extrapolated on the basis of a GNP series in 1978 U.S. prices for 1950-78 published in National Foreign Assessment Center (1979). Figures for 1979 and 1980 were derived from annual changes in national income reported in Communique on Fulfillment of 1980 Economic Plan (1981) and Communique on Fulfillment of 1979 Economic Plan (1980).

REFERENCES

Ahmad, S., Undated. "Comparisons of IMF, U.N. and IBRD Data on National Accounts." Economic and Social Data Division, World Bank.

Ahmad, S., and S. Kwon. 1981. "IMF and IBRD Data on National Accounts—Sources of Discrepancies. Division Working Paper No. 1981-5, Economic and Social Data Division, World Bank.

Aird, John S. 1982. "Population Studies and Population Policy in China." *Population and Development Review* 8, no. 2 (June): 267-97.

Alton, Thad P. 1982. "Estimates of East European Countries' GNP Structure and Growth of Factor Cost." Paper prepared for the Workshop on CPE National Income Statistics at the World Bank, Washington, D.C., June 7-8.

Alton, Thad. P.; E.M. Bass; G. Lazarcik; G.J. Steller; and W. Znayenko. 1979. *Economic Growth in Eastern Europe.* New York: L.W. International Financial Research.

————. 1982. *Economic Growth in Eastern Europe 1965, 1970, and 1975–81.* Research Project on National Income in East Central Europe, OP-70. New York: L.W. International Financial Research.

Caves, Douglas W.; L.R. Christensen; and W.E. Diewert. 1982. "Multilateral Comparisons of Output, Input and Productivity Using Superlative Index Numbers." *Economic Journal* 92 (March): 73–86.

Chenery, Hollis; M.S. Ahluwalia; C.L.G. Bell; J.H. Duloy; and R. Jolly. 1974. *Redistribution with Growth.* London: Oxford University Press.

Christensen, L.R.; D. Cummings; and D. Jorgenson. 1981. "Relative Productivity Levels, 1947–1973: An International Comparisons." *European Economic Review* 16 (May): 61–94.

Denison, E.F., and J.P. Poullier. 1967. *Why Growth Rates Differ.* Washington, D.C.: The Brookings Institution.

————. 1979. *Accounting for Slower Growth.* Washington, D.C.: The Brookings Institution.

Edwards, I.; M. Hughes; J. Noren. 1979. "U.S. and U.S.S.R.: Comparisons of GNP." *Soviet Economy in a Time of Change.* 96th Congress of the United States, 1st Session, Joint Economic Committee.

Freeman, Richard B. 1981. "The Changing Economic Value of Higher Education in Developed Economies: A Report to the O.E.C.D." Working Paper No. 820. Cambridge, Mass.: National Bureau of Economic Research.

Greenslade, R.V. 1976. "The Real Gross National Product of the U.S.S.R., 1950–75." *Soviet Economy in a New Perspective.* 94th Congress of the United States, 2nd Session, Joint Economic Committee.

International Monetary Fund. 1981. *International Financial Statistics.*

————. 1982. *International Financial Statistics.*

International Labor Organization. 1977. *Labor Force Estimates and Projections, 1950–2000.* 2d ed. Geneva:ILO.

————. 1979. *The Yearbook of Labor Statistics, 1978.* Geneva:ILO.

Kendrick, John W. 1981. "International Comparisons of Recent Productivity Trends." In *Essays in Contemporary Economic Problems: Demand, Productivity, and Population,* Washington, D.C.: The American Enterprise Institute for Public Policy Research.

Kravis, Irving B. 1979. "An Approximation of the Relative Real Per Capita GDP of the People's Republic of China." A Report of the Committee on Scholarly Communication with the People's Republic of China, National Academy of Sciences, Washington, D.C. Reprinted with additional note in 1981 *Journal of Comparative Economics* 60–78.

Kravis, I.B.; A. Heston; R. Summers. 1982. *World Product and Income: International Comparisons of Real Gross Product.* Baltimore, Md.: Johns Hopkins Press.

————. 1983. "The Share of Services in Economic Growth." in *Global Econometrics: Essays in Honor of Lawrence R. Klein,* edited by F.G. Adams and B. Hickman, pp. 188–218. Cambridge, Mass.: MIT Press.

Kravis, Irving B., and Robert E. Lipsey. 1982. "The Location of Overseas Production and Production for Exports by U.S. Multinational Firms." *Journal of International Economics* 12 (May): 201–23.

————. 1983. "Toward an Explanation of Comparative National Price Levels." Princeton Studies in International Finance, no. 52, November.

Kuznets, Simon. 1956. "Quantitative Aspects of the Economic Growth of Nations: I Levels and Variability of Growth." *Economic Development and Cultural Change.* 5, no. 1 (October).

————. 1971. *Economic Growth of Nations: Total Output and Production Structure.* Cambridge, Mass.: The Belknap Press of Harvard University Press.

————. 1972. "Problems in Comparing Recent Growth Rates for Developed and Less Developed Countries." *Economic Development and Cultural Change* 20, no. 2 (January): 185-209.

Malenbaum, Wilfred. 1982. "Modern Economic Growth in India and China: The Comparison Revisited, 1950-1980." *Economic Development and Cultural Change* 31, no. 1 (October): 45-84.

Morawetz, David. 1977. *Twenty-five Years of Economic Development.* Baltimore, Md.: Johns Hopkins Press.

National Foreign Assessment Center. 1979. *China: A Statistical Compendium.* Washington, D.C.: NFAC.

Psacharopolous, George, and K. Hinchliffe. 1973. *Returns to Education.* Amsterdam: Elsevier Scientific Publishing Co.

Shoup, Paul E. 1981. *The East European and Soviet Data Handbook.* New York: Columbia University Press.

Summers, Robert; I.B. Kravis; A. Heston. 1981. "Changes in the World Income Distribution." University of Pennsylvania Discussion Paper #407.

United Nations. 1980. *Economic Bulletin for Europe* 31, no. 2. Prepared by the Secretariat of the Economic Commission for Europe, Geneva. New York.

U.N. Conference on Trade and Development. 1976. *Handbook of International Trade Statistics, 1976.* New York: United Nations, Table 6.2.

————. 1980. *Yearbook of National Accounts Statistics, 1979.* New York: United Nations.

U.S. Bureau of the Census. 1972. *1970 Census of Population, U.S. Summary: Detailed Characteristics,* PC(1)-D1. Washington, D.C.: U.S. Government Printing Office.

World Bank. 1980. *World Tables.*

COMMENT

Laurits R. Christensen

Kravis and Lipsey have done a first-rate job of documenting the post-World War II trends in real product for essentially the whole world and for several interesting groupings of countries. This paper provides valuable perspective on how remarkably strong economic growth has been for all groups of countries. It presents a useful counterpoint to the disappointing growth record of the very recent past.

This paper would not have been possible except for the wealth of information that has been provided by the International Comparisons Project (ICP) (Kravis, Kenessey, Heston, and Summers 1975; Kravis, Heston, and Summers 1978, 1982). This project has produced three major volumes packed with useful data and insightful discussion. The first volume covered ten countries, the second covered sixteen, and the most recent volume, published in 1982, includes extensive data for thirty-four countries and lesser coverage of ninety-two additional countries.

As excellent as the ICP has been, I believe that the methods used to construct the real output figures could be improved. The volumes contain some confusion in the discussion of aggregation procedures. The discussion attempts to motivate the procedures from a utility function point of view. This is clearly inappropriate, however, since all real output, including investment goods, is being aggregated. The proper motivation would be from the point of view of a multiproduct production function. This becomes even more apparent when the discussion in the current paper turns to productivity comparisons.

In the first volume numerous index procedures were considered, but in my opinion the wrong choice was made. The method that was chosen, called the Geary-Khamis method by the authors, cannot be justified in terms of the economic theory of producer behavior. Multilateral versions of Fisher's Ideal index or the Tornqvist index (both superlative indexes, using Dierwert's [1976] terminology) would be preferable. The ICP mistakenly rejected Fisher's Ideal index as "too mechanical" and "not easy to justify in theoretical terms." On the contrary, however, it is the Geary-Khamis index that is not easy to justify theoretically, but Fisher's Ideal index can be (see Caves, Christensen, and Diewert 1982). The distinction between superlative and nonsuperlative index procedures is not just a nicety of academic interest. There can be substantial diffferences in comparisons based on the Geary-Khamis procedure and a superlative index. In comparing real product for the United Kingdom and Kenya the Geary-Khamis method understates the difference by approximately 20 percent, relative to a superlative index. This indicates that the ICP results tend to overstate the disparity between comparisons based on exchange rates versus those based on purchasing power parities (although the difference remains large even with a superlative index).

In response to the above remarks at the conference, Kravis questioned whether the use of Fisher's Ideal index would be desirable because it doesn't preserve "matrix consistency." By matrix consistency he explained that he meant the property of having constant dollar components of real product sum to subtotals of real product in constant dollars, which in turn sum to total real product in constant dollars. For example, matrix consistency requires that *real* expenditure on apples and oranges be additive in obtaining real expenditure on fruit, and that real expenditure on food and construction be additive in obtaining total real product. I disagree strongly on the desirability of such "consistency." We economists have spent our adult lives teaching students that you can't add apples and oranges. I consider it a dereliction of our duty to turn around and tell national income accountants that they must add apples and oranges. It is well known that such additivity is possible only with fixed weight indexes. And it is precisely the fixed weight nature of the Geary-Khamis that excludes it from the realm of indexes that can be justified on the basis of economic theory.

There is a related index number issue that is swept under the rug in the ICP volumes and the current paper. The point of view that is adopted is that multinational comparisons ought to be transitive or circular. That is, if country A has higher real product than country B, and country B has higher real product than country C, this ought to imply that country A has higher real product than country C. I agree wholeheartedly with this point of view. It must be recognized, however, that this view carries an obligation that is not always easy to live up to.

The problem is that circularity requires the sacrifice of some characteristics. In essence this means that comparisons must involve weighting factors that are mixtures of weights from all the countries. The ICP does this for selected benchmark years, but the annual extrapolations from the benchmarks use growth rates from country-specific data. This destroys the circularity property of the comparisons. It produces results that are inconsistent with results from true multicountry comparisons on an annual basis. If cost precludes such an annual comparison, methods could be developed that would interpolate between benchmarks using multicountry weighting factors.

The final version of the paper has been greatly improved (over the version distributed at the conference) by rounding from the excessive number of digits that were contained in the tables. I have doubts that even the remaining digits provide an accurate reflection of the precision of these figures. We economists tend to be negligent in this regard. The tables in this paper, like most others, could be further improved by organizing them to convey easily the essence of the findings. I have found the writings of Ehrenberg (1981) to be an impetus to such improvements in my own work.

Since the theme of the conference was international comparisons of productivity, I was disappointed that the paper did not provide much in this regard. I am sympathetic, however, with the response of the authors that lack of time and funding precluded them from such a pursuit. The ICP provides much of the necessary data, but additional research is clearly necessary. What is needed is that the same care be devoted to input comparisons that the ICP has devoted to output comparisons. The combination would provide the desired total factor productivity comparisions.

The paper did contain some discussion of multicountry comparisons of total factor productivity, and I would like to close with some remarks on that discussion. The authors point out that there is likely to be a correlation across countries in the levels of per capita output and per capita input, due to both better skill levels and more capital per worker. They correctly claim that this implies less disparity in total factor productivity levels than in real output levels. The interesting question is how much disparity there actually is in levels of productivity.

In the previous version of the paper they suggested that productivity levels might actually be very similar across countries. The current version backs away from that suggestion but continues to give the impression that the authors believe that productivity levels are not too disparate. My own work on international comparisons of productivity provides some useful perspective on this issue (see Christensen, Cummings, and Jorgenson 1981). I would not expect South Korea to be anywhere near the lowest countries in the world, in terms of total factor productivity. Yet in 1960 its level of productivity was less than one-quarter of the U.S. level. Even after very rapid productivity growth in the 1970s, South Korea had achieved a level only slightly higher than one-third of the U.S. level. For these same years South Korea's levels of per capita real product were one-fourteenth and one-eighth of the U.S. level. Thus, differences in real input per capita do explain a substantial part of the difference in output per capita, but I would also characterize the productivity disparity as substantial.

REFERENCES

Caves, D.W.; L.R. Christensen; and W.E. Diewert. 1982. "Multilateral Comparisons of Output, Input, and Productivity Using Superlative Index Numbers." *Economic Journal* (March).

Christensen, L.R.; D. Cummings; and D.W. Jorgenson. 1981. "Relative Productivity Levels, 1947–1973: An International Comparison." *European Economic Review* (May).

Diewert, W.E. 1976. "Exact and Superlative Index Numbers." *Journal of Econometrics*.

Ehrenberg, A.S.C. 1981. "The Problem of Numeracy." *The American Statistician* (May).

Kravis, I.B.; A. Kenessey; A. Heston; and R. Summers. 1975. *A System of International Comparisons of Gross Product and Purchasing Power*. Baltimore, Md.: Johns Hopkins Press.

Kravis, I.B.; A. Heston; and R. Summers. 1978. *International Comparisons of Real Product and Purchasing Power*. Baltimore, Md.: Johns Hopkins Press.

_____ . 1982. *World Product and Income: International Comparisons of Real Gross Product*. Baltimore, Md.: Johns Hopkins Press.

4 TRENDS AND CYCLES IN PRODUCTIVITY, UNIT COSTS, AND PRICES: AN INTERNATIONAL PERSPECTIVE

Geoffrey H. Moore and John P. Cullity[1]

Sustained long-term economic growth has been the most striking feature of U.S. business history. Growth in labor and capital resources fueled a substantial part of this growth, as did secular improvements in the use of these resources. Americans have generally taken these productivity improvements for granted. A cursory examination of the economic record of the 1970s, however, is sufficient to dispel anyone's continuing inclination to complacency on this matter. That decade was the worst since 1901–10 in terms of the growth in output per hour. Specifically, from 1971 to 1980, labor productivity in the private, nonfarm business sector grew only 9 percent, which was well below its growth in any of the preceding six decades. This development constituted a cruel irony, since in the 1960s some of the nation's ablest economists had thoroughly analyzed the problem of economic growth and put together extensive menus how to stimulate faster growth. The consequences of the dismal productivity performance made its impression on the growth of output, on the growth of real earnings, and on the behavior of costs and prices. The poor productivity performance was not a problem unique to America. The same ailment afflicted every major industrial economy. In this paper, we first examine short-run *cyclical changes* in productivity, costs, prices, and profits in the United States and other industrialized economies in recent decades, as well as in the current recession. Second, we analyze *long-term trends* in productivity, compensation, costs, and prices for their implications about levels of inflation.

157

Figure 4-1.   Growth Rates in Labor Costs, Prices, Profits, and Productivity, Nonfarm Business—United States.

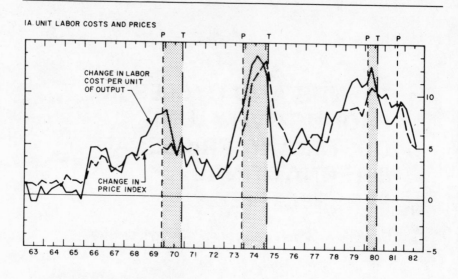

IA. UNIT LABOR COSTS AND PRICES

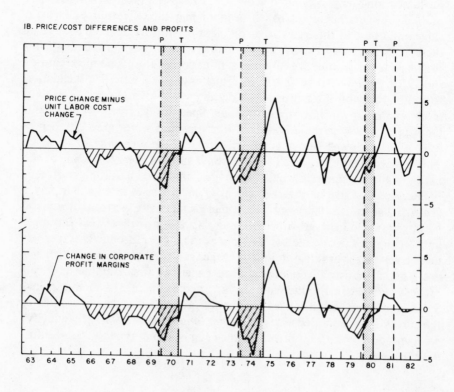

IB. PRICE/COST DIFFERENCES AND PROFITS

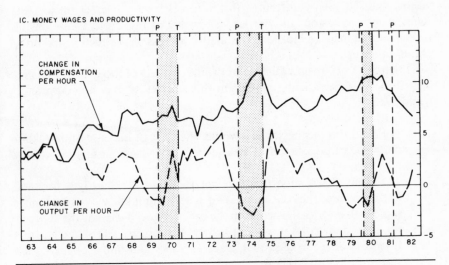

Note: Shaded areas are recessions, from peak (P) to trough (T).

CYCLICAL MOVEMENTS

Mitchell's Generalizations and Recent U.S. Business Cycles

Theoretical speculation into the etiology of the business cycle has often centered on the significance of imbalances among productivity, cost, and price changes to the process of cumulative change by which one set of business conditions transforms itself into another set. Wesley C. Mitchell (1941), for instance, recognized as far back as 1913 that these factors were important to an understanding of cyclical changes in market-oriented economies. His theoretical insights were tested extensively in the United States for many decades before the availability of statistics that securely supported his position.[2] In 1972, the U.S. Bureau of Labor Statistics began to publish quarterly data on costs and profits per unit of output for all nonfinancial corporations and on comparable prices received. The BLS series were carried back to 1948, and they now cover seven full business cycles. In each of these cycles, the changes in these variables bears a family resemblance to those described by Mitchell almost seventy years ago.

Let us now summarize Mitchell's views and then look at what happened during recent business cycles. Mitchell suggested that in the later stages of economic expansion an encroachment of costs on prices occurred and led to an eventual squeeze on aggregate profits. These developments were crucial to an understanding of the reluctance of business firms to commit themselves to new investment projects. This hesitancy to undertake new investments itself then contributed to the forces responsible for turning expansion into recession. In contrast, a reversal of this cycle occurs during recessions and helps to brake the cumulative process of contraction and bring about an upturn.

Figure 4–1 offers us a glimpse of the movements of these statistics in recent decades. The salient findings on this subject as they now appear to stand are:

1. For nonfarm businesses as a whole, the rates of increase of unit labor costs and of prices received have generally tracked one another closely (see Figure 4–1A).

2. There have been important divergences, however: Shortly before and during each of the recessions (shaded area), unit labor costs rose more rapidly than prices, whereas in the early stages of each of the recoveries, unit labor costs rose more slowly than prices. The arithmetic differences between the growth rates in prices and unit labor costs are shown in Figure 4–1B.

3. The differences between price changes and unit labor costs changes follow a cyclical pattern, which is reflected in corporate profit margins (Figure 4–1B). In general, profit margins tend to fall late in economic expansions and during recessions as businesses fail to pass through to prices some of the sharp increases they experience in unit labor costs. In contrast, margins tend to recover early in expansions.

4. The reasons for the behavior of unit labor costs can be seen when cost is subdivided into its components: average hourly compensation and output per hour (Figure 4–1C). During the late stages of contraction and the early stages of economic expansions rapid increases in output per hour occur along with a relatively slow rise in hourly compensation. Hence, changes in labor costs per unit of product fall. In contrast, as the economy approaches a peak, changes in output per hour usually decline. (For details, see Table 4–1.) At about that time, hourly compensation generally grows more rapidly. When growth in hourly compensation exceeds the increase in output per hour, changes in unit costs advance.

Mitchell's Generalizations and Growth Cycles in Europe and Japan

Another test of the power of Mitchell's generalizations, which has both scientific value and practical advantages, can be made by compiling relevant statistics in other countries and conducting similar experiments with them. If similar relationships are revealed, the case for the theory would obviously be strengthened. However, finding a similar testing ground for the theory

Table 4-1. Productivity Changes over Business Cycles, United States (percentage change at annual rate).

	Business Cycle Contractions		Business Cycle Expansions	
	1st Half	2nd Half	1st Half	2nd Half
Averages				
1919-61 (10 cycles)	0.8	2.8	5.3	3.0
1961-82 (4 cycles)	-1.9	1.4	3.2	0.7
Individual cycles				
1961-69 (expansion)	—	—	3.6	1.6
1969-70 (contraction)	1.2	1.4	—	—
1970-73 (expansion)	—	—	3.9	1.9
1973-75 (contraction)	-2.9	-0.4	—	—
1975-80 (expansion)	—	—	3.4	-0.1
1980-80 (contraction)	-2.8	3.2	—	—
1980-81 (expansion)	—	—	2.0	-0.2
1981-82 (contraction)	-3.2	—	—	—

Source: The data for 1919-61 relate to the manufacturing sector and are monthly (see Fabricant, 1969: 91). The data for 1961-82 are from the nonfarm business sector and are compiled quarterly by the Bureau of Labor Statistics.

elsewhere is a bit more difficult than it might at first appear. As noted above, the U.S. tests were conducted inside the framework of the business or classical cycle. This framework involves an absolute rise and fall in aggregate economic activity. In the 1950s and 1960s, however, many countries did not experience actual declines in activity but did experience varying rates of growth. When the work on international economic indicators now being conducted at the Rutgers Center for International Business Cycle Research was first launched at the NBER in 1973, the task was to learn more about these fluctuations. To examine these growth cycles, therefore, methods of measuring and eliminating long-run trends were developed. From the trend-adjusted data, chronologies of growth cycles were derived in the same manner that had been used in the United States to derive the business cycle chronology. The growth cycle then is simply a trend-adjusted business cycle. The expansion phase is a period when the short-run growth rate of aggregate economic activity is greater than the long-run rate, whereas in the contraction phase the short-run growth rate is less than the long-run rate.

Figures 4-2, 4-3, and 4-4 disclose information about labor costs, productivity, and prices for the United Kingdom, West Germany, and Japan within a growth cycle framework. The peak (*P*) and trough (*T*) dates iden-

Figure 4-2. Growth Rates in Labor Costs, Prices, Profits, and Productivity in Manufacturing—United Kingdom.

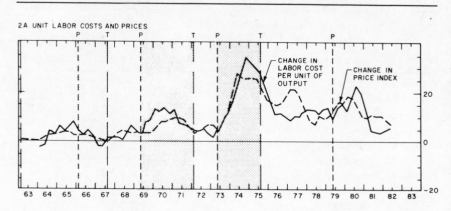

2A. UNIT LABOR COSTS AND PRICES

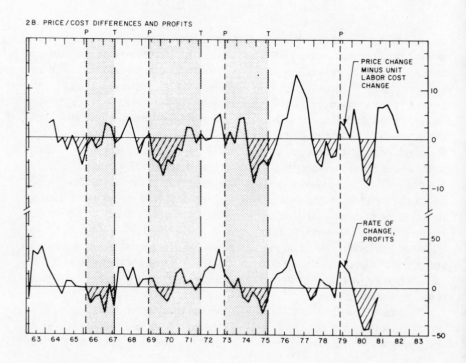

2B. PRICE/COST DIFFERENCES AND PROFITS

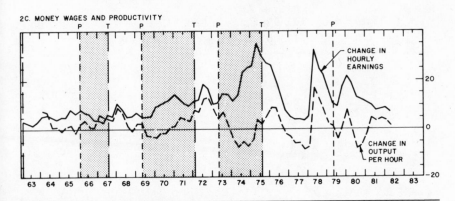

Note: Peak (P) and trough (T) dates identify periods of slowdown in economic growth.

tify periods of slowdown in economic growth in each country, not necessarily periods of recession. The salient findings for the three countries follow:

1. Although each country has its own pattern, the close relationship between rates of change in labor cost per unit of product and in prices is as visible in these three countries as in the United States.

2. For the three countries, unit labor costs rose faster than prices during each of the growth recessions since 1963. The encroachment process, however, started to take hold *before* the growth recessions in only seven of the twelve episodes.[3] Although this differs from the universal drop before U.S. business cycles, it should be borne in mind that growth cycle peaks typically occur before business cycle peaks.

3. Changes in profit margins in Japanese factories since 1963 moved downward before each of the *growth* cycle peaks and reached negative values (i.e., margins were falling) no later than one quarter after the growth cycle peak in any case. Moreover, lows of changes in profit margins preceded each of the growth cycle troughs. For the United Kingdom and West Germany we have unfortunately been unable to locate data on profit margins. As a proxy, we have computed changes in total profits for the United Kingdom and in total entrepreneurial and property income for Germany. In the United Kingdom, highs in the rate of change in profits preceded each of the growth cycle peaks, and lows occurred before growth cycle troughs. At about the same time growth cycle lows were reached, total profits were again rising. Corresponding statistics on changes in the West German series are more

Figure 4-3.   Growth Rates in Labor Costs, Prices, Profits, and Productivity in Manufacturing—West Germany.

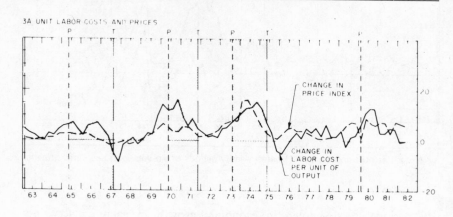

3A UNIT LABOR COSTS AND PRICES

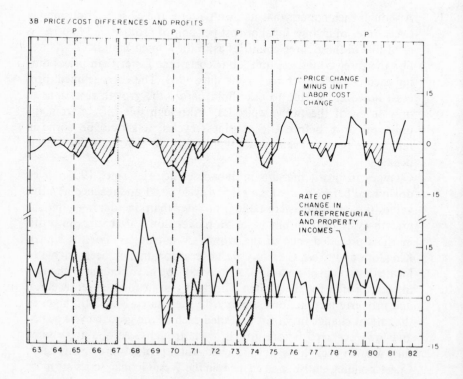

3B PRICE/COST DIFFERENCES AND PROFITS

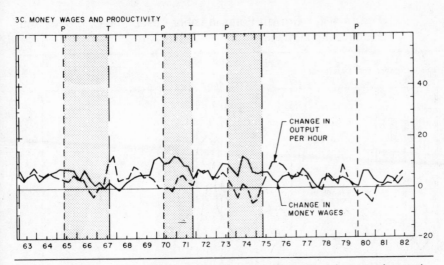

Note: Peak (P) and trough (T) dates identify periods of slowdown in economic growth.

erratic, and it is difficult to find more than traces of the cyclical pattern that shows up clearly in the price/cost differences.

4. During the early stages of growth cycle expansions, rapid increases in output per hour occur, along with a slowing of the rise in compensation; hence, increases in unit costs fall. In contrast, changes in output per hour typically decline as a growth cycle peak is approached, while hourly compensation grows more rapidly. When the growth in hourly compensation exceeds that in output per hour, changes in unit costs advance.

In general, then, costs are rising more rapidly than prices when a slowdown or recession begins, but their differences diminish during recessions. By the time a recovery begins they are usually in much closer alignment.

A principal function of economic history, which studies changes under various sets of institutional arrangements, is to test the relevance of economic generalizations and to ask which are the more widely and which are the more narrowly applicable. The historical analysis we have summarized covers a long span of U.S. history and goes far beyond our boundaries to discover new testing grounds in the United Kingdom, West Germany, Japan, and other countries. Few economic generalizations have been accorded as much testing as Mitchell's views on the cyclical behavior of costs and profits. Still fewer have been able to survive tests of this sort for so long a period of time.

Figure 4-4.　Growth Rates in Labor Costs, Prices, Profits, and Productivity in Manufacturing—Japan.

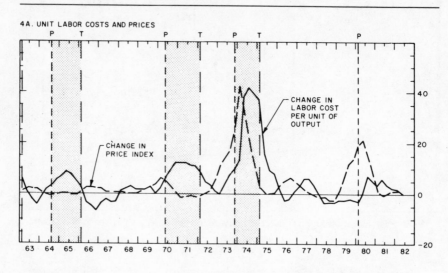

4A. UNIT LABOR COSTS AND PRICES

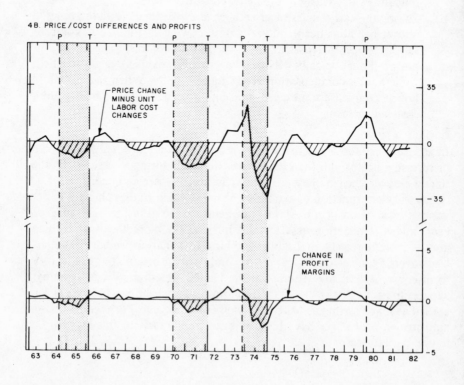

4B. PRICE/COST DIFFERENCES AND PROFITS

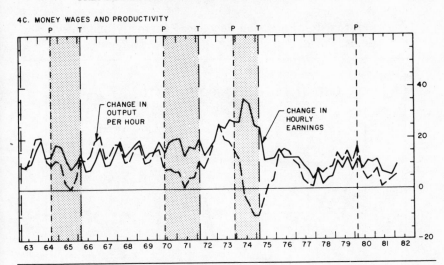

4C. MONEY WAGES AND PRODUCTIVITY

Note: Peak (P) and trough (T) dates identify periods of slowdown in economic growth.

Recession Recovery Patterns

We now turn to materials that disclose a few of the features of the disinflation processes currently affecting U.S. economic activity. Figure 4–5 depicts the movements of hourly compensation, output per hour, and various measures of costs, prices, and profits for the months before and after the business cycle peak in July 1981. The data are plotted in what is known as a recession recovery format.[4] The growth rates displayed are two-quarter smoothed changes—that is, the growth rate is derived from the ratio of the current quarter's index to the average index for the four preceding quarters. This calculation is designed to smooth out the irregularities in the short-term movements of the various statistics. The railroad-track line displays the average pattern of the series during six preceding recessions, 1948–80. The solid line represents the movements of the respective series during the current recession.

It is plain that the rate of gain in nominal hourly compensation during the 1981–82 downswing has fallen more sharply than during earlier contractions. Hourly compensation was rising at a 9 percent annual rate at the 1981 peak. A year later, it was increasing at a less than 7 percent rate. The decline to date has been more than twice as large as the average decline in previous recessions.

The slowdown in the growth of hourly pay has helped to slow the growth of labor cost per unit of product. At first, however, unit labor costs rose more rapidly, owing to the sharp decline in productivity growth when

Figure 4-5.   Recession-Recovery Patterns: Productivity, Costs, Prices, and Profits.

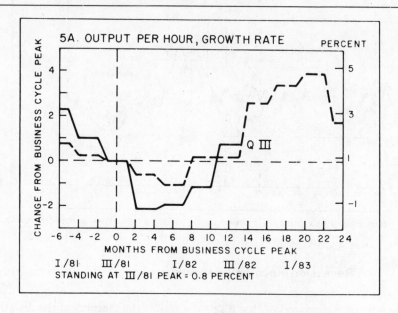

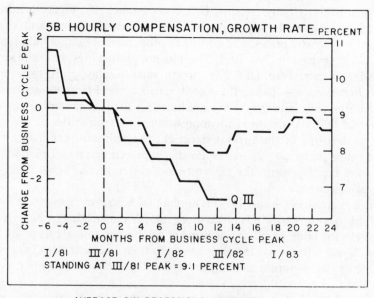

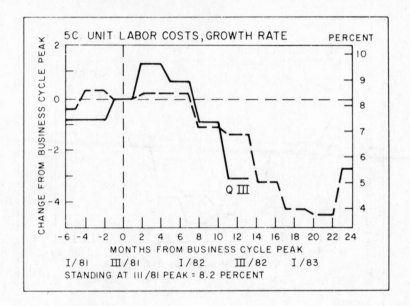

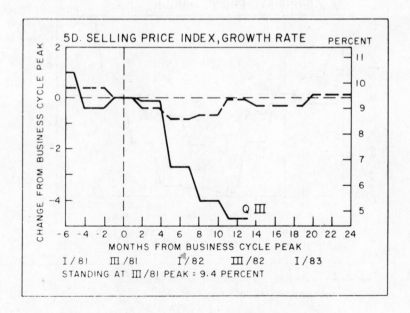

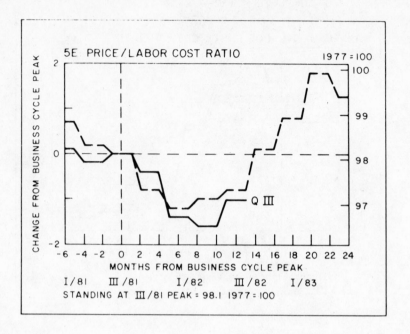

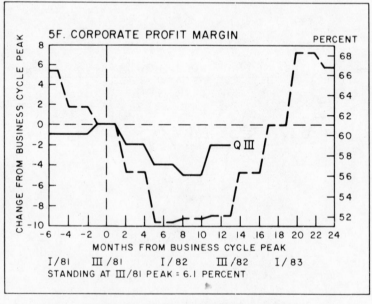

AVERAGE, SIX RECESSIONS, 1948-80

CURRENT RECESSION, 1981-82

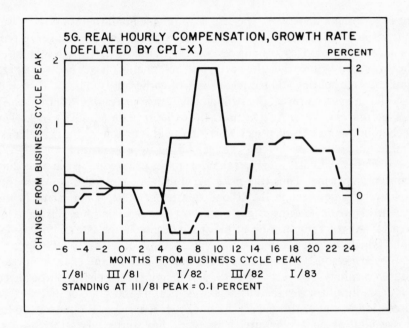

5G. REAL HOURLY COMPENSATION, GROWTH RATE
(DEFLATED BY CPI-X)   PERCENT

CHANGE FROM BUSINESS CYCLE PEAK

MONTHS FROM BUSINESS CYCLE PEAK
I/81   III/81   I/82   III/82   I/83
STANDING AT III/81 PEAK = 0.1 PERCENT

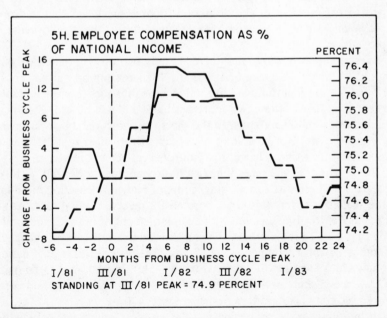

5H. EMPLOYEE COMPENSATION AS %
OF NATIONAL INCOME   PERCENT

CHANGE FROM BUSINESS CYCLE PEAK

MONTHS FROM BUSINESS CYCLE PEAK
I/81   III/81   I/82   III/82   I/83
STANDING AT III/81 PEAK = 74.9 PERCENT

Note: Data pertain to the nonfarm business sector excpet for 4-5F (all nonfinancial corporations) and 4-5H (entire employed population).

the recession got underway. The decline in private nonfarm productivity was much sharper than the typical change that occurs in the early stages of economic contraction. Hence, unit cost accelerated during the first six months of the downswing. Since then, however, unit cost changes have followed a path similar to that during comparable phases of earlier recessions.

The charts also reveal the striking changes in prices that occurred early in the economic slide. At that time, the inflation rate fell like a rock. The decline in the growth of prices working in conjunction with the stickiness (failure to decline) of the cost changes served to prolong and intensify the encroachment of costs on prices that began, as usual, during the preceding economic upswing. Thus, the price per unit labor cost ratio continued its downward slide through the second quarter of 1982, a big factor in the decline of profit margins. Since then, both the ratio and margins have increased. Another implication of the sharp decline in the rate of price inflation, which affected the economic well-being of close to 100 million employed persons, is disclosed in the movements of the changes in real hourly earnings. A sharp increase in real hourly compensation occurred about six months after the business cycle peak in the summer of 1981 (see discussion at end of this paper). Normally, real earnings do not start to increase until about a year after a recession has started. This increase has helped to offset some of the decline in income produced by the drop in employment, since real income has increased for those who remained employed.

Every economist knows that there are only two ways to increase the real earnings of labor. They can be raised by (1) increasing output per hour of work or (2) enlarging the share of total income that goes to wage and salary workers. The first of these two sources is basic and will be addressed in our discussion of long-term trends. In the short run, however, business firms in the aggregate may not be able to increase their prices as rapidly as hourly rates of pay are rising. Hence, real hourly earnings will increase.

During the 1981–82 recession, real hourly compensation fell slightly at the start, but there was a rapid quickening of real compensation afterward. In the second quarter, this series rose at a 2 percent annual rate. As suggested above, this is associated with an enlargement of the share of total income that goes to the workers. The latter effect can be seen in the lagging economic indicator, compensation of employees as a percentage of national income, which has risen of late (see Figure 4–5H). Indeed, in the first half of 1982, workers' share in the national income, at 76 percent, was higher than in any preceding six-month period save one.

In his masterpiece on business cycles, Joseph Schumpeter (1939: 142) propounded the remarkable proposition that periods of recession are times when the harvest is gathered after the strenuous efforts of the expansion. Sympathetic students of his work have usually looked at this proposition with bemusement, as something better left unexamined. But Schumpeter's formulation is at least a reminder to us that business cycle recessions are not catastrophes in all respects. The data on changes in real hourly earnings just cited provide some perspective on this matter.

The charts tell still another story, which perhaps has not received the attention it deserves. During the past year, the public's attention has been focused on the high level of nominal and real interest rates. There has been enormous speculation about the impact of these rates on the prospects for economic recovery. There is justification for this position. However, scant attention, if any, is focused on the behavior of unit labor costs and their relation to prices. Judging from past experience, economic recovery hinges as much on an upturn in price per labor cost ratios as upon a decline in interest rates.

The Link between Productivity and the Leading Indicators

We have seen that short-run movements in productivity are closely linked to costs, prices, and profits, which in turn have long been viewed as crucial factors in the generation of business cycles. One might expect, therefore, that productivity movements would show a close affinity to the so-called leading indictors, which for a variety of reasons anticipate business cycle peaks and troughs. One can think of causal relationships running in both directions. For example, an upswing in new orders, one of the leading indicators, is likely to lead to an improvement in output-per-hour because the additional ouput generated by the larger volume of orders can usually be produced without a commensurate increase in labor input. On the other hand, an improvement in productivity generated, say, by new capital equipment, can reduce costs and prices and thereby stimulate orders.

Figure 4–6 supplies a test of the strength of this two-way relationship by comparing growth rates in leading indexes with growth rates in productivity in four countries. In each country there is a general correspondence between the movements of the two series. Thus, faster growth in a country's leading index is likely to be accompanied by faster growth in output per hour. Slower growth or decline in the leading index and in productivity also go together. Both lead general business activity and by about the same amount of time (i.e., the movements of the leading indexes and productivity are roughly coincident with one another). More often than not, in fact, the turns in productivity growth have preceded those in the leading index growth rates by a few months, again attesting to the significant role of productivity in the business cycle.

One of the practical values of this relationship is that the leading indexes

Figure 4-6.   Growth Rates in Productivity and in the Leading Indexes—Four Countries.

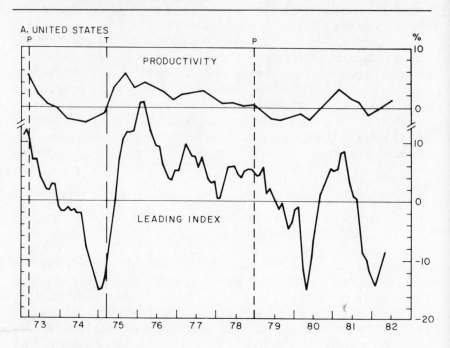

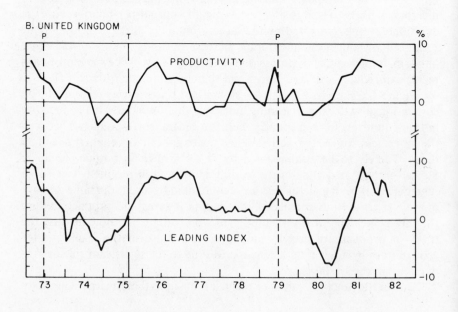

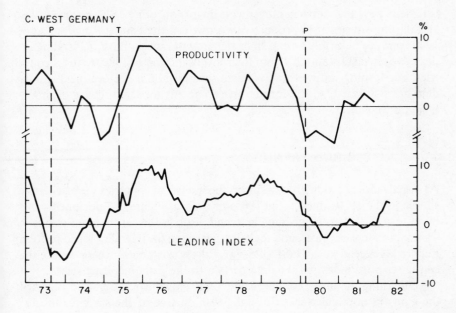

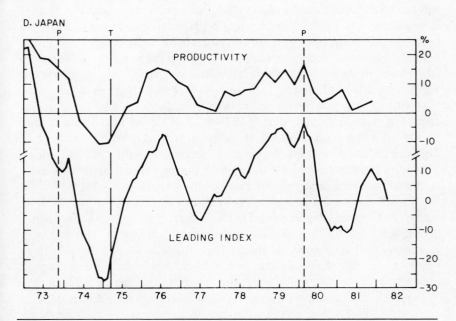

Note: Peak (P) and trough (T) dates identify periods of slowdown in economic growth.

can help appraise current movements in productivity. For example, the striking improvement in productivity growth in the United Kingdom since 1980 seems to be firmly based, since the growth rates in the U.K. leading index have risen substantially from their low at the end of 1980. In most countries, the leading indexes are available several months before productivity data are published, so the former give some advance indications of movements in the latter.

LONG-RUN TRENDS

As noted earlier, productivity gains in the industrial countries were generally slower in the 1970s than in the 1960s or before. Figure 4-7 documents this trend, using 1973 as the dividing line, and displays the concomitant trends in wages, labor costs, prices, and real earnings along the lines developed in John Kendrick's recent work (1981: 125-76). Except for prices, where we use the consumer price index, all the data pertain to the manufacturing sector.

One thing the international productivity slowdown did not do is retard the gains in nominal wages through 1980. In five of the seven countries, wage gains in manufacturing industries were higher, not lower, after 1973. Only in West Germany and Japan did wage gains follow the productivity trend. The consequence, in every country except West Germany and Japan, was an extraordinary acceleration in labor cost per unit of output. A further consequence was a faster rise in prices because labor costs constitute a big proportion of total costs in most industries. Although reductions in profit margins and other costs can temporarily offset some of the increases in labor costs, in the long run, rising labor costs are passed through to prices.[5]

A comparison of the bars in Figures 4-7C and 4-7D reveals that countries with the largest increases in unit labor costs generally had the largest increases in prices, especially during 1973-80. The United Kingdom and Italy are well above the rest in both cost and price increases. West Germany and Japan share the honors for the smallest increases in both costs and prices. They were the countries whose wage trends during the past eight years came closest to matching their reduced productivity growth.

As for real hourly earnings, growth rates were lower in the 1973-80 period than in the previous period in every country except the United Kingdom (Figure 4-7E). The reduction in real wage gains for the United States and Japan were conspicuously sharp. The enormous acceleration in money wages did not pay off in real terms. As has been established time and again, productivity growth holds the key to growth in real earnings in the long run.

Further evidence buttressing those long-run trend relationships is displayed in Figure 4-8. Here the method of putting to one side the short-run cyclical changes is to measure growth rates from one business cycle to the

Figure 4-7. International Reactions to the Productivity Slowdown.

a. Growth in Output per Hour, Manufacturing

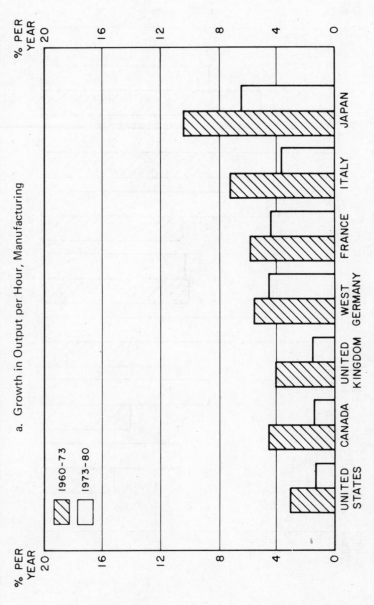

The productivity slowdown has been international in scope. . . .

Figure 4-7 continued

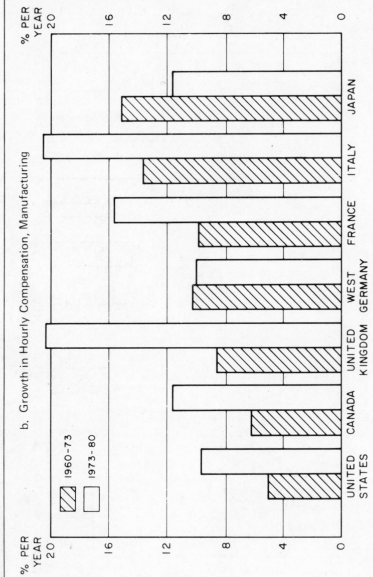

b. Growth in Hourly Compensation, Manufacturing

but hourly compensation accelerated everywhere except in Germany and Japan, far exceeding productivity growth.

Figure 4-7 continued

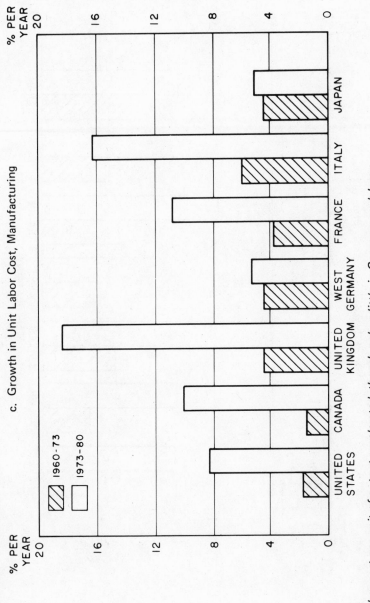

c. Growth in Unit Labor Cost, Manufacturing

So labor cost per unit of output accelerated, though only a little in Germany and Japan . . . .

Figure 4-7 continued

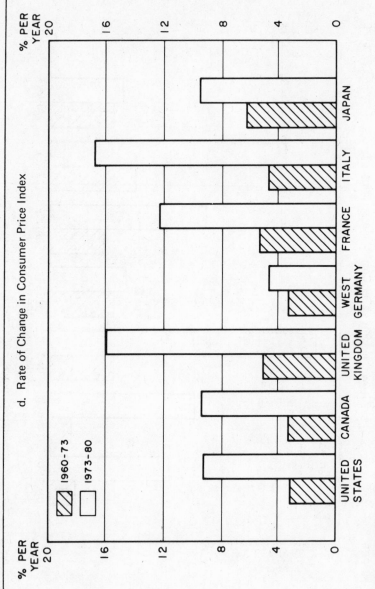

d. Rate of Change in Consumer Price Index

while prices accelerated also, but least in Germany and Japan . . . .

Figure 4-7 continued

e. Growth in Real Hourly Earnings, Manufacturing

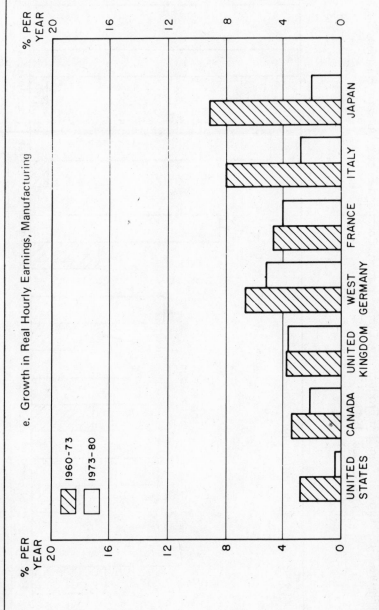

and gains in real hourly earnings slackened, like productivity.

Figure 4-8. Growth Trends in Productivity, Compensation, Costs and Prices, Nonfarm Business Sector—United States, 1948–81.

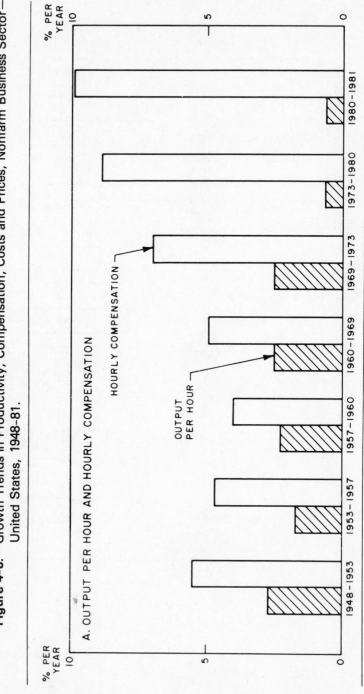

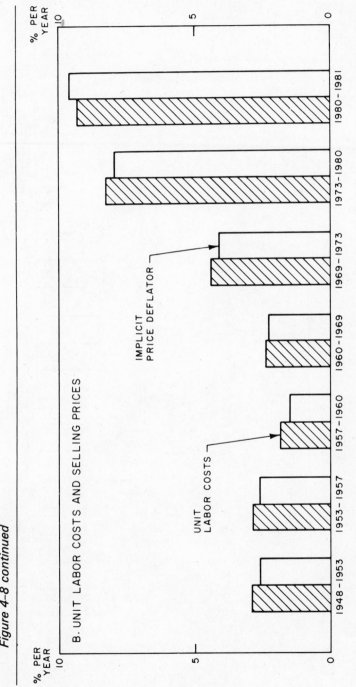

Figure 4-8 continued

B. UNIT LABOR COSTS AND SELLING PRICES

Figure 4-8 continued

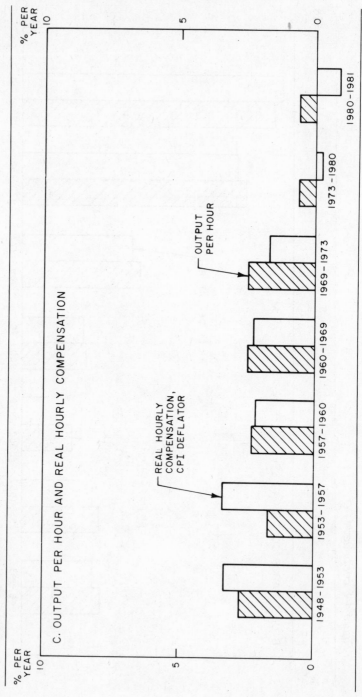

C. OUTPUT PER HOUR AND REAL HOURLY COMPENSATION

Figure 4-8 continued

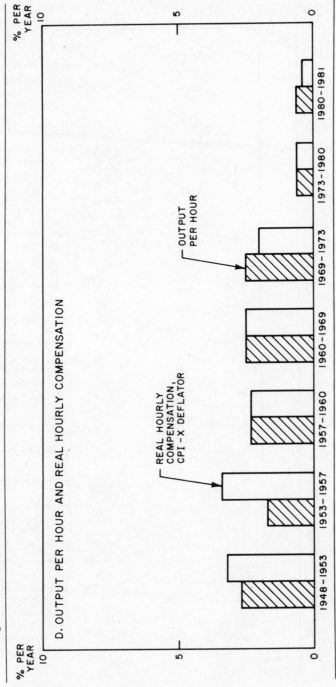

D. OUTPUT PER HOUR AND REAL HOURLY COMPENSATION

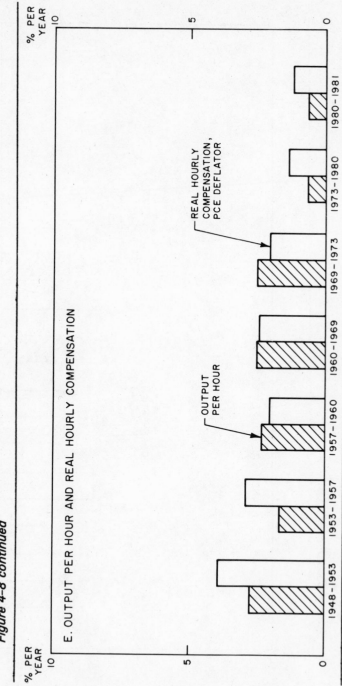

Figure 4-8 continued

E. OUTPUT PER HOUR AND REAL HOURLY COMPENSATION

Figure 4-8 continued

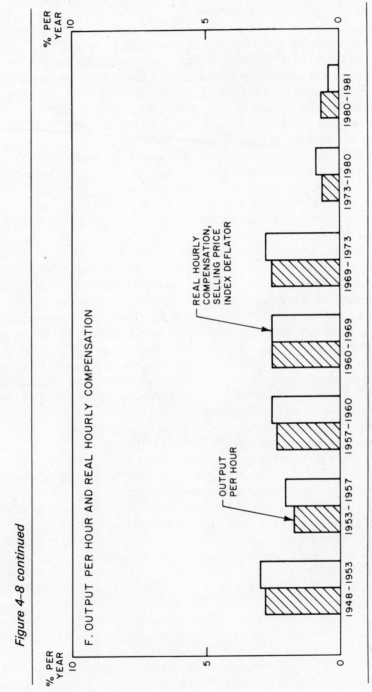

F. OUTPUT PER HOUR AND REAL HOURLY COMPENSATION

Note: Growth rates are measured between successive business cycle peaks.

next. The data cover the nonfarm business sector in the United States since 1948. Hence the industry coverage and time span is wider than in the preceding charts, while the geographic coverage is narrower.

In every one of the seven business cycles measured from peak to peak, the gains in hourly compensation in nominal terms exceeded the gains in output per hour (Figure 4-8A). In the first three cycles, from 1948 to 1960, the differential diminished. Then it increased, reaching dramatic heights in the last two cycles, 1973–80 and 1980–81. Over the entire period the relationship between growth in hourly wages and in productivity was, if anything, inverse. Perhaps "perverse" would be a better word.

This growing disparity between wages and productivity in the 1960s and 1970s showed up, of course, in unit labor costs (Figure 4-8B). The tight relation between inflation in costs and inflation in prices was maintained throughout. Whatever the ultimate source of inflation, costs and prices go together.

Finally, in Figure 4-8C, we return once again to the long-lasting marriage of real earnings and productivity. As productivity goes, so goes real earnings. This time, however, there is a slight twist. In the first two cycles, real earnings growth exceeded productivity growth. In the last five cycles (i.e., since 1957), real earnings growth fell short of productivity growth.

The reasons for this twist are worth further exploration. On the face of it, the inflation in nominal wages had a negative payoff. Not only did the gains in real earnings decline as productivity slowed, they did not even keep up with productivity. In fact, in the last two cycles, since 1973, changes in real earnings were negative, even though productivity increased slightly. This decline in real earnings, however, may reflect a problem with the consumer price index, which is used to calculate real earnings. To examine this matter, we have deflated hourly earnings with three other price indexes that have some claim to relevance, with the results shown in Figures 4-8D, 4-8E, and 4-8F. We find that in all three instances, the rates of increase in real compensation match those in productivity growth more closely than when the CPI is used. Moreover, all three of the alternative measures show that real earnings increased since 1973, albeit slowly.

One can argue, of course, about the relative merits of the various price deflators. CPI-X measures housing costs in terms of a rental equivalent concept and is to be adopted by the BLS as the official CPI for the urban population after January 1983. The PCE deflator also uses a rental equivalent concept. In addition, it is affected by changes in the composition of consumer spending. The selling price index, which is the implicit price deflator for nonfarm business output, is the same deflator that is used to derive the productivity estimates. These prices are not the prices that wage earners pay, but this measure of real earnings does represent the amount of industry's output that could be purchased with an hour's compensation. All of the alternative price deflators support the conclusion that real earnings have increased in recent years to about the same extent as productivity growth.

NOTES

1. The authors wish to thank Ted Joyce and Joyce Geiger for their valuable statistical assistance.
2. Empirical support for the hypothesis was first developed and then given stronger support by Hultgren (1952, 1965). The results of still other tests were disclosed in Moore (1962, 1975). See also Cluff (1970). Findings about the validity of the hypothesis beyond U.S. boundaries are found in Klein and Moore (1981).
3. Three of the five exceptions occurred at the start of the 1973–75 worldwide downturn when the price run-ups associated with the activities of the OPEC cartel doubtless were a contributing factor to the deviation from the usual sequence.
4. For further information on recession recovery patterns, see *Recession-Recovery Watch*, a bimonthly publication of the Center for International Business Cycle Research, Rutgers—The State University. See also Bry and Boschan (1971: 151–99).
5. Some students of economic policy drew a distinction between demand-pull and cost-push inflation that suggested that the former was a monetary phenomenon while the latter was nonmonetary. In reality, both types of inflation are monetary in the important sense that they require monetary expansion. Either M, the quantity of money, or V, its velocity of circulation, must go up. Demand-pull, as well as cost-push inflations, are phenomena that can be stopped or prevented by monetary restrictions. In modern industrial economies, price and wage policymakers often operate on the basis of an important tacit assumption that monetary policy will accommodate pricing or wage bargains that they arrange. The notion that their actions might be incompatible with moderate rates of expansion in the money supply is not often considered.

REFERENCES

Bry, Gerhard, and Charlotte Boshan. 1971. *Cyclical Analysis of Time Series: Selected Procedures and Computer Programs.* New York: Columbia University Press.

Cluff, Anthony T. 1970. "Prices, Unit Labor Costs, and Profits—An Examination of Wesley C. Mitchell's Business Cycle Theory for the Period 1947–1969." Ph.D. dissertation, George Washington University.

Fabricant, Solomon. 1969. *A Primer on Productivity.* New York: Random House.

Hultgren, Thor. 1952. "Cyclical Diversities in the Fortunes of Industrial Corporations." New York: National Bureau of Economic Research, Occasional Paper 32.

_____ . 1965. *Costs, Prices, and Profits: Their Cyclical Relations.* New York: National Bureau of Economic Research, Studies in Business Cycles No. 14.

Kendrick, John W. 1981. "International Comparisons of Recent Productivity Trends." In *Contemporary Economic Problems, 1981–1982 Edition,* edited by William Fellner, pp. 125–70. Washington, D.C.: American Enterprise Institute.

Klein, Philip A., and Geoffrey H. Moore. 1981. "Monitoring Profits during Business Cycles." In *International Research on Business Cycles—15th CIRET Conference*, edited by Helmut Laumer and Maria Ziegler, pp. 55–92. Aldershot, England: Gower Publishing.

Mitchell, Wesley C. 1941. *Business Cycles and Their Causes.* Berkeley, Calif.: University of California Press.

Moore, Geoffrey H. 1962. "Tested Knowledge of Business Cycles." In *42nd Annual Report of the National Bureau of Economic Research.* New York.

———. 1975. "Productivity, Costs, and Prices: New Light from an Old Hypothesis." *Explorations in Economic Research* 2, no. 1 (winter): 1–17.

Schumpeter, Joseph A. 1939. *Business Cycles.* Vol. 1. New York: McGraw-Hill.

COMMENT

William H. Waldorf

Moore and Cullity are attempting to establish Wesley C. Mitchell's generalizations about cyclical changes in labor productivity, unit labor costs, and prices in order to help explain postwar growth as well as the recent slowdown in productivity in the United States and other industrialized countries. I very much welcome their effort because it goes beyond the usual tautological analysis relating changes in unit labor costs to changes in hourly compensation and labor productivity. As my discussion will indicate, the evidence they present for making the leap is unfortunately more suggestive than convincing.

The first two sections of their paper discuss cyclical movements and are primarily concerned with testing Mitchell's hypothesis on the dynamics of business cycles in market-oriented economies. Their first test is for the U.S. economy where they look at growth rates of the relevant series for the nonfarm business sector during the last four recessions. In general, changes in unit labor costs, prices, and profits behaved as predicted by the hypothesis. There are, however, two points worth making here. First, the lag between the beginning of the profits squeeze and the cyclical downturns was highly variable, judging from the authors' Figure 4–1bB. The changes in corporate profit margins became—and remained—negative four years before the 1969–70 recession and about one year before both the 1973–75 and 1980 recessions, and were positive up to the time of the 1981 downturn. Thus, in the last four recessions the lag between the onset of the profits squeeze and the downturn in business activity varied from zero to four years.

The second point I would raise about this part of the analysis also concerns Figure 4–1B. Here, the authors are using "price change minus unit

191

labor cost change" to show the "encroachment of costs on prices"—and also, I believe, as an approximate measure (proxy) for profits in the non-farm business sector. As we would expect, the approximate series is highly correlated with corporate profit margins, but Figure 4–1B shows that this approximation can at times be misleading. In the mid-1960s, it would have predicted a recession in 1966 or 1967 that did not occur, and it would have signaled the 1980 recession two-and-a-half years before it happened. I believe that this second point is also relevant to the international comparisons discussed later in their paper.

As part of the international perspective, Moore and Cullity test Mitchell's generalizations against data for the United Kingdom, West Germany, and Japan. There are, however, two basic differences between these tests and the earlier one based on U.S. data. First, the test for the United States is based on "classic" cycles, whereas those for Europe and Japan are based on "growth" cycles that are measured by movements in short-run growth rates about the long-term rate (trend). Second, the tests for Europe and Japan relate to manufacturing only, apparently because statistics for non-farm business are not available for these countries. However, since manufacturing series are readily available for the United States, it would have been useful to include these in the international comparison because the cyclical movements may not be the same as for aggregate nonfarm business.

In any case, the European and Japanese experiences were not as consistent with the Mitchell hypothesis as was the U.S. To quote the authors: "For the three countries [United Kingdom, West Germany, and Japan], unit labor costs rose faster than prices during each of the growth recessions since 1963. The encroachment process, however, started to take hold *before* [authors' italics] the growth recession in only seven of the twelve episodes." This is hardly persuasive evidence in favor of Mitchell's hypothesis.

The authors also state that "Profits, whether measured as totals or as margins, usually lead growth cycle turns in the United Kingdom, West Germany, and Japan." They do not present data on profits showing this. If their analysis is based on the approximation "changes in prices minus changes in unit labor costs," then my earlier cautionary note about this possibly being a misleading measure would again apply here.

Moore and Cullity conclude their tests of the Mitchell hypothesis as follows: "Few economic generalizations have been accorded as much testing as Mitchell's views on the cyclical behavior of costs and profits. Still fewer have been able to survive tests of this sort for so long a period of time." I am not familiar with all the testing of the Mitchell hypothesis, but I would say it did not convincingly survive the tests given in their present paper.

The next section of the Moore-Cullity paper, "Recession-Recovery Patterns," is wholly concerned with comparing the U.S. disinflation experience before and after the July 1981 cyclical peak with the average pattern during the seven preceding post-World War II recessions. There is no international perspective on recession recovery patterns.

The authors are again employing Mitchell's generalizations to help explain the movements before and after the 1981 cycle peak. They compare changes in average hourly compensation and the CPI and point out that because of the sharp decline in the rate of inflation, real income of the 100 million employed rose sharply during the post-August 1981 declines in economic activity. In this context, the BLS Employment Cost Index (ECI) is conceptually better for measuring changes in real wages cyclically because it does not reflect changes in the occupational mix. As a matter of arithmetic, even if the CPI remained unchanged and there were no wage increases, laying off low-paid wage earners would show up as an increase in average real hourly compensation for those who remained employed.

Fortunately, there appears to be no bias in their analysis from this source for the particular period studied. I compared quarterly changes in the index of average hourly compensation with those for the ECI between the first quarter 1980 and the second quarter 1982, and although quarter-to-quarter changes show differences ranging from 0.1 to -0.9 percentage points, the increases for the period as a whole were the same for both series (21 percent). I must confess that finding no difference in the growth of the two indexes over the past two-and-one-half years came as a surprise. We in the BLS are currently making further comparisons of trends and cyclical movements in the two series, but we will probably need more experience with the ECI, which begins only in 1975.

In the introduction to their paper, Moore and Cullity tell us that they will be analyzing "*long-term trends* [authors' italics] in productivity, compensation, costs, and prices for their implications about levels of inflation." In the final section of the paper, they appear to do this by attributing causality to nominal wage rates. Thus, the countries that experienced the highest rates of growth in prices (United States, Canada, United Kingdom, France and Italy) were those where nominal wage rates grew much faster than productivity. On the other hand, West Germany and Japan "share the honors for the smallest increases in both costs and prices." This is presumably because nominal wage rates in the two countries grew at rates that were more in line with their slower productivity gains.

The authors fail to point out that the differential growth rates in both nominal wages and prices reflect different macroeconomic policies pursued by these countries. Both West Germany and Japan are known to have followed less inflationary policies than the other countries during the period studied. This is not to deny that changes in productivity may have affected the rates of inflation, but rather that this relationship is difficult to establish. In any case, macroeconomic policies are probably considerably more important in explaining the different inflationary experiences.

In the final pages of their paper, Moore and Cullity look at postwar trends in the United States by comparing growth rates between cyclical peaks based on data for the nonfarm business sector. There appear to be two sources of confusion here. First, the authors find an inverse relationship between growth in nominal hourly compensation and productivity, which they refer to as "perverse." I am not sure I understand what they mean by perverse. When productivity growth is related to the appropriately deflated hourly compensation series, then we see a clear correlation, as we would expect. This is shown in the authors' Figure 4–6D, where output per hour is seen to be closely correlated with hourly compensation deflated by the implicit price deflator for nonfarm business.

The second confusion in this section of the paper is that the authors seem ambivalent about whether to deflate the hourly compensation series by the implicit price deflator for the business nonfarm sector or by the CPI in order to measure changes in real wages. Besides the obvious difference in coverage, the two price series are conceptually different, and the one we use depends upon the question asked. For purposes of relating productivity growth to nominal wages and prices or "real" wages—the main theme of their paper—the appropriate price series is the implicit price deflator for nonfarm business. Although they are using an average rather than (more desirable) marginal productivity measure, the theoretical basis for the choice of deflator here is the marginal productivity theory. Using business nonfarm, hourly compensation divided by the implicit price deflator shows, in effect, the amount of nonfarm business product that the worker receives per hour. By itself, it is only a partial measure of changes in the workers' economic well-being.

The worker's welfare is affected not only by the amount of nonfarm business product he receives for his hour of labor but also by changes in the internal terms-of-trade between the nonfarm business sector and agriculture as well as by changes in the external terms-of-trade between nonfarm business output and the imports included in the worker's consumption. These are all reflected in the index of real wages based on a consumer price index that measures changes in the worker's command over a market basket of goods and services that he actually consumes. This is obviously the more appropriate real wage index for measuring changes in the economic welfare of workers in the nonfarm business sector or elsewhere.

I will conclude my discussion of the Moore-Cullity paper by referring again to their introduction. The two issues they initially raised are (1) the productivity slowdown in the 1970s (particularly as experienced in the United States) and (2) the implications of this slowdown and the long-term trend in hourly compensation for inflation. Although their tests and use of

Mitchell's hypothesis is an interesting exercise, I fear that it can do very little, if anything, to explain the two problems they posed. Most students of these problems have focused on one or a combination of factors such as the sharp rise in energy prices in 1973, tax policies, monetary policies, and fiscal policies—none of which is mentioned in the Moore-Cullity paper.

5 INTERNATIONAL COMPARISON OF TAX RATES AND THEIR EFFECTS ON NATIONAL INCOMES

George S. Tolley and
William B. Shear[1]

The advanced economies have long been concerned about the extent to which economic policies are responsible for differences in the growth and level of incomes. In recent years, the lag in productivity growth in the United States and a number of other advanced economies has led to debate over the causes of the decline and the role government policy could play in alleviating it. Those concerns have been intensified by the Reagan administration's emphasis on the supply-side effects of taxes.

A number of tax and nontax conditions can help to explain economic performance. This study evaluates the possible effects that taxes have on income growth and level by focusing on the tax systems and growth records of five advanced economies: the United States, the United Kingdom, France, West Germany, and Japan.

The first section presents measures of effective tax rates for each country on the earnings of physical capital, human capital, R&D capital, and labor. The methodology is based on the allocation of all taxes to different types of earnings based on theories of tax incidence. The second section begins by presenting estimates of how income growth is changed by taxation using a neoclassical growth model and then examines differences between these estimates and actual growth rate differences observed among the five countries. Several factors explaining these divergencies are considered, including capital stock adjustments and international capital flows.

197

MEASURING EFFECTIVE TAX RATES

This paper uses earnings, tax revenue, and tax structure data and information to make estimates of effective marginal tax rates on labor and capital earnings. Ranges will be discussed resulting from data limitations and alternative assumptions about the incidence of taxes.

How to Consider Each Type of Tax

The income base from which the income shares of labor and capital are estimated is net national product (NNP). From NNP the before-tax returns are estimated; therefore, all taxes are stated in relation to the before-tax returns. The estimates of the before-tax returns to labor and capital use the factor-share calculations of Denison (1967) for the United States, the United Kingdom, France, and West Germany and Denison and Chung (1976) for Japan. For each tax, the income base is the factor share times NNP. Taxes attributed to each income base equal (1) the summation across all taxes levied and all components of income attributed to the income base of the average marginal tax rate for the income component multiplied by (2) the level of income from that component. Subsidies and tax expenditures have not yet been included in this study. The computed tax level is divided by the relevant income base to derive the effective rax rate. Taxes at all levels of government—federal, state, and municipal—are considered.

Effective Tax Rates on Labor Earnings.   The most important component of labor taxation is the personal income tax. The progressive rate structure causes marginal tax rates to exceed average tax rates. Therefore, an average marginal tax rate must be calculated for each dollar of these earnings. The weights used in the process of averaging marginal tax rates are based on each dollar of labor income. The resulting effective tax rate is then multiplied by labor income and added to taxes attributed to labor income. Labor income includes wages and salaries and estimates of the labor share of proprietors income. For the United States, the United Kingdom, France, and West Germany, 63 percent of proprietors' income is allocated to labor based on Denison's (1967) estimate, and for Japan, 89 percent of proprietors' income is allocated based on Denison and Chung's (1976) estimate.

With respect to payroll taxes, the incidence is treated the same regardless of whether the employer or employee pays. Payroll taxes are also treated as proportional taxes. This treatment causes marginal and average tax rates to be equal and therefore allows the use of tax revenue data to calculate effective tax rates. It is a matter of controversy whether workers treat these contributions as taxes or as deferred savings. For every country lower estimates are based on treating social security as deferred savings, intermediate estimates are based on treating 50 percent as deferred savings and 50 percent as taxes, and higher estimates are based on treating social security purely as a tax. For the higher estimate, social security contributions are added to taxes on labor.

Taxes on goods and services include sales and excise taxes, and they include value added taxes in the United Kingdom, France, and West Germany. The procedure in the present study is to treat an X percent tax on output as equivalent to an X percent tax on labor and capital inputs. These taxes are also treated as being proportional. Therefore, taxes are allocated in proportion to shares in NNP.

The incidence of property taxes on housing and real estate has been analyzed by Aaron (1975), Hamilton (1975), Mieszkowski (1972), Netzer (1966), and others, with the outcome unresolved. One interpretation treats them as user fees, which are capitalized into the value of land, since local public goods and omit them in the calculations. A second interpretation treats these taxes as excise taxes; a third interpretation, as taxes on capital. This study uses the second interpretation of treating property taxes as excise taxes, with ranges allowing for other interpretations.

Effective Tax Rates on Capital Earnings.   The previous subsection establishes the treatment of taxes on goods and services and property taxes on housing and real estate. These taxes are allocated in proportion to shares in NNP, and the procedure accounts for the incidence of these taxes on the inputs used in the production of the outputs taxed. The treatment of sales, excise, and value added taxes is worthy of special consideration, in view of the fact that most investment goods are not subject to these taxes. With these taxes (which are consumption taxes), transfer of a dollar of income from consumption to saving eliminates tax liabilities on that dollar. Therefore, these taxes are included as taxes on capital but are then subtracted from capital taxes to arrive at taxes on savings of concern later in this study.

Next, consider the levying of the personal income tax on dividend, interest, rental, and proprietor's income. Just as with the treatment of the personal income tax with respect to labor income, average marginal tax rates must be computed for each of these elements of capital earnings. The weights used in the averaging process are based on each dollar of capital income for each respective element of income. With respect to proprietors' income, corresponding to its treatment in labor income discussed above, 37 percent is allocated to capital earnings in the United States, the United

Kingdom, France, and West Germany based on Denison's (1967) estimate, and 11 percent is allocated to capital earnings in Japan based on Denison and Chung's (1976) estimate. The effective tax rate on dividend income must account for the imputations system concerning dividend income in the United Kingdom, France, and West Germany. In these countries individuals who recieve dividends are allowed a tax credit (i.e., an imputation) in paying personal income taxes based on taxes paid by the corporation. The imputation lowers the effective tax rate on dividend income from the personal income tax.

The differential treatment of corporate and noncorporate capital earnings as well as corporate capital earnings from industries with different debt to equity ratios leads to conceptual problems in estimating effective tax rates from the corporate income tax. In the intermediate estimates, it is assumed that any one dollar increase in capital income will be distributed in the same proportion among industries as the existing income shares. The assumption rules out shifting of capital income shares among industries due to increases in capital income. It is further assumed that increases in capital income will not cause some corporations to be pushed into higher corporate income tax brackets. Under these assumptions, average tax rates on capital resulting from corporate income taxes on corporate profits can be interpreted as effective tax rates.

Capital gains taxes in the United States, the United Kingdom, France, and West Germany are similar to the extent that capital gains accruals are subject to a deferred tax at a special rate. As an intermediate measure of effective tax on accruals in each of these countries, 5 percent of corporate retained earnings are added to taxes on capital—based on the assumption that retained earnings act to increase corporate stock values. In Japan capital gains are taxed upon realization but at the same tax rate as ordinary income. For this reason, 10 percent of corporate retained earnings are added to taxes on capital. The effective tax rate on capital resulting from these measures is less than 2 percent in every country, so ranges on these measures will have little effect on the results. Applying the same methodology, estate, inheritance, and gift taxes are deferred until the capital income is realized, which tends to be long after accrual. The effective tax rate on this component of capital income is less than 1 percent.

The final addition to taxes on capital accounts for effective taxes on dividend and interest income from assets in private pension funds. This income faces tax rates close or equal to zero until the worker withdraws retirement funds, and therefore the effective tax rate in present value terms will be low. In the intermediate case, the calculation in the United States, the United Kingdom, France, and West Germany adds 5 percent of employers' contributions to private pension and insurance schemes. No adjustment is made in Japan because its dividend and interest income is largely unaffected by personal income taxation. The effective tax rate measure on capital connected with pension fund savings is less than 2 percent in each country, so, again, ranges on this measure will have little effect on the results.

Inflation Effects and Effective Tax Rates on Capital Earnings. Feldstein and Summers (1979) estimate that the effective tax rate on corporate sector capital income resulting from the corporate and personal income taxes in the United States in 1977 was 66 percent, while without the extra tax caused by inflation the effective tax rate would have been only 41 percent. One reason for this difference is that although corporations deduct nominal interest payments, Feldstein and Summers find that the additional taxes that lenders pay exceed the tax saving by corporate borrowers. Two other reasons they advance for the difference are that the real value of depreciation allowances are reduced and inventory profits are inflated. Inflation also causes bracket creep with regard to the individual income tax and increases nominal capital gains, which are subject to tax.

In this study, effective tax rates on capital are measured by effective tax rates on nominal capital income returns from the personal income tax, corporate tax revenues actually collected, and a percentage of retained earnings. Therefore the calculations already reflect the effects of inflation because the capital income base is derived using real returns. Also, since tax rates actually observed are used, bracket creep is accounted for. The only possible qualification based on the above considerations is that the estimates of effective tax rates on capital gains accruals may be slight underestimates.

Effective Tax Rates on Human Capital Earnings

With human capital earnings—as with physical capital, effective tax rates must take into account the tax treatment of an investment project over the lifetime of the project, from initial capital costs to the end of its benefit stream. Effective tax rates on human capital earnings are far below effective tax rates on labor earnings, with the estimation process leading to measures of 12 percent and less in each country. The major cause for this low effective tax rates on human capital is the implicit subsidy to capital costs from foregone earnings (cited by Boskin 1976), which comprise the major cost of undertaking education and training as human capital investments. The private capital cost to the individual is reduced because the earnings foregone would be subject to personal income taxation if they were not foregone.

Hansen (1972) lists (1) tuition and fees, (2) incidental school related costs, and (3) foregone earnings as the private resource costs of attending school. In the following analysis, the first two cost items will be referred to as out-of-pocket costs. From a tax standpoint, the foregone earnings are expensed immediately rather than depreciated over the life of the asset. The future earnings of the individual are subject to taxation of labor earnings. In the presence of proportional taxation of labor earnings, the same tax rate applies to the foregone earnings and the future earnings. If in addition out-of-pocket costs are zero, the rate of return is not affected and the effective tax rate equals zero.

With progressive personal income taxation, human capital investments force individuals into higher marginal tax brackets, which subjects their future earnings to a higher tax rate than would have been applied to their foregone earnings. The individual also faces out-of-pocket costs that cannot be deducted.

Following are three examples that demonstrate the low effective tax rate on the earnings of human capital. In all three examples, the individual decides whether to undertake a human capital investment at time $t = 0$. If the individual does not undertake the investment, he expects a stream of income y_{0t} in each year t until he leaves the labor force. If he does undertake the investment, his expected income stream is y_{1t} until he leaves the labor force. The calculations approximate his working lifetime by an integral from time t equal to zero to t equal to infinity. (Running the integral over a forty-year time span has little effect on the results.) While the investment is expected to raise the individual's income stream from y_{0t} to y_{1t}, both y_{0t} and y_{1t} are expected to grow between years due to life-cycle effects and the general effects of economic growth. Both y_{0t} and y_{1t} are assumed to grow at the same annual rate so that the equality $y_{1t} = \alpha y_{0t}$ holds where α is a constant greater than one. In the calculations, the time subscript is dropped.

The first example demonstrates how the effective tax rate equals zero in the presence of proportional taxation and the absence of out of pocket costs. The individual deciding to make a human capital investment faces expected net returns equal to

$$_0\int^{\infty}(y_1 - y_0)(1 - \tau)e^{-rt}dt - y_0(1 - \tau), \qquad (5.1)$$

where τ is the proportional tax rate and r is the individual's discount rate. The individual can increase future labor earnings if foregone earnings equal to $y_0(1 - \tau)$ are borne. The internal rate of return is defined as the value of r that makes the expression in equation (5.1) equal to zero. In solving, the tax terms cancel, leading to an internal rate of return measure equal to α minus one, which is the same with or without taxation.

The second example introduces progressive taxation while retaining the absence of out-of-pocket costs. The individual deciding to make a human capital investment faces expected net returns equal to

$$_0\int^{\infty}(y_1 - y_0)(1 - \tau')e^{-rt}dt - y_0(1 - \tau), \qquad (5.2)$$

where τ' is the marginal tax rate on earnings between y_0 and y_1 where τ' is greater than τ. The individual's inframarginal tax rate on income below y_0 is not affected, but he expects to face a marginal tax rate equal to τ' on income over y_0. (In the presence of a number of inframarginal tax rates, τ' and τ become average marginal tax rates.) The internal rate of return to the individual after taxes, i_H, is

$$i_H = \frac{(\alpha - 1)(1 - \tau)}{1 - \tau}, \qquad (5.3)$$

which is less than α minus one.

To compare rates of return before and after taxes, let

$$i_H = r_H(1 - \tau_H) \qquad (5.4)$$

where r_H is the before-tax return to human capital investment and τ_H is the tax rate on this return. The value of r_H is found by solving either equation (5.1) or (5.2) for the internal rate of return in the absence of taxation (i.e., $\tau' = \tau = 0$). The effective tax rate on returns to human capital investment τ_H is then found by setting equation (5.3) equal to equation (5.4) and solving for τ_H.

Estimated magnitudes may be found by using for r_H the rate of return to net investments in human capital of 11.3 percent in the United States given by Kendrick (1976). Substituting this value into equation (5.1) leads to a value of 1.113 for α. If this value of α causes τ' to equal 42 percent when τ equals 40 percent, the effective tax rate τ_H equals 3 percent.

The third example retains progressive taxation and introduces the presence of out-of-pocket costs equal to E, which cannot be deducted for tax purposes. Defining ϕ as the ratio y_0/E, ϕ can be interpreted as the ratio of deductible to nondeductible costs. The individual deciding to make a human capital investment faces expected net returns equal to

$$_0\int^{\infty}(y_1 - y_0)(1 - \tau')e^{-rt}dt - y_0(1 - \tau) - E , \qquad (5.5)$$

and the internal rate of return in this example is

$$i_H = \frac{(\alpha - 1)(1 - \tau')}{1 - \tau + 1/\phi}, \qquad (5.6)$$

which is less than the internal rate of return expressed in equation (5.3).

While ϕ is assumed to equal a constant for any one individual undertaking a given investment, ϕ would be expected to differ between different investments. Hansen (1972) estimates that foregone earnings as a fraction of total private costs, including out-of-pocket costs and foregone earnings, are 95 percent for high school education and 78 percent for college education. The 95 percent figure for high school education translates into a value of 19 for ϕ. In the example where τ' equals 42 percent and τ equals 40 percent, the effective tax rate τ_H on high school education equals 10 percent.

The 78 percent figure for college education translates into a value of 3.6 for ϕ. In the example above, the effective tax rate τ_H applicable to college education equals 33 percent.

Individuals in training programs have foregone earnings either due to the loss in hours of paid labor to attend the program or due to the lower money wage accepted for employment that includes on-the-job training. Training can also entail out-of-pocket costs to the individual if fees are collected for vocational training programs. With regard to costs associated with on-the-job training that are deductible that are borne by the employer, if the employer's tax rate for expensing equals the employee's tax rate on incremental earnings, the tax terms cancel. To the extent that out-of-pocket cost approach zero, in the example where τ' equals 42 percent and τ equals 40 percent the effective tax rate τ_H on training equals 3 percent.

Effective Tax Rates on R&D Capital Earnings

Research and development efforts play an important role in technological advance and economic growth and are subject to differing tax treatment in the five countries under consideration. Tax treatment differs with respect to whether the costs of physical capital used in R&D efforts are expensed and, if depreciated, what depreciation rate is used.

The analysis of the tax treatment of returns to R&D investment is similar to that for treatment of human capital investment. The previous discussion of effective tax rates on earnings from human capital investments showed that immediate expensing of all capital costs, followed by taxation at the same tax rate of future earnings from investment projects, amounted to a zero tax rate. Expensing and tax concessions on R&D investment leads to low tax rates in all countries.

Tax Rates for Each Country

These methods have been used below to estimate effective tax rates on labor and capital earnings in each country for the years 1970, 1973, and 1977. Effective tax rates on the earnings of human capital and R&D capital have also been estimated for each country. The discussion will illustrate the key elements of each effective tax rate measure.

The United States. The OECD (1979) tax revenue and U.N. national income statistics used in the calculations appear in Table 5-1. Based on Denison's (1967) estimates, 84 percent of NNP is allocated to labor earnings and 16 percent to capital earnings. The treasury tax model is used to calculate

Table 5-1.   Summary of Tax Revenue, United States (in millions of dollars).

Year	1970	1973	1977
Taxes on individual income	94,773	113,202	176,672
Taxes on corporate profits	35,342	39,815	61,938
Unallocable income and profits taxes	—	—	—
Social Security contributions	55,520	80,158	137,981
Other payroll taxes	—	—	—
Taxes on property	40,031	53,527	73,028
Estate, inheritance, and gift taxes	4,641	6,348	9,132
Taxes on goods and services	54,330	68,817	94,851
Other taxes	—	—	—
Paid solely by business	—	—	—
Other	—	—	—
Net national product	877,860	1,171,176	1,677,346
Tax revenue as a percentage of net national product	32	30	32

the effective tax rate on labor income from the federal personal income tax. The calculated effective tax rate is 28 percent. By allowing for state and local personal income taxes, 31 percent becomes the effective tax rate on labor income resulting from personal income taxation.

The higher estimate for social security contributions treats 100 percent as a tax on labor. The effective tax rate resulting from this estimate is approximately 7 percent, while the intermediate estimate is approximately 3.5 percent. Additions are then made for taxes on goods and services and property taxes on housing and real estate. Eighty-four percent of these taxes are added to taxes on labor (84 percent being labor's share in NNP). The calculations for the years 1970, 1973, and 1977 lead to intermediate estimates of effective tax rates on labor income of 47 percent in 1970, 46 percent in 1973, and 48 percent in 1977.

Statistics of Income data are used to calculate an average marginal tax rate on dividend income from federal personal income taxes of 51 percent. This measure is close to the measure of 53 percent found by Wright (1969). After allowing for state and municipal income taxes, the estimated average marginal tax rate for dividend income is 60 percent. Therefore, 60 percent of dividend income is added to taxes on capital.

Wright estimated an average marginal tax rate of 33 percent on taxable interest income due to federal personal income taxation. The addition of state and municipal taxes raises the effective tax rate on taxable interest income to 40 percent. Since interest income from state and local obligations is tax exempt at the federal level, 40 percent of taxable interest income (which excludes household interest income from state and local obligations) is added to taxes on capital. Since rental income and proprietors' income are received by income recipients with incomes similar to recipients of interest income, 40 percent is the estimated effective tax rate for these types of income. The estimate of the effective tax rate on capital resulting from the treatment of dividend, interest, rental, and proprietors' income is approximately 29 percent.

The United States has a classical system (i.e., no imputations) of corporate income taxation. The entire level of corporate income taxes is added into the calculation of taxes on capital. The estimated effective tax rate on capital income resulting from the corporate income tax is approximately 23 percent.

Additions accounting for capital gains taxes and taxes on dividend and interest income from assets in private pension funds have a small effect on the results. Finally, 16 percent of taxes on goods and services and property taxes on housing and real estate are added to taxes on capital (16 percent being capital's income share of NNP). Adding all of the above sources of capital income taxation, the estimated measures of effective tax rates on capital income are 67 percent in 1970, 62 percent in 1973, and 64 percent in 1977.

In the calculation of the effective tax rate on human capital earnings, the calculation of τ' minus τ uses the marginal tax rates on labor income from the personal income tax calculated by the Treasury tax model. Using this result along with the methods for estimating tax rates on returns from human capital investments described earlier, the effective tax rate for this type of capital income is calculated to be 8 percent.

The United States has the least favorable treatment of R&D of the five countries, but some capital expenditures can be amortized over sixty months, and patents sold are treated as capital gains so subject to a deferred tax at a favored tax rate. The effective tax rate on the earnings of R&D capital for the United States is estimated to be 5 percent since tax treatment comes close without replicating immediate expensing.

The United Kingdom.   The OECD (1979) tax revenue and U.N. national income statistics used in the calculations appear in Table 5-2. Based on Denison's (1967) estimates, 82 percent of NNP is allocated to labor earnings and 18 percent to capital earnings.

Since no counterpart to the treasury tax model is available for countries other than the United States, secondary sources must be used to calculate effective tax rates resulting from the personal income tax. For example, a marginal tax rate of 35 percent for the $10,000 to $15,000 tax bracket is indicated by Price Waterhouse (1977). Corroborative information is obtained from Kay and King (1978), in which it appears that personal income tax rates in the United Kingdom are similar to those in the United States with

Table 5-2. Summary of Tax Revenue, United Kingdom (in millions of pounds sterling).

Year	1970	1973	1977
Taxes on individual income	5,875	7,430	17,158
Taxes on corporate profits	1,545	1,688	3,355
Unallocable income and profits taxes	—	—	—
Social Security contributions	2,777	4,157	9,894
Other payroll taxes	844	12	838
Taxes on property	2,378	3,164	6,193
Estate, inheritance, and gift taxes	378	420	393
Taxes on goods and services	5,489	6,544	13,227
Other taxes	37	45	104
Paid solely by business	22	21	57
Other	15	24	47
Net national product	47,068	66,859	126,428
Tax revenue as a percentage of net national product	40	34	40

inclusion of state and local income taxes. The popular impression that tax rates are higher in the United Kingdom appears to be due to the greater progressivity of taxes at the highest income levels. The intermediate estimate for the United Kingdom is that the effective tax rate on labor income resulting from the personal income tax is 31 percent.

Social security contributions and payroll taxes are treated as proportional taxes on labor. For the intermediate estimate, the effective tax rate from these taxes is approximately 4 percent.

Taxes on goods and services include value added and excise taxes and are treated as being proportional. Denison's (1967) estimate of 82 percent as labor's share of NNP is used to allocate 82 percent of taxes on goods and services to labor. Likewise, 82 percent of property taxes on housing and real estate are allocated to labor.

The above calculations lead to intermediate estimates of effective tax rates on labor income of 52 percent in 1970, 49 percent in 1973, and 53 percent in 1977, levels slightly higher than effective tax rates on labor in the United States.

In the United States, 60 percent of dividend income is added to taxes on capital. An adjustment is made for the United Kingdom for 1973 and 1977 to account for its imputation system in the treatment of corporate income that began in 1973. For 1970, consideration of the classical system leads to 60 percent as the estimate. Under the imputation system in effect for the later years, dividends are treated as if a 34 percent tax had already been withheld. Thus 34 percent of gross dividend income subtracted from total gross dividend income equals the one dollar of net dividend income received, or $x - 0.34x = 1$ where x is gross dividend income giving a value of x equal to $1/(1 - 0.34)$. Since 0.34 of x of $0.34/(1 - 0.34)$ is considered to have been withheld, individual income is increased by $0.34/(1 - 0.34)$ for every dollar of dividend income received, increasing taxes in this case by the marginal personal income tax rate $0.60 \times 0.34/(1 - 0.34)$. The more than offsetting credit taken for the taxes withheld of $0.34/(1 - 0.34)$ gives a net tax reduction of $0.4 \times 0.34/(1 - 0.34)$ or 20 percent to be subtracted from the 60 percent figure in the absence of imputation. Thus 60 minus 20 or 40 percent of dividend income received is to be added to taxes on capital for years when the imputation system is in effect, rather than 60 percent when it is not in effect.

The average marginal tax rate for interest, rental, and proprietors' income is estimated to be 40 percent. Therefore, 40 percent of all interest and rental income is added to taxes on capital. The estimate of the effective tax rate on capital resulting from the treatment of dividend, interest, rental, and proprietors income is approximately 18 percent. Additionally, the estimated effective tax rate on capital income resulting from the corporate income tax is approximately 16 percent.

Eighteen percent of property taxes on housing and real estate and of taxes on goods and services, which include value added taxes, are added to taxes on capital, 18 percent being capital's share of NNP. Additions are also made for capital gains taxation and taxes on dividend and interest income from assets in private pension funds.

Addition of the above measures leads to estimated measures of effective tax rates on capital income of 62 percent in 1970, 49 percent in 1973, and 50 percent in 1977. The switch to the imputation system in 1973 accounts for approximately percent of the decline in the estimated effective tax rate. These estimates are slightly lower than the estimates of taxes on capital in the United States.

Kay and King (1978) indicate that personal income taxation in the United Kingdom is of nearly the same progressivity as that in the United States. Using this information with the methods for estimating tax rates on returns from human capital investments described earlier, the effective tax rate for this type of capital income is calculated to be 8 percent.

With respect to R&D, all current expenses as well as all capital expenditures can be expensed immediately. Therefore, the effective tax rate on the earnings of R&D capital is estimated to be zero.

France. The OECD (1979) tax revenue and U.N. national income statistics used in the calculations appear in Table 5-3. Based on Denison's (1967) estimates, 79 percent of NNP is allocated to labor earnings and 21 percent to capital earnings.

Table 5-3. Summary of Tax Revenue, France (in millions of French francs).

Year	1970	1973	1977
Taxes on individual income	32,778	44,233	97,634
Taxes on corporate profits	8,904	17,535	41,398
Unallocable income and profits taxes	258	311	697
Social Security contributions	100,926	149,223	236,915
Other payroll taxes	3,481	6,381	15,684
Taxes on property	9,975	15,751	25,486
Estate, inheritance, and gift taxes	1,944	2,282	3,723
Taxes on goods and services	105,111	142,020	226,119
Other taxes	8,286	15,660	23,802
Paid solely by business	8,237	15,558	23,747
Other	49	102	55
Net national product	712,402	1,014,849	1,671,629
Tax revenue as a percentage of net national product	38	39	40

The French personal income tax is less progressive than in the United States and United Kingdom. From Price Waterhouse (1977) personal income tax information, a single taxpayer is subject to a 29 percent tax rate in going from a $10,000 to $15,000 income. Furthermore, the marginal tax rates decline very substantially for married couples with children. The effective tax rate on labor from the personal income tax is estimated to be 30 percent. Social security contributions and payroll taxes are treated as proportional taxes on labor. For the intermediate estimate, the effective tax rate from these taxes is approximately 10 percent.

France has higher value added tax rates than the United Kingdom and West Germany, the other two countries under consideration that levy value added taxes. The basic rate in France is 20 percent in contrast to an 8 percent basic rate in the United Kingdom and an 11 percent basic rate in West Germany. Denison's (1967) estimate of 79 percent as labor's share of NNP is used to allocate 79 percent of taxes on goods and services to labor. The effective tax rate from these taxes is approximately 14 percent. Likewise, 79 percent of property taxes on housing and real estate is allocated to labor. These taxes are very low in France.

The above calculations lead to intermediate estimates of effective tax rates on labor income of 53 percent in 1970 and 1973 and 57 percent in 1977, levels slightly higher than effective tax rates on labor in both the United States and the United Kingdom.

Regarding capital income, France has an imputation system in the treatment of corporate income. A tax credit that is equivalent to a rate of imputation of one-third of dividend income is allowed in calculating personal income tax liabilities, with personal income grossed up by the amount of the tax credit. The low level of taxation and low level of progressivity in the French personal income tax leads to an estimate of one-third as the effective tax rate on dividend income resulting from the personal income tax before the tax credit. Consideration of the tax credit causes cancellation, so no addition to taxes on capital is made for dividend income.

The low level of taxation and the low level of progressivity in the French personal income tax leads to an estimate of 30 percent for interest, rental, and proprietors' income. The estimate of the effective tax rate on capital resulting from the treatment of interest, rental, and proprietors' income is approximately 14 percent. Additionally, the estimated effective tax rate on capital income resulting from the corporate income tax is approximately 12 percent.

Taxes on income and profits that are unallocable between individuals and corporations are small and are allocated based on income shares. Therefore, 21 percent of these taxes are added to taxes on capital.

Twenty-one percent of taxes on goods and services, including value added taxes and property taxes on housing and real estate, are added to taxes on capital. The estimated effective tax rate on capital resulting from these taxes is approximately 14 percent.

The estimate of the effective tax rate on capital income for 1970 is 48 percent, for 1973 is 50 percent, and for 1977 is 48 percent. These estimates are slightly lower than the estimates of taxes on capital in the United States and in the United Kingdom in 1970 when it still had a classical system of corporate income taxation. The estimates for France are fairly near to those for the United Kingdom after it converted to the imputation system of corporate income taxation.

The lesser progressivity of the personal income tax in relation to the United States and the United Kingdom leads to a lower effective tax rate on returns to human capital investment. Using the approach described in the methodological section above, the estimate of the effective tax rate on the returns to human capital is 7 percent.

France exhibits tax treatment of R&D capital that is more favorable than in the United States and less favorable than in the United Kingdom. The effective tax rate on the earnings of R&D capital is estimated to be 2 percent.

West Germany.   The OECD (1979) tax revenue and U.N. national income statistics used in the calculations appear in Table 5–4. Based on Denison's (1967) estimates, 75 percent of NNP is allocated to labor earnings and 25 percent to capital earnings.

Table 5-4.   Summary of Tax Revenue, West Germany (in millions of Deutsche marks).

Year	1970	1973	1977
Taxes on individual income	59,277	101,461	141,585
Taxes on corporate profits	12,614	17,664	24,952
Unallocable income and profits taxes	—	—	—
Social Security contributions	67,630	105,440	154,590
Other payroll taxes	1,389	2,535	3,454
Taxes on property	9,337	10,314	14,720
Estate, inheritance, and gift taxes	523	468	896
Taxes on goods and services	70,734	93,029	113,072
Other taxes	1,618	2,729	3,234
Paid solely by business	1,618	2,729	3,234
Other	—	—	—
Net national product	610,650	824,360	1,062,950
Tax revenue as a percentage of net national product	36	40	43

In West Germany, a single taxpayer in 1977 was subject to a 46 percent tax rate in going from a $15,000 to $20,000 income. Kay and King (1978) document how marginal tax rates tend to be higher under the German personal income tax than the counterparts in the United States and United Kingdom. Personal income tax information from Kay and King and Price Waterhouse (1977) lead to an intermediate estimate of 45 percent as the effective tax rate on labor from the personal income tax.

Social security contributions and payroll taxes are treated as proportional taxes on labor. For the intermediate estimate, the effective tax rate from these taxes is approximately 9 percent.

Denison's (1967) estimate of 75 percent as labor's share of NNP is used to allocate 75 percent of taxes on goods and services, including value added taxes, to labor. The effective tax rate from these taxes is about 11 percent. Of property taxes on housing and real estate, 75 percent are also allocated to labor.

The above calculations lead to intermediate estimates of effective tax rates on labor income of 64 percent in 1970, 66 percent in 1973, and 68 percent in 1977. These estimates are substantially above the estimates for the United States, the United Kingdom, and France.

West Germany has had a two-rate system of corporate income taxation since 1953, and beginning in 1977 an imputations system was also instituted. The favored corporate tax rates given dividends over retentions in 1970, 1973, and 1977 are reflected in corporate income tax liabilities. At the personal level, the estimated effective tax rate on dividend income is 60 percent in the 1970 and 1973 calculations. Beginning in 1977, individuals who receive dividends are allowed a tax credit in paying personal income tax equal to 36/64 of dividend income received, grossing up their taxable income by a like amount. If 60 percent of the increase in income is taxed, 40 percent is left as a net reduction in taxes giving a net reduction of 0.4 × 36/64 or 0.23 for every dollar of dividend income received. Subtracting 23 percent from 60 percent yields a 37 percent average marginal tax rate on dividend income from the personal income tax in 1977. A 50 percent tax rate is estimated as the effective tax rate on interest, rental, and proprietors' income due to the personal income tax. The estimate of the effective tax rate on capital resulting from the treatment of dividend, interest, rental, and proprietors' income is approximately 22 percent. The estimated effective tax rate on capital income resulting from the corporate income tax is approximately 9 percent.

Twenty-five percent of property taxes on housing and real estate and of taxes on goods and services, including value added taxes, are added to taxes on capital. Other taxes paid solely by business include the business tax faced by corporate and noncorporate enterprises and are added to taxes on capital. Additions are also made for capital gains taxation and taxes on dividend and interest income from assets in private pension funds.

The estimated measures of effective tax rates on capital income are 48 percent in 1970, 46 percent in 1973, and 47 percent in 1977. These estimates are slighlty lower than the estimates of taxes on capital in the United States and in the United Kingdom in 1970, when it still had a classical system of corporate income taxation. The estimates for West Germany are fairly near to those for France and to those for the United Kingdom after it converted to the imputation system of corporate income taxation.

Over the time period of this study, West Germany had a more progressive personal income tax system than the United States, leading to a higher estimate of the effective tax rate on the returns to human capital. The estimate of the effective tax rate on the returns to human capital is 12 percent.

West Germany exhibits more favorable tax treatment of R&D activities than the United States but less favorable than in the United Kingdom. The effective tax rate on the earnings of R&D capital is estimated to be 2 percent.

Japan. The OECD (1979) tax revenue and U.N. national income statistics used in the calculations appear in Table 5-5. Based on Denison and Chung's (1976) estimates, 73 percent of NNP is allocated to labor earnings and 27 percent to capital earnings.

Ninety-eight percent of total taxpayers face marginal tax rates below 25 percent. Many Japanese businesses also provide housing to their employees, and this in-kind income largely escapes personal income taxation. Personal

Table 5-5.   Summary of Tax Revenue, Japan (in billions of Japanese yen).

Year	1970	1973	1977
Taxes on individual income	3,125	6,738	9,379
Taxes on corporate profits	2,986	5,250	6,814
Unallocable income and profits taxes	—	—	—
Social Security contributions	3,310	5,679	13,099
Other payroll taxes	—	—	—
Taxes on property	1,125	2,165	3,760
Estate, inheritance, and gift taxes	139	310	352
Taxes on goods and services	3,314	4,778	7,438
Other taxes	975	1,609	2,058
Paid solely by business	973	1,604	2,051
Other	2	5	7
Net national product	63,483	97,515	158,280
Tax revenue as a percentage of net national product	23	27	27

income tax information from Price Waterhouse (1977) and OECD (1981) is used to estimate a 20 percent effective tax rate on labor from the personal income tax.

The effective tax rate on labor earnings from the intermediate estimate for social security contributions is approximately 4 percent. The effective tax rate resulting from addition of 73 percent of the taxes on goods and services is approximately 5 percent. Seventy-three percent of property taxes on housing and real estate are added to taxes on labor.

Intermediate estimates of effective tax rates on labor income are 30 percent in 1970, 31 percent in 1973, and 34 percent in 1977. These estimates are substantially below the estimates for the United States, the United Kingdom, France, and West Germany.

Japan has a two-rate system of corporate income taxation. Just as in West Germany, the favored corporate income tax rate given dividends over retentions is reflected in corporate income tax liabilities. An added element in Japan is the favorable treatment given dividend and interest income by the personal income tax as stated by Hayashi (1978). Taxation of dividend and interest income makes a small contribution to capital taxation.

The effective tax rate on rental and proprietors' income due to the personal income tax is estimated to be 20 percent. The estimate of the effective tax rate on capital resulting from the treatment of dividend, interest, rental, and proprietors' income is approximately 2 percent. The estimated effective tax rate on capital income resulting from the corporate income tax is approximately 18 percent.

Twenty-seven percent of property taxes on housing and real estate and of taxes on goods and services are added to taxes on capital. Other taxes paid solely by business are added to taxes on capital. The effective tax rate on capital resulting from taxes on goods and services is approximately 5 percent, as is the estimated measure based on other taxes paid solely by business. An addition is also made for capital gains taxation.

Estimates of the effective tax rate on capital income are 35 percent in 1970, 36 percent in 1973, and 29 percent in 1977. These estimates are significantly lower than estimates for the other four countries. Japan has lesser progressivity in its personal income tax rates than the United States, which leads to an estimate of the effective tax rate on the earnings of human capital of 5 percent.

With respect to research and development activities, Japan allows an extra one-third depreciation of capital facilities for approved investments in new technology. Joint research associations in mining and manufacturing get immediate write off of new machinery and equipment or to build a new facility. Tax treatment of R&D is similar to that in France and West Germany, which is more favorable than in the United States and less favorable than in the United Kingdom. In Japan the effective tax rate on the earnings of R&D capital is estimated to be 2 percent.

Summary of Effective Tax Rates

It comes as no surprise that Japan, the country with the lowest percentage of gross national product collected as tax revenue, has the lowest effective tax rates on physical capital, human capital, and labor earnings. The most surprising results in this regard are provided by the United States with its greater emphasis on the taxation of capital relative to labor. It has the highest effective tax rate on physical capital, even though the percentage of gross national product collected as total tax revenue is less than in France, West Germany, and the United Kingdom. Effective tax rates on physical capital earnings appear in Table 5-6.

Effective tax rates on returns to human and R&D investments are low and are not a major cause of variation in the five tax systems. These effective tax rates appear in Table 5-7.

Table 5-6. Effective Tax Rates on Physical Capital Earnings (percentage).

	United States	United Kingdom	France	West Germany	Japan
1970	67	62	48	48	35
1973	62	49	50	46	36
1977	64	50	48	47	29

Table 5-7. Effective Tax Rates on Human and R&D Investments, 1977 (percentage).

	United States	United Kingdom	France	West Germany	Japan
Human	8	8	7	12	5
R&D	5	0	2	2	2

Effective tax rates on labor earnings vary much more than effective tax rates on physical capital earnings as well as on human and R&D capital earnings. Lower, intermediate, and higher estimates of effective tax rates on labor earnings appear in Table 5-8.

ESTIMATION OF HOW NATIONAL INCOME IS CHANGED BY TAXATION

The previous section reported estimates of effective tax rates. These estimates will now be used in the analysis of how national income may be changed by taxation, beginning with an analysis of how income growth is affected by capital taxation in a neoclassical growth model. One version of the model centers on taxation and accumulation of physical capital. The second version of the model centers on taxation and accumulation of aggregate measures of physical, human, and R&D capital. Results from these

Table 5-8. Effective Tax Rates on Labor Earnings (percentage).

	United States	United Kingdom	France	West Germany	Japan
Lower Estimates					
1970	43	47	39	50	26
1973	42	44	39	52	27
1977	44	48	43	54	30
Intermediate Estimates					
1970	47	52	53	64	30
1973	46	49	53	66	31
1977	48	53	57	68	34
Higher Estimates					
1970	50	60	63	78	34
1973	49	57	63	80	35
1977	51	61	67	82	38

models are then compared to empirical observation of tax and growth rates. Tax and nontax explanations are then advanced in the attempt to reconcile the disparities.

Taxation of Capital Earnings in a Neoclassical Growth Model

The first version of the model centers on the role of physical capital accumulation in the economic growth process considering a Cobb-Douglas production function with (physical) capital and labor inputs. Total income Y is expressed

$$Y = aK^{\beta}M^{1-\beta}, \qquad (5.7)$$

where a is a production function shifter, K is capital, and M is hours of labor input. Income per labor hour y becomes

$$y = ak^{\beta}, \qquad (5.8)$$

where k is capital per labor hour. To consider changes over time, take percentage rates of change with respect to time to obtain the yearly percentage rate of growth of per capita income (dots indicate percentage rates of change per year)

$$\dot{y} = \dot{a} + \beta\dot{k}, \qquad (5.9)$$

where β is the elasticity of output with respect to capital.

In this model, taxes can affect growth through affecting savings which in turn determine the change in the capital stock per labor hour k. To provide an upper bound on these estimated changes, the experiments are based on the comparison of current levels of taxation with situations where a zero tax on savings prevails. (Other taxes such as those on labor can still exist.) Subtracting the version of equation (5.9) using values for situation 0 without taxes from the version using values for situation 1 with taxes gives

$$\dot{y}_1 - \dot{y}_0 = \beta(\dot{k}_1 - \dot{k}_0), \qquad (5.10)$$

which will be negative when taxes reduce capital formation. Since savings S is the change in the capital stock, the difference in income growth is

$$\dot{y}_1 - \dot{y}_0 = \beta(S_1 - S_0)/K, \qquad (5.11)$$

or output elasticity multiplied by the absolute difference in savings as a fraction of the capital stock. Multiplying and dividing the right side by S_0 yields

$$\dot{y}_1 - \dot{y}_0 = \beta(S_0/K)\{(S_1 - S_0)/S_0\}, \qquad (5.12)$$

showing how the effect of taxes on income growth depends multiplicatively on the elasticity of output with respect to capital, the addition to the capital stock as a percentage of total capital, and the percentage difference between the addition to capital in the tax and no tax situations.

The analysis looks at income growth at a given point in time where the capital stock k is given, leading to a given marginal product of capital equal to the before tax return to capital. Letting τ be the marginal tax rate on savings as a result of all forms of taxation, the saver's interest rate return i received after taxes is the fraction of the extra dollar of capital earnings received after taxes $1 - \tau$ times the before tax rate of return on capital r:

$$i = (1 - \tau)r , \tag{5.13}$$

where i corresponds to the saver's rate of return in the presence of taxation and r the saver's rate of return in the absence of taxation.

When δ is the elasticity of savings with respect to the interest rate received by the saver,

$$(S_1 - S_0)/S_0 = -\delta\tau . \tag{5.14}$$

Substituting equation (5.11) into equation (5.9) for the difference in income growth rates gives

$$\dot{y}_1 - \dot{y}_0 = -\delta\beta(S_0/K)\tau . \tag{5.15}$$

Since β is equal to capital's relative income share or alternatively $\beta = rK/Y$, equation (5.15) can be expressed as

$$\dot{y}_1 - \dot{y}_0 = -r\delta\tau(S_0/Y) , \tag{5.16}$$

which leads to parameters on the right-hand side that are more readily observable. The difference in growth rates depend on the before-tax rate of return that would be earned on the savings lost due to taxation r and the reduction of the savings to income ratio $\delta\tau(S_0/Y)$. This equation provides the basis of the estimations.

The value of τ for each country represents an estimate of the effective tax rate on savings. This estimate starts with the 1977 estimate of the effective tax rate on capital earnings. Since the transfer of a dollar of income from consumption to savings reduces tax liabilities resulting from consumption-based taxes, the effective tax rates on capital earnings resulting from taxes on goods and services and property taxes on housing and real estate are subtracted to obtain τ—which is equal to 55 percent in the United States, 35 percent in the United Kingdom, 34 percent in France, 36 percent in West Germany, and 24 percent in Japan.

For each country, the same values of the before-tax rate of return r of 0.10 and of the elasticity of savings with respect to the interest rate δ of 0.2 are used. The estimate of 0.2 is consistent with Wright (1969), whose estimates are intermediate among investigators who have been concerned with the response of savings to interest rates. Recent ratios of net savings to national income for each country are reported in OECD (1980) and are obtained as they appear in Kendrick (1981). Since these ratios are from observed conditions with taxes and therefore represent S_1/Y, equations (5.13) and (5.14) are used to solve for S_0 leading to the equality of $S_0 = S_1/(1 - \delta\tau)$. Table 5-9 presents recent growth rates and estimates of what growth rates would have been in the absence of taxation for each of the five countries.

The estimates imply that taxation of capital earnings subtracts on the order of 0.1 from the yearly percentage rate of growth of income per labor hour. For the United States, the estimate is that the recently observed growth rate of 1.2 percent per year would be raised to about 1.3 percent per year. Using a higher estimate of δ equal to 0.4 as suggested by Boskin (1978) would lead to estimated tax effects on the growth rate on the order of 0.2 percent. These estimates are based on the constancy of the parameters in equation (5.13) under the unlikely situation of an abolition of taxes on savings.

Attention now turns to entertain the possibility that taxes on physical, human, and R&D capital have greater effects on income growth. Define the measure of capital input appearing in the production function of equation (5.7) as total wealth equal to the sum of physical capital, human capital, and R&D capital. Equation (5.16) can again be used to estimate the tax effects on the income growth rate, but the parameters will differ. The measure of savings, S_0, becomes the sum of savings in increasing each type of capital. Data for S_1 from OECD (1980) as presented by Kendrick (1976, 1981) are used. Estimates of effective tax rates on physical, human, and R&D capital are then weighted by the share of total savings represented by each respective type of capital to derive an effective tax rate τ_w on savings in this aggregate measure of capital—which equals 24 percent in the United States, 16 percent in the United Kingdom, 26 percent in France, 21 percent in West Germany, and 16 percent in Japan.

Estimates of how τ_w affects income growth are based on values of δ equal to 0.2 and r equal to 0.10. It should be noted that no empirical studies of δ as

Table 5-9. Effects of Taxation on Saving Using Growth Model with Physical Capital (percentage).

Country	Recent Growth Rate	Growth Rate without Taxes
United States	1.20	1.30
United Kingdom	2.00	2.06
France	4.00	4.09
West Germany	4.20	4.30
Japan	3.60	3.69

it relates to this aggregate form of savings have been made. Furthermore, tax reductions could increase the share of savings going to capital with higher before-tax rates of return, possibly rendering the value of r equal to 10 percent too low. Table 5-10 presents results involving the aggregate measure of capital, which are very similar to the results presented in Table 5-9 for the definition of capital restricted to physical capital.

A simple example, using the physical capital version of the model, may help to elucidate the reasons for the basic results that the effects of taxes on growth are small. Consider the following magnitudes:

Symbol	Definition	Example
τ	Tax rate on earnings from savings	0.50
δ	Elasticity of savings with respect to the interest rate earned on savings	0.20
S/Y	Fraction of income saved	0.10
r	Before-tax interest rate on savings	0.10

Referring again to equation (5.16), the marginal tax rate τ lowers the saver's rate of return. Multiplying τ of 0.50 by δ of 0.20 gives the proportionate change in savings due to the tax rate, which equals 0.10 or a 10 percent change in savings. Multiplying the proportionate change in savings ($\tau\delta$) by the fraction of income saved (S/Y) of 0.10 gives the change in savings as a fraction of income or the change in the percentage of income saved equal to 0.01 or 1 percent. Multiplying the change in the percentage of income saved ($\tau\delta S/Y$) by earnings on the savings r of 0.10 gives the change in income as a percentage of income or the change in income growth, which equals 0.001 or one-tenth of 1 percent.

For example, if the income growth rate is 0.02 or 2 percent per year, then the growth rate is changed from 2 percent to 2.1 percent per year. Four numbers are multipled together to obtain the change in the income growth rate due to taxes: (1) tax rate, (2) elasticity of savings with respect to the

Table 5-10. Effects of Taxation on Saving Using Growth Model with Physical, Human, and R&D Capital (percentage).

Country	Recent Growth Rate	Growth Rate without Taxes
United States	1.20	1.32
United Kingdom	2.00	2.08
France	4.00	4.20
West Germany	4.20	4.32
Japan	3.60	3.70

saver's rate of interest, (3) savings rate, and (4) before-tax interest rate. The numbers are all less than one and when multiplied together give an extremely small number. The greatest uncertainty attaches to the elasticity of savings with respect to the interest rate. Serious econometric estimates in the literature vary from zero to 0.4. The value of 0.4 would double the effect on the growth rate. Note again, this result occurs when reducing the tax rate to zero, so any realistic change in tax rates would have more minimal effects.

Estimates of how taxation of savings affects income growth are small using the two versions of the neoclassical growth model. The estimates do little to explain differences in recent income growth rates between the five countries. These results imply that nontax considerations are nearly the sole source of differences in growth rates. While this may indeed be the case, taxes may affect income growth in ways not captured in the neoclassical growth model. Such a possibility is suggested by the apparent negative correlation between effective tax rates on physical capital and recent growth rates among the five countries. Attention now turns to consider other avenues through which tax effects can enter. The discussion serves as a proposed agenda for future research on how taxation affects productivity and income growth.

The Capital Stock Approach

In the neoclassical growth model, growth is determined by a savings function, and savings is affected by how taxation changes the after-tax rate of return on savings. The alternative approach proposed here is one in which the key behavior is the demand to hold capital. The rationale for this model is provided by considering the explicit aggregation of savings over all individuals in an economy in a life-cycle context. Younger individuals tend to accumulate asset holdings, while dissavings becomes more dominant among older, retired individuals. Further motives to hold stocks of capital include bequeathment and provision for unexpected contingencies. Summing over all individuals, the stock of capital held becomes a function of income.

Taxes may lower the stock of capital as a percentage of income by lowering the after-tax return to capital earnings. If this occurs, the level of income made possible by the determinants of factor productivity will be lowered. Using steady state comparisons, taxes will affect only the level and not the growth rate of income. Only in a non-steady state in the movement between two steady state levels of capital stock and income level would income growth be affected.

The capital stock approach can be applied based on a purely physical capital measure of the capital stock or based on an aggregate measure of physical, human, and R&D capital. Unfortunately, few if any attempts have been made to empirically estimate how after-tax rates of return affect capital held.

In a neoclassical growth model the marginal product of capital is fixed at a point in time because investment in any one year is a small percentage of the capital stock. When approaching an equilibrium capital stock one must consider the elasticity of the marginal product curve. Income level will be reduced by taxes more when the marginal product curve is more elastic. When using an aggregate measure of capital in this regard, one would also desire evidence on how taxes alter the composition of the capital stock between low and high before tax rate of return industries. The elasticity of substitution between different types of capital would then be of interest. As an example, the taxation of bequests may only cause individuals to invest more in their children's human capital without a loss in future income level if the elasticity of substitution between physical and human capital is high.

Perceived Income and Social Security Effects

Discussion has been limited to marginal tax rates in the evaluation of how taxation affects income growth and level. Government expenditures may also affect capital formation, and concepts of average tax rates are relevant to such considerations. If defense expenditures are not viewed as income, or if the benefits of other government expenditures are not fully perceived by persons in the economy as adding to their incomes, then the measure of aggregate income influencing their behavior will be affected—with a resulting income effect on savings and/or capital holding.

Define ω as the fraction of income produced in the economy that is perceived by persons in the economy as being income to them. For each of the five countries, an estimate of ω is obtained by subtracting the sum of national defense expenditures plus 20 percent of nondefense government expenditures on goods and services from NNP and dividing the difference by NNP. The percentage estimate of ω is 91 for the United States, 92 for the United Kingdom, 94 for France, 93 for West Germany, and 97 for Japan. The high estimate of ω for Japan may partially account for its growth success.

It has also been contended that the net effect of social security programs is to reduce savings. Social security contributions as a percentage of NNP in 1977 went from a high of 19 percent in France to 16 percent in West Germany, 10 percent in the United States, and 8 percent in the United Kingdom and Japan. These figures do not appear to be correlated with recent growth rates. The issue, however, is a controversial one requiring more research. Included in the debate are arguments by Barro (1974, 1976) that social security effects on savings are small and Feldstein (1974, 1976) that these effects are substantial. If social security acts to reduce stocks of capital held by individuals rather than saving per se, a capital stock approach would provide further avenue to analyze these effects.

International Capital Flows

The analysis has not taken account of the international mobility of capital. As a result, there will be a tendency for before-tax rates of return to be equalized among countries. Feldstein and Horioka (1980) find a high correlation between savings and investment rates out of income over time in a cross-section of countries and conclude that international capital mobility is minimal. Harberger (1980) finds no apparent correlation between savings rates and capital to labor ratios and concludes that the world capital market is well functioning and has international capital mobility.

While the issue of whether before-tax rates of return equalize has not been resolved, the capital stock approach is appropriate in considering possible effects from such a process. If such a process holds, a country's equilibrium capital stock is at a level where the marginal product of capital equates with a before-tax rate of return in the world economy. Furthermore, tax rate changes over time could exert large effects on income level because of the elastic supply of capital.

The after-tax rate of return available in considering investment among different countries depends on tax reciprocity arrangements among countries. Customary foreign tax credit allowances tend to result in the taxpayer's being taxed on personal income at the rates in his own country. If there is a tendency for rates of return to capital among countries to be equalized before personal income tax rates are deducted but after all other taxes on capital are deducted, an interesting result is that taxes on goods and services are included in the calculation of taxes on capital. Such a measure of tax rates on international capital earnings shows less favorable tax treatment in France and Japan, two countries with relatively high recent growth rates, because of their high reliance on taxes on goods and services.

Effects of Taxation on Labor Earnings

Past studies on the effects of taxation on labor supply, some of which are reviewed by OECD (1975), tended to predict the lack of much effect. More recent work by Hausman (1981) using piecewise linear budget constraints suggest that the substitution effect elasticity of hours of work with respect to wage is in the range of 0.4. If this result is correct, taxes on labor earnings could have a significant effect on income level in light of estimates of the effective tax rate on labor earnings reported in the first section of this discussion. Changes in these tax rates over time would be necessary to affect recent growth rates.

CONCLUSIONS

The first section allocated the incidence of a country's entire structure of taxes to capital and labor income for the United States, the United Kingdom, France, West Germany, and Japan. Effective tax rates on earnings from human capital and R&D capital were also estimated.

In two versions of a neoclassical growth model presented in the second section, the removal of taxes on savings leads to small estimated changes in the rate of income growth. Although these estimated changes are small, one should not necessarily conclude that taxes have an insignificant effect. The results indicate only that in our traditional model stressing savings, little effect of taxes on growth rates are found using interest rate responses in or near those seriously estimated in the literature. However, taxes could be significant in a number of other ways. First, taxes may affect the size of the capital stock as suggested by the capital stock approach. Second, taxes on labor affect income level. For example, applying Hausman's (1981) wage elasticity of 0.4 to the intermediate tax rates on labor earnings of 66 percent in West Germany and 31 percent in Japan reported in Table 5–8, leads to estimated income level reductions of 19.8 percent and 9.1 percent, respectively. According to these estimates, if the taxation of labor earnings in Japan was equivalent to that in West Germany, the level of income in Japan would be over 10 percent below its current level. Third, taxes on capital affect the composition of the capital stock in relation to the productivity of different types of capital. All three of these considerations could lead to a greater effect of taxes on income level than on income growth rate.

NOTE

1.   This research was financed, in part, by a grant from the U.S. Department of the Treasury. The opinions are solely those of the authors.

REFERENCES

Aaron, Henry J. 1975. *Who Pays the Property Tax?* Washington, D.C.: The Brookings Institution.
Barro, Robert J. 1974. "Are Government Bonds Net Wealth?" *Journal of Political Economy* 82 (November): 1095–117.

Barro, Robert J. 1976. "Reply to Feldstein and Buchanon." *Journal of Political Economy* 84 (April): 337–42.

Boskin, Michael J. 1976. "Notes on the Tax Treatment of Human Capital." Paper prepared for a conference on tax policy presented by the U.S. Department of the Treasury, Washington, D.C.

———. 1978. "Taxation, Saving, and the Rate of Interest." *Journal of Political Economy* 86 (April): S3–S27.

Denison, Edward F. 1967. *Why Growth Rates Differ: Postwar Experience in Nine Western Countries*. Washington, D.C.: The Brookings Institution.

Denison, Edward F., and William K. Chung. 1976. *How Japan's Economy Grew So Fast*. Washington, D.C.: The Brookings Institution.

Feldstein, Martin S. 1974. "Social Security, Induced Retirement and Aggregate Capital Accumulation." *Journal of Political Economy* 82 (September): 905–26.

———. 1976. "Perceived Wealth in Bonds and Social Security: A Comment." *Journal of Political Economy* 84 (April): 331–36.

Feldstein, Martin, and Charles Horioka. 1980. "Domestic Saving and International Capital Flows." *Economy Journal* 90 (June): 314–29.

Feldstein, Martin, and Lawrence Summers. 1979. "Inflation and the Taxation of Capital Income in the Corporate Sector." *National Tax Journal* 32 (December): 445–70.

Hamilton, Bruce W. 1975. "Property Taxes and the Tiebout Hypothesis: Some Empirical Evidence." In *Fiscal Zoning and Land Use Controls*, edited by Edwin S. Mills and William E. Oates, pp. 13–29. Lexington, Mass.: D.C. Heath.

Hansen, W. Lee. 1972. "Total and Private Rates of Return to Investment in Schooling." In *An Anthology of Labor Economics: Readings and Commentary*, edited by Ray Marshall and Richard Perlman, pp. 785–96. New York: John Wiley & Sons.

Harberger, Arnold C. 1980. "Vignettes on the World Capital Market." *American Economic Review* 70 (May): 331–37.

Hausman, Jerry A. 1981. "Labor Supply." In *How Taxes Affect Economic Behavior*, edited by Henry J. Aaron and Joseph A. Pechman, 27–83. Washington, D.C.: The Brookings Institution.

Hayashi, Taizo. 1978. *Guide to Japanese Taxes, 1978–79*. Tokyo: Zikei Shoho Sha.

Kay, J.A., and M.A. King. 1978. *The British Tax System*. Oxford: Oxford University Press.

Kendrick, John W. 1976. *The Formation and Stocks of Total Capital*. New York: National Bureau of Economic Research.

———. 1981. "International Comparisons of Recent Productivity Trends." In *Essays in Contemporary Economic Problems*, edited by William Fellner, pp. 125–170. Washington, D.C.: American Enterprise Institute.

Mieszkowski, Peter M. 1972. "The Property Tax: An Excise Tax or a Profits Tax?" *Journal of Public Economics* 1 (April): 73–96.

Netzer, Dick. 1966. *Economics of the Property Tax*. Washington, D.C.: The Brookings Institution.

Organisation for Economic Co-operation and Development. 1975. *Theoretical and Empirical Aspects of the Effects of Taxation on the Supply of Labour*. Paris: OECD.

———. 1979. *Revenue Statistics of OECD Member Countries: 1965–1978*. Paris: OECD.

———. 1980. *Productivity Trends in the OECD Area*. Paris: OECD.

———. 1981. *Income Tax Schedules: Distribution of Taxpayers and Revenues*. Paris: OECD.

Price Waterhouse. 1977. *Individual Taxes in 80 Countries*. Washington, D.C.
U.N. Statistical Office. Undated. National Income Accounts System of National
    Accounts Data. New York: United Nations.
Wright, Colin. 1969. "Saving and the Rate of Interest." In *The Taxation of Income
    from Capital*, edited by Arnold C. Harberger and Martin J. Bailey, pp.
    275–300. Washington, D.C.: The Brookings Institution.

COMMENT

Charles S. Friedman[1]

As the tax burden became an unusually large proportion of the GNP in the United States and other industrial countries during the last decade, economists and others debated whether the high rate of taxation had hindered the rate of economic growth. The answer is no, according to Professors Tolley and Shear. Their paper, based on a neoclassical model, argues that aggregate tax rates have negligible effects on the rates of economic growth in the United States, United Kingdom, Japan, Germany, and France.

I have several problems with their paper. A major one is with their use of tax aggregates, since the various kinds of taxes (especially direct and indirect taxes) are not likely to affect growth rates similarly. Furthermore, they do not consider any of the alternatives to taxation (i.e., changes in the various kinds of government expenditures, government debt, inflation, crowding out, and so on). Taxation's effects on the economy should be related to its alternatives and also to the circumstances surrounding it.

Thus, it might be more useful to study separately the effects on growth of various kinds of taxes and some of their alternatives before it would be possible to learn whether and how high rates of taxation, given the circumstances, tend to affect rates of economic growth. Various steps in this direction could be taken. As one step I propose to study the effects on growth of the taxation and deductibility of interest. The cessation of both taxation and deductibility at the same time could increase federal tax revenue, since itemized deduction of interest payments from taxable income for individuals and nonfinancial corporations in 1979 exceeded taxable receipts by about $4 billion and for nonfinancial corporations by about $46 billion.

227

Taxation and deductibility of interest tend to influence interest rates, incentives to consumption, production, and various kinds of investment—and, thus, the rate of economic growth.

In the following discussion, I present my views on the Tolley-Shear paper in more detail and then attempt to analyze the consequences of the U.S. tax treatment of interest compared with the elimination of such taxation—and what it would mean to individuals, corporations, and governments, and to consumption, production, investments, and economic growth.

The Effect of Taxation

Two-thirds of the Tolley-Shear paper presents calculations of the "effective marginal tax rates on labor and capital earnings." The aggregate rates are substituted in their single equation neoclassical model, from which they conclude that the growth rate of real product per labor hour is not significantly altered by taxation in any of the five major OECD countries.

It should be noted that they do not present any test to show that the model is able to "explain" growth rates in any country at any time. Furthermore, their model is not sensitive to substitution of even large changes in the three explanatory variables other than taxation. Substitution of large changes in these variable generates almost negligible effect on growth rates.

Finally, there are problems with the estimates they substitute for the explanatory variables, such as:

1. Their estimate for the interest elasticity of savings is 0.2, which is presented as the "intermediate" figure (i.e., middle of the range) among available estimates. However, the estimate is questionable, since many investigators doubt the existence of any significant interest elasticity of savings.
2. The average rate of return on savings is presented as 0.10—without explanation.
3. The authors substitute the actual rate of savings as a percentage of national income instead of the rate in the absence of taxation called for by their equation.
4. The same numbers are used for interest elasticity and for average return on savings for each of the countries without reasonable proof that the average for these variables is about the same in each of the five countries—a very unlikely occurrence.
5. The distribution of the tax burden between labor and capital is based on Denison's 1967 estimates of distribution of real income between capital and labor, while the tax data are from the 1970s. This may result in a

bias, since the 1970s were more inflationary than the 1960s and the interaction of inflation and taxation tends to hurt capital incomes more than labor incomes. For example, the effect of interaction on capital income may result in negative real incomes, while the interaction is unlikely to reduce real labor incomes nearly that much.

Since the meaning of the effects of the aggregate of all taxes on economic growth is doubtful, it might be more useful to study special tax effects, such as the consequences on economic growth of taxing interest receipts and deducting interest payments from taxable income as compared to economic growth without such taxation. One important way these tax rules influence economic growth is through their effects on interest rates.

CONSEQUENCES OF ELIMINATING
INTEREST TAXATION

Some of the probable consequences of eliminating taxation on interest receipts and deduction of interest payments from taxable income include the following:

1. Taxpayers would have fewer incentives to borrow and more incentives to lend, resulting in interest rates that would be lower than otherwise.

2. Investment in "tax shelters" would decline because one of their most important incentives is deductibility of interest payments from taxable income derived from other sources, which enables the tax shelter investors to reduce and/or postpone their tax liabilities.

3. Investment in precious metals, real estate, anticipatory purchases of consumer goods and other "inflation shelters" would decline, as their cost would increase for high-bracket taxpayers who use borrowed funds. Even when they use their own funds, they might consider lending as an alternative when interest receipts are tax exempt.

4. As these and other distortions are reduced, a given expansion of demand may be translated into a somewhat stronger expansion in the rate of growth of real product and a somewhat lower rate of growth of prices, provided that capacity is not yet strained.

5. High tax bracket lenders and low tax bracket borrowers would tend to gain. Tax benefits for high tax bracket lenders would probably exceed the decline in interest rates. Low tax bracket or nontaxpaying borrowers would benefit from the decline in interest rates with little if any loss as a result of the elimination of the tax deduction.

6. In contrast to most other nontaxpaying borrowers, state and local governments would not gain because these governments would lose their exclusivity of issuing tax exempt obligations. When this possibility becomes

available to other borrowers, governments would no longer be able to pay interest rates below those of borrowers of similar or better credit rating. This would be especially significant for their short-term borrowing, since the interest rate differential for their long-term borrowing already fell in 1982. In any case they would not be able to take advantage of their special status by borrowing to place the proceeds in taxable bonds or to lend the proceeds to favorite borrowers.

7. The federal government, as a very big borrower, would gain from lower interest rates, but it would lose the income tax paid on interest receipts on U.S. obligations by those holders who pay U.S. taxes. Since a large part of U.S. obligations is owned by nontaxpayers, the two effects might offset each other.

8. Demand for homes and automobiles by high bracket taxpayers would be affected negatively to the extent that they are influenced by an increase in their after-tax interest cost. On the other hand, demand for homes and automobiles by low tax bracket households could be affected positively to the extent that they are influenced by lower after-tax interest costs. Changes in the total demand for homes or automobiles will depend on the relative strength of these effects.

9. The elimination of the deductibility of interest payments would create incentives to shift from debt to equity financing by corporations. Such a shift would reduce their problems when earnings decline. The incentive to shift from debt to equity financing would further strengthen if dividends received would also become tax-exempt (which could be offset by the revenue from the elimination of interest taxation). As a result, distributions of corporate profits would not be taxed to recipients. All profits would be taxed on the corporate level, regardless of whether the financing is equity, long-term debt, or short-term debt, and regardless of the tax status of the owner of corporate securities. In contrast, if only the owners were taxed, the tax base would be eroded because of a shift in ownership of corporate securities to tax exempt entities. Furthermore, if all distributions become tax-free, it would be harder for corporate managers to retain profits without the likelihood of earning returns that are higher than those available elsewhere. Increased capital mobility and more efficient use of funds may result.

Related Measures

10. When interest taxation (including deductions for interest paid and other related expenditures to secure interest income) is eliminated, banks, credit agencies and many other financial corporations would have no income tax liabilities. A 3 to 4 percent excise tax on the currently taxable gross interest revenue of banks and nonbank credit agencies would be sufficient to provide the same revenue to the treasury as under the current tax system.

For other financial industries, such as nonbank holding and investment companies, insurance, and brokers and services dealing with insurance securities, commodities, and so forth, a split of their tax accounting into interest related and other activities might be the solution. Their interest-related activities would be subject to excise tax and their other activities to income tax. One may note here that the 1979 tax liabilities of these industries were less than 5 percent of the total corporate income tax liabilities, while the tax liabilities of all financial industries were about 9 percent of the total.

11. In order to achieve a transition without unduly hurting those whose interest obligation was undertaken with the expectation of deductibility of interest payments, all obligations outstanding at the time of enactment would remain deductible for up to twenty years after the enactment providing that these are registered with the IRS. Interest received from registered obligations would remain taxable. This would preserve revenue and eliminate windfall gains on outstanding credit instruments.

Refinancing of registered outstanding obligations with interest deductibility (and taxation of interest received) would be permitted up to a maturity of not more than five years after the enactment, provided that the original outstanding amount is not exceeded. The refinancing of registered obligations that have more than five years maturity at the time of the enactment would also be permitted with deductibility of interest paid and taxation of interest received, provided that the outstanding amount and the maturity of the original obligation is not exceeded. In any case, interest deductibility ends twenty years after enactment.

12. As long as taxation abroad remains what it is, interest and dividend receipts from foreign sources would remain taxable to U.S. recipients according to present laws and regulations. Recipients of U.S. source interest and dividends who are nonresident aliens would be treated the same as U.S. recipients: They would not have to pay U.S. income taxes. These rules may somewhat increase incentives for those nonresident aliens who now pay U.S. income taxes on U.S. source interest or dividend receipts to lend in the U.S. or to buy U.S. stocks. Since interest income from foreign sources would remain taxable, nonresident aliens (including corporations and governments) might have to pay somewhat higher interest rates for their U.S. dollar borrowings. The differences would be small, since they can borrow from non-U.S. lenders abroad or from nontaxpaying U.S. lenders in the United States.

CONCLUSIONS, WITH INTERNATIONAL COMPARISONS

The above discussion indicates that the current system of interest taxation in the United States is likely to have had adverse consequences on resource allocation and economic growth. The effects became especially bad when the creeping inflation of the 1950s and early 1960s turned virulent after 1965. When inflation and market interest rates are high, the taxation of interest results in large subsidies to borrowings and strong disincentives to lending and productive investments. Furthermore, taxation of interest was likely to have made market interest rates higher than they would have been in the absence of taxation.

Eliminating the taxation of the portion of interest that is equal to the current rate of inflation may be one solution. However, taxation of the inflation-adjusted portion of interest rates also tends to have adverse consequences. Elimination of the taxation of only the inflation-adjusted portion of interest rates would be much more difficult to administer than full elimination because of the constantly changing inflation rates. Finally, full elimination of the taxation of interest could be accomplished in the United States without increasing the federal deficit and could provide enough revenue to finance the elimination of the taxation of dividends.

Elimination of the taxation of interest in the other major OECD countries would also be desirable. However, the benefits would not be as great as in the United States because their tax systems are different. A major difference is that in these countries interest on home mortgages is either not deductible, as in Japan; or it cannot exceed imputed incomes from homes, as in Germany; or it is limited to the interest liability from a home mortgage of no more than $25,000 (about $38,000 in 1983), as in the United Kingdom; or the maximum yearly deduction is limited to FFrs 7,000 plus FFrs 1,000 for each dependent ($1,400 for a four-person household), as in France. Interest on consumer loans is not deductible in any of these four countries. In contrast, home mortgage interest deduction in the United States in 1979 amounted to $46 billion (i.e., more than two-thirds of all reported taxable interest received, and a large part of the $25 billion other itemized interest deductions for individuals was likely to be interest on consumer loans).

Further, one should note that Japanese taxpayers may limit the maximum tax rates on interest receipts from Japanese sources to 35 percent and Japanese source interest received is tax exempt on certain deposits and credit instruments with face value of up to Y14,000,000 ($60,000). Despite all these tax benefits some Japanese lenders prefer to lend outside Japan when considerably higher interest rates are available abroad. Another interesting feature of the Japanese tax code is that real property is liable to capital gains taxes, and securities generally are not. This provision may shift some incentives away from real estate investments.

Finally, I will comment on the views on the elimination of interest taxation of M. Pierre Uri, professor of economics at the University of Paris-Dauphine who was appointed to develop new French policies on savings and investments. Professor Uri, in an article published in *Le Monde* and republished in the *Guardian* on 26 July 1981 entitled "How to Lower Interest Rates," suggests that "the Americans might temporarily suspend both the tax deductibility of interest on loans and the taxation of interest accruing from savings accounts. The result of this is obvious. The nominal interest rate could not possibly stay at its present incredibly high level: we could expect it to drop by 50 percent."

In my opinon, a *temporary*, partial suspension of taxation and deductibility of interest in the United States might induce a rapid drop of interest rates because loan demand would fall abruptly. When the suspension ends, interest rates would spring back rapidly. Thus, the whole experience would be destabilizing, similar to the Carter administration's experiment with credit controls in 1980. In contrast, a gradual and complete elimination of interest taxation would be more efficient and equitable.

NOTE

1. The analysis and conclusions expressed in this comment are those of the author and do not reflect those of the U.S. Department of Commerce.

6 INTERNATIONAL COMPARISONS OF RESEARCH AND DEVELOPMENT EXPENDITURES

Rolf Piekarz, Eleanor Thomas,
and *Donna Jennings*[1]

This paper describes and compares patterns of R&D spending by thirteen OECD countries over the past twenty years. The available data are described in the context of our understanding of (1) the contribution of R&D to productivity growth and (2) the role of government policy in funding and stimulating R&D expenditures.

There are a number of reasons that patterns of R&D spending should be examined in the course of a thorough attempt to understand international productivity growth records. First and most obvious, R&D is a major contributor to technological progress, which, in turn, is a key contributor to productivity growth. Though some of the causal pathways may elude our statistical searches, we know R&D is important. Second, R&D-based industries such as chemicals and electronics represent a growing share of the output and exports of the manufacturing sector of advanced industrial countries. Thus, R&D spending patterns may underlie shifts in international competitiveness and some compositional aspects of productivity growth. Third, there are discussions among informed observers about the importance of the role of R&D spending in many countries' productivity growth deceleration, and arguments about changes in government policies toward business based on propositions about R&D and productivity. Discussants of these topics should be informed by whatever evidence exists about spending patterns and about the effects of government efforts to change them.

Economists agree that, as far as we can measure, domestic R&D expenditures have not been a major factor in the recent world slowdown of productivity growth (Kendrick 1981; Denison 1977: 122–26). But one approach

235

to identifying important organizational differences across countries is to document differences in practice and then try to understand why they come about. References are frequently made to facts about aggregate R&D spending in different nations, but detailed looks at patterns of R&D spending are rare. This paper attempts to gather up some of the available evidence that is often thought relevant to current discussions about productivity growth and competitiveness.

In the study of R&D and productivity growth, it is important to consider the effectiveness of R&D efforts, not just the amount of resources devoted to them or policies directed at increasing those resources. Effectiveness of both R&D performance and the application of R&D results may vary across countries. A major policy issue is how to make the R&D system more efficient. The effectiveness issue is a most difficult one to study, and this paper does not do it. It examines instead the more frequently discussed issue of resources. As an astute observer fears (Vernon 1980: 152), "emphasis on the amount and quality of U.S. R&D threatens to be a red herring. . . . History shows repeatedly that countries with an outstanding record in science and technology are not necessarily those that shine in productivity and competitiveness." But the paper can be thought of as an attempt to set the stage for thinking about the issue of the effectiveness of the R&D performance and use system.

The first Section offers a context for a summary of the available international R&D data with a brief sketch of some current ideas about the economic contributions of R&D. The second section looks at recent trends and distributions over several dimensions of R&D spending by the United States and twelve other OECD countries. The next section presents some information at the current state of cross-national comparisons of government actions to increase R&D through expenditure and tax mechanisms, and the final section discusses some implications.

ECONOMIC CONTRIBUTIONS OF R&D

Summarizing some current ideas about the relationship between R&D and productivity growth helps indicate why certain apsects of R&D activities among industrial nations are of interest. Sketching the complexities surrounding the contributions to productivity growth of science and technology and of the role of R&D helps explain the difficulties in assessing R&D performances across nations. Our discussion is not intended to be a review of the underlying literature; it is intended only to present some ideas that can provide a context for interpreting R&D spending data.

First, some definitions. Organized activities intended to add to and test scientific ideas and technological understanding are classified as research and development. Two classes of research are distinguished: basic and applied. The National Science Foundation defines research and development as "[b]asic and applied research in the sciences and engineering and the design and development of prototypes and processes." This definition excludes quality control, routine product testing, market research, sales promotion, and sales service. Basic research is defined as "[o]riginal investigations for the advancement of scientific knowledge not having specific commercial objectives." Applied research is defined as "[i]nvestigations directed to the discovery of new scientific knowledge having specific commercial objectives with respect to products or processes." Development is defined as "[t]echnical activities of a nonroutine nature concerned with translating research findings or other scientific knowledge into products or processes" (NSF 1978: 40–41).

R&D and Productivity Growth

Studies at the line of business, firm, industry, and economy levels consistently have shown a significant relationship between industrial R&D spending and subsequent industrial productivity growth.[2] Recent work has taken into account that there are different kinds of R&D, and the findings from these efforts are beginning to confirm that the composition of industrial R&D makes a difference to subsequent productivity growth. An industry's rate of productivity growth is positively related to the extent that its R&D was *long term* and also to the percentage of its research that was *basic*, total R&D expenditures being held constant (Mansfield 1980; Link 1981). Also, R&D financed by an industry (firm) that is devoted to new or improved processes has greater impact on that industry's (firm's) own productivity growth than does R&D devoted to new or improved products (Link 1982a; Terleckyj 1982b). For the productivity of industries that buy goods from the R&D performing industry, product-related R&D tends to be more important (Sherer 1981; Link 1982b).

Use of foreign R&D also can lead to productivity growth. Japanese reliance on imported science and technology as a basis for technical development of product or process improvements has been widely documented. For Japan, drawing on foreign science and technology (and thereby shaping domestic R&D) has varied by sector (more in chemicals, less in steel) and over time (more in the 1960s and less in the 1980s). Technology developed in other nations is becoming a more important factor in the U.S. economy. In a study of U.S. firms' overseas laboratories, Edwin Mansfield (1981) found that the percent of those laboratories' R&D resulting in technology transfer to the United States increased from 1965 to 1979. He also found that a U.S. firm's R&D performed in its overseas laboratories has a significant positive effect on the firm's productivity growth in the United States. W. Halder Fisher (1977) found that foreign subsidiaries in the United States exploit their superior technology in U.S. markets—examples are firms in the chemical and consumer electronic industries. Other studies find that "[t]rade in technology is clearly increasing for all countries" (Peck and Goto 1981: 226).

Various classes of government-funded R&D contribute to productivity growth. But the effects are not as measureable as for industry-funded R&D, and the linkages are more complex and less direct. This diversity of effects has been partly documented for the United States. The effects of government-funded basic research on economic growth have been documented primarily by studies of the linkage-revealed-by-cases type. Econometric studies in the United States at the industry level have in general found no significant productivity impact of government R&D spending. Researchers agree that part of the reason for this finding is the predominance of federal government R&D funding for purposes unrelated to industrial productivity growth. However, one econometric study has found indications that when the R&D funds received by a firm from the government are disaggregated into funds for carrying out *basic* research, as opposed to those going for applied research and for development, the basic research spending is positively related to the firm's productivity growth (Link 1982a). Another finds that government R&D contracts to firms seem to have a positive effect on industrial productivity growth at the macroeconomic level, perhaps reflecting the indirect effects of producer goods developed under government contract R&D on the productivity of industries that use them (Terleckyj and Levy 1982).

The strong positive effects of federally funded agricultural research on agricultural productivity growth have been well documented.[3] (Agriculture is a case where the lack of incentive for individual firms to do R&D combined with the clear potential social benefits from such activities, gives a strong reason for government investment.) Cases of spinoffs from government R&D spending in other industries have been noted as well. Defense Department R&D spending (as well as procurement) is known to have been instrumental in the early development of the computer, semiconductor, and numerically controlled machine tool industries (Nelson 1983). Recent work has shown that federal government R&D spending in firms has been associated with increased private R&D spending in those firms. This work suggests that government funded R&D probably should be viewed as a factor that facilitates and expands the possibilities and potential profitability of privately funded R&D (Mansfield and Switzer 1982; Terleckyj and Levy 1982).

There are a number of special conceptual difficulties in empirically relating R&D to productivity growth that will not be taken up here. Two examples: (1) The fruits of R&D take time to be used productively, thus there are varying lags between R&D spending and resultant productivity changes; and (2) an important output of R&D often is changed, or entirely new, characteristics in the products processes or services produced. Thus, the measurement of output in R&D intensive industries, in order to properly reflect the contribution of R&D, is a problem (Griliches 1979). Nevertheless, studies have consistently shown the positive relationships between R&D and productivity growth referred to above.

Ascribing causality is a bit tricky—on the one hand, results from R&D patently contribute to productivity growth. On the other hand, R&D and fast productivity growth naturally occur together in firms and industries for which there are technological opportunities, often in science-based industries. In other words, it is not simply the R&D that spurs productivity, it is the R&D taking advantage of technological (combined with economic) opportunities. Without them, R&D spending would have little economic payoff. It appears that most industrialized countries spend the most for R&D in the same industries, and that those industries tend to have the fastest productivity growth (Okubo, Piekarz, and Thomas 1977).[4] In a rough sense, then, industrial R&D spending both reflects technological-economic possibilities and realizes some of them (Nelson 1981: 1029–64).

Certainly R&D spending is not sufficient for subsequent productivity growth. Consistent with that fact, most economic researchers agree that the slowdown in the growth of total R&D funding accounted for, at most, only a small part of the observed decline in the rate of American productivity growth in the last decade. Not only does composition of R&D matter, as we have seen, but there are other factors of major importance—including labor skills, amount of plant and equipment per worker, management of available productive resources, legal constraints or incentives, and general economic conditions. These factors do not operate uniformly in all industries of a nation or across all nations for a particular industry. In sum, R&D, in a great variety of types, affects productivity growth in a great variety of ways, some of which are more likely to be captured in standard measurements and models than others, and some of which are better understood than others.

Limitation of R&D as an Indicator for Science and Technology Inputs to Productivity Growth

R&D expenditures are measurable, but it is scientific and technological advances that have economic consequences. Their patterns and interactions are much harder to measure. Science and technology are concurrent enterprises that feed upon each other. They are not clearly distinguishable. For a rough distinction, let us say that science seeks understanding and that technology seeks new uses—that is, to learn how to do something new or better. Scientific advances are neither necessary nor sufficient for technological advances, and vice versa. There are cases in which scientific research has resulted in significant unexpected applications or potential applications (NSF 1979, 1980). There are cases in which technological developments have had significant effects on what research is doing (computer power has greatly changed many kinds of research), or in which technological developments for use in one field (lasers for atomic physics) have changed research in others (chemistry). There are cases in which existing knowledge has new value because of emerging problems or in which technical problems spurred new scientific breakthroughs.

Many kinds of interaction between science and technology have been documented. Science and technology interact through publications, education, mobility of scientists and engineers, and special institutions such as industry/university research arrangements. And some barriers to the interaction between science and technology also are known. For instance "important differences between universities and industry with respect to patents, publications, and freedom of research direction . . . may hinder the transfer of results . . . [though] solutions [to these substantial problems] have been found in the past" (Magee 1980: 276). Ways to improve the contribution of science to technology are being sought and experimented with, as through the NSF's industry/university programs.

Science and technology, then, are complicated enterprises with a large variety of patterns and interactions. R&D activities are important parts of the processes of scientific and technological advance, but they are not synonymous with that advance or even with the activities leading to that advance, especially on the technology side. In a recent article, Jordan Lewis (1982: 1204-11) discussed the various sources of technological knowledge within firms, and the importance of factors other than R&D to technological progress, such as marketing, time horizons of managers, regulation, inflation, and social factors. Unlike technological or scientific advance, R&D has two handy measuring devices, namely the dollars or manpower expended on those activities. But a great oversimplification is clearly involved in looking at R&D expenditures as a lone indicator of scientific and technological enterprises, especially in comparisons at a single point in time.

R&D SPENDING PATTERNS IN THIRTEEN INDUSTRIALIZED COUNTRIES

For a number of years, diminished U.S. R&D commitment and position vis-à-vis other advanced industrial nations (especially France, Germany, and

Japan) have been cited frequently as important factors in the decline in the status of the United States in the world economy. We do not intend to debate the relative position of the U.S. economy among industrial nations at present as compared to 1960 or 1970. A look at the available R&D funding data for advanced industrial nations provides an idea of how the U.S. R&D effort since the mid-1960s compares with the R&D spending experience of its major industrial competitors.

Our summary of the data shows that indeed U.S. R&D funding remained fairly constant from the mid-1960s through the early 1970s, while most other advanced industrial nations increased their expenditures. But since the mid-1970s, the U.S. funding of R&D has increased in real terms at a rate comparable to the growth rate of R&D among the other advanced industrial nations. In addition, the available data indicate that the lack of real growth of U.S. R&D efforts during the late 1960s and early 1970s was attributable primarily to a cutback in government funding of R&D efforts. The U.S. recovery in R&D expenditures in contrast derives largely from steady growth in private sector R&D funding, combined with a growth rate in government funding that moved from negative to (slightly) positive.

The OECD Research and Development Statistics

Before turning to the data, a few points should be made about the data set that was the primary source for estimates. Our comparisons of R&D efforts among advanced industrial nations use estimates derived predominantly from data put out by the Organization for Economic Cooperation and Development (OECD). Data on R&D efforts come from the biennial OECD surveys of R&D performance, funding, and personnel of member states. We rely primarily on this source for three reasons. First, the data for the different countries use reasonably comparable standards of measurement.[5] The OECD secretariat translates individual country data into similar concepts of R&D, comparable units of deflated values, similar standard industrial classification breakdowns, comparable classes of R&D performance and funding. (That comparability is far from complete; it is less good the less aggregate the phenomena being estimated.) Second, the OECD figures present comprehensive coverage of R&D performance of advanced industrial nations with a market orientation and thereby include all important international economic competitors of U.S. firms. Third, these data represent a reasonably long time period, especially the period during which the U.S. relative international economic position has declined. These series span the period from 1963–64 through 1979–80.

Estimates of economic activity used to standardize R&D spending across countries and sectors of different sizes by translating it to a proportion of some measure of economic size also come largely from OECD sources. Wherever estimates are expressed in terms of a single currency at constant prices, we adopt the OECD convention of using as a base 1975 prices and 1975 exchange rates in terms of U.S. dollars.

Thirteen countries are included in our discussion. We incorporate all the large advanced industrial nations, six by our division: United States, France, Germany, Italy, Japan, and United Kingdom. Small countries include Belgium, Canada, Denmark, Netherlands, Norway, Sweden, and Switzerland. These countries cover most of the European Economic Community, Scandinavia, and the important international competitors of the United States for industrial products, especially for high technology goods and services.

Despite all the advantages of the OECD data, a number of its shortcomings and limitations should be cited. First, there are major differences among the nations in the measurement of R&D inputs. Most important, in academic research, U.S. estimates cover only funding specifically earmarked for research projects in the natural and social sciences. Other countries, in addition to specific project support, apportion a fraction of all university faculty salaries to research and include humanities as a part of academic research and development activity. Second, with regard to plant and equipment, U.S. estimates reflect current-year expenditures, whereas estimates for other countries include estimated depreciation. Third, industry breakdowns of enterprise R&D represent the main product class of the firm surveyed and not the product line associated with the R&D activity. National Science Foundation data on industry research and development performance are classified by product line as well as the SIC of the main product of the firm. Fourth, this paper develops its estimates from the uncorrected submissions by the OECD member governments in the biennial surveys. In many cases, governments have made corrections to these data in subsequent years as the capabilities for collecting R&D data have improved among member states. These corrected data have recently been compiled into a consistent data set by the OECD secretariat, but the tapes have not as yet been made available to member countries.

Total Research and Development

Total national R&D efforts may be compared across countries in two ways: relative to a broad-based indicator of economic activity, or in absolute magnitudes and changes in these magnitudes as measured by a given set of prices and exchange rates. Most comparisons of R&D efforts with those of other advanced industrial nations cite the ratio of R&D to gross national product or gross domestic product over a period of years. This method of comparison has a serious shortcoming. It is quite possible for one nation to experience a high rate of real growth of R&D and for the real R&D spending of another nation to be constant while both will show similar ratios (such is the situation, in fact, for Japan and the United Kingdom in recent years). It is quite obvious that the scientific and technological capabilities of the first nation are likely to progress relative to the second nation under these circumstances. Besides, as Denison (1977: 123) so aptly asks, "[j]ust because the size of the economy is, say, twice as big, does it take twice as much R&D to obtain the same annual productivity gain?"

Comparison of absolute magnitudes of R&D spending overcomes such difficulties. The method adopted by the OECD in this situation has been to deflate R&D expenditures by the 1975 gross domestic product price deflator and to convert these estimates into dollars using 1975 exchange rates. This procedure permits a rough comparison of the size R&D efforts of a single advanced industrial country in relation to all other advanced industrial countries for different points in time. In terms of national currencies, the deflated estimates permit comparison of the rates of change in the R&D efforts of the different nations between different points in time. We were particularly interested in comparing the average annual rates of change of R&D efforts (as measured by expenditures in constant prices) for the periods 1963–64 to 1972 and 1972 to 1979–80, in order to get a tentative picture of whether or not growth of R&D investment was affected by the adverse macroeconomic environment among advanced industrial nations during the post-energy crisis years. However, the use of deflated values of R&D as indexes of "real" magnitudes also has its limitations because of the deficiencies of price indexes as deflators for R&D, which presents special output measurement problems.

Percentage of R&D in Gross Domestic Product.   Figure 6-1A presents the ratio of R&D expenditures to GDP for the six large advanced industrial nations for the period 1963–64 through 1979–80. Figure 6–1B presents similar ratios over the same time for the small advanced countries. These ratios provide little information about the patterns of R&D spending or their effects on economic growth. There is no obvious relationship between the proportion of its output a nation devotes to R&D and the productivity growth rate. The United States, United Kingdom, and Sweden are large R&D spenders but have modest long-term productivity growth rates. Italy and Norway are modest R&D spenders but have relatively high productivity growth rates. In addition, the economic size of a nation, as measured by total gross domestic product or by population is not necessarily a factor in determining the proportion of economic output spent for R&D.

For the large countries, Figure 6-1A shows that since 1974 R&D expenditures have increased at about the same rate as gross domestic product. In

Figure 6-1A. R&D as a Percentage of Gross Domestic Product for Six Large Industrial Nations, 1963-80.

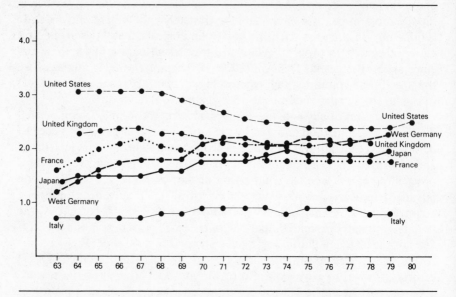

Source: Data source 19:7-9, 96-98 (listed at the back of the paper).

addition, except for Italy, the share of gross domestic product devoted to R&D falls within a narrow range of values ranging from 1.8 to 1.9 percent for France to 2.4 to 2.5 percent for the United States (which spends relatively large amounts for defense and space R&D). During the period 1963-64 through 1972-73, these countries have dissimilar patterns of growth of R&D spending relative to gross domestic product. Figure 6-1A shows that in Germany, Italy, and Japan, R&D spending grew more rapidly than gross domestic product. In France and the United Kingdom, they increased at about the same rate. Only in the United States did R&D spending increase more slowly than the gross domestic product.

Figure 6-1B shows a more diverse pattern of R&D spending relative to the gross domestic product for small countries. These estimates do indicate that in a large number of instances small advanced industrial countries expend as large a portion of their gross domestic product for R&D as do the high-spending advanced industrial large countries. Patterns of growth of R&D relative to gross domestic product also have differed more among the small nations. For example, these countries have the only case—the Netherlands—where R&D grew more slowly than gross domestic product throughout the 1970s. In addition, for three small countries—Belgium,

Figure 6-1B.   R&D as a Percentage of Gross Domestic
Product for Seven Small Industrial Nations, 1963-80.

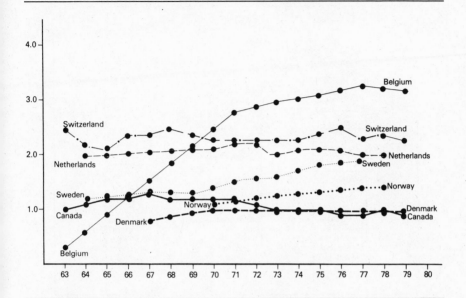

Source: Data source 19:7-9, 96-98 (listed at the back of the paper).

Norway, and Sweden—the percentage has been increasing during the 1970
to 1980 period.

Levels and Growth of R&D in Constant Prices.   Viewing the R&D efforts
of advanced industrial countries in terms of absolute levels, as measured in
constant prices, provides different information. Figure 6-2 shows first, that
the R&D efforts of the advanced industrial nations increased by about one-
third from 1969 to 1979. Second, during this period, the United States spent
about as much on R&D as all other twelve industrial nations combined. The
U.S. share did decline substantially from 1969 to 1975 but seems to have
stabilized since then. As a result, the United States still dominates in the
R&D activities of the advanced industrial nations. Third, German and
Japanese R&D efforts increased substantially relative to those of the United
States during the 1969 to 1975 period, but they gained little ground from
1975 through 1979. These estimates also indicate that the United Kingdom
and France have fallen far behind in R&D relative to Germany and Japan.
Whereas France, Germany, Japan, and the United Kingdom spent about
the same amounts on R&D at the end of the 1960s, by the end of the 1970s
Germany and Japan had moved far ahead as R&D performers. The changing

Figure 6-2.   Total R&D for Thirteen Industrial Nations in Terms of 1975 Prices and Dollars, 1969, 1975, 1979.

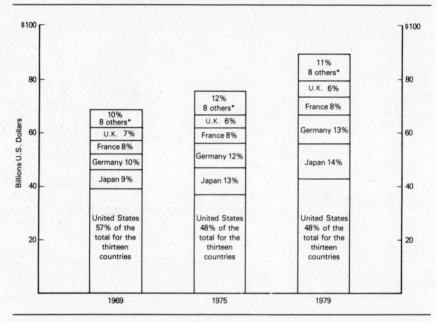

*Other countries are: Belgium, Canada, Denmark, Italy, Netherlands, Norway, Sweden, and Switzerland.

Note: Interpolations were done for the following: 1969—United States, Denmark, and Norway; 1975—Denmark; 1979—Netherlands, Norway, and United Kingdom.

Source: Data sources 19:7-9, 92; 21:82 (listed at the back of the paper).

status of the four countries is even more striking if one begins with 1963–64, when France and the United Kingdom had substantially higher levels of R&D activity than Japan. Figure 6–3, which traces the levels of real R&D spending for each country from 1963 through the end of the 1970s, highlights this change in the status among these countries. This finding contrasts sharply with the impression given by the approach that looks at R&D spending relative to gross domestic product.

The estimates presented in Figures 6–2 and 6–3 highlight the dominating influence of five countries in R&D activities. Despite the changing positions among them between 1969 and 1979, the United States, Japan, Germany, France, and the United Kingdom had 90 percent of the R&D efforts of the thirteen advanced industrial nations both at the beginning and at the end of the 1970s. The top three spenders—United States, Germany, Japan—of the

Figure 6-3. Annual R&D for Thirteen Industrial Nations in 1975 Prices and Dollars, 1963-80.

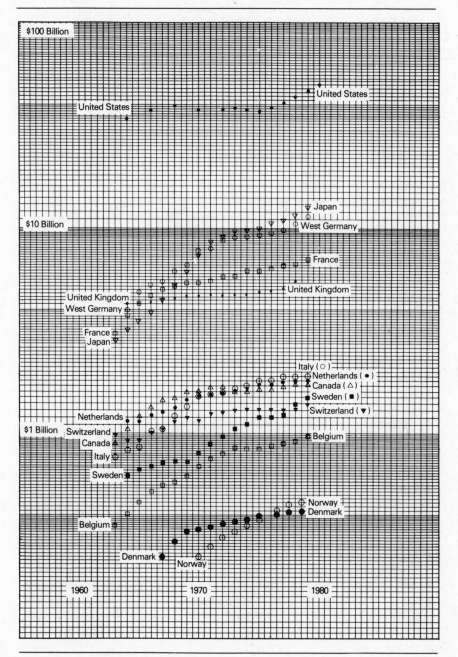

Sources: Data sources 19:7-9, 92; 21:82 (listed at the back of the paper).

thirteen advanced industrial nations increased their share of R&D expenditures from 71 percent in 1969 to 75 percent in 1979.

Some National Patterns of R&D

Looking at the major sources of funding and the allocation of funds between research activities and development may provide some additional insights about the broad patterns of R&D across the advanced industrial nations. Here the data are sketchy but permit a rough comparison across the large advanced nations and for selected small nations for the 1963–64 to 1980 period.

Funds for R&D come predominantly from two sources: government and business enterprises. It is generally acknowledged that government funding of R&D is intended to focus on such broad social objectives as advancement of knowledge, health, and defense. In contrast, enterprises fund R&D to advance the interests of the business. This difference in interests has an important influence on the projects selected and, in turn, on the patterns of scientific and technological advances and their economic consequences. As a result, a major change in the distribution of R&D funding between government and business would tend to result in a shift in the source of decisions for the nation's technological development and the characteristics of technological advance. Analogously, funds for research are for the purpose of advancing scientific knowledge, while funds for development are for the purpose of translating scientific knowledge into products, processes, or services. Allocation of funds to one activity or another involves different projects, possibly different approaches to technological advancement, and different levels of responsibility.

Government and Business as a Source of Funds.   The data suggest that government funds tend to represent on the order of 50 percent of the national R&D spending among major industrial countries. Table 6–1 shows that by the end of the 1970s, government provided 45 to 53 percent of the funds for R&D in five of the six large nations. Only for Japan did government account for a substantially smaller share—25 to 30 percent. Also, during the period 1963–64 to 1980, for two of these nations—France and the United States—government funding was a declining share of the R&D expenditures. Table 6–2 presents the scattered estimates of the percentage of national R&D expenditures funded by government that we could compute for the small advanced industrial nations for the 1970s. These estimates indicate that for six of the seven small nations, government provided between 43 to 63 percent of the funds for R&D during selected years in the 1970s. In contrast, the government in Switzerland accounted for only 14 to 21 percent of the national spending on R&D.

Table 6-1. Percentage of Government Funds in National R&D Expenditures for Six Large Industrial Countries, 1963-81.

Year	France	West Germany	Italy	Japan	United Kingdom	United States
1963	65.8	48.8	43.7	27.8	—	65.7
1964	64.5	48.6	—	29.5	53.7	66.5
1965	66.2	47.4	42.1	30.8	—	64.9
1966	66.2	47.7	—	32.0	49.1	63.9
1967	67.3	49.2	40.9	30.3	48.8	62.2
1968	66.6	47.0	41.4	28.2	48.6	60.7
1969	63.1	46.3	43.7	26.3	50.6	58.1
1970	60.1	46.6	42.7	25.2	—	56.9
1971	59.2	48.3	41.1	27.1	—	56.1
1972	58.6	49.9	41.7	27.0	48.7	55.4
1973	57.7	50.6	45.1	26.4	—	53.3
1974	57.4	50.9	41.6	26.5	—	51.2
1975	55.2	48.8	43.1	27.5	51.9	51.4
1976	52.8	47.8	45.6	27.2	—	50.9
1977	52.7	45.5	47.8	27.4	—	50.5
1978	—	46.1	—	28.0	47.0	49.8
1979	—	48.0	—	—	—	49.0
1980	—	47.8	—	—	—	47.9
1981	—	—	—	—	—	47.3

Sources: Data sources 13:57; 18; 19:7-9 (listed at the back of the paper).

The marked decline of the government in national R&D in France and the United States suggests an increased importance of commercial technological projects to technological advance in both countries in recent years. For example, frequently cited examples of important U.S. commercial

Table 6-2. Percentage of Government Funds in National R&D Expenditures for Seven Small Industrial Countries, 1970-79, Selected Years.

Year	Belgium	Canada	Denmark	Netherlands	Norway	Sweden	Switzerland
1970	—	52.3	53.4	44.4	59.4	—	13.9
1971	51.8	51.3	—	44.5	—	41.2	14.2
1972	—	53.0	—	44.4	63.6	—	14.9
1973	47.0	53.5	54.1	44.6	—	46.8	15.5
1974	—	50.7	—	43.3	61.7	—	16.7
1975	—	47.5	—	44.9	59.1	43.3	17.4
1976	—	47.7	—	45.6	—	—	18.0
1977	—	47.5	—	47.0	61.7	—	21.1
1978	—	47.9	—	—	62.7	—	—
1979	—	47.9	—	—	—	—	—

Sources: Data sources 1:42-3; 4:24; 7:28; 8:22; 11:34; 12:44; 13a-1; 18; 19:7-9 (listed at the back of the paper).

technological contributions from military and space R&D usually date from the 1950s and 1960s when government funding dominated U.S. R&D activities. The experience of more recent years is for military technology to build on commercial technological developments.

Table 6-3, which presents the share of business funding in national R&D expenditures, shows the expected related trends. For France, business funds increase from about 30 percent to over 40 percent of R&D expenditures, and for the United States they increase from about 30 percent to nearly 50 percent.

These findings are reinforced by the estimates in Table 6-4 of the growth in constant prices of government and business R&D funding for the six large advanced industrial nations for the periods 1964–72 and 1972–80. These data indicate that the lack of real R&D growth in the United States in the late 1960s through early 1970s may be attributed predominantly to the real decline in government-funded R&D activity. Interestingly, the acceleration of U.S. R&D spending in the 1970s can also be thought of as due to a change in the rate of growth of government R&D funding, despite the continuing decline in the government funding role in national R&D. Government

Table 6-3. Percentage of Business Funds in National R&D Expenditures for Six Large Industrial Countries, 1963–81.

Year	France	West Germany	Italy	Japan	United Kingdom	United States
1963	31.3	49.6	53.3	–	–	32.0
1964	32.6	49.9	–	–	41.2	31.2
1965	30.2	51.3	50.2	–	44.3	32.7
1966	28.1	50.9	–	–	44.3	35.5
1967	29.1	49.4	48.2	–	44.9	36.2
1968	30.7	51.7	49.3	–	43.0	39.6
1969	32.4	52.2	48.9	–	–	39.1
1970	36.5	51.4	51.2	66.8	–	40.1
1971	36.8	48.5	52.2	66.8	43.5	40.6
1972	37.3	47.7	52.3	66.8	–	41.2
1973	38.3	47.0	49.3	67.3	–	43.4
1974	38.1	46.4	51.7	65.5	40.8	44.3
1975	39.1	47.9	51.0	65.5	–	46.0
1976	41.5	49.0	49.6	66.1	–	45.4
1977	41.1	50.9	47.3	65.5	44.2	46.9
1978	–	50.4	–	–	–	46.5
1979	–	48.7	–	–	–	47.3
1980	–	49.1	–	–	–	48.2
1981	–	–	–	–	–	49.0

Sources: Data sources 1:42–43; 4:24; 7:28; 8:22; 11:34; 12:44; 13:a-1; 18; 19:7-9 (listed at the back of the paper).

Table 6-4. Average Annual Real Growth of Business and Government-Funded R&D for Six Large Industrial Nations, 1964–72 and 1972–80 (percentage).

	Business-Funded		Government-Funded	
Countries	1964–72	1972–80ᶜ	1964–72	1972–80ᶜ
France	7.3	4.2	4.3	0.1
West Germany	9.1	3.0	10.0	2.1
Italyᵃ	10.5	7.4	9.6	12.6
Japanᵇ	13.7	4.7	12.5	5.7
United Kingdom	1.7	3.1	-0.2	2.2
United States	4.8	4.4	-1.0	3.2

[a]1965–72.
[b]1963–72.
[c]1980 or latest year available. France: 1977, Italy: 1977, Japan: 1978, United Kingdom: 1978.

Sources: Data sources 13:57F; 18; 21:82 (listed at the back of the paper).

funding moved from a period of (slight) real decline to a period of real growth. But for both the periods, business funded R&D grew at close to the same annual rate. Thus the rate of growth of the R&D spent by business and government combined increased. Also, importantly, the data in Table 6–4 show that since 1972, the growth of U.S. business-funded R&D has compared favorably with the growth rates of business R&D funding of other major competing large industrial nations. This stems from the deceleration of R&D growth of business-funded R&D among most of the other nations. These observations are contrary to the often heard assertions about a slowdown of U.S. business-funded R&D and a lag in its growth compared to the other major industrial nations during the 1970s. Also, while the growth of government-funded R&D slowed for a number of countries, it accelerated for the United States.

A look at another dimension reenforces the impression of a strong U.S. business commitment to R&D. From the perspective of the share of net output devoted to R&D and the ratio of R&D expenditures to gross fixed capital formation, the allocation of funds by U.S. manufacturing firms to R&D is higher than for comparable firms in other countries. About 95 percent of business-funded R&D comes from the manufacturing sector. Figures 6–4A and 6–4B show business-funded R&D as a percentage of manufacturing gross domestic product for large and small countries, respectively, during the 1964 through 1978 period. These data show that U.S. manufacturing firms devote over 4 percent of their gross domestic product to R&D. Moreover, this ratio has been increasing over time. Only Japan and Sweden have begun to approach this 4 percent level. In contrast to the increasing R&D commitment of these countries, firms in Canada and the Netherlands have been directing a declining share of their factor inputs to R&D.

Figure 6-4A. Business-Funded R&D as a Percentage of Manufacturing Gross Domestic Product for Five Large Nations, 1964-78.

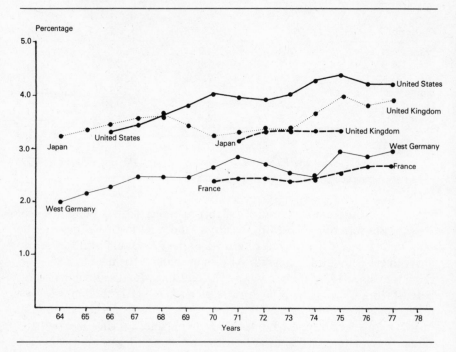

Source: Data sources 1; 4; 7; 8; 11; 12; 13; 20 (listed at the back of the paper).

Figure 6-5 presents business-funded R&D as a percentage of gross fixed capital formation for the manufacturing sector for the few nations where the data permit. These estimates indicate that for the United States, business expenditures for R&D fluctuated between 40 to 50 percent of expenditures for gross fixed capital formation by the manufacturing sector. The shares for the most other nations for which data were available ranged between 10 and 30 percent. The relatively high ratio for the United States cannot be wholly attributed, especially in recent years, to a lower rate of plant and equipment investment. Since the mid 1970s, the U.S. ratio of gross fixed capital formation to gross domestic product in the manufacturing sector has approached that of the European OECD nations. During the 1960s and early 1970s U.S. gross fixed capital formation in manufacturing did represent a much lower share of gross domestic product in manufacturing than for other OECD countries.

Figure 6-4B. Business-Funded R&D as a Percentage of Manufacturing Gross Domestic Product for Five Small Nations, 1963-78.

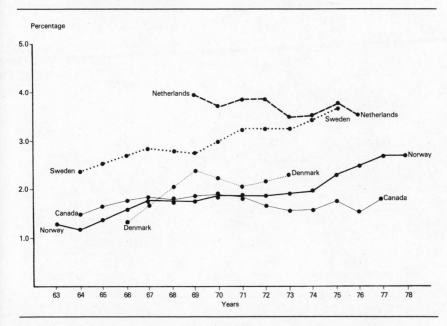

Sources: Data sources 1; 4; 7; 8; 11; 12; 13; 20 (listed at the back of the paper).

Research vs. Development Objectives. Time series data showing the breakdown of R&D expenditures between research activities and development over the period 1963 through 1980 also have limitations. Data are not available for Belgium, Germany, and Switzerland; for other countries data exist only for a few years during the period. In addition, special caution must be exercised in making these comparisons across nations because of major differences in the interpretation and measurement of research across countries. For example, in Europe and Japan a portion of the national expenditures for all university faculty salaries is apportioned to research. In the United States, only direct government and business funding for research projects at universities is incorporated into research expenditures.

With these limitations in mind, we present in Table 6-5 the average of the percentage of R&D apportioned to research for each of the advanced industrial nations during the 1967-77 period. Averages are presented for total national research, business-funded research, and government-funded research. (Averages seemed a good approach, given the absence of obvious

Figure 6-5.   Business-Funded R&D as a Percentage of
Gross Fixed Capital Formation in Manufacturing for
Seven Industrial Nations, 1963-78.

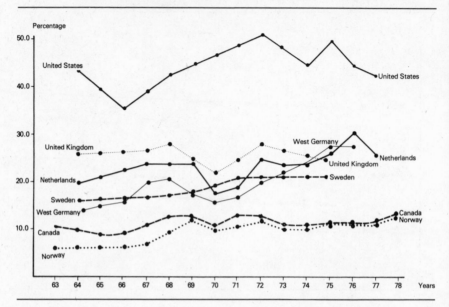

Sources: Data sources 1; 4; 7; 8; 11; 12; 13; 20 (lsited at the back of the paper).

trends in the data, the relatively small annual fluctuation, and the missing data points.)

These data show that in all countries the percentage of government-funded R&D devoted to research substantially exceeds the percentage of business-funded R&D spent for research. In fact, with the exception of the United States, the governments of all other countries apportioned 50 to 80 percent of their R&D funds for research. The figure for the United States was somewhat below 50 percent, and the figure for the United Kingdom is slightly above. In contrast, business spent only 20 to 40 percent of its R&D budget for basic and applied research. This result probably reflects the economic and profit orientation of business R&D in contrast to the social orientation of government R&D with its concomitant greater interest in advancing and disseminating scientific knowledge. Table 6-5 also indicates that Japan, Sweden, United Kingdom, and the United States devote a substantially smaller fraction of their R&D funds to research than do the other countries. For these four countries research is a bit over 35 percent of R&D as compared to 50 to 60 percent for the other countries. This finding

Table 6-5.   Research as a Percentage of R&D Expenditures for Ten Industrial Countries, Average for Available Years between 1967-77.

	Total Research as a Percentage of Total R&D	Business-Funded Research as a Percentage of Business-Funded R&D	Government-Funded Research as a Percentage of Government-Funded R&D
Large countries			
France	53.5	36.7	64.1
Italy	60.0	41.5	82.1
Japan	44.8	30.8	57.1
United Kingdom	36.1	25.9	53.0
United States	37.5	21.8	47.6
Small countries			
Canada	60.0	31.3	74.5
Denmark	48.9	18.6	69.9
Netherlands	51.9	30.0	74.4
Norway	54.3	30.7	61.0
Sweden	36.6	15.3	66.1

Sources: Data sources 4:52, 58-59; 7:72-73; 8:42-44; 11:70-71; 12:74-77; 13:b-d, f-j; 1 (listed at the back of the paper).

does not square with the popular view of Japan having a longer-term perspective for R&D as compared to other industrial nations. Advances in scientific (as opposed to technological) knowledge often require additional investments in time as well as resources in order to be exploited for economic ends.

A further breakdown of R&D to basic research expenditures provides an additional perspective. Recall that basic research involves ". . . investigations for the advancement of new scientific knowledge not having specific commercial objectives." The bulk of this research is conducted by universities and scientific research institutes. Table 6-6 presents the percentage of R&D approtioned to basic research for selected years during the 1964-79 period for eight industrial nations. These data indicate that six nations increased the proportion of their R&D for basic research in the 1967-79 period: France, Germany, Italy, Japan, Sweden, and the United Kingdom. The United States in the 1970s maintained basic research as a rather stable fraction of R&D. This pattern suggests that a strengthening of the scientific position of Europe and Japan relative to the United States probably occurred during the 1970s. To our knowledge, the increase in scientific capability has not as yet been examined in a systematic fashion to check our whether the output data provide results consistent with these input data.

Table 6-6.   Basic Research as a Percentage of R&D for Eight
Industrial Nations, 1967-77, Selected Years.

Year	France	West Germany	Italy	Japan	Norway	Sweden	United Kingdom	United States
1967	17.7	14.7	10.3	–	–	–	9.2	–
1968	–	–	–	–	–	–	9.3	–
1969	17.8	15.5	19.5	7.7	–	12.7	–	–
1970	–	–	–	–	14.7	–	–	–
1971	17.8	19.6	14.0	7.7	–	15.4	–	–
1972	–	–	–	–	–	–	–	–
1973	21.9	23.9	–	6.0	–	18.5	–	11.9
1974	–	–	–	–	–	–	–	–
1975	21.4	22.3	18.0	11.2	22.6	19.3	14.1	12.2
1976	–	–	–	–	–	–	–	–
1977	21.1	21.7	17.9	15.1	19.4	18.8	–	12.2
1978	–	–	–	–	–	–	–	–

Sources: Data sources 4:48-49; 7:64-65; 8:34-35; 11:64-65, 72; 12:72-79; 13:b-d, f-j, 1;
19:7-9 (listed at the back of the paper).

Distributions of R&D over Industries
and Social Objectives

Debates about governmental actions that influence R&D lead to comparisons of how different nations apportion R&D funds among industries or of categories of government programs. How the R&D funds of a nation are allocated among industries reflects which industries are favored for growth or which get government support in an effort to retard decline. Looking at a breakdown of government R&D budgets in terms of a common classification of social objectives provides some information about the similarities and differences among nations in the use of R&D for public policy purposes.

The available data are spotty; we attempt a summary comparison by pooling observations over the 1963-64 through 1979 time period. At least a tentative picture emerges of how nations apportion their total and industry R&D funds among classes of industries, and of how they allocate their government R&D budgets in terms of a standard classification of social objectives. In pooling we compute the average percentage over the period (for the available observations) that R&D in an industry (or devoted to a social objective) represents of total R&D funds. Two conditions made this method a responsible approach for measuring the data gaps: (1) Annual percentages for individual industries or objectives fluctuate within a relatively narrow range where there are observations; and (2) with just a few exceptions, we could not identify trends in the percentage allocations during the period of observation.

Industrial Composition of Business R&D.   Do advanced industrial nations concentrate their R&D activities in the same few industries? Studies of international trade or competitiveness in manufactures of industrial nations usually presume that R&D intensive industries for advanced industrial countries are the same as in the United States. On the other hand, officials of small industrial countries sometimes state that small countries apportion their R&D activities differently than do large countries. Industrial R&D activities in the United States tend to be concentrated in five broad sectors: electric and electronic equipment and components, chemicals and drugs, aircraft, automobiles, and machinery. The industrial breakdown of R&D activities and funding data of the OECD for the 1963–64 through 1979 period should provide a tentative overview.

Table 6–7 presents for each of nine industrial nations the average percentage share of an industry for 1963–64 through 1977 in the nation's total manufacturing R&D activity. The estimates are presented only for the five industries usually considered to be the major U.S. R&D performing industries. Table 6-8 presents for the same countries and industries the average percentage share of business-funded R&D for an industry in the manufacturing sector. The important difference between the estimates of the two tables is that Table 6–7 includes government R&D funds provided to industries; for countries where government is an important source of R&D funds, the R&D distribution over industries might be different from the distribution of industry-funded R&D alone.

The estimates of both tables indicate that the five industries account for 60 percent or more of the manufacturing R&D for all advanced industrial countries where data are available for all five industrial groups. In fact, for most countries these five industries conduct 75 percent or more of either total- or business-funded R&D in the manufacturing sector. But within this class of industries there are major differences in distributions. For example, for the United States, if one looks at total manufacturing sector R&D, aircraft accounts for about 30 percent of the average share of the manufacturing R&D during the 1963–64 through 1979 period. (The U.S. aircraft industry was one of the few industries with a trend pattern during this period. Its share declined.) Excluding government funding, aircraft's share of business-funded manufacturing R&D becomes a more modest 10 percent. A similar situation holds in France and the United Kingdom, where the aircraft industry accounts for about 25 percent of industrial R&D for government funding of industrial R&D. For business funding of industrial R&D, the aircraft industry accounts for only 5 to 10 percent of manufacturing R&D.

Looking across countries, one striking feature is the dominance of chemicals and drugs in the R&D of Germany's manufacture sector, since with or without government funding this industry accounts for about 30 percent of its manufacturing R&D. In Italy and Japan this industry tends to

Table 6-7. R&D in Five Industries as a Percentage of Total Manufacturing R&D in Nine Nations, Average for Available Years between 1963–64 to 1977.

	Large Nations						Small Nations		
	France	West Germany	Italy	Japan	United Kingdom	United States	Canada	Norway	Sweden
Electrical and electronic equipment and components	24.8	26.8	19.4	24.9	23.0	22.1	24.3	23.2	22.3
Chemicals and drugs	13.9	27.2	22.7	21.1	13.4	10.2	12.2	13.1	9.4
Aircraft and missiles	22.2	7.4	—	NA	25.3	29.3	11.7	NA	NA
Motor vehicles	8.9	12.1	24.4[a]	10.4	6.7	10.0	2.1	NA	NA
Machinery	5.6	12.3	3.3	7.2	6.9	10.4	6.2	9.4	15.6
Total	75.4	85.8	69.8	(63.6)	75.3	82.0	56.5	—	—

[a]Includes shipbuilding, aircraft, and other transportation.

Sources: Data sources 1:98–99; 2:21–22; 5:26–27; 9:47–49; 12:146–47; 13:b, d–g; i, j, 1 (listed at the back of the paper.)

Table 6–8. R&D in Five Industries as a Percentage of Business-Funded Manufacturing R&D in Nine Nations, Average for Available Years between 1963-64 to 1977.

	Large Nations						Small Nations		
	France	West Germany	Italy	Japan	United Kingdom	United States	Canada	Norway	Sweden
Electrical and electronic equipment and components	21.7	28.2	17.8	25.1	21.5	19.0	23.1	26.0	24.3
Chemicals and drugs	18.6	32.5	25.8	21.9	19.0	16.1	15.0	17.1	12.3
Aircraft and missiles	9.4	1.1	NA	NA	4.1	9.7	8.5	NA	NA
Motor vehicles	12.0	14.8	32.3[a]	10.3	10.7	14.5	3.0	6.2	NA
Machinery	6.9	11.6	3.1	7.2	9.7	14.4	5.4	10.3	19.0
Total	68.6	88.2	(79.0)	(64.5)	65.0	73.7	55.0	(59.6)	—

[a]Includes shipbuilding, aircraft, and other transportation.

Sources: Data sources 1:100–01; 2:23; 5:28–29; 12:148–54; 13:b, d–g, i, j, 1 (listed at the back of the paper).

account for 20 to 30 percent of manufacturing R&D, a higher fraction than for the other countries. One noticeable similarity among these industrial nations is the heavy concentration of R&D activity in electric and electronic equipment and components. In all cases this industry grouping accounts for 20 to 30 percent of the manufacturing R&D. In addition, other data show that for all these countries this industry grouping tends to absorb 20 to 25 percent of the government R&D funds obtained by the manufacturing sector. Finally, there is no obvious pattern of industrial distribution of R&D spending that differentiates small countries from large countries.

These findings suggest there is a tendency among industrial countries for firms to pursue technological opportunities or at least to distribute R&D by industry, along broadly similar lines. Large-scale government funding focused on an industry can have an important impact on the composition of industrial R&D activity (e.g., aircraft in France, the United Kingdom, and the United States). Such a large-scale intrusion probably enhances the international competitive position of these nations for this sector. However, some studies suggest this focused government attention may potentially detract from the competitive position of other high technology sectors of these countries by diverting scientific and engineering talent and capital investment (Melman 1974; Pavitt and Soete 1980). With regard to matters of scale, the data suggest that nations differing greatly in economic size and commitment of resources to R&D tend to diversify their R&D across industries in about the same proportions. It is obvious that vast differences exist among nations in the magnitude of resources each commits to R&D; to succeed, the firms in countries with relatively small R&D efforts probably pursue a different strategy for technological development and exploitation than do firms in countries when the industry makes large R&D investments. This phenomenon has been discussed informally but has not been subject to systematic study.

Government R&D in Terms of Social Objectives.   Governments of various nations allocate their R&D budgets among different objectives in different ways, as has been mentioned in discussions of industrial policy and of science and technology policy. For example, a point raised frequently in the United States is that other countries allocate a larger proportion of government R&D funds for industrial development purposes. On the other hand, foreign officials frequently refer to the high proportion of U.S. government R&D funds assigned to defense objectives and the presumed benefits to industrial technology that U.S. firms derive therefrom. They also cite the high priority that the U.S. government gives to agricultural R&D and the economic advantages that U.S. farming gains as a result.

The only attempt we know of to compare systematically how governments of industrial countries allocate their R&D budgets among social objectives is an OECD study completed in 1975 (OECD 1975). Since then the classification and collection of data about government R&D funding have been changed and substantially improved. We shall look at these recent data to see what they tell us about the patterns of government R&D funding among social objectives for advanced industrial nations. Nine of the thirteen classes of the OECD objectives for government R&D funding will be presented: agriculture, forestry and fishing; industrial development; energy; transport and telecommunications; environment protection; health; advancement of knowledge; civil space; defense. These classes were singled out because they are the major types of government R&D spending focused on in policy discussions. We collapsed the three remaining classes of objectives into an "other" category: urban and rural planning; social development and services; earth and atmosphere.

Table 6–9 presents the distribution in percentage terms of government-funded R&D for the thirteen advanced industrial nations for these nine classes of social objectives. The percentage figures are the average values for 1975 and 1979, the only two years for which we had the data. These estimates show that, except for Canada, two social objectives account for more than half of the government-funded R&D in advanced industrial nations. In the United States and the United Kingdom, "defense" makes up about 50 percent of the use of government R&D funds. In seven countries—Belgium, Denmark, Germany, Italy, Japan, Netherlands, and Norway—45 to 55 percent of government expenditures are for the "advancement in knowledge." For France, Sweden, and Switzerland, "defense" and "advancement in knowledge" combined comprise 50 to 60 percent of the use of government funds. For the most part, the other categories of social objectives usually absorb 2 to 10 percent of the government R&D funds. In other words, for eleven of the social objectives, each accounts for only a small fraction of the government R&D budget.

Except for the United States and Switzerland, in countries where "advancement of knowledge" absorbs a large percentage of government R&D funds, the category includes general university funds. These general university funds constitute a substantial fraction, somewhere between 25 to 40 percent of government expenditures for the general operations of universities.[6] "General university funds" includes faculty salaries, cost of supplies, library, and general university overheads. Incorporating these funds into the government R&D budget makes an enormous difference in its size and in the picture of the distribution of government funds among the various social objectives, other than "advancement of knowledge." Prior to 1975, during the period when OECD incorporated only government expenditures specifically designated for R&D, "advancement in knowledge" absorbed 5 to 10 percent of the government R&D funds for most countries and at most 15 to 20 percent for three countries. For the most part, the

Table 6-9. Distribution of Government R&D Funding among Nine Social Objectives for Thirteen Industrial Nations, Average for 1975 and 1979.

A. Large Countries	France	West Germany	Italy	Japan[a]	United Kingdom	United States
Agriculture	3.9	1.9	4.0	13.5	4.0	2.2
Industrial growth	12.1	8.5	10.1	6.2	8.3	0.4
Energy	8.3	12.1	20.2	8.5	7.0	9.9
Transportation and telecommunication	2.9	1.7	0.5	1.5	0.7	3.1
Environment	1.0	1.5	0.9	1.4	0.8	2.0
Health	4.2	3.7	4.0	3.1	2.3	11.6
Advancement of knowledge	24.1	47.0	43.5	55.3	20.0	3.9
Civil space	5.1	4.1	9.2	5.3	2.3	13.4
Defense	32.5	11.4	3.3	2.3	50.9	48.9
Other	5.9	8.3	4.6	3.0	4.0	5.0

B. Small Countries	Belgium	Canada	Denmark	Netherlands	Norway	Sweden	Switz
Agriculture	4.0	16.9	8.7	8.7	8.3	2.2	10
Industrial growth	11.5	17.1	11.6	5.3	11.7	6.7	4
Energy	12.3	11.8	5.6	3.3	4.0	7.6	10
Transportation and telecommunication	1.2	4.2	0.5	1.8	4.4	3.1	6
Environment	8.3	2.4	2.0	5.9	2.7	1.5	3
Health		8.4	8.5		5.5	7.1	2
Advancement of knowledge	47.8	15.6	48.1	56.6	48.9	37.3	36
Civil space	3.2	3.8	3.9	3.1	0.5	2.3	5
Defense	0.4	7.5	0.6	3.3	5.3	21.8	16
Other	11.4	14.4	10.1	12.4	8.8	10.5	3

[a]1974–75 only available.

Sources: Data sources 14; 16; 17 (listed at the back of the paper). Canada's distribution sums t○ than 100 percent because "civil space" is not broken out in 1979; we show the 1975 figure.

proportion of expenditures on "advancement of knowledge" were not much than the U.S. figure of about 4 percent. Eliminating general university funds government R&D spending would then reduce substantially the size of govern▪ R&D for the seven countries that include them under "advancement of knowled The reduction could be on the order of 30 to 40 percent for these countries. Als○ government R&D funds estimates for the other OECD data would be more parable to what is included for the United States.

It also may be instructive to see the average distribution of government R&D f for 1975 and 1977 among the social nine objectives if general university funds eliminated from "advancement of knowledge expenditures." Such estimates

Table 6-10. Distribution of Government R&D Funding Net of General University Funds among Nine Social Objectives for Ten Industrial Nations, Average for 1975 and 1979.

Large Countries	France	West Germany	Italy	Japan	United Kingdom	United States
Agriculture	4.3	3.3	5.4	30.2	4.8	2.2
Industrial growth	13.6	14.6	13.7	13.9	10.0	0.4
Energy	9.3	20.7	27.3	19.0	8.3	9.9
Transportation and communication	3.3	2.8	0.6	3.4	0.8	3.1
Environment	1.1	2.6	1.2	3.1	0.9	2.0
Health	4.7	6.3	5.4	6.9	2.8	11.6
Advancement of knowledge	14.5	8.8	23.4	0	4.2	3.9
Civil space	5.7	7.1	12.4	11.9	2.8	13.4
Defense	36.6	19.5	4.5	5.1	61.0	48.9
Other	6.6	14.3	6.2	6.7	4.7	5.0
B. Small Countries	Canada	Netherlands	Norway	Sweden		
Agriculture	18.2	17.5	14.0	3.3		
Industrial growth	18.4	10.6	19.7	10.2		
Energy	12.7	6.6	6.8	11.5		
Transportation and telecommunications	4.5	3.5	7.3	4.6		
Environment	2.5	11.8	4.5	2.3		
Health	9.1		9.3	10.8		
Advancement of knowledge	9.0	12.1	13.7	4.9		
Civil space	4.1	6.3	0.8	3.4		
Defense	8.0	6.7	8.9	33.1		
Other	15.5	25.1	14.9	15.9		

Sources: Data sources 16; 17 (listed lat the back of the paper). Canada's distribution sums to more than 100 percent because "civil space" is not broken out in 1979; we show the 1975 figure.

obtained by assuming that the average 1963-64 to 1972 share of expenditures for advancement of scientific knowledge (which excluded general university funds) in government R&D funding continued to prevail in the 1975-79 period. Under this assumption government funding of university R&D (as opposed to "general university funds") for other countries approximates the concept used by the United States. These estimates are presented in Table 6-10. With these estimates, it would appear that two nations in addition to the United States and the United Kingdom have their governments spend major shares of the remaining R&D budget for defense: France spends about 37 percent, and Sweden about 33 percent. In addition, industrial development absorbs a substantial portion—on the order of 10 to 20 percent—of the government R&D budgets for most other nations.

For the other classes of social objectives, there are some additional surprises. U.S. government funding of agricultural R&D is usually viewed as a major government R&D program. Yet agriculture represents only about 2 percent of U.S. government R&D budgets. With the revised estimates from eliminating general university funding, apparently the governments of all other advanced industrial nations devote a substantially higher proportion of their R&D funds to agriculture R&D. In a few cases (Canada, Japan, Netherlands, and Norway) agriculture accounts for over 10 percent of the remaining government R&D funds. Also, three countries—Germany, Italy and Japan—devote on the order of 20 percent of government R&D funds to energy R&D. This exceeds the relative effort to energy of the other nations.

GOVERNMENT TAX AND SPENDING POLICIES FOR R&D

More and more attention is being directed in science and technology policy debates to the use and contribution of government expenditures and tax incentives as measures to stimulate technical progress. Governments of all advanced industrial countries use tax and expenditure measures to encourage business R&D and technical progress. Though claims are made about policies and their effects in other industrialized countries, there actually exists little empirical information about the value and characteristics of these measures and their influence on business R&D and technical change.

Government Expenditures

Efforts by governments to help underwrite R&D for commercial purposes are widespread but have not been assessed systematically. Many are not included in national statistics as government expenditures for R&D. Examples are expenditures by European governments for the design and development of commercial jet aircraft and aircraft engines, U.S. government allowances for "independent research and development" (IR&D) under Defense Department and National Aeronautics and Space Agency contracts, and soft loans by the Japanese government to businesses for the development of certain products.

In addition, evidence of the effectiveness of government funding of R&D in industry for technological development leading to economic progress is not clearcut. As we saw earlier in this paper, investigations of the economic effects of government R&D performed in industry provide us with a confusing array of descriptive information. Usually they include some speculations about the factors influencing their findings but lack systematic assessment. In the end what we know is that the outcome of government funding of R&D in industry for technological development and economic growth depends on a host of factors: the role played by government officials in specifying the technology to be developed; the financial contribution of the firm to the technological development; the structure of the domestic market for the product; the use of the original product. It would take a number of pages to list the factors claimed to have a role. The role of government R&D spending at universities in promoting private industrial R&D spending is even less well studied.

Tax Incentives

Unlike the area of government expenditures, there has been a bit of progress for some countries in systematically cataloging and measuring tax incentives to encourage R&D. Prominent here is a recently completed survey by the National Science Foundation (1981) of corporate tax measures relating to business R&D spending among six industrial nations. It was prepared by Eileen Collins, who is responsible for work on tax policies for R&D in the Division of Policy Research and Analysis at NSF, in collaboration with Richard Hammer at Price Waterhouse and Company.

In summary, based on the NSF documentation to date, no country's corporate income tax code can be said to offer uniformly more favorable treatment for R&D activities. Individual features of one country's tax code can be identified as more favorable than another's, but the overall balance is not clear. To reach this conclusion, it is necessary to consider two aspects of the corporate tax code. One is a set of baseline provisions against which the treatment of business R&D can be compared. This baseline covers the corporation income tax rate structure and treatment of capital gains, and investment expenditures. The other aspect consists of the major provisions that directly relate to R&D activities (i.e., the tax treatment of R&D expenditures, venture capital investment in new technology-based firms, sale or license of technology and donations to and activities of nonprofit scientific organizations).

Regarding baseline provisions, highlights of the study's findings for the four major industrial countries (United States, France, Germany, Japan) include:

Rate Structure. All four countries have some form of differential rate structure. The simplest is Germany, where the tax rate is 56 percent on retained earnings and 36 percent on (the "pretax" amount of) distributed earnings. The Japanese rate structure is similar; the rate is 40 percent on retained earnings and 30 percent on income earmarked for dividends. In addition, there are lower rates on the first Y7 million (about $33,000) of small business income; retained earnings are taxed at 28 percent and income earmarked for dividends at 22 percent.

The U.S. top bracket rate is 46 percent, with graduated rates ranging from 17 percent on the first $25,000 of income to 40 percent on the fourth $25,000. The United States does not have a preferential rate for distributed earnings, but there is a preferential rate of 28 percent for net long-term capital gains. In France, the standard rate is 50 percent. For net long-term capital gains held in a reserve account, the rate is 15 percent. This amounts to a tax deferral rather than a tax reduction because if the gains are later distributed, an equilization tax is imposed to cover the difference between the capital gains 15 percent tax rate and the standard 50 percent rate.

Investment in Plant and Equipment. In all four countries, expenditures for plant and equipment may be deducted as depreciated allowances over the life of the asset. The basic depreciation method is straight-line. Declining-balance and other methods are also used, subject to rules specified by the tax code and government authorities. All four countries offer *special* tax incentives for particular investment objectives such as pollution abatement or regional development. Such special incentives are often in the form of special accelerated depreciation. Two countries offer a more *general* investment tax incentive. The United States provides a 10 pecent tax credit for investment in new equipment with a useful life of seven or more years (6.7 percent for five or six years, and 3.3 percent for three or four years). France provides an additional first-year tax deduction of 10 percent for fixed investment.

Regarding tax treatment of measures relating to R&D, highlights of the study's findings for the four major industrial countries include:

Expenditures for R&D. In all four countries, current R&D costs may be deducted in the year incurred; in the United States and Japan, a firm has an option to capitalize and amortize them over five or more years. In all four countries, capital costs of R&D are treated under the tax code's depreciation rules. In France and Japan, these include special treatment for plant or equipment used in R&D. In Japan, useful lives are regulated separately by the ministry of finance, which provides faster write-off. In France, a first-year deduction of 50 percent is allowed for the cost of buildings for R&D; the balance is written off over the remainder of useful life. The same treatment is available for R&D equipment and tools purchased by small companies. Japan also offers a special tax credit to firms which file a "blue return" (a device intended to set certain accounting standards). The credit is 20 percent of the excess in eligible R&D expenses above the amount in an earlier base period. Eligible expenses include current costs, depreciation on equipment, and overhead for R&D. This provision of Japan is similar to the United States under the 25 percent tax credit for increased R&D allowed under the Economic Recovery Tax Act (ERTA).

Venture Capital Investments in New Technology-Based Firms.   Only the United States and France offer any special treatment for venture capital investments in new techology-based firms. In the United States, corporations that meet the requirements for "regulated investment companies" (two common examples are mutual funds and "venture capital companies") can avoid income tax if all income is distributed to shareholders. Also, long-term capital gains distributed by the company are taxed as long-term capital gains (rather than as ordinary income) in the hands of shareholders. In France, business purchasers of shares in "qualified research companies" or "innovation finance companies" may deduct 50 percent of their cost in the year of acquisition.

Sale or License of Technology.   In all four countries, the costs and revenues associated with the sale or license of technology generally receive "standard" treatment. However, intercountry differences in other parts of the tax code create some differences in treatment of proceeds from the sale of technology. Most notable is the U.S. preferential 28 percent tax rate of long-term capital gains, which also applies in sales of patents or technology. In addition, patent sales by individual inventors and those who finance individual inventors receive the more favorable capital-gains tax rate, regardless of how long the patent was held. In France, long-term capital gains on the sale of a patent or technology (and in some cases royalty income) are taxed at the preferential 15 percent capital gains tax rate (recall, however, that this amounts to a deferral rather than a reduction in the tax liability). In all four countries, royalty payments are tax deductible, and expenditures for intangible assets may be amortized over useful life.

Contributions to Nonprofit Scientific Organizations.   In all four countries, contributions to nonprofit scientific organizations are deductible within certain limits, and there is some form of preferential treatment for such organization's income.

Turning to the effectiveness of tax incentives for encouraging R&D, we find a lack of evidence just as in the case of government funding of industry R&D. At present the argument for tax incentives directed to business R&D activities relies heavily on untested propositions about the behavior of firms (Collins 1982; NSF 1981, esp. Mansfield). First, evidence is sparse about the links between innovative activities, such as R&D, and tax-induced changes in net-of-cost R&D and in cash flow. Second, experience suggests that estimated tax effects for R&D are sensitive both to estimating procedures and to underlying assumptions about behavior of enterprises' expectations. In fact, a recent study of tax incentive effects on investment has shown a tendency for empirical studies to start out with elasticities substantially higher than estimates derived from later examination, and for these different initial conditions to alter the results (Chirinko and Eisner 1981). Third, qualitative analysis has demonstrated that the efficacy of tax incentives depend on business expectations and the general economic climate. Unfortunately, we lack generally validated estimated relationships. Finally, there are the indirect effects to be considered in assessing the influence of an existing tax code or when there are extensive changes to such a code. For example, in the Economic Recovery Tax Act of 1981 the new R&D tax credit "competes" with the new tax incentives for investment; on the other hand, the investment incentives can be viewed as complementary to R&D incentives, since application of R&D results usually require capital investment.

CONCLUSIONS

Despite the great public policy attention given to R&D expenditures, it is not clear that accelerating growth in U.S. R&D activity is a prerequisite for increasing the rate of U.S. economic growth or for improving the international competitiveness of its industries. Improved productivity depends on factors beyond improved technology. In turn, U.S. efforts to improve technology involve more than research and development activities (e.g., acquisition of foreign technology). Granted that R&D plays an important role, the U.S. R&D effort during the period when the nation has experienced a substantial slowdown in productivity improvement has compared favorably with the past levels of U.S. R&D activity and with the R&D inputs of other major industrial nations. It is not surprising that Denison could attribute to R&D spending only a minor fraction of the slowdown in U.S. productivity improvement during the 1970s. A look at some other advanced industrial nations shows most as having substantially higher rates of productivity growth than the United States, with substantially smaller proportionate outlays for R&D. Much more than R&D activity seems to be involved.

    The available evidence also does not support a move toward higher government R&D expenditures and favorable tax treatment for R&D as ways to accelerate technological progress in industry. Much of the advocacy for more U.S. government R&D spending derives from claims about large foreign government R&D involvement relative to the efforts of the U.S. government and from assertions about the importance of the government role. We know little about the magnitude and characteristics of government

R&D funding for commercial technology both here and abroad. In addition, the evidence about the economic effectiveness of major government R&D funding for commercial technology does not provide a strong case for large-scale U.S. government involvement. We know a bit more about the tax treatment of R&D among major industrial countries, but the information leads us to conclude that on the whole, the United States provides its firms with as favorable tax treatment for R&D as do other industrial countries. Although these tax measures are expensive in terms of loss of revenues, we know little about their effectiveness for stimulating R&D (though the magnitude of the incentive effects are influenced by enabling factors).

What may be more worthwhile is to develop information and approaches for increasing the economic effectiveness of R&D activity for the purpose of industrial development and economic growth. U.S. R&D spending for commercial technology has remained at relatively high levels and grown throughout the 1960s and 1970s. Some recent looks at foreign experience suggest that other countries are more effective than the United States in adopting current scientific discoveries and technological advances to productivity growth and industrial development (Vernon 1980, 1982; Peck and Goto 1981). In recent years, the U.S. government has initiated a few modest programs in an attempt to accelerate the application of scientific discoveries to industry: These are the NSF programs for joint industry/university research projects, industry/university centers for applied research, and small business research. But we have not really explored the role of the different factors that influence how well a firm or industry applies scientific discoveries and technological advances to improve its market positions. New approaches for government actions relating to R&D can only benefit from increased knowledge about the effectiveness of R&D application.

NOTES

1. Any opinions, findings, conclusions, or recommendations expressed in this paper are those of the authors and do not necessarily reflect the views of the National Science Foundation (NSF).
2. That literature is not reviewed here; for a survey, see NSF (1977). More recent examples include Griliches and Lichtenberg (1984) and Terleckyj (1982).
3. Evenson, Waggoner, and Ruttan (1979) summarize many such studies. Their article notes that "science-oriented research does not have a significant independent effect. The high payoff to science-oriented research is achieved only when it is directed toward increasing the productivity of technology-oriented research" (1979: 1103).
4. That paper also reports that a look at the relationship between industrially funded R&D as a fraction of value added and productivity growth, for a given industry but across several industrialized countries, showed little direct relationship.

5.   For a discussion of the guidelines and procedures used to compile the OECD R&D data, see OECD (1980).
6.   A telephone call to OECD (9/17/82) elicited this verbal estimate. The percentage varies between countries and fields.

DATA SOURCES

The sources listed on each table or graph refer to the following publications by the numbers assigned them on these pages.

1.   *International Statistical Year for Research and Development, A Study of Resources Devoted to R&D in OECD Member Countries in 1963/64.* Statistical Tables and Notes, Volume 2. Paris: OECD, 1968.
2.   *International Survey of the Resources Devoted to R&D in 1967 by OECD Member Countries.* Statistical Tables and Notes, Volume 1, Business Enterprise Sector. Paris: OECD, May 1970.
3.   *International Survey of the Resources Devoted to R&D in 1967 by OECD Member Countries.* Statistical Tables and Notes, Volume 2, General Government Sector. Paris: OECD, June 1970.
4.   *International Survey of the Resources Devoted to R&D in 1967 by OECD Member Countries.* Statistical Tables and Notes, Volume 5, Total Tables. Paris: OECD, August 1970.
5.   *International Survey of the Resources Devoted to R&D in 1969 by OECD Member Countries.* Statistical Tables and Notes, Volume 1, Business Enterprise Sector. Paris: OECD, June 1972.
6.   *International Survey of the Resources Devoted to R&D in 1969 by OECD Member Countries.* Statistical Tables and Notes, Volume 2, General Government Sector. Paris: OECD, April 1972.
7.   *International Survey of the Resources Devoted to R&D in 1969 by OECD Member Countries.* Statistical Tables and Notes, Volume 5, Total Tables. Paris: OECD, June 1973.
8.   *International Statistical Year 1971, Survey of the Resources Devoted to R&D by OECD Member Countries.* Volume 5, Total Tables, Statistical Tables and Notes. Paris: OECD, August 1974.
9.   *International Statistical Year 1973, Survey of the Resources Devoted to R&D by OECD Member Countries.* Volume 1, Business Enterprise Sector, Statistical Tables and Notes. Paris: OECD, October 1976.
10.   *International Statistical Year 1973, Survey of the Resources Devoted to R&D by OECD Member Countries.* Volume 2(A), General Government Sector, Statistical Tables and Notes. Paris: OECD, October 1976.
11.   *International Statistical Year 1973, Survey of the Resources Devoted to R&D by OECD Member Countries.* International Statistical Year 1973, Volume 5, Total Tables, Statistical Tables and Notes. Paris: OECD, September 1976.
12.   *International Statistical Year 1975, International Survey of the Resources Devoted to R&D by OECD Member Countries.* International Volume, Statistical Tables and Notes. Paris: OECD, March 1979.
13.   *International Statistical Year 1977, International Survey of the Resources Devoted to R&D by OECD Member Countries.* Country Volumes. Paris: OECD.

a. Belgium   DSTI/SPR/79.28/03 March 1980
b. Canada   ”   ”   ”   /04 August 1980
c. Denmark   ”   ”   ”   /05 October 1980
d. France   ”   ”   ”   /08 March 1980
e. Germany   ”   ”   ”   /01 April 1980
f. Italy   ”   ”   ”   /12 November 1980
g. Japan   ”   ”   ”   /21 December 1979
h. Netherlands ”   ”   ”   /15 November 1980
i. Norway   ”   ”   ”   /14 June 1980
j. Sweden   ”   ”   ”   /18 April 1980
k. Switzerland ”   ”   ”   /19 December 1979
l. United States ”   ”   ”   /07 November 1979

14. *Changing Priorities for Government R&D: An Experimental Study of Trends in the Objectives of Government R&D Funding in 12 OECD Member Countries 1961-1972.* Paris: OECD, 1975.

15. *The Measurement of Scientific and Technical Activities: Proposed Standard Practice for Surveys of Research and Experimental Development ("Frascati Manual"), 1980.* Paris: OECD, 1981.

16. *Science Resources/Newsletter,* no. 2. Directorate for Science, Technology and Industry, Science Resources Unit. Paris: OECD, Spring 1977.

17. *Science Resources Newsletter,* no. 5. Directorate for Science, Technology and Industry, Science and Technology Indicators Unit. Paris: OECD, summer 1980.

18. Science Resources Studies Division, National Science Foundation, unpublished country tables.

19. *OECD Science and Technology Indicators I.* Part A, Annex 2 to DSTI/SPR/ 81.27. Draft November 6, 1981.

20. *National Accounts of OECD Countries, 1961-1978.* Volume II, Detailed Tables. Paris: OECD, 1980.

21. *National Accounts of OECD Countries, 1951-1980.* Vol. I. Paris: OECD, 1982.

REFERENCES

Chirinko, Robert S., and Robert Eisner. 1981. "The Effects of Tax Parameters on the Investment Equations in Macroeconomic Econometric Models." Office of Tax Analysis Paper 47. Washington, D.C.: U.S. Treasury Department.

Collins, Eileen. 1982. "Tax Policy and Innovation: A Synthesis of the Evidence." PRA Research Report 82-1. Washington, D.C.: National Science Foundation.

Denison, Edward F. 1977. *Accounting for Slower Economic Growth.* Washington, D.C.: The Brookings Institution.

Evenson, Robert; Paul Waggoner; and Vernon Ruttan. 1979. "Economic Benefits from Research: An Example from Agriculture." *Science* 205 (September): 1101-07.

Fisher, W. Halder. 1977. "Technology Transfer as a Motivation for United States Direct Investment by Foreign Firms." Washington, D.C.: National Science Foundation. NTIS summary #PB-284792/9SL A02; report #PB-284793/7SL A07.

Griliches, Zvi. 1979. "Issues in Assessing the Contribution of Research and Development to Productivity Growth." *The Bell Journal of Economics* 10, no. 1 (spring): 92-116.

Griliches, Zvi, and Frank Lichtenberg. 1984. In *R&D, Patents, and Productivity,* edited by Zvi Griliches. Chicago: National Bureau of Economic Research.

Kenrick, John W. 1981. "International Comparisons of Recent Productivity Trends." In *Essays in Contemporary Economic Problems,* edited by William Fellner, pp. 125-70. Washington, D.C.: American Enterprise Institute.

Lewis, Jordan. 1982. "Technology, Enterprise, and American Economic Growth." *Science* 215 (March): 1204-11.

Link, Albert. 1981. "Basic Research and Productivity Increase in Manufacturing: Additonal Evidence." *American Economic Review* 71 (December): 111-12.

_____ . 1982a. "A Disaggregated Analysis of Industrial R&D: Product versus Process Innovation." In *The Transfer and Utilization of Technical Knowledge,* edited by D. Sahal, pp. 45-62. Lexington, Mass.: D.C. Heath.

_____ . 1982b. "Interfirm Technology Flows and Productivity Growth." University of North Carolina. Working paper.

Mansfield, Edwin. 1980. "Basic Research and Productivity Increase in Manufacturing." *American Economic Review* 70 (December): 863-73.

_____ . 1981. "International Technology Transfer: Rates, Benefits, Costs, and Public Policy." Paper presented at a meeting of the American Economic Association, Washington, D.C., December.

Mansfield, Edwin, and Lorin Switzer. 1981. "Effects of Federal Support on Company-Financed R and D: The Case of Energy." Paper prepared for a meeting of the Southern Economic Association, Atlanta, November.

Melman, Seymour. 1974. *The Permanent War Economy.* New York: Simon and Schuster.

Mogee, Mary Ellen. 1980. "The Relationship of Federal Support of Basic Research in Universities to Industrial Innovation and Productivity." In *Special Study on Economic Change,* vol. 3, *Research and Innovation: Developing a Dynamic Nation,* pp. 257-79. Prepared for the Joint Economic Committee of the U.S. Congress, 96th Cong., 2nd Sess. Washington, D.C.: U.S. Government Printing Office.

National Science Foundation. 1977. *Preliminary Papers for a Colloquium on the Relationship between R&D and Economic Growth/Productivity.* Washington, D.C., November.

_____ . 1978. *Research and Development in Industry.* Washington, D.C.: NSF.

_____ . 1979. "Unanticipated Benefits from Basic Research." Washington, D.C.: NSF.

_____ . 1980. "How Basic Research Reaps Unexpected Rewards." Washington, D.C.: NSF.

_____ . 1981. *Corporation Income Tax Treatment of Investment and Innovation Activities in Six Countries.* PRA Research Report 81-1. Washington, D.C.: NSF.

Nelson, Richard. 1981. "Research on Productivity Growth and Productivity Differences: Dead Ends and New Departures." *Journal of Economic Literature* 19 (September): 1029-64.

Nelson, Richard, and Richard Langlois. 1983. "Industrial Innovation Policy: Lessons from American History." *Science* 219 (February): 814-18.

Okubo, Sumiye; Rolf Piekarz; and Eleanor Thomas. 1977. "International Comparison of Enterprise-Funded Research and Development in Manufacturing." In *Proceedings of a Conference on Engineering and Science for Industrial Development.* Easton, Md.: The Engineering Foundation.

Organization for Economic Cooperation and Development. 1975. *Changing Priorities for Government R&D: An Experimental Study of Trends in the Objectives*

of Government R&D Funding in 12 OECD Member Countries 1961-1972.
Paris: OECD.

———. 1980. *The Measurement of Scientific and Technical Activities ("Frascati Manual").* Paris: OECD.

Pavitt, K., and L. Soete. 1980. "Innovative Activities and Export Shares: Some Comparisons between Industries and Countries." In *Technical Innovation and British Economic Performance,* edited by K. Pavitt, pp. 38-66. London: Macmillan.

Peck, Merton J., and Akira Goto. 1981. "Technology and Economic Growth: The Case of Japan." *Research Policy* 10 (July): 226.

Scherer, F.M. 1981. "Inter-Industry Technology Flows and Productivity Growth." Northwestern University, working paper.

Terleckyj, Nestor. 1982a. "National Planning Association Working Paper 5-18-82." Washington, D.C.: National Planning Association.

———. 1982b. "R&D and the U.S. Industrial Productivity in the 1970s." In *The Transfer and Utilization of Technical Knowledge,* edited by D. Sahal, pp. 63-99. Lexington, Mass.: D.C. Heath.

Terleckyj, Nestor, and David Levy. 1982. "Effects of Government R&D in Private R&D Investment and Productivity: A Microeconomic Analysis." Paper prepared for a meeting of the Southern Economic Association, Atlanta, November.

Vernon, Raymond. 1980. "Gone Are the Cash Cows of Yesteryear." *Harvard Business Review* 58, no. 6 (November/December): 152 n.21.

———. 1982. "The Analytical Challenge." Harvard University. Draft paper.

COMMENT

John K.L. Thompson

The Title

Dr. Piekarz's paper addresses the subjects indicated by the title and is almost wholly concerned with international comparisons of R&D and funding thereof, together with government policies on R&D. The object of the conference, however, was to look at international comparisons of productivity, not simply R&D. Dr. Piekarz claims that there is a linkage between R&D and productivity, though government policies on matters other than R&D may be of greater importance.

Introduction

Dr. Piekarz states that "R&D is a major contributor to technological progress, which in turn is a key contributor to productivity growth." I agree with this, but it does not follow that any country wishing to derive productivity growth must perform the R&D itself. If a country relies on the R&D efforts of other countries, the efficiency of the R&D systems is less important than the availability and exploitation of R&D results.

Economic Contributions and Policy Determinants of R&D

I entirely agree with his statement that "scientific advances are neither necessary nor sufficient for technological advances, and vice versa." Eco-

275

nomic growth is much more dependent upon the application of science and technology than upon its generation. The mechanism of technology transfer seems to me to be far more important than the management of basic research. Between 1950 and 1980 Japan, under the guidance of MITI, effectively bought all of the usable technology in the world at a cost of $9 billion—a very low price compared to the current annual R&D expenditure in the United States of $75 billion. In the form of such transactions as licenses and know-how agreements, the United States is selling ten times as much technology as it buys, with Japan doing approximately the reverse. A trend is now discernible, however, whereby Japan is starting to export more technology in fields where it has become the world leader. This is particularly true in the steel industry, where several U.S. companies are now hiring Japanese consultants to help improve their technology.

The American farming industry is probably the most efficient in the world, which has enabled the United States to feed not only itself but much of the rest of the world as well. This has been assisted by considerable federal government assistance to the farming industry for one hundred years or so, which has involved not merely sponsoring appropriate research and development but also providing a direct consultancy service that helps individual farmers to apply the knowledge that has been obtained. This avoids the problem that some government laboratories have encountered in attempting to transfer their technology to potential users who may be unaware of the laboratories' existence. Many valuable developments in technology have been made in defense programs and the space program, such as microcircuitry and new materials. In both cases the federal government has had to address the problem of getting this technology out of the federal laboratories and out of the defense and space contractors' establishments into the rest of the manufacturing industry.

Government Policies and Comparisons of National R&D Aggregates

Piekarz's paper is concerned with government policies on R&D rather than productivity. The presentation of the various national R&D aggregates is exceptionally well done and will provide good source material for other researchers. No obvious relationship is demonstrated between R&D expenditure and economic growth. Funding of R&D by business as opposed to government appears to be more productive, as is demonstrated by the data on Japan, Switzerland, and Sweden.

The ratio of R&D expenditure to GNP seems to me to be irrelevant. For any particular bit of R&D there is a fixed cost that has to be borne and that needs to be recovered by loading the price of products utilizing this R&D.

This "entry fee" is much smaller in the case, say, of designing a new knitting needle than it would be in designing a new supersonic aircraft. Since very few products can carry a load of more than 3 percent to cover R&D costs, market research can indicate just how much a country or a company should be prepared to spend on a particular development. Another problem arises from the time lag in converting a piece of research into a saleable product. The average time lag is probably about ten years, and in some cases it may be more like twenty years. Hence, what is spent on R&D today is not likely to affect anything that will happen in the next five years, though it may be of considerable importance in ten years' time. Again, however, I would stress that the R&D does not necessarily have to be done by the ultimate user. The totals of R&D expenditure for a country can be misleading unless they are broken down into particular subject areas. The total R&D expenditure of the United States and the United Kingdom is greatly reduced when one takes out expenditures on defense, space, and nuclear. Although the United States in particular has done quite well in selling the products of defense, space, and nuclear industries' R&D, most other countries have not and are not likely to. Japan and Switzerland in particular have spent very little in those three fields but have spent a fair amount in straightforward industrial development. In those two countries the bulk of the finance for R&D comes from industry rather than the government and therefore is directed by those concerned with making and selling products. Governments are notoriously bad at deciding what to make and how to sell it. Another fact explaining Japanese and Swiss success is that their R&D is carried out predominantly in industry rather than in government laboratories. This avoids the technology transfer problem.

Industrial Composition of Business R&D

Table 6-7 shows how the United States spent a considerably higher percentage of its total manufacturing R&D on five particular industries than does Japan or Sweden. It would be interesting to see how the balance of R&D expenditure is allocated in these two countries, both of which are very successful in trade terms. In fact, a more comprehensive international comparison of R&D expenditures as related to trade would be interesting. There is considerable trade in food and drink, though neither is reknown for high R&D expenditures.

Government R&D in Terms of Social Objectives

The figures given comparing U.S. and U.K. funding related to industrial growth may be misleading. Certainly, the U.S. figures are understated. The

U.S. Department of Defense's expenditure on the manufacturing technology and ICAM programs are probably not included in the "industrial growth" totals. Similarly the massive expenditure by the DOD and NASA on engine and aircraft development, which has fed into civil engines and aircraft production, is probably not stated.

Tax Measures

The paper deals with tax measures related to R&D but not those related to productivity. Most of the tax measures described involve reductions in the amount of corporate tax paid by a company. As we have found in Britain and is now being discovered in the United States, such measures are irrelevant if a company is not making any profit and hence not paying any corporate taxes.

Conclusions

I agree with the conclusions as stated. I believe that three additional points should be made as follows:

1. In improving productivity, technology transfer may be more important than R&D. Studies of various mechanisms to stimulate technology transfer would be very worthwhile. In Britain we have mounted various schemes to improve technology transfer in the fields of robotics, CAD/CAM, and microcircuitry. In due course, a study of these measures would be worthwhile.
2. Nothing is said about the time lag in progressing from research to production. In most products the minimum time lag is five years and may be as much as twenty; therefore, any attempt to correlate R&D expenditure with productivity year by year is bound to be difficult.
3. It is bound to be more difficult to treat macro—rather than micro—effects. Studies of particular industries or particular companies are more likely to reveal usable conclusions.

7 THE ROLE OF ENERGY IN PRODUCTIVITY GROWTH

Dale W. Jorgenson[1]

The objective of this paper is to analyze the role of energy in the growth of productivity. The special significance of energy in economic growth was first established in the classic study, *Energy and the American Economy 1950–1975*, by Schurr and his associates (1960) at Resources for the Future.[2] For the period from 1920 to 1955, Schurr noted that energy intensity of production had fallen while both labor and total factor productivity were rising. The simultaneous decline in energy intensity and labor intensity of production ruled out the possibility of explaining the growth of productivity solely on the basis of substitution of less expensive energy for more expensive labor. Since the quantity of both energy and labor inputs required for a given level of output had been reduced, technical change is also a critical explanatory factor.

An alternative explanation for growth of output with declining energy and labor intensity required an examination of the character of technical change. This examination was motivated by the fact that from 1920 to 1955 the utilization of electricity had expanded by a factor of more than ten, while consumption of all other forms of energy only doubled. Two key features of technical change during this period were that the thermal efficiency of conversion of fuels into electricity increased by a factor of three and that "the unusual characteristics of electricity had made it possible to perform tasks in altogether different ways than if the fuels had to be used directly" (Schurr 1983: 3). Schurr illustrated this point by the impact of electrification on industrial processes, which led to much greater flexibility in the application of energy to industrial production.

279

The importance of electrification in productivity growth has also been documented by Rosenberg (1983: 24):

Increasingly, the spreading use of electric power in the 20th century has been associated with the introduction of new techniques and new arrangements which reduce total costs through their saving of labor and capital. Perhaps the most distinctive features of these new techniques are (1) that they take so many forms as to defy easy categorization, and (2) that they occur in so many industries that they defy a simple summary.

Rosenberg has illustrated this point with examples drawn from the production of iron and steel, the making of glass, and the production and utilization of aluminum.

Rosenberg, like Schurr and his associates, has drawn attention to the significance of electrification of industrial processes that took place during the first several decades of the twentieth century. Electrical motors have provided greater flexibility in the supply of power to industrial processes and in the organization and layout of production processes. Rosenberg (1983: 36) reaches this overall conclusion:

It seems obvious that there has been a very wide range of labor saving innovations throughout industry which have taken an electricity using form. As a consequence, greater use of electricity is, from an historical point of view, the other side of the coin of a labor-saving bias in the innovation process.

Schurr (1981) has recently extended the analysis of *Energy and the American Economy 1950–1975* through 1981. For the period through 1969 his conclusions are as follows (Schurr 1982: 6):

Although the inverse relationship between total factor productivity and energy intensity virtually disappeared during the 1953–1969 period, it is still noteworthy that high rates of improvement in total factor productivity were essentially not associated with increases in energy intensity.

Schurr has analyzed the experience of the U.S. economy in the aftermath of the oil embargo of 1973. He points out that energy intensity of production has fallen steadily since 1973 and that the rate of decline accelerated sharply after the second oil price shock in 1979, following the Iranian revolution. He goes on to point out that (1982: 10):

While energy productivity has been improving at a very high rate during the past decade, the overall productivity efficiency side of the story has been highly unfavorable, and has become a matter of great concern. The post-1979 years that witnessed a new high in the rate of growth of national energy productivity also saw a decline in productive efficiency with a *fall* in total factor productivity of about 0.3 percent per year between 1979 and 1981.

We can summarize the evidence on energy intensity and productivity growth by saying that energy intensity was falling while productivity was rising for the period 1920–53. Between 1953 and 1969 energy intensity was relatively stable, while productivity continued to rise. After 1973 energy intensity has resumed its downward trend with a sharp acceleration after 1979, while productivity growth has fallen off since 1973 and has given way to productivity decline since 1979. In exploring the determinants of trends in energy intensity and in productivity growth a useful framework is provided by Schurr and his associates (1979) in the study *Energy in America's Future*. This study emphasizes the role of change in the composition of the national output, trends in energy intensity within industrial sectors, the significance of changing energy forms, and the role of price developments.

Focusing on historical experience through 1975 and 1977, Schurr and his associates conclude that the perspective provided by change in the composition of the national output "offers a useful but, at best, limited insight" (Schurr et al. 1979: 88). Similarly, they find that energy intensity has declined in some sectors and risen in others (Schurr et al. 1979: 89–90). They find that the transformation of energy forms, especially toward greater electrification and the use of fluid forms of energy such as petroleum and natural gas, has played an important role (Schurr et al. 1979: 92). "The changes have made possible shifts in production techniques and locations within industry, agriculture, and transportation that greatly enhanced the growth of national output and productivity," and finally, they argue that " . . . quite apart from energy prices, technology developed its own momentum."

The framework suggested by Schurr and his associates and the historical evidence on trends in energy intensity and productivity growth suggests that an explanation of these trends must encompass a wide range of determinants. First, the gradual decline in real energy prices through the early 1970s and the sharp increases in energy prices that have followed the oil shocks of 1973 and 1979 suggest an important role for substitution between energy and other productive inputs, especially labor input. While the real price of labor input rose steadily through the early 1970s, this price has been declining since that time. These price trends would suggest the possibility of substitution of energy for labor through the early 1970s and substitution of labor for energy afterward.

Second, technical change is an important component of any explanation of trends in energy intensity and productivity. Schurr (1982: 9) has suggested a possible role for technical change in reviewing U.S. experience through 1969, as follows:

> The net result, then, was that strong improvements in both energy productivity and overall productive efficiency were achieved without any special efforts being made to bring about this desirable combination of circumstances. Energy was abundantly available, and its price was low and, for the most part, falling during this period. Simple economic reasoning would tell us that the intensity of energy use should have risen because favorable energy prices would have encouraged energy consumption. But even though energy use rose relative to labor inputs, it fell in relationship to the final output of the economy. Did this decline in energy intensity take place in spite of low energy prices, or somehow because of them?

The mechanisms of technical change, as described above by Schurr and by Rosenberg, indicate a specific role for electrification. For this reason it is essential to analyze the role of both the price of electricity and the price of nonelectrical energy in the determination of productivity growth.

Another potential determinant of changes in energy intensity and changes in productivity growth in the U.S. economy is the change in the composition of the national output. The role of this change in stimulating and retarding U.S. productivity growth is suggested by a review of postwar U.S. economic history. The growth of the U.S. economy in the postwar period has been very rapid by historical standards. The rate of economic growth reached its maximum during the period 1960 to 1966. Growth rates have slowed substantially since 1966 and declined further since 1973. A decomposition of the growth of output into contributions of capital input, labor input, and productivity growth shows that capital input has made the most important contribution to postwar growth of output, while growth in productivity and labor input are less significant. Focusing on the period since 1973, the fall in the rate of economic growth is due to a dramatic decline in productivity growth. Declines in the contributions of capital and labor input are much less significant in explaining the slowdown.[3]

To analyze the potential sources of the decline in productivity growth since 1973 it is useful to decompose productivity growth into components that can be identified with productivity growth at the sectoral level and with reallocations of output, capital input, and labor input among sectors. For the period up to 1973 the contribution of reallocations of output and inputs among sectors is insignificant relative to sectoral productivity growth. For the period since 1973 the contributions of these reallocations was positive rather than negative, but relatively small. Declines in productivity growth for the individual industrial sectors of the U.S. economy must bear the full burden of explaining the slowdown in productivity growth for the economy as a whole.

The overall conclusion from our review of postwar U.S. economic history is that the key to understanding the role of energy in the advance of productivity is to analyze the growth of productivity at the level of individual industrial sectors in the United States. As Rosenberg and Schurr have indicated, special attention must be devoted to the substitution of electricity for other forms of energy. An important force in electrification has been identified by Schurr as the cheapening of electricity relative to other forms of energy that has accompanied the dramatic increases in the thermal change through innovations that have occurred throughout the whole range of industrial activity.

Second, our review of postwar history shows that growth in productivity at the level of individual industrial sectors is the primary explanation of productivity growth for the economy as a whole. Furthermore, the decline in economic growth that has taken place since 1973 can be attributed almost entirely to a decline in productivity growth at the level of individual industrial sectors. To revive the growth of sectoral productivity it will be necessary to revive the process of innovation at the sectoral level. Given the importance of electrification in stimulating innovation, it is essential to assess the potential of electrification for generating a revival in innovation and in productivity growth.

In order to assess the role of energy in stimulating productivity growth, it will be necessary to go behind trends in energy utilization and productivity. For this purpose we employ an econometric model of sectoral productivity growth for individual industrial sectors in the United States. In order to assess the significance of changing forms of energy, we divide inputs in each sector among capital, labor, electricity, nonelectrical energy, and materials. Our econometric model encompasses substitution among productive inputs in response to changes in relative prices. Our model also determines the growth of sectoral productivity as a function of relative prices.

ECONOMETRIC MODELS

For each industry our model of production will be based on a sectoral price function that summarizes both possibilities for substitution among inputs and patterns of technical change. Each price function gives the price of output of the corresponding industrial sector as a function of the prices of capital, labor, electricity, nonelectrical energy, and materials inputs and time, where time represents the level of technology in the sector.[4] Obviously an increase in the price of one of the inputs, holding the prices of the other inputs and the level of technology constant, necessitates an increase in the price of output. Similarly, if productivity of a sector improves and the prices of all inputs into the sector remain the same, the price of output must fall. Price functions summarize these and other relationships among the prices of output, capital, labor, electricity, nonelectrical energy, and materials inputs, and the level of technology.

The sectoral price functions provide a complete model of production patterns for each sector, incorporating both substitution among inputs in response to changes in relative prices and technical change in the use of inputs to produce output. To characterize both substitution and technical change it is useful to express the model in an alternative and equivalent form. First, we can express the shares of each of the five inputs—capital, labor, electricity, nonelectrical energy, and materials—in the value of output as functions of the prices of these inputs and time, again representing the level of technology.[5] Second, we can add to these five equations for the value shares an equation that determines productivity growth as a function of the prices of all five inputs and time. This equation is our econometric model of sectoral productivity growth.[6]

Like any econometric model, the relationships determining the value shares of capita, labor, electricity, nonelectrical energy, and materials inputs and the rate of productivity growth involve unknown parameters that must be estimated from data for the individual industries. Included among these unknown parameters are biases of productivity growth that indicate the effect of change in the level of technology on the value shares of each of the five inputs. For example, the bias of productivity growth for capital input gives the change in the share of capital input in the value of output in response to changes in the level of technology, represented by time. We say that productivity growth is capital using if the bias of productivity growth for capital input is positive. Similarly, we say that productivity growth is capital saving if the bias of productivity growth for capital input is negative.

For the purposes of a study of the role of electrification in productivity growth the key parameter in our econometric model is the bias of productivity growth for electricity. This bias gives the change in the share of electricity in the value of output in response to changes in the level of technology. We say that productivity is electricity using, as suggested by Rosenberg, if the bias of productivity growth for electricity is positive. Similarly, we say that productivity growth is electricity saving if the bias of productivity growth for electricity input is negative. To test the hypothesis that technical change is electricity using for an individual industrial sector, we fit the bias of productivity growth for electricity, together with other parameters that describe substitution and technical change in that sector. We then test the hypothesis that the bias of productivity growth is positive.

It is important to observe that the sum of the biases of all five inputs must be precisely zero, since the changes in all five shares with any change in technology must sum to zero. To put this another way, if productivity growth is electricity using, then productivity growth must be input saving in some other input. For example, productivity growth could be labor saving and electricity using, as suggested by Rosenberg. This would correspond to a positive bias of productivity growth for electricity and a negative bias of productivity growth for labor. Our econometric model will make it possible to classify each of the thirty-six industries included in our study of technical change among the thirty logically possible patterns of productivity growth that correspond to positive or negative values of each of the five biases. Only the possibility that all five biases are negative or all five are positive can be ruled out on the basis of purely analytical considerations.

We have pointed out that our econometric model for each industrial sector of the U.S. economy includes an equation giving the rate of sectoral productivity growth as a function of the prices of the five inputs and time. The biases of technical change with respect to each of the five inputs appear as the coefficients of time, representing the level of technology, in the five equations for the value shares of all five inputs. The biases also appear as coefficients of the prices in the equation for the negative of sectoral productivity growth. This feature of our econometric model makes it possible to use information about changes in the value shares with time and information about changes in the rate of sectoral productivity growth with prices in determining estimates of the biases of technical change.

The biases of productivity growth express the dependence of the value shares of the five inputs on the level of technology and also express the dependence of the rate of productivity growth on the input prices. We say that capital-using productivity growth, associated with a positive bias of productivity growth for capital input, implies that an increase in the price of capital input decreases the rate of productivity growth. Similarly, capital-saving productivity growth, associated with a negative bias for capital input, implies that an increase in the price of capital input increases the rate of productivity growth. Analogous relationships hold between the biases of labor, electricity, nonelectrical energy, and materials inputs on the one hand and the impact of changes in the prices of each of these inputs on the other.

The dual role of the bias of productivity growth—expressing the impact of a change in technology on the value share of an input and the impact of a change in the price of that input—is the key to an assessment of the role of electrification in productivity growth. Historical evidence, as summarized by Rosenberg, suggests that much of the innovation in the twentieth century is electricity using so that it increases the share of electricity in the value of output for a given set of input prices, including the price of electricity. Entirely different evidence, analyzed by Schurr and his associates, has linked the reduction in the cost of electricity resulting from increased thermal efficiency in electricity generation to enhanced productivity growth. Within our econometric model these two pieces of historical evidence are both consistent with the hypothesis that the bias of productivity growth for electricity is positive.

Electricity using productivity growth, associated with a positive bias of productivity growth for electricity, implies that the utilization of electricity increases as technology changes. This is precisely what happened over the first several decades of this century, according to the evidence reviewed by Rosenberg. Electricity-using productivity growth also implies that the overall rate of productivity growth increases as the price of electricity declines, which is consistent with historical evidence on the growth of output, productivity, and energy consumption analyzed by Schurr. Our overall conclusion is that this historical evidence suggests the hypothesis that technical change at the level of individual sectors of the U.S. economy is electricity using. This implies a central role for electrification in the growth of productivity.

Empirical Results

We provide a detailed description of our econometric models of production and technical change in the appendix. To implement these models we have assembled a data base for the thirty-five industrial sectors of the U.S. economy listed in Table 7–1.[7] The thirty-five industries encompass all sectors of the U.S. economy. Manufacturing is subdivided among twenty-one two-digit industries. These industries differ greatly in their relative importance to the economy and in their energy intensity. The thirty-five industries also include the primary production sectors of agriculture and mining, the

Table 7–1.   Industrial Sectors.

1.	Agriculture, forestry, and fisheries.
2.	Metal mining
3.	Coal mining
4.	Crude petroleum and natural gas
5.	Nonmetallic mining and quarring, except fuel
6.	Construction
7.	Food and kindred products
8.	Tobacco manufactures
9.	Textile mill products
10.	Apparel and other fabricated textile products
11.	Lumber and wood products
12.	Furniture and fixtures
13.	Paper and allied products
14.	Printing, publishing, and allied industries
15.	Chemicals and allied products
16.	Petroleum refining
17.	Rubber and miscellaneous plastic products
18.	Leather and leather products
19.	Stone, clay, and glass products
20.	Primary metal industries
21.	Fabricated metal products
22.	Machinery, except electrical
23.	Electrical machinery
24.	Motor vehicles and motor vehicles equipment
25.	Transportation equipment and ordnance, except motor vehicles
26.	Instruments
27.	Miscellaneous manufacturing industries
28.	Transportation
29.	Communication
30.	Electric utilities (including federal, state, and local)
31.	Gas utilities
32.	Trade
33.	Finance, insurance, and real estate
34.	Services (including water and sanitary services)
35.	Government enterprises (excluding electric utilities)

energy intensive transportation and public utilities industries, and the construction, communications, trade, and service industries.

For capital and labor inputs we have first compiled data by sector on the basis of the classification of economic activities employed in the U.S. National Income and Product Accounts. We have then transformed these data into a format appropriate for the classification of activities employed in the U.S. Interindustry Transactions Accounts. For electricity, nonelectrical energy, and materials inputs we have compiled data by sector on interindustry transactions among the thirty-five industrial sectors. For this purpose we have used the classification of economic activities employed in the U.S. Interindustry Transactions Accounts.[8]

For each sector we have compiled data on the value shares of capital, labor, electricity, nonelectrical energy, and materials inputs, annually, for the period 1958–79. We have also compiled indexes of prices of sectoral output and all four sectoral inputs for the same period. Finally, we have compiled translog indexes of sectoral rates of technical change. There are twenty-one observations for each behavioral equation, since unweighted two period averages of all data are employed.

The parameters $\{\alpha_K^i, \alpha_L^i, \alpha_E^i, \alpha_N^i, \alpha_M^i\}$ can be interpreted as average value shares of capital, labor, electricity, nonelectrical energy, and materials inputs for the corresponding sector. Similarly, the parameters $\{\alpha_T^i\}$ can be interpreted as averages of the negative of rates of technical change. The parameters $\{\beta_{KK}^i, \beta_{KL}^i, \beta_{KE}^i, \beta_{KN}^i, \beta_{KM}^i, \beta_{LL}^i, \beta_{LE}^i, \beta_{LN}^i, \beta_{LM}^i, \beta_{EE}^i, \beta_{EN}^i, \beta_{EM}^i, \beta_{NN}^i, \beta_{NM}^i, \beta_{MM}^i\}$ can be interpreted as constant share elasticities with respect to price for the corresponding sector. Similarly, the parameters $\{\beta_{KT}^i, \beta_{LT}^i, \beta_{ET}^i, \beta_{NT}^i, \beta_{MT}^i\}$ can be interpreted as constant biases of technical change with respect to price. Finally, the parameters $\{\beta_{TT}^i\}$ can be interpreted as constant rates of change of the negative of the rates of technical change.

In estimating the parameters of our sectoral models of production and technical change we retain the average of the negative of the rate of technical change, biases of technical change, and the rate of change of the negative of the rate of technical change as parameters to be estimated for all thirty-five industrial sectors. Estimates of the share elasticities with respect to price are obtained under the restrictions implied by the necessary and sufficient conditions for concavity of the price functions presented in the appendix. Under these restrictions the matrices of constant share elasticities $\{U^i\}$ must be negative semidefinite for all industries. To impose the concavity restrictions we represent the matrices of constant share elasticities for all sectors in terms of their Cholesky factorizations. The necessary and sufficient conditions are that the diagonal elements $\{\delta_1^i, \delta_2^i, \delta_3^i, \delta_4^i\}$ of the matrices $\{D^i\}$ that appear in the Cholesky factorizations must be nonpositive. We present estimates subject to these restrictions for all thirty-five industrial sectors in Table 7–2.

Table 7-2. Parameter Estimates.

Parameter	Agriculture, Forestry, and Fisheries	Industry	
		Metal Mining	Coal Mining
AK	0.179 (0.00301)	0.226 (0.00770)	0.242 (0.00743)
AL	.243 (.00587)	.328 (.0134)	.494 (.00537)
AE	.00341 (.000469)	.0253 (.00141)	.0140 (.000306)
AN	.0215 (.00105)	.0143 (.000567)	.102 (.00120)
AM	.553 (.00374)	.407 (.0133)	.148 (.00684)
AT	-.0201 (.0318)	-.0681 (.107)	-.0213 (.0512)
BKK			
BKL			
BKE			
BKN			
BKM			
BKT	.00362 (.000430)	.00206 (.00110)	.00923 (.00106)
BLL	-.0586 (.0307)	.422 (.247)	.00803 (.000767)
BLE	-.00189 (.00466)	-.00217 (.0246)	-.000240 (.000158)
BLN	-.0168 (.00592)	.0294 (.00827)	-.00321 (.000981)
BLM	.0735 (.0350)	.394 (.219)	-.00345 (.00114)
BLT	-.00271 (.00149)	.0178 (.00688)	-.000830 (.0000522)
BEE	-.00886 (.00528)	-.0000111 (.000259)	.0429 (.00522)
BEN	-.000661 (.00193)	-.000151 (.00177)	.0461 (.00502)
BEM	.00630 (.00317)	.00203 (.0231)	-.00612 (.000237)
BET	-.0000677 (.000216)	.000765 (.000669)	-.0495 (.00500)
BNN	-.00484 (.00274)	-.00205 (.000570)	-.0103 (.000990)
BNM	.0210 (.00816)	-.0275 (.00720)	
BNT	-.000714 (.000277)	-.000884 (.000238)	
BMM	-.101 (.0406)	.369 (.194)	
BMT	-.00155 (.00149)	-.0197 (.00615)	
BTT	.000868 (.00455)	-.00835 (.0153)	-.00130 (.00731)

Table 7-2 (continued).

Parameter	Crude Petroleum and Natural Gas		Industry			
			Nonmetallic Mining		Construction	
AK	0.471	(0.00299)	0.281	(0.00318)	0.0715	(0.000650)
AL	.109	(.00247)	.314	(.00539)	.449	(.00427)
AE	.00870	(.000764)	.0296	(.000894)	.000294	(.000176)
AN	.0492	(.00150)	.0486	(.000392)	.0261	(.000767)
AM	.362	(.00388)	.327	(.00482)	.453	(.00474)
AT	−.00510	(.0489)	−.0600	(.114)	.00585	(.0482)
BKK						
BKL						
BKE						
BKN						
BKM						
BKT	.00203	(.000428)	.00329	(.000455)	.000667	(.0000929)
BLL			−.377	(.109)	−.311	(.0333)
BLE			.0441	(.0146)	.00622	(.000915)
BLN			−.0131	(.00938)	−.0563	(.00378)
BLM			.346	(.109)	.361	(.0355)
BLT	−.000124	(.000353)	.0102	(.00294)	−.00377	(.000998)
BEE	−.0231	(.0112)	−.00514	(.00401)	−.000124	(.0000405)
BEN	.00475	(.00590)	.00153	(.00163)	.00112	(.000213)
BEM	.0184	(.00588)	−.0404	(.0119)	.00722	(.00107)
BET	−.000151	(.000169)	−.000624	(.000418)	−.0000649	(.0000297)
BNN	−.000977	(.00198)	−.000454	(.000728)	.0102	(.00125)
BNM	−.00378	(.00393)	.0120	(.00861)	.0654	(.00465)
BNT	−.000880	(.000224)	.00185	(.000262)	−.00152	(.000120)
BMM	−.0146	(.00341)	−.318	(.109)	.420	(.0378)
BMT	−.00264	(.000555)	−.0147	(.00291)	.00455	(.00108)
BTT	−.000571	(.00699)	−.00657	(.0162)	−.00113	(.00688)

Table 7-2 (continued).

	Industry					
Parameter	Food and Kindred Products		Tobacco Manufactures		Textile Mill Products	
AK	0.0578	(0.000656)	0.171	(0.00381)	0.0730	(0.000969)
AL	.159	(.00192)	.130	(.00462)	.210	(.00206)
AE	.00441	(.000306)	.00211	(.000246)	.00977	(.000120)
AN	.00679	(.000151)	.00121	(.0000986)	.00586	(.000102)
AM	.772	(.00243)	.696	(.00620)	.701	(.00254)
AT	-.0152	(.0279)	-.00138	(.0912)	-.0215	(.00742)
BKK						
BKL						
BKE						
BKN						
BKM						
BKT	-.000900	(.0000938)	.00224	(.000544)	.00000139	(.000138)
BLL	-.0656	(.0165)	-.133	(.0279)		
BLE	-.00209	(.00462)	.0000237	(.00155)		
BLN	.00138	(.00214)	-.000447	(.000626)		
BLM	.0663	(.0167)	.133	(.0282)		
BLT	.000638	(.000487)	.0108	(.00142)	.00104	(.000294)
BEE	-.00973	(.00563)	-.000601	(.000756)		
BEN	.00167	(.00253)	-.000962	(.000577)		
BEM	.0101	(.00334)	.00154	(.00187)		
BET	.0000834	(.000154)	.000127	(.0000787)	.000215	(.0000172)
BNN	-.000302	(.000689)	-.00154	(.000212)		
BNM	-.00275	(.00149)	.00295	(.000652)		
BNT	.0000285	(.0000650)	.000938	(.0000314)	.000159	(.0000146)
BMM	-.0737	(.0178)	-.138	(.0287)		
BMT	.000150	(.000535)	.0132	(.00156)	-.00142	(.000363)
BTT	-.00162	(.00399)	.00464	(.0130)	-.00136	(.00105)

Table 7-2 (continued).

Parameter	Industry		
	Apparel and Other Fabricated Textile Products	Lumber and Wood Products	Furniture and Fixtures
AK	0.0429 (0.000668)	0.160 (0.00260)	0.0675 (0.000516)
AL	.315 (.00318)	.287 (.00574)	.295 (.00725)
AE	.00414 (.0000818)	.00790 (.000203)	.00351 (.000207)
AN	.00221 (.0000676)	.0109 (.000377)	.00262 (.000214)
AM	.636 (.00366)	.534 (.00760)	.631 (.00739)
AT	.00542 (.0301)	-.0308 (.0485)	-.00895 (.0158)
BKK			
BKL			
BKE			
BKN			
BKM			
BKT	.000551 (.0000954)	.00586 (.000372)	-.000150 (.0000738)
BLL	-.0775 (.0321)		-.0160 (.00564)
BLE	.00159 (.00124)		.00808 (.00122)
BLN	-.00365 (.000668)		.000440 (.00117)
BLM	.0796 (.0330)		.00750 (.00426)
BLT	.000839 (.000831)	.00146 (.000820)	-.00783 (.00104)
BEE	-.0000324 (.0000618)		-.00408 (.00130)
BEN	.0000747 (.0000880)		-.000222 (.000540)
BEM	.00163 (.00126)		.00378 (.00116)
BET	.000105 (.0000308)	.000280 (.0000290)	.00358 (.0000427)
BNN	-.000402 (.000259)		-.000121 (.0000617)
BNM	.00398 (.00812)		-.000206 (.000576)
BNT	.000202 (.0000215)	.000483 (.0000538)	-.0000593 (.0000425)
BMM	-.0820 (.0341)		-.00351 (.00279)
BMT	-.00170 (.000889)	-.00808 (.00109)	.00840 (.00106)
BTT	-.000187 (.00430)	-.00245 (.00692)	.00109 (.00226)

Table 7-2 (continued).

	Industry		
Parameter	Paper and Allied Products	Printing Publishing and Allied Industries	Chemicals and Allied Products
AK	0.116 (0.000498)	0.109 (0.00192)	0.135 (0.000976)
AL	.266 (.00178)	.384 (.00532)	.209 (.00335)
AE	.0117 (.0000739)	.00478 (.000139)	.0191 (.000788)
AN	.0215 (.000185)	.00351 (.000119)	.0741 (.000440)
AM	.584 (.00193)	.499 (.00703)	.562 (.00386)
AT	−.0327 (.0528)	.0103 (.0191)	−.0321 (.0527)
BKK			
BKL			
BKE			
BKN			
BKM			
BKT	−.00137 (.0000712)	.00116 (.000274)	−.00449 (.000139)
BLL		−.360 (.0742)	.121 (.0249)
BLE		.00338 (.00242)	.0884 (.0114)
BLN		−.0170 (.00300)	−.0179 (.0116)
BLM		.373 (.0765)	.0504 (.0162)
BLT	.000649 (.0000254)	.0134 (.00249)	.00246 (.00105)
BEE		−.00955 (.00186)	−.0646 (.0122)
BEN		.00369 (.000673)	.0131 (.00989)
BEM		.00249 (.00243)	−.0369 (.00899)
BET	.000267 (.0000106)	.0000269 (.0000813)	−.00301 (.000435)
BNN		−.00211 (.000332)	−.00264 (.00361)
BNM		.0154 (.00323)	.00745 (.00555)
BNT	.000351 (.0000264)	.000688 (.000101)	.00257 (.000436)
BMM		−.391 (.0791)	−.0210 (.00982)
BMT	.000104 (.000276)	−.0153 (.00265)	.00247 (.000821)
BTT	−.00183 (.00755)	.000566 (.00272)	−.000930 (.00753)

Table I-2 (continued).

		Industry	
Parameter	Petroleum Refining	Rubber and Miscellaneous Plastic Products	Leather and Leather Products
AK	0.111 (0.00299)	0.104 (0.00131)	0.0491 (0.000770)
AL	.0393 (.00302)	.269 (.00398)	.356 (.00471)
AE	.00311 (.000202)	.00983 (.000318)	.00451 (.000101)
AN	.635 (.00378)	.0139 (.000243)	.00346 (.000114)
AM	.211 (.00172)	.603 (.00486)	.587 (.00477)
AT	−.0433 (.0839)	−.0320 (.0585)	−.00547 (.0144)
BKK			
BKL			
BKE			
BKN			
BKM			
BKT	.000913 (.000427)	−.00284 (.000187)	−.0000830 (.000110)
BLL	−.350 (.0151)	−.337 (.0624)	
BLE	.00722 (.00293)	−.0215 (.00622)	
BLN	.145 (.00894)	−.0416 (.00568)	
BLM	.198 (.0173)	.400 (.0685)	
BLT	−.00246 (.000377)	.00578 (.00145)	.000452 (.000673)
BEE	−.0216 (.00309)	−.00750 (.00465)	
BEN	.0149 (.00106)	−.00228 (.00290)	
BEM	−.000549 (.00367)	.0313 (.00745)	
BET	−.000392 (.0000516)	.000732 (.000153)	.000110 (.0000144)
BNN	−.0746 (.00818)	−.00516 (.00164)	
BNM	−.0848 (.00303)	.0490 (.00752)	
BNT	.00436 (.000453)	.00116 (.000146)	.000113 (.0000163)
BMM	−.113 (.0155)	−.481 (.0759)	
BMT	−.00243 (.000283)	−.00484 (.00163)	−.000592 (.000681)
BTT	−.00343 (.0120)	−.00110 (.00836)	−.00128 (.00206)

Table 7-2 (continued).

	Industry		
Parameter	Stone, Clay, and Glass Products	Primary Metal Industries	Fabricated Metal Products
AK	0.125 (0.00134)	0.0930 (0.000960)	0.0926 (0.00231)
AL	.373 (.00382)	.291 (.00262)	.356 (.00569)
AE	.0156 (.000368)	.0154 (.000158)	.00659 (.000102)
AN	.0302 (.000379)	.0270 (.000277)	.00602 (.0000956)
AM	.456 (.00497)	.574 (.00285)	.538 (.00796)
AT	-.00767 (.0215)	-.0135 (.0168)	-.00781 (.0170)
BKK			
BKL			
BKE			
BKN			
BKM			
BKT	-.00323 (.000192)	-.00179 (.000137)	.000890 (.000329)
BLL	-.440 (.0698)		-.441 (.0260)
BLE	.120 (.00716)		-.00667 (.00122)
BLN	-.0202 (.00587)		.0214 (.00121)
BLM	.339 (.0629)		.469 (.0264)
BLT	.0152 (.00186)	.00348 (.000375)	.0135 (.000898)
BEE	-.0330 (.00393)		-.000101 (.0000349)
BEN	.00554 (.00208)		-.000323 (.0000657)
BEM	-.0930 (.00711)		.00709 (.00132)
BET	-.00303 (.000193)	.000186 (.0000226)	.000297 (.0000237)
BNN	-.000930 (.000614)		-.00103 (.000140)
BNM	.0156 (.00450)		.0227 (.00139)
BNT	.000347 (.000171)	-.00365 (.0000396)	.000485 (.0000236)
BMM	.262 (.0558)		-.499 (.0270)
BMT	-.00933 (.00177)	-.00151 (.000406)	.0151 (.00120)
BTT	.000437 (.00307)	-.00151 (.00240)	.000575 (.00243)

Table 7-2 (continued).

	Industry		
Parameter	Machinery Except Electrical	Electrical Machinery	Motor Vehicles and Motor Vehicle Equipment
AK	0.103 (0.00232)	0.0978 (0.00220)	0.115 (0.00396)
AL	.305 (.00312)	.348 (.00211)	.205 (.00176)
AE	.00441 (.000144)	.00528 (.0000610)	.00317 (.0000720)
AN	.00622 (.000236)	.00491 (.000194)	.00424 (.000107)
AM	.581 (.00244)	.544 (.00210)	.673 (.00383)
AT	-.00623 (.00916)	-.00979 (.0119)	.0127 (.0250)
BKK			
BKL			
BKE			
BKN			
BKM			
BKT	-.000751 (.000331)	.000426 (.000314)	.000385 (.000566)
BLL	.240 (.0843)		-.00230 (.00207)
BLE	.0156 (.00288)		-.00350 (.00151)
BLN	-.0131 (.00271)		.00164 (.000680)
BLM	.237 (.0887)	-.00189 (.000302)	.00416 (.00289)
BLT	.00176 (.00203)		.00501 (.000258)
BEE	-.00102 (.000690)		-.00532 (.000935)
BEN	.000854 (.000315)		.00249 (.000314)
BEM	-.0155 (.00251)		.00633 (.00167)
BET	-.00378 (.0000747)	.0000817 (.000000872)	.000134 (.0000542)
BNN	-.000716 (.000178)		-.00116 (.000165)
BNM	.0130 (.00297)		-.00296 (.000650)
BNT	.000401 (.0000723)	.0000873 (.0000277)	.0000755 (.0000286)
BMM	-.235 (.0931)		-.00753 (.00379)
BMT	-.00103 (.00212)	.00130 (.000300)	-.00561 (.000553)
BTT	.000201 (.00130)	.00170 (.00169)	.00305 (.00357)

Table 7-2 (continued).

	Industry		
Parameter	Transportation Equipment and Ordinance	Instruments	Miscellaneous Manufacturing Industries
AK	0.0400 (0.00138)	0.132 (0.00541)	0.0955 (0.00195)
AL	.384 (.00335)	.355 (.00607)	.333 (.00248)
AE	.00473 (.0000796)	.00414 (.0000939)	.00502 (.000177)
AN	.00500 (.000121)	.00278 (.0000659)	.00567 (.000130)
AM	.567 (.00386)	.505 (.0106)	.561 (.00327)
AT	−.00680 (.0217)	−.0179 (.0468)	−.0161 (.0177)
BKK			
BKL			
BKE			
BKN			
BKM			
BKT	−.00135 (.000197)	−.000224 (.000773)	.000794 (.000278)
BLL		−.674 (.0643)	.375 (.0430)
BLE		−.000538 (.00148)	.00507 (.00350)
BLN		−.0101 (.00108)	−.0317 (.00243)
BLM		.685 (.0653)	.401 (.0447)
BLT	−.000162 (.000478)	.0140 (.00116)	.00845 (.00104)
BEE		−.000000429 (.00000233)	−.0000686 (.0000979)
BEN		−.00000802 (.0000218)	.000429 (.000322)
BEM		.000546 (.00150)	−.00543 (.000372)
BET	.0000710 (.0000114)	.0000842 (.0000227)	−.0000444 (.000876)
BNN		−.000150 (.0000346)	−.00269 (.000480)
BNM		.0102 (.00112)	.0340 (.00276)
BNT	.000110 (.0000173)	.000199 (.0000169)	.000901 (.0000620)
BMM		−.695 (.0664)	−.430 (.0468)
BMT	.00133 (.000552)	−.0141 (.00171)	−.0101 (.00112)
BTT	−.000433 (.00310)	−.000652 (.00668)	.000307 (.00253)

Table 7-2 (continued).

Parameter	Industry					
	Transportation		Communications		Electric Utilities	
AK	0.178	(0.00195)	0.353	(0.00296)	0.342	(0.00487)
AL	.444	(.00288)	.364	(.00357)	.241	(.00289)
AE	.00374	(.0000450)	.00844	(.000209)	.104	(.00473)
AN	.0519	(.00130)	.00667	(.000379)	.149	(.00211)
AM	.322	(.00365)	.268	(.00568)	.164	(.00793)
AT	−.00181	(.0163)	−.0355	(.0255)	−.0159	(.0309)
BKK						
BKL						
BKE						
BKN						
BKM						
BKT	.000354	(.000278)	−.00420	(.000423)	−.00367	(.000696)
BLL					.0901	(.0508)
BLE					−.00168	(.0401)
BLN					.00984	(.0165)
BLM					.0819	(.0385)
BLT	.00123	(.000411)	−.00306	(.000509)	−.00353	(.00162)
BEE					.115	(.0689)
BEN					.0355	(.0315)
BEM					.0816	(.0581)
BET	.0000108	(.00000642)	.000134	(.0000298)	.00216	(.00155)
BNN			−.00108	(.000708)	.0119	(.0144)
BNM			.00108	(.000708)	−.0335	(.0240)
BNT	.000784	(.000186)	.0000148	(.0000450)	.000592	(.000666)
BMM			−.00108	(.000708)	−.130	(.0599)
BMT	−.00239	(.000521)	.00712	(.000811)	−.000874	(.00152)
BTT	.00173	(.00232)	−.00164	(.00364)	.00198	(.00441)

Table 7-2 (continued).

Parameter	Gas Utilities	Industry: Trade	Finance Insurance and Real Estate
AK	0.220 (0.00211)	0.154 (0.00101)	0.260 (0.00596)
AL	.167 (.00363)	.585 (.00698)	.254 (.00121)
AE	.00347 (.000140)	.0129 (.000278)	.00711 (.000229)
AN	.546 (.00264)	.0105 (.000434)	.0115 (.000166)
AM	.0644 (.00340)	.238 (.00738)	.468 (.00663)
AT	−.0188 (.0398)	−.00507 (.0116)	−.0233 (.0354)
BKK			
BKL			
BKE			
BKN			
BKM			
BKT	−.00599 (.000302)	.000916 (.000144)	−.00215 (.000851)
BLL	−.161 (.0403)	−1.032 (.217)	
BLE	−.00897 (.00164)	.0188 (.109)	
BLN	.0728 (.0122)	.0145 (.0113)	
BLM	.0970 (.0322)	.999 (.218)	
BLT	.0100 (.000876)	.0355 (.00672)	.00255 (.000174)
BEE	−.00266 (.00118)	−.000343 (.000457)	
BEN	.00220 (.000802)	−.000264 (.000144)	
BEM	.00942 (.00120)	.0182 (.0104)	
BET	.000407 (.0000460)	−.000708 (.000343)	.000106 (.0000327)
BNN	−.0345 (.00584)	−.000203 (.000287)	
BNM	−.0405 (.0100)	.0140 (.0109)	
BNT	.000724 (.000413)	−.000833 (.000354)	.0000380 (.0000237)
BMM	−.0660 (.0249)	.966 (.219)	
BMT	−.00516 (.000739)	−.0349 (.00676)	−.000550 (.000947)
BTT	−.00173 (.00568)	.00129 (.00166)	.00238 (.00504)

Table 7-2 (continued).

Parameter	Services	Government Enterprises	Industry
AK	0.103 (0.000468)	0.105 (0.00403)	
AL	.538 (.00368)	.597 (.00796)	
AE	.0129 (.000168)	.0149 (.000822)	
AN	.00804 (.000126)	.0168 (.00100)	
AM	.338 (.00367)	.266 (.00668)	
AT	−.00244 (.0231)	−.0339 (.0420)	
BKK			
BKL			
BKE			
BKN			
BKM			
BKT	.00125 (.0000668)	.00567 (.000575)	
BLL		−.0435 (.0174)	
BLE		.0512 (.0114)	
BLN		−.0290 (.00553)	
BLM		.0213 (.0143)	
BLT	.00714 (.000525)	.0173 (.00152)	
BEE		−.0602 (.0161)	
BEN		.0341 (.00692)	
BEM		−.0251 (.0106)	
BET	.000225 (.0000240)	−.00346 (.000679)	
BNN		−.0194 (.00324)	
BNM		.0142 (.00645)	
BNT	−.0000313 (.0000180)	.00140 (.000328)	
BMM		−.0104 (.0103)	
BMT	−.00859 (.000525)	−.0209 (.00129)	
BTT	.0000208 (.00330)	−.00310 (.00600)	

Substitution

Our interpretation of the parameter estimates reported in Table 7-2 begins with an analysis of the estimates of the parameters $\{\alpha_K^i, \alpha_L^i, \alpha_E^i, \alpha_N^i, \alpha_M^i\}$. It is useful to recall that if the sectoral price functions are increasing in the prices of capital, labor, electricity, nonelectrical energy, and materials inputs, the average value shares are nonnegative for each sector. These conditions are satisfied for all thirty-five sectors included in our study. The sectoral price functions are not universally decreasing in time. The negative of the estimated average rate of technical change is negative in thirty-one sectors and positive in four sectors. Negative signs characterize the construction, apparel, printing and publishing, and motor vehicles industries.

The estimated share elasticities with respect to price $\{\beta_{KK}^i, \beta_{KL}^i, \beta_{KE}^i, \beta_{KN}^i, \beta_{KM}^i, \beta_{LL}^i, \beta_{LE}^i, \beta_{LN}^i, \beta_{LM}^i, \beta_{EE}^i, \beta_{EN}^i, \beta_{EM}^i, \beta_{NN}^i, \beta_{NM}^i, \beta_{MM}^i\}$ describe the implications of patterns of substitution among capital, labor, electricity, nonelectrical energy, and materials inputs for the relative distribution of the value of output among these five inputs. Positive share elasticities imply that the corresponding value shares increase with an increase in price; negative share elasticities imply that the value shares decrease with an increase in price; share elasticities equal to zero imply that the value shares are independent of price. It is important to keep in mind that we have fitted these parameters subject to the restrictions implied by concavity of the price function. These restrictions imply that all share elasticities be set equal to zero for ten of the thirty-five industries listed in Table 7-2. For all industries the share elasticities of all inputs with respect to the price of capital input are set equal to zero. For thirteen of the thirty-five industries the share elasticities of all inputs with respect to the price of labor input are set equal to zero. For eleven industries all share elasticities with respect to the price of electricity input are set equal to zero. Finally, for ten industries all share elasticities with respect to the price of nonelectrical energy input are set equal to zero. Of the five hundred twenty-five share elasticities for the thirty-five industries included in our study 234 are fitted without constraint and 291 are set equal to zero.

Our interpretation of the parameter estimates given in Table 7-2 continues with the estimated elasticities of the share of each input with respect to the price of the input itself $\{\beta_{KK}^i, \beta_{LL}^i, \beta_{EE}^i, \beta_{NN}^i, \beta_{MM}^i\}$. Under the necessary and sufficient conditions for concavity of the price function for each sector, these share elasticities are nonpositive. The share of each input is nonincreasing in the price of the input itself. This condition together with the condition that the sum of all the share elasticities with respect to a given input is zero implies that only two of the elasticities of the shares of each input with respect to the prices of the other four inputs $\{\beta_{KL}^i, \beta_{KE}^i, \beta_{KN}^i, \beta_{KM}^i, \beta_{LE}^i, \beta_{LN}^i, \beta_{LM}^i, \beta_{EN}^i, \beta_{EM}^i, \beta_{MM}^i\}$ can be negative. All ten of these share elasticities can be nonnegative, and this condition holds for eleven of the thirty-five industries included in our study.

We have already pointed out that the share elasticities of all inputs with respect to the price of capital input are equal to zero. The share elasticity of labor with respect to the price of electricity $\{\beta_{LE}^i\}$ is nonnegative for twenty-seven of the thirty-five industries. By symmetry this parameter can also be interpreted as the share elasticity of electricity with respect to the price of labor. The share elasticity of labor with respect to the price of nonelectrical energy $\{\beta_{LN}^i\}$ is nonnegative for twenty-one of the thirty-five industries. Finally, the share elasticity of labor with respect to the price of materials $\{\beta_{LM}^i\}$ is nonnegative for all thirty-five industries. Considering the share elasticities of electricity, nonelectrical energy, and materials inputs, we find that the share elasticity of electricity with respect to the price of nonelectrical energy $\{\beta_{EN}^i\}$ is nonnegative for twenty-eight of the thirty-five industries, while the share elasticity of electricity with respect to the price of materials $\{\beta_{EM}^i\}$ is nonnegative for twenty-four of these industries. Finally, the share elasticity of nonelectrical energy with respect to the price of materials $\{\beta_{NM}^i\}$ is nonnegative for twenty-six of the thirty-five industries.

Technical Change

We continue the interpretation of parameter estimates given in Table 7-2 with the estimated biases of technical change with respect to the price of each input $\{\beta_{KT}^i, \beta_{LT}^i, \beta_{ET}^i, \beta_{NT}^i, \beta_{MT}^i\}$. These parameters can be interpreted as the negative of the change in the rate of technical change with respect to the price of each input or, alternatively, as the change in the share of each input with respect to time. The sum of the five biases of technical change with respect to price is equal to zero, so that we can rule out the possibility that the five biases are all negative or all positive. Of the thirty remaining logical possibilities, only fifteen actually occur among the results presented in Table 7-2. Of these, only nine occur for more than one industry, and only four occur for more than two industries. It is important to note that the biases of technical change are not affected by the concavity of the price function. All five parameters are fitted for thirty-five industries, subject to the constraint that their sum is equal to zero.

We first consider the bias of technical change with respect to the price of capital input. If the estimated value of this parameter is positive, technical change is capital using. Alternatively, the rate of technical change decreases with an increase in the price of capital input. If the estimated value is negative, technical change is capital saving, and the rate of technical change increases with the price of capital. Technical change is capital using for twenty of the thirty-five industries included in our study; it is capital saving for fifteen of these industries. We conclude that the rate of technical change decreases with the price of capital input for twenty industries and increases with this price for fifteen industries.

The interpretation of the biases of technical change with respect to the prices of labor, electricity, nonelectrical energy, and materials inputs is analogous to the interpretation of the bias with respect to the price of capital input. If the estimated value of the bias is positive, technical change uses the corresponding input; alternatively, the rate of technical change decreases with an increase in the input price. If the estimated value is negative, technical change saves the corresponding input; alternatively, the rate of technical change decreases with the input price. Considering the bias of technical change with respect to the price of labor input, we find that technical change is labor using for twenty-six of the thirty-five industries and labor saving for nine of these industries. The rate of technical change decreases with the price of labor input for twenty-six industries and increases with this price for nine industries.

Considering the bias of technical change with respect to the price of electricity input, we find that technical change is electricity using for twenty-three of the thirty-five industries included in our study and electricity saving for twelve of these industries. The rate of technical change decreases with the price of electricity for twenty-three industries and increases with this price for twelve industries. Turning to the bias of technical change with respect to the price of nonelectrical energy input we find that technical change is nonelectrical energy using for twenty-eight of the thirty-five industries and nonelectrical energy saving for only seven of these industries. We conclude that the rate of technical change increases with the price of nonelectrical energy for twenty-eight industries and decreases with this price for the remaining seven. Finally, technical change is materials using for eight of the thirty-five industries included in our study and materials saving for the other twenty-seven, so that the rate of technical change increases with the price of materials for twenty-seven industries and decreases with this price for the remaining eight.

Patterns of Technical Change

A classification of industries by patterns of the biases of technical change is given in Table 7-3. The pattern that occurs with the greatest frequency is capital using, labor using, electricity using, nonelectrical energy using and materials saving technical change. This pattern occurs for eight of the thirty-five industries included in our study. For this pattern the rate of technical change decreases with the prices of capital, labor, electricity, and nonelectrical energy inputs and increases with the price of materials input.

Table 7-3. Classification of Industries by Biases of Technical Change.

Pattern of Biases	Industries
Capital using Labor using Electricity using Nonelectrical energy using Materials saving	Tobacco, textiles, apparel, lumber and wood, printing and publishing, fabricated metal, motor vehicles, transportation
Capital using Labor saving Electricity using Nonelectrical energy using Materials using	Electrical machinery
Capital using Labor using Electricity using Nonelectrical energy saving Materials saving	Metal mining, services
Capital using Labor using Electricity saving Nonelectrical energy using Materials saving	Nonmetallic mining, miscellaneous manufacturing, government enterprises
Capital using Labor saving Electricity using Nonelectrical energy saving Materials using	Construction
Capital using Labor using Electricity saving Nonelectrical energy saving Materials saving	Coal mining, trade
Capital using labor saving Electricity saving Nonelectrical energy using Materials saving	Agriculture, crude petroleum and natural gas, petroleum refining
Capital saving Labor using Electricity using Nonelectrical energy using Materials using	Food, paper
Capital saving Labor using Electricity using Nonelectrical energy using Materials saving	Rubber, leather, instruments, gas utilities, finance, insurance, and real estate

Table 7-3 (continued).

Pattern of Biases	Industries
Capital saving Labor using Electricity saving Nonelectrical energy using Materials using	Chemicals
Capital saving Labor saving Electricity using Nonelectrical energy using Material using	Transportation equipment and ordnance, communications
Capital saving Labor using Electricity saving Nonelectrical energy using Materials saving	Stone, clay and glass, machinery
Capital saving Labor using Electricity using Nonelectrical energy saving Materials saving	Primary metals
Capital saving Labor saving Electricity using Nonelectrical energy using Materials saving	Electric utilities
Capital saving Labor saving Electricity saving Nonelectrical energy saving Materials using	Furniture

The pattern that occurs next most frequently is capital saving, labor using, electricity using, nonelectrical energy using, and materials saving technical change. This pattern occurs for five industries. For this pattern the rate of technical change decreases with the prices of labor, electricity, and non-electrical energy inputs and increases with the prices of capital and materials inputs. These two patterns of technical change differ only in the role of the price of capital input.

Our interpretation of the parameter estimates given in Table 7-2 concludes the rates of change of the negative of the rate of technical change $\{\beta^i_{TT}\}$. If the estimated value of this parameter is positive the rate of technical change is decreasing; if the value is negative the rate is increasing. For fifteen of the thirty-five industries included in our study the estimated value is positive and the rate of technical change is decreasing; for twenty industries the fitted value is negative, so that the rate of technical change is increasing.

SUMMARY AND CONCLUSION

In this paper we have analyzed the role of electrification in the growth of productivity. For this purpose we have developed and implemented a new econometric model of productivity growth. We have estimated the unknown parameters of this model from data for thirty-five individual industries of the United States for the period 1958–79. Our econometric model determines the growth of sectoral productivity as a function of the relative prices of sectoral inputs. To capture the impact of electrification we have divided inputs for each sector among capital, labor, electricity, nonelectrical energy, and materials inputs.

To represent the impact of the relative prices of sectoral inputs on productivity growth we have defined biases of technical change as the negative of changers in the rate of technical change with respect to proportional changes in input prices. Biases of technical change can also be defined in an alternative and equivalent way as changes in the value shares of each input with respect to time. Biases of technical change can be employed to derive the implications of changes in the relative prices of sectoral inputs on the rate of technical change. They can also be used to derive the implications of patterns of technical change for the distribution of the value of sectoral output among the inputs.

The Role of Electrification

We have estimated biases of technical change with respect to prices of capital input, labor input, electricity input, nonelectrical energy input, and materials input. These biases are unknown parameters of the econometric models for the thirty-five industrial sectors included in this study. In order to test the hypothesis advanced by Schurr and Rosenberg about the importance of electrification in productivity growth, we can focus on the bias of technical change with respect to electricity input. If this bias is positive, then technical change is electricity using; if the bias is negative, technical change is electricity saving. If technical change is electricity using, the share of electricity input in the value of output increases with technical change, while the rate of technical change increases with a decrease in the price of electricity.

We have found that technical change is electricity using for twenty-three of the thirty-five industries included in our study. Our first and most important conclusion is that electrification plays a very important role in productivity growth. A decline in the price of electricity stimulates technical change in twenty-three of the thirty-five industries and dampens productivity growth in only twelve. Alternatively and equivalently, we can say that technical change results in an increase in the share of electricity input in the value of output, holding the relative prices of all inputs constant, in twenty-three of the thirty-five industries included in our study. Technical change results in a decrease in the share of electricity input in only twelve of these industries.

Our empirical results provide strong confirmation for the hypothesis advanced by Schurr and Rosenberg about the interrelationship of electrification and productivity growth in a wide range of industries. Schurr and his associates in the study *Energy in America's Future* have shown that the price of electricity fell in real terms through 1971. This decline in real electricity prices has promoted electrification through the substitution of electricity for other forms of energy and through the substitution of energy for other inputs, especially for labor input. In addition, the decline in the real price of electricity has stimulated the growth of productivity in a wide range of industries. The spread of electrification and the rapid growth of productivity through the early 1970s are both associated with a decline in real electricity prices. This decline was made possible in part by advances in the thermal efficiency of electricity generation.

Beginning in the early 1970s the downward trend in the real price of electricity was reversed. The reversal in the trend of real electricity prices has been associated with a marked slowdown in advances in the thermal efficiency of electricity generation that can be traced back to the late 1960s. However, the reduction in the rate of technical change in the electric generating industry is only part of the explanation of the reversal in the trend of real electricity prices. In addition, prices of primary energy sources employed in electricity generation have risen sharply in the aftermath of the oil price shocks of 1973 and 1979. Rising electricity prices have slowed the growth of productivity in U.S. industries throughout the 1970s. These price increases have an important role to play in the explanation of the slowdown of U.S. productivity growth since 1973.

In linking electrification and productivity growth, Schurr has advanced an important subsidiary hypothesis. This hypothesis is that electrification is especially significant in stimulating the growth of productivity in the manufacturing industries. Schurr's hypothesis is supported by the fact that technical change is electricity using in fifteen of the twenty-one manufacturing industries included in our study, while technical change is electricity using in only eight of the fourteen nonmanufacturnig industries. Schurr's explanation for this phenomenon is that electrification of industrial processes led to much greater flexibility in the application of energy. Rosenberg's examples of the importance of electrification—iron and steel, glass, and aluminum production—are also drawn from manufacturing.

Rosenberg has advanced a second subsidiary hypothesis in analyzing the link between electrification and productivity growth. This hypothesis is that electricity using technical change is the "other side of the coin" of labor saving technical change. We have been unable to find support for this hypothesis in our empirical results. In fact, technical change is labor saving for only nine of the thirty-five industries included in our study and labor using for the remaining twenty-six of these industries. However, we have pointed out that the sum of biases of technical change for all five inputs must be equal to zero. The predominance of technical change that uses electricity must be balanced by technical change that saves other inputs. We have found that technical change is materials saving for twenty-seven of the thirty-five industries included in our study and materials using for the remaining eight. For all other inputs, including labor and electricity, technical change is predominantly input using. We conclude that technical change that uses electricity input and inputs of capital labor, and nonelectrical energy is balanced by technical change that saves materials.

Utilization of Nonelectrical Energy

We have found that electrification plays an important role in productivity growth and we have also examined the utilization of nonelectrical energy. Our findings are that technical change is nonelectrical energy using for twenty-eight of the thirty-five industries included in our study and energy saving for seven of these industries. Our second conclusion is that greater utilization of nonelectrical energy plays an even more significant role in productivity growth than electrification. A decline in the price of nonelectrical energy stimulates technical change in twenty-eight of the thirty-five industries and dampens productivity growth in only seven. Alternatively, we can say that technical change results in an increase in the share of nonelectrical energy input in the value of output in twenty-eight of the thirty-five industries and results in a decrease in the nonelectrical energy input share in only seven.

Again considering the evidence on energy price developments presented by Schurr and his associates, we find that the price of nonelectrical energy has fallen in real terms through the early 1970s, reaching a minimum for natural gas and fuel oil in 1970 and for gasoline in 1972. This decline in nonelectrical energy prices in real terms has promoted greater utilization of nonelectrical energy through the substitution of these forms of energy for capital, labor, and materials inputs. In addition, the decline in the real price of nonelectrical energy, like the decline in electricity prices we have examined earlier, has stimulated the growth of productivity in a wide range of industries. We conclude that the greater utilization of nonelectrical energy in relation to other inputs such as labor and the rapid growth of productivity through the early 1970s are associated with the decline in the real price of nonelectrical energy.

Beginning in the early 1970s the downward trend in the real price of nonelectrical energy has been reversed and the increase in utilization of nonelectrical energy relative to other inputs in U.S. industries has slowed dramatically. The reversal in the trend of nonelectrical energy prices, as well as an important part of the reversal in the trend of electricity prices we have examined above, has been associated with the oil price shocks of 1973 and 1979. Rising prices of nonelectrical energy have reinforced the negative impact of rising prices of electricity on the growth of productivity throughout the 1970s. Increases in the real prices of both electricity and nonelectrical energy have a role to play in the explanation of the slowdown in U.S. productivity growth since 1973.

In linking greater utilization of nonelectrical energy and productivity growth, Schurr and his associates in the study *Energy in America's Future* have advanced an important subsidiary hypothesis. This hypothesis is that greater utilization of fluid forms of energy has enhanced productivity in agriculture, transportation, and manufacturing. We find that technical change is nonelectrical energy using in agriculture and transportation, as suggested by Schurr and his associates. We also find that technical change is nonelectrical energy using for nineteen of the twenty-one manufacturing industries included in our study. Technical change in nonelectrical energy using for only seven of the twelve industries other than agriculture, manufacturing, and transportation. We conclude that greater utilization of nonelectrical energy has a significant role in productivity growth for an even wider range of industries than electrification.

Conclusion

We have now completed our analysis of the role of electrification and the utilization of nonelectrical energy in productivity growth. For this purpose we have employed an econometric model of production and technical change. Within the framework provided by our model we can offer a tentative explanation of the disparate trends in energy intensity and productivity growth. These trends first drew the attention of Schurr and his associates to the special role of electrification. Over the period 1920–53 energy intensity of production was falling while productivity was rising. While the fall in real prices of electricity and nonelectrical energy resulted in the substitution of energy inputs for other inputs, especially for labor input, these price trends also generated sufficient growth in output per unit of energy input that the energy intensity of production actually fell. This explanation is completely in accord with the explanation advanced by Schurr and his associates.

Between 1953 and 1973 energy intensity was stable, while productivity continued to grow. During this period real energy prices continued to fall, but at slower rates than during the period 1920–53. As before, the fall in real prices of electricity and nonelectrical energy resulted in the substitution of energy inputs for other inputs. But this was almost precisely offset by the growth in output per unit of energy input, leaving the energy intensity of production unchanged. Finally, real energy prices began to rise in the early 1970s, increasing dramatically after the first oil shock in 1973 and again after the second oil shock in 1979. These price trends resulted in the substitution of capital, labor, and materials inputs for inputs of electricity and nonelectrical energy, thereby reducing energy intensity of production. At the same time, the energy price trends contributed to a marked slow-down in productivity growth.

Although much research remains to be done before we obtain a complete understanding of the role of energy utilization in productivity growth, it is important to emphasize that we have made important progress toward this goal. We have analyzed the character of technical change in a wide range of industries covering the whole of the U.S. economy. We have confronted hypotheses advanced in earlier research by Schurr and his associates and by Rosenberg with new empirical evidence. We have found support for the hypothesis that electrification and productivity growth are interrelated. Somewhat surprisingly, we have found that the utilization of nonelectrical energy and productivity growth are even more strongly interrelated. Finally, we have identified new research objectives that will make it possible to obtain a deeper understanding of the interrelationship between energy utilization and productivity change.

Given the support for the hypothesis that technical change is electricity using and nonelectrical energy using, we can assess the potential for electrification and greater utilization of nonelectrical energy in reviving the growth of productivity at the level of individual industries in the United States. Schurr (1983: 7) has summarized this potential as follows:

> If this line of theorizing is correct, one of the keys to reconciling the future growth of energy productivity and labor and total factor productivity would be (a) through the vigorous pursuit of these energy supply technologies which assure the renewed future availability, on favorable terms, of those energy forms which possess the highly desirable flexibility features that have characterized liquid fuels and electricity, and (b) through the search for counterpart energy consumption technologies that can put these characteristics to efficient use in industrial, commercial, and household application.

APPENDIX

The development of our econometric model of production and technical change proceeds through two stages. We first specify a functional form for the sector price functions, say $\{P^i\}$, taking into account restrictions on the parameters implied by the theory of production. Secondly, we formulate an error structure for the econometric model and discuss procedures for estimation of the unknown parameters.

Our first step in formulating an econometric model of production and technical change is to consider specific forms for the sectoral price function $\{P^i\}$:

$$
\begin{aligned}
q_i = \exp [\alpha_O^i &+ \alpha_K^i \ \ell n \ p_K^i + \alpha_L^i \ \ell n \ p_L^i + \alpha_E^i \ \ell n \ p_E^i + \alpha_N^i \ \ell n \ p_N^i + \alpha_M^i \ \ell n \ p_M^i + \alpha_T^i \cdot T \\
&+ \frac{1}{2} \beta_{KK}^i \big(\ell n \ p_K^i\big)^2 + \beta_{KL}^i \ \ell n \ p_K^i \ \ell n \ p_L^i + \beta_{KE}^i \ \ell n \ p_K^i \ \ell n \ p_E^i \\
&+ \beta_{KN}^i \ \ell n \ p_K^i \ \ell n \ p_N^i + \beta_{KM}^i \ \ell n \ p_K^i \ \ell n \ p_M^i + \beta_{KT}^i \ \ell n \ p_K^i \cdot T + \frac{1}{2} \beta_{LL}^i \big(\ell n \ p_L^i\big)^2 \\
&+ \beta_{LE}^i \ \ell n \ p_L^i \ \ell n \ p_E^i + \beta_{LN}^i \ \ell n \ p_L^i \ \ell n \ p_N^i + \beta_{LM}^i \ \ell n \ p_L^i \ \ell n \ p_M^i + \beta_{LT}^i \ \ell n \ p_L^i \cdot T \\
&+ \frac{1}{2} \beta_{EE}^i \big(\ell n \ p_E^i\big)^2 + \beta_{EN}^i \ \ell n \ p_E^i \ \ell n \ p_N^i + \beta_{EM}^i \ \ell n \ p_E^i \ \ell n \ p_M^i + \beta_{ET}^i \ \ell n \ p_E^i \cdot T \\
&+ \frac{1}{2} \beta_{NN}^i \big(\ell n \ p_N^i\big)^2 + \beta_{NM}^i \ \ell n \ p_N^i \ \ell n \ p_M^i + \beta_{NT}^i \ \ell n \ p_N^i \cdot T \\
&+ \frac{1}{2} \beta_{MM}^i \big(\ell n \ p_M^i\big)^2 + \beta_{MT}^i \ \ell n \ p_M^i \cdot T + \frac{1}{2} \beta_{TT}^i \cdot T^2], \quad (i = 1, 2 \ldots n).
\end{aligned}
$$

For these price functions, the prices of outputs are transcendental or, more specifically, exponential functions of the logarithms of the prices of capital (K), labor (L), electricity (E), nonelectrical energy (N), and materials (M) inputs. We refer to these forms as *transcendental logarithmic price functions* or, more simply, translog price functions, indicating the role of the variables that enter into the price functions.

Homogeneity and Symmetry

The price functions $\{P^i\}$ are homogeneous of degree one in the input prices. The translog price function for an industrial sector is characterized by homogeneity of degree one if and only if the parameters for that sector satisfy the conditions

$$
\begin{aligned}
\alpha_K^i + \alpha_L^i + \alpha_E^i + \alpha_N^i + \alpha_M^i &= 1, \\
\beta_{KK}^i + \beta_{KL}^i + \beta_{KE}^i + \beta_{KN}^i + \beta_{KM}^i &= 0, \\
\beta_{LK}^i + \beta_{LL}^i + \beta_{LE}^i + \beta_{LN}^i + \beta_{LM}^i &= 0, \\
\beta_{EK}^i + \beta_{EL}^i + \beta_{EE}^i + \beta_{EN}^i + \beta_{EM}^i &= 0, \\
\beta_{NK}^i + \beta_{NL}^i + \beta_{NE}^i + \beta_{NN}^i + \beta_{NM}^i &= 0, \\
\beta_{MK}^i + \beta_{ML}^i + \beta_{ME}^i + \beta_{MN}^i + \beta_{MM}^i &= 0, \\
\beta_{KT}^i + \beta_{LT}^i + \beta_{ET}^i + \beta_{NT}^i + \beta_{MT}^i &= 0, \quad (i = 1, 2 \ldots n).
\end{aligned}
$$

For each sector the value shares of capital, labor, electricity, nonelectrical energy, and materials inputs, say $\{v_K^i\}$, $\{v_L^i\}$, $\{v_E^i\}$, $\{v_N^i\}$, and $\{v_M^i\}$, can be expressed in terms of logarithmic derivatives of the sectoral price functions with respect to the logarithms of price of the corresponding input:

$$v_K^i = \alpha_K^i + \beta_{KK}^i \ln p_K^i + \beta_{KL}^i \ln p_L^i + \beta_{KE}^i \ln p_E^i + \beta_{KN}^i \ln p_N^i + \beta_{KM}^i \ln p_M^i + \beta_{KT}^i \cdot T,$$

$$v_L^i = \alpha_L^i + \beta_{KL}^i \ln p_K^i + \beta_{LL}^i \ln p_L^i + \beta_{LE}^i \ln p_E^i + \beta_{LN}^i \ln p_N^i + \beta_{LM}^i \ln p_M^i + \beta_{LT}^i \cdot T,$$

$$v_E^i = \alpha_E^i + \beta_{KE}^i \ln p_K^i + \beta_{LE}^i \ln p_L^i + \beta_{EE}^i \ln p_E^i + \beta_{EN}^i \ln p_N^i + \beta_{EM}^i \ln p_M^i + \beta_{ET}^i \cdot T,$$

$$v_N^i = \alpha_N^i + \beta_{KN}^i \ln p_K^i + \beta_{LN}^i \ln p_L^i + \beta_{EN}^i \ln p_E^i + \beta_{NN}^i \ln p_N^i + \beta_{NM}^i \ln p_M^i + \beta_{NT}^i \cdot T,$$

$$v_M^i = \alpha_M^i + \beta_{KM}^i \ln p_K^i + \beta_{LM}^i \ln p_L^i + \beta_{EM}^i \ln p_E^i + \beta_{NM}^i \ln p_N^i + \beta_{MM}^i \ln p_M^i + \beta_{MT}^i \cdot T,$$

$$(i = 1, 2 \ldots n).$$

Finally, for each sector the rate of technical change, say $\{v_T^i\}$, can be expressed as the negative of the rate of growth of the price of sectoral output with respect to time, holding the prices of capital, labor, electricity, nonelectrical energy, and materials inputs constant. The negative of the rate of technical change takes the following form:

$$-v_T^i = \alpha_T^i + \beta_{KT}^i \ln p_K^i + \beta_{LT}^i \ln p_L^i + \beta_{ET}^i \ln p_E^i + \beta_{NT}^i \ln p_N^i + \beta_{MT}^i \ln p_M^i + \beta_{TT}^i \cdot T,$$

$$(i = 1, 2 \ldots n).$$

Given the sectoral price functions $\{P^i\}$, we can define the *share elasticities with respect to price*[9] as the derivatives of the value shares with respect to the logarithms of the prices of capital, labor, electricity, nonelectrical energy, and materials inputs. For the translog price functions the share elasticities with respect to price are constant. We can also characterize these forms of *constant share elasticity* or CSE price functions indicating the interpretation of the fixed parameters that enter the price functions. The share elasticities with respect to price are symmetric, so that the parameters satisfy the conditions

$$\beta_{KL}^i = \beta_{LK}^i, \qquad \beta_{LN}^i = \beta_{NL}^i,$$

$$\beta_{KE}^i = \beta_{EK}^i, \qquad \beta_{LM}^i = \beta_{ML}^i,$$

$$\beta_{KN}^i = \beta_{NK}^i, \qquad \beta_{EN}^i = \beta_{NE}^i,$$

$$\beta_{KM}^i = \beta_{MK}^i, \qquad \beta_{EM}^i = \beta_{ME}^i,$$

$$\beta_{LE}^i = \beta_{EL}^i, \qquad \beta_{NM}^i = \beta_{MN}^i, \qquad (i = 1, 2 \ldots n).$$

Similarly, given the sectoral price functions $\{P^i\}$, we can define the *biases of technical change with respect to price* as derivatives of the value shares with respect to time.[10] Alternatively, we can define the biases of technical change with respect to price in terms of the derivatives of the rate of technical change with respect to the logarithms of the price of capital, labor, electricity, nonelectrical energy, and materials inputs. Those two definitions of biases of technical change are equivalent. For the translog price functions the biases of technical change with respect to price are constant; these parameters are symmetric and satisfy the conditions

$$\beta_{ET}^i = \beta_{TE}^i \quad ,$$
$$\beta_{LT}^i = \beta_{TL}^i \quad ,$$
$$\beta_{ET}^i = \beta_{TE}^i \quad ,$$
$$\beta_{NT}^i = \beta_{TN}^i \quad ,$$
$$\beta_{MT}^i = \beta_{TM}^i \quad , \qquad (i = 1, 2 \ldots n).$$

Finally, we can define the *rate of change of the negative of the rate of technical change* β_{TT}^i ($i = 1, 2 \ldots n$) as the derivative of the negative of the rate of technical change with respect to time.[11] For the translog price functions these rates of change are constant.

Concavity

Our next step in considering specific forms of the sectoral price functions $\{P^i\}$ is to derive restrictions on the parameters implied by the fact that the price functions are increasing in all five input prices and the concave in the five input prices. First, since the price functions are increasing in each of the five input prices, the value shares are nonnegative:

$$v_K^i \geqq 0 ,$$
$$v_L^i \geqq 0 ,$$
$$v_E^i \geqq 0 ,$$
$$v_N^i \geqq 0 ,$$
$$v_M^i \geqq 0 , \qquad (i = 1, 2 \ldots n).$$

Under homogeneity these value shares sum to unity:

$$v_K^i + v_L^i + v_E^i + v_N^i + v_M^i = 1 , \qquad (i = 1, 2 \ldots n).$$

Concavity of the sectoral price functions $\{P^i\}$ implies that the matrices of second-order partial derivatives $\{H^i\}$ are negative semidefinite. This implies, in turn, that the matrices $\{U^i + v^i v^{i\prime} - V^i\}$ are negative semidefinite:[12]

$$\frac{1}{P^i} \cdot Q^i \cdot H^i \cdot Q^i = U^i + v^i v^{i\prime} - v^i , \qquad (i = 1, 2 \ldots n),$$

where

$$Q^i = \begin{bmatrix} P_K^i & 0 & 0 & 0 & 0 \\ 0 & P_L^i & 0 & 0 & 0 \\ 0 & 0 & P_E^i & 0 & 0 \\ 0 & 0 & 0 & P_N^i & 0 \\ 0 & 0 & 0 & 0 & P_M^i \end{bmatrix}, \quad V^i = \begin{bmatrix} v_K^i & 0 & 0 & 0 & 0 \\ 0 & v_L^i & 0 & 0 & 0 \\ 0 & 0 & v_E^i & 0 & 0 \\ 0 & 0 & 0 & v_N^i & 0 \\ 0 & 0 & 0 & 0 & v_M^i \end{bmatrix}, \quad v^i = \begin{bmatrix} v_K^i \\ v_L^i \\ v_E^i \\ v_N^i \\ v_M^i \end{bmatrix}$$

$$(i = 1, 2 \ldots n),$$

and $\{U^i\}$ are matrices of constant share elasticities, defined above.

Without violating the nonnegativity restrictions on value shares we can set the matrices $\{v^i v^{i\prime} - V^i\}$ equal to zero, for example, by choosing the value shares:

$$v_K^i = 1,$$
$$v_L^i = 0,$$
$$v_E^i = 0,$$
$$v_N^i = 0,$$
$$v_M^i = 0.$$

Necessary conditions for the matrices $\{U^i + v^i v^{i\prime} - V^i\}$ to be negative semidefinite are that the matrices of share elasticities $\{U^i\}$ must be negative semidefinite. These conditions are also sufficient, since the matrices $\{v^i v^{i\prime} - V^i\}$ are negative semidefinite for all nonnegative value shares summing to unity and the sum of two negative semidefinite matrices is negative semidefinite.

To impose concavity on the translog price functions the matrices $\{U^i\}$ of constant share elasticities can be represented in terms of their Cholesky factorizations, as shown on page 314.

Under constant returns to scale the constant share elasticities satisfy symmetry restrictions and restrictions implied by homogeneity of degree one of the price function. These restrictions imply that the parameters of the Cholesky factorizations $\{\lambda_{21}^i, \lambda_{31}^i, \lambda_{41}^i, \lambda_{51}^i, \lambda_{32}^i, \lambda_{42}^i, \lambda_{52}^i, \lambda_{43}^i, \lambda_{53}^i, \lambda_{54}^i, \delta_1^i, \delta_2^i, \delta_3^i, \delta_4^i, \delta_5^i\}$ must satisfy the following conditions:

$$1 + \lambda_{21}^i + \lambda_{31}^i + \lambda_{41}^i + \lambda_{51}^i = 0,$$
$$1 + \lambda_{32}^i + \lambda_{42}^i + \lambda_{52}^i = 0,$$
$$1 + \lambda_{43}^i + \lambda_{53}^i = 0,$$
$$1 + \lambda_{54}^i = 0,$$
$$\delta_5^i = 0, \quad (i = 1, 2 \ldots n).$$

$$
\begin{bmatrix}
\beta^i_{KK} & \beta^i_{KL} & \beta^i_{KE} & \beta^i_{KN} & \beta^i_{KM} \\
\beta^i_{KL} & \beta^i_{LL} & \beta^i_{LE} & \beta^i_{LN} & \beta^i_{LM} \\
\beta^i_{KE} & \beta^i_{LE} & \beta^i_{EE} & \beta^i_{EN} & \beta^i_{EM} \\
\beta^i_{KN} & \beta^i_{LN} & \beta^i_{EN} & \beta^i_{NN} & \beta^i_{NM} \\
\beta^i_{KM} & \beta^i_{LM} & \beta^i_{EM} & \beta^i_{NM} & \beta^i_{MM}
\end{bmatrix}
=
\begin{bmatrix}
1 & 0 & 0 & 0 & 0 \\
\lambda^i_{21} & 1 & 0 & 0 & 0 \\
\lambda^i_{31} & \lambda^i_{32} & 1 & 0 & 0 \\
\lambda^i_{41} & \lambda^i_{42} & \lambda^i_{43} & 1 & 0 \\
\lambda^i_{51} & \lambda^i_{52} & \lambda^i_{53} & \lambda^i_{54} & 1
\end{bmatrix}
\begin{bmatrix}
\delta^i_1 & 0 & 0 & 0 & 0 \\
0 & \delta^i_2 & 0 & 0 & 0 \\
0 & 0 & \delta^i_3 & 0 & 0 \\
0 & 0 & 0 & \delta^i_4 & 0 \\
0 & 0 & 0 & 0 & \delta^i_5
\end{bmatrix}
\begin{bmatrix}
1 & \lambda^i_{21} & \lambda^i_{31} & \lambda^i_{41} & \lambda^i_{51} \\
0 & 1 & \lambda^i_{32} & \lambda^i_{42} & \lambda^i_{52} \\
0 & 0 & 1 & \lambda^i_{43} & \lambda^i_{53} \\
0 & 0 & 0 & 1 & \lambda^i_{54} \\
0 & 0 & 0 & 0 & 1
\end{bmatrix}
$$

$$
=
\begin{bmatrix}
\delta^i_1 & \lambda^i_{21}\delta^i_1 & \lambda^i_{31}\delta^i_1 & \lambda^i_{41}\delta^i_1 & \lambda^i_{51}\delta^i_1 \\[4pt]
\lambda^i_{21}\delta^i_1 & \lambda^i_{21}\lambda^i_{21}\delta^i_1+\delta^i_2 & \lambda^i_{21}\lambda^i_{31}\delta^i_1+\lambda^i_{32}\delta^i_2 & \lambda^i_{41}\lambda^i_{21}\delta^i_1+\lambda^i_{42}\delta^i_2 & \lambda^i_{51}\lambda^i_{21}\delta^i_1+\lambda^i_{52}\delta^i_1 \\[4pt]
\lambda^i_{31}\delta^i_1 & \lambda^i_{31}\lambda^i_{21}\delta^i_1+\lambda^i_{32}\delta^i_2 & \lambda^i_{31}\lambda^i_{31}\delta^i_1+\lambda^i_{32}\lambda^i_{32}\delta^i_2+\delta^i_3 & \lambda^i_{41}\lambda^i_{31}\delta^i_1+\lambda^i_{42}\lambda^i_{32}\delta^i_2+\lambda^i_{43}\delta^i_3 & \lambda^i_{51}\lambda^i_{31}\delta^i_1+\lambda^i_{52}\lambda^i_{32}\delta^i_2+\lambda^i_{53}\delta^i_1 \\[4pt]
\lambda^i_{41}\delta^i_1 & \lambda^i_{41}\lambda^i_{21}\delta^i_1+\lambda^i_{42}\delta^i_2 & \lambda^i_{41}\lambda^i_{31}\delta^i_1+\lambda^i_{42}\lambda^i_{32}\delta^i_2+\lambda^i_{43}\delta^i_3 & \lambda^i_{41}\lambda^i_{41}\delta^i_1+\lambda^i_{42}\lambda^i_{42}\delta^i_2+\lambda^i_{43}\lambda^i_{43}\delta^i_3+\delta^i_4 & \lambda^i_{41}\lambda^i_{51}\lambda^i_1+\lambda^i_{42}\lambda^i_{52}\lambda^i_2+\lambda^i_{43}\lambda^i_{53}\delta^i_3+\lambda^i_{54}\delta^i_4 \\[4pt]
\lambda^i_{51}\delta^i_1 & \lambda^i_{51}\lambda^i_{21}\delta^i_1+\lambda^i_{52}\delta^i_2 & \lambda^i_{51}\lambda^i_{31}\delta^i_1+\lambda^i_{52}\lambda^i_{32}\delta^i_2+\lambda^i_{53}\delta^i_3 & \lambda^i_{51}\lambda^i_{41}\delta^i_1+\lambda^i_{52}\lambda^i_{52}\delta^i_2+\lambda^i_{53}\lambda^i_{53}\delta^i_3+\lambda^i_{54}\delta^i_4 & \lambda^i_{51}\lambda^i_{51}\delta^i_1+\lambda^i_{52}\lambda^i_{52}\delta^i_2+\lambda^i_{53}\lambda^i_{53}\delta^i_3+\lambda^i_{54}\delta^i_4+\delta^i_5
\end{bmatrix}
$$

Under these conditions there is a one-to-one transformation between the constant share elasticities $\{\beta^i_{KK}, \beta^i_{KL}, \beta^i_{KE}, \beta^i_{KN}, \beta^i_{KM}, \beta^i_{LL}, \beta^i_{LE}, \beta^i_{LN}, \beta^i_{LM}, \beta^i_{EE}, \beta^i_{EN}, \beta^i_{EM}, \beta^i_{NN}, \beta^i_{NM}, \beta^i_{MM}\}$ and the parameters of the Cholesky factorizations. The matrices of share elasticities are negative semidefinite if and only if the diagonal elements $\{\delta^i_1, \delta^i_2, \delta^i_3, \delta^i_4\}$ of the matrices $\{D^i\}$ are nonpositive. This completes the specification of our model of production and technical change.

Index Numbers

The negative of the average rates of technical change in any two points of time, say T and T-1, can be expressed as the difference between successive logarithms of the price of output, less a weighted average of the differences between successive logarithms of the prices of capital, labor, electricity, nonelectrical energy, and materials inputs, with weights given by the average value shares:

$$-\bar{v}^i_T = \ell n q_i(T) - \ell n q_i(T - 1) - \bar{v}^i_K[\ell n p^i_K(T) - \ell n p^i_K(T - 1)]$$

$$-\bar{v}^i_L[\ell n p^i_L(T) - \ell n p^i_L(T - 1)] - \bar{v}^i_E[\ell n p^i_E(T) - \ell n p^i_E(T - 1)]$$

$$-\bar{v}^i_N[\ell n p^i_N(T) - \ell n p^i_N(T - 1)] - \bar{v}^i_M[\ell n p^i_M(T) - \ell n p^i_M(T - 1)],$$

$$(i = 1, 2 \ldots n),$$

where

$$\bar{v}^i_T = \frac{1}{2}[v^i_T(T) + v^i_T(T - 1)], \qquad (i = 1, 2 \ldots n),$$

and the average value shares in the two periods are given by

$$\bar{v}^i_K = \frac{1}{2}[v^i_K(T) + v^i_K(T - 1)],$$

$$\bar{v}^i_L = \frac{1}{2}[v^i_L(T) + v^i_L(T - 1)],$$

$$\bar{v}^i_E = \frac{1}{2}[v^i_E(T) + v^i_E(T - 1)],$$

$$\bar{v}^i_N = \frac{1}{2}[v^i_N(T) + v^i_N(T - 1)],$$

$$\bar{v}^i_M = \frac{1}{2}[v^i_M(T) + v^i_M(T - 1)], \qquad (i = 1, 2 \ldots n).$$

We refer to the expressions for the average rates of technical change $\{\bar{v}^i_T\}$ as the *translog price index of the sectoral rates of technical change*.

Similarly, we can consider specific forms for prices of capital, labor, electricity, nonelectrical energy, and materials inputs as functions of prices of individual capital, labor, electricity, nonelectrical energy, and materials inputs into each industrial sector. We assume that the price of each input can be expressed as a translog function of the price of its components. Accordingly, the difference between successive logarithms of the price of the input is a weighted average of differences between successive logarithms of prices of its components. The weights are given by the average value shares of the components. We refer to these expressions of the input prices as *translog indexes of the price of sectoral inputs.*[13]

Stochastic Specification

To formulate an econometric model of production and technical change we add a stochastic component to the equations for the value shares and the rate of technical change. We assume that each of these equations has two additive components. The first is a nonrandom function of capital, labor, electricity, nonelectrical energy, and materials inputs and time; the second is an unobservable random disturbance that is functionally independent of these variables. We obtain an econometric model of production and technical change corresponding to the translog price function by adding random disturbances to all six equations:

$$v_K^i = \alpha_K^i + \beta_{KK}^i \ell n \, p_K^i + \beta_{KL}^i \ell n \, p_L^i + \beta_{KE}^i \ell n \, p_E^i + \beta_{KN}^i \ell n \, p_N^i + \beta_{KM}^i \ell n \, p_M^i + \beta_{KT}^i \cdot T + \epsilon_K^i,$$

$$v_L^i = \alpha_L^i + \beta_{KL}^i \ell n \, p_K^i + \beta_{LL}^i \ell n \, p_L^i + \beta_{LE}^i \ell n \, p_E^i + \beta_{LN}^i \ell n \, p_N^i + \beta_{LM}^i \ell n \, p_M^i + \beta_{LT}^i \cdot T + \epsilon_L^i,$$

$$v_E^i = \alpha_E^i + \beta_{KE}^i \ell n \, p_K^i + \beta_{LE}^i \ell n \, p_L^i + \beta_{EE}^i \ell n \, p_E^i + \beta_{EN}^i \ell n \, p_N^i + \beta_{EM}^i \ell n \, p_M^i + \beta_{ET}^i \cdot T + \epsilon_E^i,$$

$$v_N^i = \alpha_N^i + \beta_{KN}^i \ell n \, p_K^i + \beta_{LN}^i \ell n \, p_L^i + \beta_{EN}^i \ell n \, p_E^i + \beta_{NN}^i \ell n \, p_N^i + \beta_{NM}^i \ell n \, p_M^i + \beta_{NT}^i \cdot T + \epsilon_N^i,$$

$$v_M^i = \alpha_M^i + \beta_{KM}^i \ell n \, p_K^i + \beta_{LM}^i \ell n \, p_L^i + \beta_{EM}^i \ell n \, p_E^i + \beta_{NM}^i \ell n \, p_N^i + \beta_{MM}^i \ell n \, p_M^i + \beta_{MT}^i \cdot T + \epsilon_M^i,$$

$$v_T^i = \alpha_T^i + \beta_{KT}^i \ell n \, p_K^i + \beta_{LT}^i \ell n \, p_L^i + \beta_{ET}^i \ell n \, p_E^i + \beta_{NT}^i \ell n \, p_N^i + \beta_{MT}^i \ell n \, p_M^i + \beta_{TT}^i \cdot T + \epsilon_T^i,$$

$$(i = 1, 2 \ldots n),$$

where $\{\alpha_K^i, \alpha_L^i, \alpha_E^i, \alpha_N^i, \alpha_M^i, \alpha_T^i, \beta_{KK}^i, \beta_{KL}^i, \beta_{KE}^i, \beta_{KN}^i, \beta_{KM}^i, \beta_{KT}^i, \beta_{LL}^i, \beta_{LE}^i, \beta_{LN}^i, \beta_{LM}^i, \beta_{LT}^i, \beta_{EE}^i, \beta_{EN}^i, \beta_{EM}^i, \beta_{ET}^i, \beta_{NN}^i, \beta_{NM}^i, \beta_{NT}^i, \beta_{MM}^i, \beta_{MT}^i, \beta_{TT}^i\}$ are unknown parameters and $\{\epsilon_K^i, \epsilon_L^i, \epsilon_E^i, \epsilon_N^i, \epsilon_M^i, \epsilon_T^i\}$ are unobservable random disturbances.

Since the value shares sum to unity, the unknown parameters satisfy the same restrictions as before and the random disturbances corresponding to the four value shares sum to zero:

$$\epsilon_K^i + \epsilon_L^i + \epsilon_E^i + \epsilon_N^i + \epsilon_M^i = 0, \qquad (i = 1, 2 \ldots n),$$

so that these random disturbances are not distributed independently.

We assume that the random disturbances for all six equations have expected value equal to zero for all observations:

$$E \begin{pmatrix} \epsilon_K^i \\ \epsilon_L^i \\ \epsilon_E^i \\ \epsilon_N^i \\ \epsilon_M^i \\ \epsilon_T^i \end{pmatrix} = 0, \qquad (i = 1, 2 \ldots n).$$

We also assume that the random disturbances have a covariance matrix that is the same for all observations; since the random disturbances corresponding to the five value shares sum to zero, this matrix is positive semidefinite with rank at most equal to five.

We assume that the covariance matrix of the random disturbances corresponding to the first four value shares and the rate of technical change, say Σ^i, has rank five, where

$$V \begin{pmatrix} \epsilon_K^i \\ \epsilon_L^i \\ \epsilon_E^i \\ \epsilon_N^i \\ \epsilon_T^i \end{pmatrix} = \Sigma^i, \qquad (i = 1, 2 \ldots n),$$

so that the Σ^i is a positive definite matrix. Finally, we assume that the random disturbances corresponding to distinct observations in the same or distinct equations are uncorrelated. Under this assumption that the matrix of random disturbances for the first four value shares and the rate of technical change for all observations has the Kronecker product form,

$$V \begin{pmatrix} \epsilon_K^i(1) \\ \epsilon_K^i(2) \\ \cdot \\ \cdot \\ \cdot \\ \epsilon_K^i(N) \\ \epsilon_L^i(1) \\ \cdot \\ \cdot \\ \epsilon_T^i(N) \end{pmatrix} = \Sigma^i \otimes I, \qquad (i = 1, 2 \ldots n).$$

Since the rates of technical change $\{v_T^i\}$ are not directly observable, the equation for the rate of technical change can be written

$$-\bar{v}_T^i = \alpha_T^i + \beta_{KT}^i \overline{\ell n\ p}_K^i + \beta_{LT}^i \overline{\ell n\ p}_L^i + \beta_{ET}^i \overline{\ell n\ p}_E^i + \beta_{NT}^i \overline{\ell n\ p}_N^i + \beta_{MT}^i \overline{\ell n\ p}_M^i + \beta_{TT}^i \cdot T + \bar{\epsilon}_T^i,$$
$$(i = 1, 2 \ldots n),$$

where $\bar{\epsilon}_T^i$ is the average disturbance in the two periods

$$\bar{\epsilon}_T^i = \frac{1}{2}[\epsilon_T^i(T) + \epsilon_T^i(T - 1)], \qquad (i = 1, 2 \ldots n).$$

Similarly, the equations for the value shares of capital, labor, electricity, nonelectrical energy, and materials inputs can be written

$$\bar{v}_K^i = \alpha_K^i + \beta_{KK}^i \overline{\ln p_K^i} + \beta_{KL}^i \overline{\ln p_L^i} + \beta_{KE}^i \overline{\ln p_E^i} + \beta_{KN}^i \overline{\ln p_N^i} + \beta_{KM}^i \overline{\ln p_M^i} + \beta_{KT}^i \cdot \bar{T} + \bar{\epsilon}_K^i,$$

$$\bar{v}_L^i = \alpha_L^i + \beta_{KL}^i \overline{\ln p_K^i} + \beta_{LL}^i \overline{\ln p_L^i} + \beta_{LE}^i \overline{\ln p_E^i} + \beta_{LN}^i \overline{\ln p_N^i} + \beta_{LM}^i \overline{\ln p_M^i} + \beta_{LT}^i \cdot \bar{T} + \bar{\epsilon}_L^i,$$

$$\bar{v}_E^i = \alpha_E^i + \beta_{KE}^i \overline{\ln p_K^i} + \beta_{LE}^i \overline{\ln p_L^i} + \beta_{EE}^i \overline{\ln p_E^i} + \beta_{EN}^i \overline{\ln p_N^i} + \beta_{EM}^i \overline{\ln p_M^i} + \beta_{ET}^i \cdot \bar{T} + \bar{\epsilon}_E^i,$$

$$\bar{v}_N^i = \alpha_N^i + \beta_{KN}^i \overline{\ln p_K^i} + \beta_{LN}^i \overline{\ln p_L^i} + \beta_{EN}^i \overline{\ln p_E^i} + \beta_{NN}^i \overline{\ln p_N^i} + \beta_{NM}^i \overline{\ln p_M^i} + \beta_{NT}^i \cdot \bar{T} + \bar{\epsilon}_N^i,$$

$$\bar{v}_M^i = \alpha_M^i + \beta_{KM}^i \overline{\ln p_K^i} + \beta_{LM}^i \overline{\ln p_L^i} + \beta_{EM}^i \overline{\ln p_E^i} + \beta_{NM}^i \overline{\ln p_N^i} + \beta_{MM}^i \overline{\ln p_M^i} + \beta_{MT}^i \cdot \bar{T} + \bar{\epsilon}_M^i,$$

where

$$\bar{\epsilon}_K^i = \frac{1}{2}[\epsilon_K^i(T) + \epsilon_K^i(T-1)],$$

$$\bar{\epsilon}_L^i = \frac{1}{2}[\epsilon_L^i(T) + \epsilon_L^i(T-1)],$$

$$\bar{\epsilon}_E^i = \frac{1}{2}[\epsilon_E^i(T) + \epsilon_E^i(T-1)],$$

$$\bar{\epsilon}_N^i = \frac{1}{2}[\epsilon_N^i(T) + \epsilon_N^i(T-1)],$$

$$\bar{\epsilon}_M^i = \frac{1}{2}[\epsilon_N^i(T) + \epsilon_M^i(T-1)], \qquad (i = 1, 2 \ldots n).$$

As before, the average value shares $\{\bar{v}_K^i, \bar{v}_L^i, \bar{v}_E^i, \bar{v}_N^i, \bar{v}_M^i\}$ sum to unity, so that the average disturbances $\{\bar{\epsilon}_K^i, \bar{\epsilon}_L^i, \bar{\epsilon}_E^i, \bar{\epsilon}_N^i, \bar{\epsilon}_M^i\}$ sum to zero:

$$\bar{\epsilon}_K^i + \bar{\epsilon}_L^i + \bar{\epsilon}_E^i + \bar{\epsilon}_N^i + \bar{\epsilon}_M^i = 0, \qquad (i = 1, 2 \ldots n).$$

The covariance matrix of the average disturbances corresponding to the equation for the rate of technical change for all observations, say Ω, is a Laurent matrix:

$$V \begin{pmatrix} \bar{\epsilon}_T^i(2) \\ \bar{\epsilon}_T^i(3) \\ \cdot \\ \cdot \\ \cdot \\ \bar{\epsilon}_T^i(N) \end{pmatrix} = \Omega,$$

where

$$\Omega = \begin{pmatrix} \frac{1}{2} & \frac{1}{4} & 0 & \cdots & 0 \\ \frac{1}{4} & \frac{1}{2} & \frac{1}{4} & \cdots & 0 \\ 0 & \frac{1}{4} & \frac{1}{2} & \cdots & 0 \\ \cdot & \cdot & \cdot & & \cdot \\ \cdot & \cdot & \cdot & & \cdot \\ \cdot & \cdot & \cdot & & \cdot \\ 0 & 0 & 0 & \cdots & \frac{1}{2} \end{pmatrix}$$

The covariance matrix of the average disturbance corresponding to each equation for the four value shares is the same, so that the covariance matrix of the average disturbances for the first four value shares and the rate of technical change for all observations has the Kronecker product form

$$V \begin{pmatrix} \bar{\epsilon}_K^i(2) \\ \bar{\epsilon}_K^i(3) \\ \cdot \\ \cdot \\ \cdot \\ \bar{\epsilon}_K^i(N) \\ \bar{\epsilon}_L^i(2) \\ \cdot \\ \cdot \\ \cdot \\ \bar{\epsilon}_T^i(N) \end{pmatrix} = \Sigma^i \otimes \Omega, \qquad (i = 1, 2 \ldots n).$$

Estimation

Although disturbances in equations for the average rate of technical change and the average value shares are autocorrelated, the data can be transformed to eliminate the autocorrelation. The matrix Ω is positive definite, so that there is a matrix T such that

$$\begin{aligned} T\Omega T' &= I, \\ T'T &= \Omega^{-1}. \end{aligned}$$

To construct the matrix T we can first invert the matrix Ω to obtain the inverse matrix Ω^{-1}, a positive definite matrix. We then calculate the Cholesky factorization of the inverse matrix Ω^{-1},

$$\Omega^{-1} = LDL',$$

where L is a unit lower triangular matrix and D is a diagonal matrix with positive elements along the main diagonal. Finally, we can write the matrix T in the form

$$T = D^{1/2} L',$$

where $D^{1/2}$ is a diagonal matrix with elements along the main diagonal equal to the square roots of the corresponding elements of D.

We can transform the equations for the average rates of technical change by the matrix $T = D^{1/2} L'$ to obtain equations with uncorrelated random disturbances:

$$D^{1/2} L' \begin{pmatrix} \bar{v}_T^i(2) \\ \bar{v}_T^i(3) \\ \cdot \\ \cdot \\ \cdot \\ \bar{v}_T^i(N) \end{pmatrix} = D^{1/2}L' \begin{pmatrix} 1\overline{\ell n\, p_K^i}(2)\ldots 2 - \frac{1}{2} \\ 1\overline{\ell n\, p_K^i}(3)\ldots 3 - \frac{1}{2} \\ \cdot \\ \cdot \\ \cdot \\ 1\overline{\ell n\, p_K^i}(N)\ldots N - \frac{1}{2} \end{pmatrix} \begin{pmatrix} \alpha_T^i \\ \beta_{KT}^i \\ \cdot \\ \cdot \\ \cdot \\ \beta_{TT}^i \end{pmatrix} + D^{1/2} L \begin{pmatrix} \bar{\epsilon}_T^i(2) \\ \bar{\epsilon}_T^i(3) \\ \cdot \\ \cdot \\ \cdot \\ \bar{\epsilon}_T^i(N) \end{pmatrix},$$

$$(i = 1, 2 \ldots n),$$

since

$$T\Omega T' = (D^{1/2} L') \,\Omega\, (D^{1/2} L')' = I.$$

The transformation $T = D^{1/2} L'$ is applied to data on the average rates of technical change $\{\bar{v}_t^i\}$ and data on the average values of the variables that appear on the right hand side of the corresponding equation.

We can apply the transformation $T = D^{1/2} L'$ to the first four equations for average value shares to obtain equations with uncorrelated disturbances. As before, the transformation is applied to data on the averge values shares and the average values of variables that appear in the corresponding equations. The covariance matrix of the transformed disturbances from the first four equations for the average value shares and the equation for the average rate of technical change has the Kronecker product form

$$(I \otimes D^{1/2} L')(\Sigma^i \otimes \Omega)(I \otimes D^{1/2}L')' = \Sigma^i \otimes I,$$
$$(i = 1, 2 \ldots n).$$

To estimate the unknown parameters of the translog price function we combine the first four equations for the average value shares with the equation for the average rate of technical change to obtain a complete econometric model of production and technical change. We estimate the parameters of the equations for the remaining average value shares, using the restrictions on these parameters given above. The complete model involves twenty unknown parameters. A total of twenty-two additional parameters can be estimated as functions of these parameters, given the restrictions. Our estimates of the unknown parameters of the econometric model of production and technical change will be based on the nonlinear three-stage least squares estimator introduced by Jorgenson and Laffont (1974).

NOTES

1.   This research was supported by the Electric Power Research Institute under RP 1152-6. Able research assistance was provided by Kun-Young Yun. Very useful comments on an earlier draft were made by Ernst Berndt, John Kendrick, and Sam Schurr. All responsibility for opinions expressed or for any deficiencies in the research remain with the author.
2.   This summary is based on Schurr (1983).
3.   This summary of the sources of postwar economic growth in the United States is based on Jorgenson (1983).
4.   The price function was introduced by Samuelson (1953).
5.   Our sectoral price functions are based on the translog price function introduced by Christensen, Jorgenson, and Lau (1971, 1973). The translog price function was first employed at the sectoral level by Berndt and Jorgenson (1973) and Berndt and Wood (1975). References to sectoral production studies incorporating energy and materials inputs are given by Berndt and Wood (1979).
6.   This model of sectoral productivity growth is based on that of Jorgenson and Lau (1983). A useful survey of studies of energy prices and productivity growth is given by Berndt (1982).
7.   These industries have been employed by Jorgenson and Fraumeni (1981).
8.   Data on energy and materials are based on annual interindustry transactions tables for the United States, 1958-74, compiled by Jack Faucett Associates (1977). Data on capital and labor input are based on estimates by Fraumeni and Jorgenson (1980).
9.   The share elasticity with respect to price was introduced by Christensen, Jorgenson, and Lau (1971, 1973) as a fixed parameter of the translog production function. An analogous concept was employed by Samuelson (1973). The terminology is from Jorgenson and Lau (1983).
10.   The bias of productivity growth was introduced by Hicks (1932). An alternative definition of the bias of productivity growth was introduced by Binswanger (1974a, 1974b). The definition of bias of productivity growth to be employed in our econometric model is based on that of Jorgenson and Lau (1983).
11.   The rate of change was introduced by Jorgenson and Lau (1983).
12.   The following discussion of share elasticities with respect to price and concavity follows that of Jorgenson and Lau (1983). Representation of conditions for concavity in terms of the Cholesky factorization is due to Lau (1978).

13.   The price indexes were introduced by Fisher (1922). These indexes were first derived from the translog price function by Diewert (1976). The corresponding index of technical change was introduced by Christensen and Jorgenson (1970). The translog index of technical change was first derived from the translog price function by Diewert (1980) and by Jorgenson and Lau (1983).

REFERENCES

Berndt, Ernst R. 1982. "Energy Price Increases and the Productivity Slowdown in United States Manufacturing." In *The Decline in Productivity Growth*, pp. 60–89. Boston: Federal Reserve Bank of Boston.

Berndt, Ernst R., and Dale W. Jorgenson. 1973. "Production Structures." In *U.S. Energy Resources and Economic Growth*, edited by Dale W. Jorgenson and Hendrik S. Houthakker, Washington, D.C.: Energy Policy Project.

Berndt, Ernst R., and David O. Wood. 1975. "Technology, Prices, and the Derived Demand for Energy." *Review of Economics and Statistics* 56, no. 3 (August): 259–68.

_____. 1979. "Engineering and Econometric Interpretations of Energy-Capital Complementarity." *American Economic Review* 69, no. 3 (September): 342–54.

Binswanger, Hans P. 1974a. "The Measurement of Technical Change Biases with Many Factors of Production." *American Economic Review* 64, no. 5 (December): 964–76.

_____. 1974b. "A Microeconomic Approach to Induced Innovation." *Economic Journal* 84, no. 336 (December): 940–58.

Christensen, Laurits R., and Dale W. Jorgenson. 1970. "U.S. Real Product and Real Factor Input, 1929–1967." *Review of Income and Wealth*, ser. 16, no. 1 (March): 19–50.

Christensen, Laurits R.; Dale W. Jorgenson; and Lawrence J. Lau. 1971. "Conjugate Duality and the Transcendental Logarithmic Production Function." *Econometrica* 39, no. 3 (July): 255–56.

_____. 1973. "Transcendental Logarithmic Production Frontiers." *Review of Economics and Statistics* 55, no. 1 (February): 28–45.

Diewert, W. Erwin. 1976. "Exact and Superlative Index Numbers." *Journal of Econometrics* 4, no. 2 (May): 115–46.

_____. 1980. "Aggregation Problems in the Measurement of Capital." In *The Measurement of Capital*, edited by Dan Usher, pp. 433–528. Chicago: University of Chicago Press.

Fisher, I. 1922. *The Making of Index Numbers.* Boston: Houghton Mifflin.

Fraumeni, Barbara M., and Dale W. Jorgenson. 1980. "The Role of Capital in U.S. Economic Growth, 1948–1976." In *Capital, Efficiency and Growth*, edited by George M. von Furstenberg, pp. 9–250. Cambridge, Mass.: Ballinger.

Hicks, John R. 1932. *The Theory of Wages.* 2d ed. 1963. London: Macmillan.

Jack Faucett Associates. 1977. *Development of 35 Order Input-Output Tables, 1958–1974, Final Report.* Washington, D.C.: Federal Preparedness Agency.

Jorgenson, Dale W. 1983. "Energy Prices and Productivity Growth." In *Energy, Productivity, and Economic Growth*, edited by Sam Schurr, Sidney Sonenblum, and David O. Wood, pp. 133–154. Cambridge, Mass.: Oelgeschlager, Gunn, and Hain.

Jorgenson, Dale W., and Barbara M. Fraumeni. 1981. "Relative Prices and Technical Change." In *Modeling and Measuring Natural Resource Substitution*, edited by E.R. Berndt and B. Field, pp. 17–47. Cambridge, Mass.: M.I.T. Press.

Jorgenson, Dale W., and Jean-Jacques Laffont. 1974. "Efficient Estimation of Non-Linear Simultaneous Equations with Additive Disturbances." *Annals of Social and Economic Measurement* 3, no. 4 (October): 615–40.

Jorgenson, Dale W., and Lawrence J. Lau. 1983. *Transcendental Logarithmic Production Functions.* Amsterdam: North-Holland.

Lau, Lawrence J. 1978. "Testing and Imposing Monotonicity, Convexity, and Quasi-Convexity Constraints." In *Production Economics: A Dual Approach to Theory and Applications*, vol. 1, edited by Melvin Fuss and Daniel McFadden, pp. 409–53. Amsterdam: North-Holland.

Rosenberg, Nathan. 1983. "The Effects of Energy Supply Characteristics on Technology and Economic Growth." In *Energy, Productivity, and Economic Growth*, edited by Sam Schurr, Sidney Sonenblum, and David O. Wood, pp. 279–306. Cambridge, Mass.: Oelgeschlager, Gunn, and Hain.

Samuelson, Paul A. 1953. "Prices of Factors and Goods in General Equilibrium." *Review of Economic Studies* 21, no. 1 (October): 1–20.

————. 1973. "Relative Shares and Elasticities Simplified: Comment." *American Economic Review* 63, no. 4 (September): 770–71.

Schurr, Sam. 1982. "Energy Efficiency and Productive Efficiency: Some Thoughts Based on American Experience." *Energy Journal*, 3, no. 3 (July): 3–14.

————. 1983. "Energy Efficiency and Economic Efficiency: An Historical Perspective." In *Energy, Productivity, and Economic Growth*, edited by Sam Schurr, Sidney Sonenblum and David O. Wood, pp. 203–214. Cambridge, Mass.: Oelgeschlager, Gunn and Hain.

Schurr, Sam; Joel Darmstadter; Harry Perry; William Ramsay; and Milton Russell. 1979. *Energy in America's Future.* Baltimore: Johns Hopkins University Press.

Schurr, Sam; Bruce C. Netschert; Vera E. Elizasberg; Joseph Lerner; and Hans H. Landsberg. 1960. *Energy in the American Economy.* Baltimore: Johns Hopkins University Press.

Comment

Ernst R. Berndt

Dale Jorgenson has made seminal contributions in developing the underlying theory of productivity, implementing it empirically, and in interpreting recent productivity trend phenomena. It is therefore a pleasure to comment on this paper, which illustrates again the rich interaction of theory, measurement, and interpretation.

Since 1973 in most U.S. industries, both labor and multifactor measures of productivity growth have fallen considerably from their previous high rates. At times in the last decade productivity growth has even been negative. Because of the coincidence in timing with the worldwide OPEC-induced energy price increases, because the productivity growth slowdown occurred simultaneously throughout the industrialized world, and because other traditional analyses could not adequately explain the magnitude, duration, and timing of the productivity growth decline, energy price increases have been singled out by a number of writers and analysts as being a possible significant cause of the productivity slowdown. Some have even named energy price increases as the principal villain. In these comments I want to address the issue of precisely how energy (both electric and nonelectric) price increases might have affected productivity growth adversely—a principal finding of Dale Jorgenson—and whether such hypotheses square well with intuition and the recent data.

Let me begin with a few background observations. One of the most robust findings of empirical productivity analysis is that both labor and multifactor productivity growth trends tend to be procyclical. As the economy reaches peak performance and full capacity, labor and multifactor

325

productivity growth all grow at relatively rapid growth rates, whereas when the economy experiences a recession, productivity growth tends to decline. There are a number of reasons that help explain this classic finding of productivity analysis; the most compelling, in my judgment, are those that recognize that in the short run, the stocks of capital plant and equipment, as well as the stocks of salaried white-collar labor, are to some extent fixed and not instantaneously adjustable. As a consequence, when rapid economic growth takes place, output increases more rapidly than capital input, total labor input, or aggregate input, thereby inducing a procyclical pattern to measured productivity growth.

There are two important implications of this. First, one must be very careful in interpreting short-term movements in productivity trends as representing major structural changes or significant new developments, for quite simply, short-term productivity growth is affected considerably by short-term economic conditions. Second, changes in long-term trends are of course very important. Indeed, our long-run welfare depends critically on sustained productivity improvements. Although it may appear to be tautological, it is of course true that analysis and detection of changes in long-term or secular (as distinct from cyclical) trends in productivity growth require data from a longer time period—often as long as half-centuries, as Moses Abramovitz (1956), John Kendrick (1961), and Solomon Fabricant (1973) have often emphasized. Typically, such long time series of data are not available; Jorgenson's data, for example, spans a twenty-one-year time interval between 1958 and 1979.

To understand long-term trends with a limited time span of data, some productivity analysts such as Denison (1979) attempt to adjust annual data for short-run variations in capacity utilization. Precisely how one adjusts such data remains a troublesome and difficult issue within the economics profession, and turns out in some cases to be decisive. For example, Denison adjusts his data for cyclical variations in intensity of use and concludes that the productivity growth slowdown in the United States began suddenly and dramatically in 1973. Why this occurred in 1973 Denison is unable to explain, and instead he has concluded that "What happened is, to be blunt, a mystery." By contrast, Randy Norsworthy and his associates (1979) formerly at BLS make no adjustment for cyclical variations in capacity utilization and conclude that the productivity growth slowdown in the United States began much earlier than 1973—indeed, in 1965—and in particular does not coincide with the OPEC energy price increases. Jorgenson's measure of capital input is unaffected by changes in utilization, and elsewhere he has reported results that concur with Norsworthy, rather than Denison. Hence the dating of the productivity growth slowdown is critically affected by how and whether one adjusts for cyclical variations in capacity utilization.

Because of this problem of properly adjusting data for utilization, some productivity analysts compare growth patterns only between "peak" years when capacity utilization rates are perceived as being high, thereby reducing considerably the role of cyclical effects. Unfortunately, the validity of this procedure is of course dependent on the assumption that to some extent all peaks represent equal rates of recovery or capacity utilization, an assumption whose validity is somewhat questionable.

Bearing these two observations in mind—that in the short run some inputs are fixed rather than instantaneously adjustable, thereby yielding a procyclical pattern to productivity growth, and that long-term analysis of productivity growth trends is impeded by the fact that it is difficult to adjust data for short-run cyclical variations in utilization—let us now briefly examine Jorgenson's and several others' stories of how energy price increases since 1973 have adversely affected labor and multifactor productivity growth. There are basically two schools of thought—one is that energy can't be that important because its share in total costs is just too small to be significant; the other, that energy is much more important than its share would indicate. I, like Jorgenson, tend to believe the latter, but let's begin with the former.

One argument, advanced by some, is that energy price increases have induced substitution of labor (human energy) for energy, thereby have increased the labor to output ratio and depressed labor productivity growth. George L. Perry of the Brookings Institution (1977) has examined this argument in considerable detail. Using a number of different estimates of energy price-responsiveness in the private business sector, he computes the implied value of energy saved due to energy price increases and then assumes that all energy savings were used to purchase additional labor. He then asks how much additional labor could be purchased if there were this dollar-for-dollar energy-labor substitutability and by how much would it depress average labor productivity? Briefly, Perry finds that since in the overall private business sector energy is but a small proportion of capital-labor costs (at most 10 percent), even substantial energy price responsiveness and energy cost savings would free up only a small amount of funds to hire labor. Perry calculates at most a 0.2 percent increase, which implies that at most labor productivity growth would fall by 0.2 percent—a relatively small proportion of the post-1973 labor productivity growth decline. While there are problems with this type of reasoning (for example, there is no reason why total costs should remain unchanged after energy price increases), Perry's explicit recognition that the cost share of energy is very small is an important insight, and it implies that at least in a static context, it is unlikely that the tail can wag the dog. Related arguments within a static environment have been made, incidentally, by Alan Manne and William Hogan (1977), who find a substantial effect on labor productivity due to energy price increases only if the energy substitution response is rather large.

One set of authors who arrived at a strikingly different set of conclusions is Robert H. Rasche and John A. Tatom (1977). These authors specify an aggregate production function of a Cobb-Douglas form that implies substantial energy-labor and energy-capital substitutability, and then argue that economic capacity output has been reduced considerably by energy price increases, thereby clearly lowering labor productivity growth and perhaps even multifactor productivity growth. As Denison has noted, however, the energy price elasticities assumed by Rasche-Tatom in their production function specification would imply that over the 1973–76 time period, instantaneously energy consumption per unit of output should have decreased 36 percent (alternatively, energy productivity should have increased by 36 percent). However, one of the sobering features of the last decade is that while real energy price increases since 1973 have increased 200 percent, the ratio of energy consumption to output in the industrial sector has only dropped 20 percent. In other words, energy productivity has increased at a much slower rate, in spite of substantial real energy price increases. Hence, for the energy versus labor productivity argument to be of the correct quantitative magnitude, substantially more energy conservation would have been necessary than has actually occurred. Next, let's examine the "energy is more important than you'd think" story.

One line of reasoning linking energy price increases and the productivity growth slowdown in a theoretically defensible manner is often called the energy-capital complementarity hypothesis, and initially was based on the empirical work of E.R. Berndt, David O. Wood, Edward Hudson, Dale W. Jorgenson, and J.R. Norsworthy and his research associates. The energy-capital complementarity hypothesis has gone through a number of stages, not all of which are worth detailing here. Hudson and Jorgenson (1974) have argued that since in a substantial number of empirical studies of various industries, energy and capital were found to be complementary rather than substitutable inputs, other things equal it is the case that energy price increases reduce not only the demand for energy but also the demand for capital, and thereby reduce the demand for investment. Further, since one important view shared by both economists and technologists is that new investment goods embody technical progress, which facilitates productivity gains, it follows that the reduced investment brought about by energy price increases would result in lower multifactor productivity growth. Moreover, since future capital/labor ratios would be smaller than in the absence of energy price increases, labor productivity growth would also fall.

This Hudson-Jorgenson dynamic argument must be distinguished clearly from the essentially static analyses of the previously noted energy-labor substitution advocates. However, precisely because the Hudson-Jorgenson view is dynamic, in my judgment it cannot explain the sharpness of the labor productivity slowdown since 1973. After all, investment is *gradual* and takes time, whereas the labor productivity decline in 1973 was quite substantial. In brief, while energy-capital complementarity might have an adverse effect on productivity growth in the long run, surely such effects could not be expected to be important quantitatively so soon after 1973. Moreover, in the relatively energy-intensive manufacturing sector of the U.S. economy, investment in new plant and equipment has been surprisingly robust since 1973, a fact not easily explained by the simple energy-capital complementarity hypothesis.

A more recent and different line of reasoning linking energy price increases and the productivity slowdown is that of Dale W. Jorgenson and Barbara Fraumeni (1981), which is extended considerably in the current paper by Jorgenson. Jorgenson finds empirically in almost all U.S. industries over the 1958–79 time period (especially the manufacturing industries), bias of technical change has been both electric and nonelectric energy-using. Note that when technical progress occurs, the same level of output can be produced with less of one or more inputs. When technical change results in all input demands' being reduced by the same proportion, technical change is said to be neutral. If demand for the ith input is reduced by a proportion greater than the average reduction in the other inputs, technical change is said to be input i-saving. On the other hand, if as a consequence of technical progress the demand for the jth input is reduced by a proportion less than the average reduction in the other inputs, technical change is said to be input j-using. The using- or saving-bias is relative, not absolute. An implication of the Jorgenson-Fraumeni and Jorgenson findings of energy-using technical progress is that, other things equal, energy price increases (both electric and nonelectric) directly reduce the rate of multifactor productivity growth. To the best of my knowledge, however, Jorgenson-Fraumeni estimates have not yet been presented of just how much of the productivity slowdown can be explained quantitatively by this energy bias argument. Were it calculated, I suspect it would be quite small. As I shall explain shortly, I believe even this novel Jorgenson approach understates the adverse effects of energy price increases on productivity growth.

Although the analytical economic reasoning underlying the Jorgenson-Fraumeni energy-using technical change bias argument is relatively straightforward, in my judgment this line of reasoning lacks persuasiveness because it simply transforms the mystery of the productivity slowdown to the mystery of the energy-using bias of technical change. The mystery has not been solved or explained, but rather has simply been shifted. What does an electric energy-using or nonelectric energy-using bias of technical change really mean? Why was the bias of technical change energy-using during the 1958–79 time period, and why must this bias be fixed forever? But that the bias of technical change could vary is ruled out in the constant-bias translog framework of Jorgenson-Fraumeni. Moreover, it seems eminently reasonable to believe that such changes in technical progress are slow and gradual, and therefore are unlikely to be very helpful in explaining the sharper productivity slowdowns of 1973–75 and 1979–80.

The final line of reasoning linking energy price increases with the productivity slowdown is indirect rather than direct and follows the "energy is more important than you think" line of reasoning. Specifically, OPEC price increases could be viewed as an unexpected tax increase reducing U.S. (and, for that matter, the non-OPEC world's) disposable income, thereby leading to decreased levels of domestic consumption, saving, production and employment. In turn, since productivity growth has long been known to be procyclical, the energy price-induced recession could via this indirect "OPEC tax" route be partly responsible for the productivity growth slowdown.

Although this Keynesian type of indirect effect argument seemed eminently plausible in the 1973–75 time period and still has adherents today, it has become clear that its empirical or quantitative foundations are rather limited. For as real energy prices fell in the 1975–76 time period and as production and employment levels rose, productivity growth failed to perform as well as expected given the history of previous recoveries from recession. Hence, while there may be plausibility in the indirect OPEC-tax argument, the economic recoveries since 1973 have provided less stimulus to productivity growth than would be expected based on earlier recoveries. Something more, apparently, is involved.

But then where does this leave us? All the above arguments linking energy price increases to the productivity growth slowdown suffer to varying extents from serious flaws: (1) They rest on the assumption that a great deal of energy conservation has taken place, when in fact the recent figures demonstrate disappointingly low and at best only modest rates of improvement in energy productivity, especially in relation to the quadrupling of real energy price increases since 1973; (2) they are more long run in nature and are unable to explain how energy price increases could lead to the sudden and dramatic changes in labor productivity growth that occurred after 1973; (3) they cannot adequately explain why investment in energy-intensive consuming sectors has been as large as experienced since 1973; and (4) they are unable to explain why in the 1974–78 time period productivity growth failed to return to rates expected based on earlier recoveries, even as real energy prices fell in 1975–78 following the 1974–75 shock.

While I do not have the complete answer to the very important problem of better understanding the post-1973 productivity slowdown, and while undoubtedly a number of factors may simultaneously have contributed to the recent productivity slowdown, I do believe quite strongly that one somewhat nontraditional but plausible line of reasoning indirectly involving energy price increases is compelling and persuasive.

In my view, what is missing from all the above arguments is recognition that OPEC may have had an important capital *stock* effect—diminishing much of its economic value. This argument, buried in the pages of the 1977 *Economic Report of the President*, and considered more recently by Martin Baily (1981), has not yet been examined with the care it deserves. Although a great deal of work on economic (as opposed to technological) depreciation has been done using secondhand market data, this research on economic depreciation such as that by Hulten and his co-workers (1981) needs to be extended to incorporate effects of energy price increase on the value or price of physical capital. Once OPEC-induced unexpected energy price increases are viewed as reducing the economic value of much of the nation's capital stock, one can argue more credibly that (1) substantial productivity declines can occur even with only limited gains in energy conservation; (2) energy price increases had sudden and dramatic effects in 1973–74 and 1979; (3) part of the reason for the only partial recovery of productivity growth rates during the 1975–78 time period is that while real energy prices fell in this time interval, they fell only slightly to levels certainly much higher than in the 1960s—thereby resuscitating only part of the critically wounded capital stock; and (4) the substantial investment activity in energy-intensive consuming sectors has in effect tried to replace the capital OPEC destroyed. Let me elaborate briefly on this theme.

When the Huns invaded and conquered Europe, they took as spoils from war, wives, children, and numerous valuable possessions. It is time we realize, I believe, that OPEC has won a recent war with the United States and her other allied industrialized countries, that in fact we have lost, and that in this case the analog to spoils of war consists primarily of the lost economic value of our capital stock. To some extent, this is difficult to believe, for it surely *appears* that the capital stock is still here—our machines, plants, and generating units are physically still present—and most are even operating. But their economic value has subtly vanished. The growth in demand for output of energy and capital intensive industries in the United States has dropped substantially since 1973, and much of the capital stock in these industries was constructed predicated on assumptions of higher growth rate in output and sales. As a consequence, the implicit economic value of this fixed plant and equipment has also fallen sharply. In addition, further economic depreciation of capital has taken place in some of these U.S. industries because in certain cases foreign companies are blessed with more energy-efficient fixed capital and thus have not fared as poorly when energy price increases occurred.

But what does this have to do with productivity? In economic terms, energy price-induced economic depreciation since 1973 has undoubtedly been much larger than the technical, engineering-based, or physical deterioration of capital plant and equipment. However, the way we typically measure capital is to assume that physical deterioration and economic depreciation occur at a constant geometric rate (the "net capital stock" procedure), or else to assume that capital depreciation follows a "one hoss shay" pattern with a constant mortality probability distribution (the "gross capital stock" procedure using the Winfrey mortality distribution). Neither of these capital stock measurement procedures accounts for the substantial economic depreciation induced by post-OPEC energy price increases.

To the extent that the economic value of our nation's industrial capital stock (especially its older, energy-inefficient stock) has been rendered economically obsolete and impotent by the victorious OPEC energy forces, our *multifactor* productivity measures are biased downward, and our *labor* productivity measures must be completely reinterpreted. The "true" multifactor productivity growth slowdown since 1973 is probably considerably less in the United States than that being measured today, simply because our capital measurement techniques fail to account for the substantial economic depreciation of capital caused by OPEC. This downward bias in measured multifactor productivity growth may be larger for the United States than for a country like Japan, which has a younger, more energy-efficient capital stock. Hence U.S.-Japanese productivity comparisons may be overstating the relative decline of productivity growth in U.S. industry.

With respect to labor productivity, the argument is somewhat different. One can partially "explain" the slowdown in measured labor productivity growth for the United States as being due to the fact that the "true" value of capital per hour at work has actually fallen considerably in the last decade due to the OPEC-induced energy price increases, even though the measured capital-per-hour-at-work figures do not necessarily reveal such a phenomenon.

I want to emphasize here that the above remarks should not be interpreted as yet another academic nuance—the leisure of the theory class—but instead have very significant implications for understanding economic developments of the last decade and for constructing effective policies today. Let me begin with economic growth policy. In the last decade we have used the wrong capital data for assessing investment incentives. Using traditional measurement procedures, one might conclude that for certain energy-intensive sectors like manufacturing, net investment (gross investment minus traditionally estimated depreciation) since 1973 has been surprisingly healthy. Conventionally measured, today's capital stock is substantially larger than that of 1973. Such calculations pretend, however, that the capital stock is still entirely here. We must reassess and revalue our capital. Because of the lost wars with OPEC, our capital stock may be smaller than that of 1973 and may even be no larger than that of, say, 1968. Rather than having been substantial in the last decade, net investment in plant and equipment may actually have been negative. Policies designed so as to stimulate investment effectively should receive highest priority, for in this way we can rebuild from our lost was with OPEC and once again achieve healthy rates of economic growth.

Next let me turn to the evaluation of industrial and worker performance in the last decade. There are two important points here. First, because of the OPEC-induced loss of economic value of much of our nation's capital, we likely have a work force today with smaller capital-labor ratios than they had a decade earlier. Partly because her capital plant and equipment are more energy-efficient and of more recent vintages, Japan's labor force has not suffered as greatly from the OPEC encounters. We cannot expect sustained major gains in labor productivity growth until we again equip our labor force with more economically vital capital. Second, in evaluating the performance of energy and capital intensive industries in the United States, such as manufacturing and electricity, we must be sensitive to the fact that it is these workers and management who in particular have fought at the front lines, have borne the brunt of the encounter with OPEC, and have suffered disproportionately in their loss of capital value. The productivity performance of these industries in the last decade must be evaluated using data which clearly recognize the war losses from OPEC. If one equates industry with worker/management performance, at the present time it is not clear whether these veterans of the OPEC war should be awarded citations for heroism or should be shot at sunrise.

Finally, the above remarks have clear implications for regulation and energy policy. I noted earlier that energy industries are often capital-intensive and their capital has been particularly decimated by OPEC. Pretending that either old or new energy-inefficient equipment is still alive will do us little benefit and considerable harm in adjusting to the hard fact that the spoils from this war consist of the lost economic value of our nation's capital. Depreciation policy, especially in the regulatory setting, must reflect new economic realities. As an example, in hearings before utility rate commissions, electric generating plant and equipment should be revalued to reflect vastly changed economic values. Allowable life calculations based only on engineering data must also be redone. Rate increases must provide clear, unambiguous, and significant incentives for new investment in order to recover losses from the OPEC war.

Above all, in constructing effective policies for the 1980s, it is imperative that we recognize and then act on the basis that much of the economic value of our nation's capital stock has been lost in the 1970s from two encounters with OPEC.

REFERENCES

Abramovitz, Moses. 1956. "Resource and Output Trends in the United States since 1870," *American Economic Review* 44, no. 2 (May): 5–23.

Baily, Martin N. 1981. "The Productivity Growth Slowdown and Capital Accumulation," *American Economic Review* 71, no. 2 (May): 326–31.

Berndt, Ernst R., and Dale W. Jorgenson. 1973. "Production Structure," in D.W. Jorgenson, et al., eds., *U.S. Energy Resources and Economic Growth*, Final Report to the Ford Foundation Energy Policy Project, Washington, D.C., October.

Berndt, Ernst R., and David O. Wood. 1979. "Engineering and Economic Interpretations of Energy-Capital Complementarity," *American Economic Review* 69, no. 3 (June): 342–54.

Denison, Edward F. 1979. *Accounting for Slower Economic Growth: The United States in the 1970's.* Washington, D.C.: The Brookings Institution.

Economic Report of the President, 1977. Washington, D.C.: U.S. Government Printing Office.

Fabricant, Solomon. 1973. "Perspectives on Productivity Research," in *Proceedings of a Conference toward an Agenda for Econmoic Research on Productivity.* Washington, D.C.: National Commission on Productivity, pp. 6–14.

Hudson, Edward A., and Dale W. Jorgenson. 1974. "U.S. Energy Policy and Economic Growth, 1975-2000," *Bell Journal of Economics and Management Science* 5 (Autumn): 461–514.

Hulten, Charles R., and Frank C. Wykoff. 1981. "The Measurement of Economic Depreciation," in Charles R. Hulten, ed., *Depreciation, Inflation, and the Taxation of Income from Capital.* Washington, D.C.: The Urban Institute, pp. 81–125.

Jorgenson, Dale W., and Barbara M. Fraumeni. 1981. "Relative Prices and Technical Change," in E.R. Berndt and B.C. Field, eds, *Modeling and Measuring Natural Resource Substitution.* Cambridge: MIT Press, pp. 17–47.

Kendrick, John. 1961. *Productivity Trends in the United States.* Princeton: Princeton University Press for the National Bureau of Economic Research.

Manne, Alan, and William Hogan. 1977. "Energy-Economy Interactions: The Fable of the Elephant and the Rabbit?" in Charles J. Hitch, ed., *Modeling Energy-Economy Interactions: Five Approaches.* Washington, D.C.: Resources for the Future, pp. 247–77.

Norsworthy, J.R.; Michael J. Harper; and Kent Kunza. 1979. "The Slowdown in Productivity Growth: Analysis of Some Contributing Factors," *Brookings Papers on Economic Activity,*" pp. 387–421.

Perry, George L. 1977. "Potential Output and Productivity," *Brookings Papers on Economic Activity,* pp. 11–60.

Rasche, Robert H., and John A. Tatom. 1977. "The Effects of the New Energy Regime on Economic Capacity, Production and Prices," *Federal Reserve Bank of St. Louis Review* 59, no. 5 (May): 2–12.

8 THE CONTRIBUTION OF EDUCATION TO ECONOMIC GROWTH: INTERNATIONAL COMPARISONS

George Psacharopoulos[1]

Since the concept of human capital was invented (or perhaps reinvented) in the late 1950s, we have been flooded with papers written about the contribution of education to economic growth. The most often cited early references are Schultz (1961) for the United States, Denison (1967) for the United States and other advanced countries, and Krueger (1968) and Nadiri (1972) for less advanced countries. After a rather long pause in the 1970s, triggered by lack of economic growth and ambivalence about the role of education in development, the topic has begun attracting renewed interest. Thus we have the less known recent works of Hicks (1980), Wheeler (1980), Easterlin (1981) and Marris (1982).

In this paper I first summarize past efforts to estimate the contribution of education to economic growth. Then I augment and reinforce this evidence by examining recent related analyses of the role of education in society that do not formally come under the popular heading of "the contribution of education to economic growth." The paper concludes with a response to recent attacks on the economic value of education, especially with reference to developing countries.

THE EXISTING EVIDENCE

Traditionally, estimates of the contribution of education to economic growth are arrived at by using one or another variant of the same basic accounting

335

framework. Assuming there exists an aggregate production function linking output (Y) to various inputs such as physical capital (K) and labor (L),

$$Y = f(K,L) , \qquad (8.1)$$

the observed average annual rate of growth (g_y) of the economy over a given time period can be disaggregated into capital and labor components (right-handed-side of equation (8.2), respectively),

$$g_y = \frac{I}{Y} r + g_L \cdot s_L , \qquad (8.2)$$

where I/Y stands for the investment-output ratio, r is the rate of return to investment, g_L is the average annual rate of growth of the labor force, and s_L is the share of labor in national income.[2]

Early attempts to empirically balance the two sides of equation (8.2) have resulted in the well known sizeable "residual," and it has since become a scholarly sport to try to reduce it by introducing other variables, such as education.

Education can enter into equation (8.2) either per Denison:

$$\Sigma_i {}^g L_i {}^s L_i ,$$

where L_i refers to labor with educational level i, or per Schultz:

$$\sum_i \frac{(I_i)r_i}{Y} ,$$

where I_i is the level of investment in the i type of education and r_i the rate of return to this type of education. The two methods are logically equivalent since they use wage differentials by level of education either as weights to derive the share of different types of labor to national income (Denison) or as income ratios to derive the rate of return to particular levels of education (Schultz).[3] Computational differences may arise in using the two methods because of discrepancies in the counting of physical increments of labor with given educational attainments (Denison) and the value invested in a particular type of education (Schultz).

First-Generation Estimates

Table 8-1 gives a compilation of the various first-generation estimates of the contribution of education to economic growth using one or another of the above accounting frameworks, expressed as the percentage of the observed rate of economic growth "explained" by education. It will be immediately noted that no easy generalizations can be made on the basis of

Table 8-1.   The Contribution of Education to Economic Growth (percentage).

Country	Growth Rate Explained
North America	
Canada	25.0
United States	15.0
Europe	
Belgium	14.0
Denmark	4.0
France	6.0
Germany	2.0
Italy	7.0
Greece	3.0
Israel ˹	4.7
Netherlands	5.0
Norway	7.0
United Kingdom	12.0
USSR	6.7
Latin America	
Chile	4.5
Argentina	16.5
Colombia	4.1
Brazil	3.3
Equador	4.9
Honduras	6.5
Peru	2.5
Mexico	0.8
Venezuela	2.4
Asia	
Japan	3.3
Malaysia	14.7[a]
Philippines	10.5
South Korea	15.9[a]
Africa	
Ghana	23.2[a]
Kenya	12.4[a]
Nigeria	16.0[a]

[a]Estimates based on "Schultz-type" growth accounting.

Source: Psacharopoulos (1973: 116) and Nadiri (1972: 138).

Note: Unless otherwise noted, estimates are based on Denison-type growth accounting.

this table. Education seems to have contributed substantially to the growth rate of some highly advanced countries—such as the United States, Canada, and Belgium—as well as to the growth rate of African and Asian countries (with the exception of Japan). In Latin America, Argentina notably stands out from the rest with a much higher contribution of education to growth.

Second-Generation Estimates

Characteristic of second-generation estimates is the use of econometric techniques relating inputs to output, rather than the growth accounting decomposition found in the work of Schultz and Denison. Such estimates cannot be easily summarized (as in Table 8-1), since each author followed a different estimating technique.

Hicks (1980) compared the growth rate of different countries in the 1960-77 period with each country's deviation from the 1960 expected literacy level. The latter was found by regressing the 1960 literacy level with the 1967 per capita income and its square in a sample of sixty-three developing countries. Table 8-2 shows that the top eight growth performers had clearly positive literacy deviations from the norm. In the case of the eight fastest growing countries, a 16 percent literacy advantage is associated with a higher growth rate of 3.3 percentage points. For all countries, Hicks found on the average that an increase in the literacy rate by 20 percentage points is associated with 0.5 percent higher growth rate.

Wheeler (1980) addressed the simultaneity problem inherent in previous analyses—namely, that the level of income might be influencing the level of education rather than the other way around. Pooling data from eighty-eight countries and working with differences in the variables (rather than levels) and simultaneous equation techniques, he found that education has an independent effect on income. For example, on the average, an increase of the literacy rate from 20 to 30 percent is the cause of an increase in real GDP by 8 to 16 percent. In the case of African countries the estimated elasticity of output with respect to literacy is double relative to the sample of all developing countries.

Table 8-2. Economic Growth and Literacy (percentage).

Top Eight Countries Ranked by Growth of GNP	Growth Rate of GNP Per Capita, 1960-77	Literacy Deviation from the Norm
South Korea	7.6	43.6
Hong Kong	6.3	6.4
Greece	6.1	7.5
Portugal	5.7	1.7
Spain	5.3	1.2
Yugoslavia	5.2	16.7
Brazil	4.9	8.6
Thailand	4.5	43.5
Average, top eight countries	5.7	16.2
Average, all LDC's	2.4	0.0

Source: Based on Hicks (1980), as cited in World Bank (1980: 38).

Marris's (1982) work is in effect an extension of Wheeler's. Using data from sixty-six developing countries in the 1965–79 period and a chain model of output determination, he confirmed previous results that the benefits of education in terms of economic growth are very high—and in particular that general investment plays a weak role when not supported by education. Costing the coefficients of the model, he estimated benefit/cost ratios for education (measured by the primary enrollment rate) ranging from 3.4 to 7.4. The benefit-cost ratios for education stood in a class of their own as compared, for example, with the corresponding ratios for investment in physical capital, which ranged from 0.4 to 1.0.

Finally, it should be noted that in a recent Denison-type growth accounting exercise by Kendrick (1981) splitting the 1960–79 period into two subperiods, it was found that in seven out of nine industrial countries, the contribution of education to economic growth was higher during the slowdown period of 1973–79 relative to 1960–73.

AN ENLARGEMENT

This section argues that the above evidence, especially the first-generation evidence, underestimates the true effect of education on economic growth and on social welfare in general. This point is made by raising a number of issues and by examining supplementary evidence that does not formally come under the heading of the contribution of education to economic growth.

To start with, let us abstract from the so-called interaction effects or complementarities between human and physical capital. The simply additive decomposition of the economic growth rate in the first-generation estimates has necessarily disregarded the interaction between education and other independent variables in promoting economic growth. For example, in an extremely macro exercise Krueger (1968) has shown that three variables normally associated with the concept of human capital (education, age, and sectoral distribution of the population) can explain more than half of the difference in income levels between the United States and a group of twenty-eight developing countries. Education alone was found to contribute one-quarter to one-third in explaining income differences, and its interaction with other variables was nearly equal to its direct effect. And it has repeatedly been found that human and physical capital complement each other in the process of economic growth. Griliches (1969), Psacharopoulos (1973), and Fallon and Layard (1975), among others, report results consistent with the hypothesis that a higher stock of human capital enhances the rental value of machines. Of course, the complementarity argument could be interpreted the other way around—namely, that an increasing stock of physical capital boosts the efficiency of educational investment, although Marris (1982), using a recursive path model, found that general investment plays a weak role in economic growth when not supported by education.

I want to abstract from interaction effects and complementarities because a correctly measured marginal product of labor used as a weight in growth accounting captures the mutually enhancing effect of an increased quantity of any input on other inputs. Also, if there exist nonlinearities in the sense of a mathematically more sophisticated growth decomposition than the one derived from Euler's theorem, one could, in fact, explain a greater part of the residual. However, it is not easy to attribute the extra-explanatory power of the nonlinear formulation to a particular factor of production like education (Nelson 1981). Instead, let us proceed on safer ground and make a distinction between the contribution of education to measured economic growth on the one hand and to a wider concept of social welfare on the other.

Contribution to Economic Growth

Typical growth accounting exercises underestimate the total effect of education for the following reasons:

The Maintenance Component.   Denison-type growth accounting, as commonly applied, underestimates the true contribution of education to economic growth because it neglects the educational maintenance component of a growing labor force. This is a fundamental distinction made by Bowman (1964) and Selowsky (1969) but that has not been followed up in the more recent literature. The distinction is important in the case of fast population growth developing countries where the educational system has a double burden: first, to maintain constant the level of educational attainment of the labor force and second, to augment its level of educational attainment. Denison-type accounting, as commonly applied, captures only the net increments of educated labor, neglecting the maintenance component. As shown in Table 8–3 the resulting underestimate errors of the contribution of education to economic growth are substantial, especially in developing countries.

The Educated Farmer.   The basic link between education and economic growth in typical growth accounting exercises is the classification of wages of labor by level of schooling. These wages are derived mainly from employment surveys in the modern sector of the economy. In developing countries, however, the majority of the economically engaged population does not work for wages but makes a living from agriculture or from self-employment in the informal sector of the economy.

Table 8-3. Downward Bias of the Estimated Contribution of Education to Economic Growth Because of Omission of the Maintenance Component (percentage).

Country	Downward Bias
Chile	58
Mexico	66
India	90
United States	38

Source: Selowsky (1969: 463).

Although the positive relationship between farmers' education and agricultural productivity was one of the first and repeatedly documented propositions in the empirical literature on human capital, such evidence has failed to be integrated into growth models. Landmarks of past analyses in this respect are the works of Griliches (1964) and Welch (1970) for U.S. agriculture and Hayami and Ruttan (1970) on cross-country comparisons. Thus, the output elasticities with respect to education in the United States are of the order of 0.3 to 0.5, as compared to 0.1 to 0.2 for land, fertilizer, and machinery. And nearly one-third of the difference in labor productivity between developed and less developed countries has been accounted for by differences in the human capital stock.

Of particular importance to this review is the recent work of Jamison and Lau (1982). Mastering the results of thirty-one data sets that related schooling to agricultural productivity, they concluded that, on the average, the latter increases by 8.7 percent as a result of a farmer completing four years of primary education. The importance of this finding stems from the fact that (1) productivity measurements in agriculture are in real (physical) output terms and (2) the usual objections raised when using wages as proxies for productivity in other studies have no relevance in a farm setting. Jamison and Lau also report that in Thailand the marginal effect of education on output is greater in rural than in urban areas. To the extent this is true in other countries, as one might reasonably suspect, past-growth accounting exercises using urban wage differentials must have underestimated the contribution of education to economic growth, especially in developing countries.

One of the prime indirect ways in which education contributes to economic growth is that it enhances the adoption and efficient use of new inputs. Whether the argument is cast in terms of the allocative efficiency of farmers (Schultz 1964) or the more general ability to "deal with disequilibria" (Schultz 1975), the literature is full of evidence that schooling acts as a catalyst in behavioral change conducive to growth. For example, Jamison and Lau (1982) report that in Thailand the probability of a farmer adopting a technology using chemical inputs is about 60 percent greater if the farmer has four years of education rather than none. In traditional Denison-type exercises this source of the contribution of education to growth is lumped into the unexplained residual.

The Use of Public Sector Weights. The wage differentials by level of schooling used in typical growth accounting are heavily influenced by salaries paid by the civil service, especially in developing countries. Although the salary level for some categories of labor might be higher than its marginal product in the noncompetitive sector of the economy, the salary *differential* by level of schooling is not. Comparisons of public-to-private sector wage differentials by educational level have shown that the earnings advantage of the more educated is higher in the private sector (see Table 8-4). To the extent earnings in the competitive sector are good proxies for the marginal product of labor, typical growth accounting studies, by using flatter differentials as weights, must have underestimated the true contribution of education to economic growth.

The Case of Women. For a variety of reasons, women earn substantially less than men. Thus it would appear that using male earnings—as the only data available in growth accounting—would overstate the contribution of education. However, the opposite is likely to be the case. For what matters in growth accounting is the within-sex earnings differential by level of education, or the rate of return to women's education. To the casual observer it comes as a surprise that the profitability of investing in education is higher for women than for men (see Table 8-5 for some examples).

There are two reasons for this apparently paradoxical finding. First, in the case of females the effect of education is not restricted to just raising their earnings; it also increases their chance of participating in the labor force. For example, Table 8-6 shows that in Puerto Rico the chances of a woman being formally engaged in economic activity is three times as much

Table 8-4.   The Earnings Differential by Economic Sector.

Country	Economic Sector	
	Public	*Private*
Portugal	0.99	1.12
Brazil	1.59	1.92
Colombia	1.07	1.48
Malaysia	0.62	1.13

Source: Psacharopoulos (1982: Table 3).

Note: Figures are ratios of mean earnings of employees with primary and less than primary educational qualifications.

Table 8-5. The Returns to Education by Sex (percentage).

Country	Educational Level/Type	Rate of Return	
		Males	Females
Colombia	Vocational	35.4	39.8
Puerto Rico	Secondary	26.3	44.9
New Zealand	Secondary	19.3	25.3
Germany	Vocational	9.0	11.3

Source: Woodhall (1973: Table 1).

as if she has received some college education rather than one to four years of primary schooling. Second, females tend to have lower foregone earnings, and this raises the rate of return. A third possibility is that discrimination against better educated women results in female wages that are lower than their true marginal product. This proposition could be documented by shadow pricing female labor by level of schooling. But perhaps the most persuasive evidence comes again from agriculture. Moock (1976) studied 152 maize farmers in Kenya and concluded that the impact of schooling on output, other factors remaining the same, is greater for the women than for the men. Considerations such as those listed above suggest that the use of male wages as weights in growth accounting understates the contribution of education to economic growth.

The Use of an Ability Adjustment. The cornerstone of the contribution of education to economic growth is the earnings differential between well-educated and less well-educated labor. Such observed earnings differential has been typically discounted by as much as 40 percent before entering the growth accounting equation to allow for effects other than education, like differential ability. Although the so-called alpha coefficient adjustment has been both plausible and intuitive, recent econometric evidence does not support its use.

Table 8-6. Female Labor Force Participation by Level of Education (percentage).

Educational Level	Participation Rate
Elementary 1-4	16.3
Elementary 5-6	21.6
Elementary 7-8	23.5
High school 1-3	31.8
High school 4	38.6
College 1+	53.6

Source: Shields (1977: 65).

Earnings functions analysis using schooling and ability measures, such as IQ, point that the effects of education on earnings is substantial, even after controlling for ability (e.g., Griliches 1970). A review of the empirically derived alpha coefficient found that its value is more likely to be 0.90 rather than the originally assumed 0.67 used in typical growth accounting (Psacharopoulos 1975). Also, a recent study using nearly experimental data of farmers in Nepal found not only that education has a significant effect on increased efficiency in wheat production but also that its effect does not diminish when the farmers' family background and measures of ability were introduced as additional control factors (Jamison and Moock 1984).

On-the-Job Training (OJT). If "education" is given an all-inclusive definition encompassing all forms of formal and informal learning, then OJT should be included in growth accounting. In spite of Mincer's (1962) early findings, however, that (1) in terms of costs, investment in on-the-job training in the United States is as important as formal education and that (2) the rate of return to on-the-job training investment is of the same order of magnitude as the return to investment in conventional schooling, no efforts have been made to incorporate OJT in formal growth models.

The observed wage level of a given type of labor certainly includes returns to OJT. To the extent a higher formal educational attainment facilitates investment in OJT, it reinforces the view that observed wage differentials between categories of labor classified by educational level should be attributed to one or another form of human capital.

Furthermore, the Beckerian distinction between general and specific training raises the question of second-round interaction effects between formal education and the trainability of the employee, and also brings to the surface the unrecorded benefits later reaped by the firm that has invested in specific employee training (Bowman 1980). A well-known proposition in the economics of education is that in the case of specific training, posttraining wages are less than the marginal product of the employee, the difference being the returns to the investment made by the employer. Since the latter appears in capital profits, failure to take OJT into account results to an underestimate of the contribution of education to economic growth.

Life Expectancy. Once human capital is created via education or training it has to be preserved so that it yields a stream of benefits throughout its theoretical lifetime (which in this case is of the order of fifty years). Cochrane (1980) reports significant partial effects of literacy on life expectancy in a number of countries, after standardizing for the level of income. Also, Hicks (1980) reports positive deviations from norm life expectancy associated with a higher rate of growth of GNP per person. As shown in Table 8-7, a nine-year positive deviation of life expectancy from the income-

Table 8-7.   Economic Growth and Life Expectancy.

Top Ten Countries Ranked by Life Expectancy in Relation to Income	Life Expectancy Deviation from the Norm, 1960	Growth Rate of GNP per Person, 1960–77
Sri Lanka	22.5	1.9
South Korea	11.1	7.6
Thailand	9.5	4.5
Malaysia	7.3	4.0
Paraguay	6.9	2.4
Philippines	6.8	2.1
Hong Kong	6.5	6.3
Panama	6.1	3.7
Burma	6.0	0.9
Greece	5.7	6.1
Average, Top ten countries	8.8	4.0
Average, eighty-three developing countries	0.0	2.4

Source: Hicks (1980) as reported in World Bank (1980: 38).

predicted value is associated with a 1.6 percent higher growth rate in per capita GNP. Typical growth accounting exercises neglect the indirect effect of education in lengthening the number of years during which individuals are productive; hence, they underestimate its real contribution to economic growth.

Migration.   Rural-urban and rural-rural migration is the process par excellence by which labor is reallocated to more productive uses. The migration literature is full of findings pointing at the positive relationship between education and the decision to move to another area (e.g., Greenwood 1975). This has been explained in terms of the "information hypothesis," which assumes that the economic attractiveness of a location is an increasing function of the level of education (Schwartz 1971). Growth accounting models do not take into account the effect of education on migration, hence they underestimate the indirect contribution mainly rural schools make to national output.

The Use of Literacy as Education Proxy.   Second-generation econometric estimates of the contribution of education to economic growth have typically used a basic education indicator, like the literacy rate of the population or the primary enrollment rate, as a proxy for the education variable. First-level education in developing countries carries a heavy weight in the construction of any educational quantity index (for an exception see Harbison and Myers 1964), and its benefits are more important relative to secondary and university education. On the other hand, the neglect of postprimary levels of schooling must underestimate the contribution of education to economic growth. Of course, second-generation econometric growth models have necessarily traded off the availability of more observations for the comprehensiveness of the education index.

Contribution to Social Welfare

The dependent variable in growth accounting exercises has typically been changes in the measured level of income (GNP or GDP). It is common knowledge, however, that part of the total income employed by households is not captured in the national accounts statistics and that there exist other welfare indicators, such as per capita income and distributive equity, that could be used as dependent variables in explaining well-being. Such considerations point to additional reasons why classic estimates, such as those presented above, are likely to underestimate the true contribution of education to economic growth and social welfare in general.

Fertility. This is one of a long series of demographic effects of schooling. Education affects fertility through different channels, such as the demand for children, contraception, and the child-bearing potential of women. Cochrane (1979) reports that the majority of case studies seem to conclude that education has a fertility reduction effect (see Table 8–8). Thus education has an important effect in *per capita* income increases in otherwise fast-growing population that goes unrecorded in ordinary growth accounting.

Table 8-8. The Relationship between Education and Fertility: Results of Case Studies.

Variable	Relation of Education to Variable	Probable Relation of Education through the Variable	Results (Number of Cases)	
			Supporting	Not Supporting
Age of marriage	Direct	–	59	12
Desired family size	Inverse	–	17	8
Perceived costs of children	Direct	–	2	0
Perceived costs to afford children	Direct	+	9	3
Contraceptive use	Direct	–	26	11
Knowledge of birth control	Direct	–	28	1

Source: Based on Cochrane (1979: 146).

Infant and Child Mortality.   Cochrane, Leslie, and O'Hara (1980) summarized evidence from a number of developing countries and reported partial effects of mother's literacy on infant and child mortality, as in Table 8-9. To the extent such considerations enter the social welfare function, they remain uncaptured in ordinary growth accounting.

Income Distribution.   If one is willing to accept a wider notion of development, the latter including not only the level of income but its distribution as well, education makes a further contribution to social welfare. Several studies in both advanced and developing countries have found that an increased level of educational attainment of the population or the labor force is associated with a more equal income distribution. For example, Marin and Psacharopoulos (1976) report that in the case of Mexico's giving primary education to 10 percent of those without would reduce the variance of the logarithm of earnings (a standard measure of income inequality) by nearly 5 percent. Also, Blaug, Dougherty, and Psacharopoulos (1982) found that the most recent (1972) raising of the minimum school-leaving age in England by one year, other things equal, is likely to reduce income inequality in a future steady state by 12 to 15 percent.

Household Production.   What households consume and the goods and services actually enjoyed by its members is not totally captured in national accounts statistics. This proposition is more relevant in developing countries where a great part of household income is in kind.

There are many ways a higher level of educational attainment of the members of the household contributes to income, other than through the labor market or agricultural production. For example, education embodied in nonformally economically active females is likely to have a great payoff in terms of household production activities, such as better sanitation conditions, more nutritious meals for the family, better educated children, and more efficient consumption behavior. Also, of particular importance is the effect of a more educated mother imparting early abilities to preschool age children (Selowsky 1982). Although the beneficial effect of education in this respect has been mainly documented in advanced countries (Schultz 1974;

Table 8-9.   The Effect of Literacy on Mortality, Per 1,000 Population.

Population Reference	$\frac{\partial \, (Mortality)}{\partial \, (Literacy)}$
Infants	-0.55
Children	-0.25

Source: Cochrane, Leslie, and O'Hara (1980: 86).

Michael 1982), one might validly extrapolate that the corresponding effect of education in developing countries must be even greater given the relative scarcities of human capital in the two types of countries.

Corroborating Evidence

For the results of macro-growth accounting models to be credible they have to agree with other evidence on the economic effect of education, such as microstudies at the individual plant level, the returns to investment in education, and evidence drawn from the economic history of nations.

Evidence from Microstudies. Detailed microstudies on the effect of schooling on individual employees at the firm level are not as abundant in the literature as the more popular Denison-type aggregate exercises. However, several of them have documented the positive effect of education and training on productivity. Thus Aryee (1976) found a positive correlation between output and the educational level of industrial entrepreneurs in Ghana, net of capital inputs. Fuller (1972) studied millers and grinders in two Indian factories and reported positive correlations between time taken to complete a given task and the educational level of the worker.

The Returns to Education. Evidence on the returns to investment in education in many respects complements, corroborates, and also highlights the possible underestimates of Denison-type growth accounting calculations. Furthermore, it increases our understanding of the particular types of education that are more likely to contribute to economic growth, especially in developing countries. Table 8–10 presents a summary of the available evidence on the returns to education around the world. The rate of return (r) figures have been arrived at by solving the following equation for r:

$$\sum_{t=1}^{n} \frac{(Y_{st} - Y_{s-1,t} - C_{st})}{(1 + r)^t} = 0$$

where Y_{st} is the earnings of labor with s level of education in year t, $Y_{s-1,t}$ is the earnings of the control group (lower level of schooling), and C_{st} is the direct cost of educational level s in year t. The difference between the private and social rates of return is that the latter are calculated on gross of income tax earnings and the direct cost includes the full amount of resources committed to a given level of education. The returns to primary education, although conservatively estimated, are the highest among the three levels that point to the relative importance of this kind of education for economic development. The absolute size of the private returns in

Table 8-10.   The Returns to Education by Region and Country Type (percentage).

Region or Country Type	N	Private			Social		
		Primary	Secondary	Higher	Primary	Secondary	Higher
Africa	(9)	29	22	32	29	17	12
Asia	(8)	32	17	19	16	12	11
Latin America	(5)	24	20	23	44	17	18
LDC average	(22)	29	19	24	27	16	13
Intermediate	(8)	20	17	17	16	14	10
Advanced	(14)	[a]	14	12	[a]	10	9

[a]Not computable because of lack of a control group of illiterates.

Source: Psacharopoulos (1981: 329).

Notes: N = number of countries in each group. Figures are not horizontally strictly comparable because in a given country the returns to education might not be available for all levels.

African countries: Ethiopia, Ghana, Kenya, Malawi, Morocoo, Nigeria, Rhodesia, Sierra Leone, and Uganda.

Asian countries: India, Indonesia, South Korea, Malaysia, Philippines, Singapore, Taiwan, and Thailand.

Latin America countries: Brazil, Chile, Colombia, Mexico, and Venezuela.

LDC countries are all listed above.

Intermediate countries: Cyprus, Greece, Spain, Turkey, Yugoslavia, Israel, Iran, and Puerto Rico.

Advanced countries: Australia, Belgium, Canada, Denmark, France, Germany, Italy, Japan, Netherlands, New Zealand, Norway, Sweden, United Kingdom, and United States.

general is consistent with the unsatisfied demand for school places, especially in poor countries. The declining pattern of the rate of return by educational level adds credibility to treating school expenditures and foregone student earnings as investment. And although the social returns are based mostly on observed market wages, shadow pricing and evidence from self-employment and agriculture lend support to the economic value of education, net of other influences.

Educational Quality.   The education variable has been measured in a great variety of ways in growth models such as the level of educational attainment of the population, the number of years of schooling of the labor force, the percentage of literacy in a given country or the primary enrollment rate. Although it might appear that reference to the labor force is most relevant to growth accounting, the general population educational attainment measures are also pertinent in the sense of capturing economic effects of education other than through the labor market, as in the case of females and household production mentioned above.

One dimension that is typically missing in quantitative measures of education used in growth accounting is its quality, although other studies have shown that not only the quantity of education is productive but its quality is, as well. Regardless of whether educational quality has been measured in terms of school buildings, laboratories, textbooks, teacher qualifications, nature of the curriculum, class size, composition of the student body, or per-pupil expenditures, the evidence shows that such measures have an impact on student achievement and later earnings (Solmon 1975; Wachtel 1975; Rizzuto and Wachtel 1980). With respect to the former, the impact is greater in low-income countries (Heyneman and Loxley 1983).

Consideration of school quality might help explain the widening gap in economic performance between developing and advanced countries or the alleged failure of some economies to grow in spite of the rising educational attainment of the population. Jamison, Searle, Galda, and Heyneman (1981) report that whereas in 1960 the average OECD country invested sixteen times more per pupil than did any of the thirty-six countries with per capita income below $265, by 1970 the difference grew to 22:1, and by 1975 to 31:1. According to unpublished estimates this ratio stood at 50:1 by 1977.

The View of Economic Historians.   Economic historians have often been intrigued by the relationship between education and economic development. Three pieces of evidence are worth citing. First, Landes and Solmon (1972) have found that minimum schooling legislation did not cause the observed increases in the level of schooling in late nineteenth and early twentieth century United States. This finding runs against the popular hypothesis that schooling follows economic development. Second, Saxonhouse (1977) in a study of the Japanese cotton spinning industry from 1891 to 1935 found that education, among other factors, had a large and significant impact on productivity growth. Third, Easterlin (1981) looked at the chicken-egg problem of the relationship between educational development and economic growth by examining historical data for twenty-five of the largest countries of the world. His conclusion was that the spread of technology in modern economic growth depended on the learning potentials and motivation that were linked to the development of formal schooling—or that the most likely causal link is from education to economic growth rather than the other way around.

CONCLUDING REMARKS

Without resorting to externalities, institution building, or other difficult-to-estimate but certainly positive effects of education in society, it is possible to substantially enlarge and reinforce the traditional evidence on the contribution of education to economic growth. This conclusion does not coincide with recent attacks on the role of education on productivity growth and income distribution. Screening for ability, job competition, labor market segmentation, nonclearing wages, nonprofit maximizing public sector pay scales, social class, and youth unemployment allegedly provide alternative explanations of the observed earnings advantage of the more educated or have been used to cast doubts on the social role of schooling. Such explanations are, at first sight, intuitively plausible and have often influenced the decision of policymakers and administrators against spending on schooling. Also, what might be partially true in the case of highly advanced industrial countries is often casually extrapolated to apply in developing countries.

To the careful reader of the literature, however, the challenges to the beneficial role of education in development are mostly superficial and in most cases have not been rigorously tested, especially in developing countries. Thus, the screening hypothesis (Taubman and Wales 1973) diminishes in importance when reference is made to the self-employed or the direct social product of education in agriculture (Jamison and Lau 1982). The job competition model (Thurow 1972) has never addressed or considered the possibility of a more educated person being more productive within a given occupational title.

The popular labor market segmentation or duality hypothesis (Gordon 1972) has faded away, following the critique by Cain (1976). When a distinction is made between nonclearing and competitive labor markets, as mentioned earlier, it is found that wage differentials in the public sector understate the true productive advantage of the more educated as the latter is measured by earnings differentials in the competitive private sector (Psacharopoulos 1982). In the sociological literature, social class is not the main determinant of earnings, net of the effect of education (Psacharopoulos and Tinbergen 1978). And unemployment does not permanently diminish the earnings advantage of the more educated because it is a sharply declining function of time since graduation, often measured in terms of weeks rather than years (Psacharopoulos and Sanyal 1981). When reference is made to developing countries, the argument for investment in schools and training becomes even stronger given the relative scarcity of human capital and the low score of such countries on any indicator of educational development.

NOTES

1.   The author is grateful to Mary Jean Bowman, Marcelo Selowsky, and Finis Welch for reading a first draft of this paper and offering suggestions for improvement. The views and interpretations are those of the author and should not be attributed to The World Bank.

2. For a proof of this and related growth accounting derivations, see Selowsky (1969), Robinson (1971), and Psacharopoulos (1972).
3. For a proof of this proposition, see Psacharopoulos (1973: 113–14). For the most elaborate discussion of the differences between the two methods, see Bowman (1964).

REFERENCES

Aryee, G.A. 1976. "Effects of Formal Education and Training on the Intensity of Employment in the Informal Sector: A Case Study of Kumasi, Ghana." Geneva: International Labor Organization, World Employment Program, WP No. 14.

Blaug, M.; C.R.S. Dougherty; and G. Psacharopoulos. 1982. "The Distribution of Schooling and the Distribution of Earnings: Raising the School Leaving Age in 1972." *The Manchester School* 50 (March): 24–39.

Bowman, M.J. 1964. "Schultz, Denison and the Contribution of 'Eds' to Economic Growth." *Journal of Political Economy* 72, no. 9 (October): 450–64.

_____. 1980. "Education and Economic Growth: An Overview." In *Education and Income,* edited by T. King, pp. 1–71. Washington, D.C.: World Bank, Staff Working Paper No. 402.

Cain, G. 1976. "The Challenge of Segmented Labor Market Theories to Orthodox Theory: A survey." *Journal of Economic Literature* 14 (December): 1215–17.

Cochrane, S.H. 1979. *Fertility and Education: What Do We Really Know?* Baltimore, Md.: Johns Hopkins University Press, for the World Bank.

_____. 1980. "The Socioeconmic Determinants of Mortality: The Cross-National Evidence." In *The Effects of Education on Health,* by S.H. Cochrane, D.J. O'Hara, and J. Leslie, pp. 3–33. Washington, D.C.: World Bank, Staff Working Paper No. 405.

Cochrane, S.H.; J. Leslie; and D.J. O'Hara. 1980. "Parental Education and Child Health: Intra-Country Evidence." In *The Effects of Education on Health,* edited by pp. 56–95. Washington, D.C.: World Bank, Staff Working Paper No. 405.

Denison, E. 1967. *Why Growth Rates Differ: Post-War Experience in Nine Western Countries.* Washington, D.C.: The Brookings Institution.

Easterlin, R. 1981. "Why Isn't the Whole World Developed?" *The Journal of Economic History* 41, no. 1 (March): 1–19.

Fallon, R.P., and R. Layard. 1975. "Capital-Skill Complementarity, Income Distribution and Growth Accounting." *Journal of Political Economy* 83 (April): 279–302.

Fuller, W.P. 1972. "Evaluating Alternative Combinations of Education and Training for Job Preparation: An Example from Indian Industry." *Manpower Journal* 3: 7–38.

Gordon, E. 1972. *Theories of Poverty and Unemployment.* Lexington, Mass.: Lexington Books.

Greenwood, M.J. 1975. "Research on Internal Migration in the U.S.: A Survey." *Journal of Economic Literature* 3, no. 2 (June): 397–433.

Griliches, Z. 1964. "Research Expenditures, Education, and the Aggregate Agricultural Production Function." *American Economic Review* 54 (December): 961–74.

_____. 1969. "Capital-Skill Complementarity." *Review of Economics and Statistics* 51: 465–68.

_____ . 1970. "Notes on the Role of Education in Production Functions and Growth Accounting." In *Education, Income and Human Capital,* edited by W. Lee Hansen. New York: National Bureau for Economic Research.

Harbison, F., and C.A. Myers. 1964. *Education, Manpower and Economic Growth.* New York: McGraw Hill.

Hayami, Y., and V.W. Ruttan. 1970. "Agricultural Productivity Differences among Countries." *American Economic Review* 60 (December): 985–11.

Heyneman, S., and W. Loxley. 1983. "The Effect of Primary-School Quality on Academic Achievement across Twenty-nine High and Low Income Countries." *American Journal of Sociology* 88, no. 6: 11–62.

Hicks, N. 1980. "Economic Growth and Human Resources." Washington, D.C.: World Bank, Staff Working Paper No. 408.

Jamison, D., and L. Lau. 1982. *Farmer Education and Farm Efficiency.* Baltimore, Md.: Johns Hopkins University Press.

Jamison, D., and P. Moock. 1984. "Farmer Education and Farm Efficiency in Nepal: The Role of Schooling, Extension Services and Cognitive Skills." *World Development* 12, no. 1: 67–86.

Jamison, D.T.; B. Searle; K. Galda; and S. Heyneman. 1981. "Improving Elementary Mathematics Education in Nicaragua: An Experimental Study of the Impact of Textbooks and Radio on Achievement." *Journal of Education Psychology* 73, no. 4 (August): 556–67.

Kendrick, J.W. 1981. "International Comparisons of Recent Productivity Trends." In *Essays in Contemporary Economic Problems: Demand, Productivity and Population,* edited by William Fellner, pp. 125–70. Washington, D.C.: American Enterprise Institute for Public Policy Research.

Krueger, A.O. 1968. "Factor Endowments and Per Capital Income Differences among Countries." *Economic Journal* 78 (September): 641–59.

Landes, W.M., and L.C. Solomon. 1972. "Compulsory Schooling Legislation: An Economic Analysis of Law and Social Change in the Nineteenth Century." *Journal of Economic History* 32, no. 1 (March): 54–91.

Marin, A., and G. Psacharopoulos. 1976. "Schooling and Income Distribution." *Review of Economics and Statistics* 58, no. 3 (August): 332–38.

Marris, R. 1982. "Economic Growth in Cross-Section." Department of Economics, Birbeck College. Mimeo.

Michael, R.T. 1982. "Measuring Non-Monetary Benefits of Education: A Survey." In *Financing Education,* edited by W.W. McMahon and T.G. Geske, pp. 119–49. Urbana: University of Illinois Press.

Mincer, J. 1962. "On-the-Job Training: Costs, Returns and Some Implications." *Journal of Political Economy* 70, no. 5, pt. 2 (October): 50–80.

Moock, P. 1976. "The Efficiency of Women as Farm Managers: Kenya." *American Journal of Agricultural Economics* (December): 831–35.

Nadiri, M.I. 1972. "International Studies of Total Factor Productivity: A Brief Survey." *Review of Income and Wealth* 18, no. 2 (June): 129–54.

Nelson, R. 1981. "Research on Productivity Growth and Productivity Differences: Dead Ends and New Departures." *Journal of Economic Literature* 19 (September): 1029–64.

Psacharopoulos, G. 1972. "Measuring the Marginal Contribution of Education to Economic Growth." *Economic Development and Cultural Change* 20, no. 4 (July): 641–58.

_____ . 1973. *Returns to Education: An International Comparison.* Amsterdam: Elsevier-Jossey Bass.

_____. 1975. *Earnings and Education in OECD Countries.* Paris: OECD.

_____. 1981. "Returns to Education: An Updated International Comparison." *Comparative Education* 17 (October): 321–41.

_____. 1982. "Education and Society: Old Myths versus New Facts." In *The Mixed Economy,* edited by Lord Roll of Ipsden, pp. 145–61. New York: Mac-Millan.

Psacharopoulos, G., and B. Sanyal. 1981. *Higher Education and Employment: The IIEP Experience in Five Less Developed Countries.* Paris: UNESCO, International Institute for Educational Planning.

Psacharopoulos, G., and J. Tinbergen. 1978. "On the Explanation of Schooling, Occupation and Earnings: Some Alternative Path Analyses." *De Economist* 126, no. 4 (December): 505–20.

Rizzuto, R., and P. Wachtel. 1980. "Further Evidence on the Returns to School Quality." *Journal of Human Resources* 15, no. 2 (winter): 240–54.

Robinson, S. 1971. "Sources of Growth in Less Developed Countries: A Cross-Section Study." *Quarterly Journal of Economics* 85 (August): 391–408.

Saxonhouse, G.R. 1977. "Productivity Change and Labor Absorption in Japanese Cotton Spinning, 1891–1935." *Quarterly Journal of Economics* 91, no. 2 (May): 195–200.

Schultz, R.W. 1961. "Education and Economic Growth." In *Social Forces Influencing American Education,* edited by N.B. Henry, National Society for the Study of Education, pp. 46–88. Chicago: University of Chicago Press.

Shultz, T.W. 1964. *Transforming Traditional Agriculture.* New Haven, Conn.: Yale University Press.

_____, ed. 1974. *The Economics of the Family.* New York: National Bureau of Economic Research.

_____. 1975. "The Value of the Ability to Deal with Disequilibria." *Journal of Economic Literature* 13, no. 3 (September): 827–46.

Schwartz, A. 1971. "On Efficiency of Migration." *Journal of Human Resources* 6, no. 2 (spring): 193–205.

Selowsky, M. 1969. "On the Measurement of Education's Contribution to Growth." *Quarterly Journal of Economics* (August): 449–63.

_____. 1982. "The Economic Effects of Investment in Children: A Survey of the Quantitative Evidence." In *Child Development Information and the Formation of Public Policy,* edited by T.E. Jordan, pp. 186–210. Springfield: Charles Thomas.

Shields, N. 1977. "Female Labor Force Participation and Fertility: Review of Empirical Evidence from LDC's." Washington, D.C.: World Bank, Population and Human Resources Division, February. Mimeo.

Solmon, L. 1975. "The Definition of College Quality and Its Impact on Earnings." *Explorations in Economic Research* 2, no. 4 (fall): 537–87.

Taubman, P.F., and T. Wales. 1973. "Higher Education, Mental Ability and Screening." *Journal of Political Economic* 81 (January/February): 28–55.

Thurow, L. 1972. *Generating Inequality.* New York: Basic Books.

Wachtel, P. 1975. "The Effect of School Quality on Achievement, Attainment Levels and Lifetime Earnings." *Explorations in Economic Research* 2, no. 4 (fall): 502–36.

Welch, F. 1970. "Education in Production." *Journal of Political Economy* 78 (January/February): 32–59.

Wheeler, D. 1980. "Human Resource Development and Economic Growth in Developing Countries: A simultaneous Model." Washington, D.C.: World Bank, Staff Working Paper No. 407.

Woodhall, M. 1973. "Investment in Women: A Reappraisal of the Concept of Human Capital." *International Review of Education* (spring): 9–29.
World Bank. 1980. *World Development Report 1980.* Washington, D.C.: World Bank.

A COMMENT ON EDUCATION AND ECONOMIC GROWTH

Theodore W. Schultz

It now can be told that those two oldtimers Denison and Schultz severely underestimated the true contributions of education to economic growth and social welfare. I am sure that Denison and I are both pleased and relieved that the exposure is put so graciously. Both of us used old-fashioned simple economics and elementary data. Omissions abound in what we did. Psacharopoulos speaks with authority—to wit, his recent "Returns to Education: An Updated International Comparison" and his other new published papers, which extend and enhance the findings set forth in his 1973 book.

The first two sections of Psacharopoulos's paper give us evidence that advances in the art of economics have added to our knowledge of the contributions of education to economic growth. Although the international comparisons are very brief, they provide results of various approaches to the evidence.

In these approaches theory and data talk to each other, which I applaud. But there are always questions about the parts of the theory from which a particular model is derived. The economic growth that fashions the data is a dynamic process, whereas the theory that guides the analysis is, as a rule, based on equilibrium assumptions. Actual private and public investments in education are responses to opportunities that occur as a consequence of the disequilibria that characterize economic growth. Steady-state equilibrium growth is rare indeed. Questions about the data on which we all are dependent are fairly obvious. Statistical aggregates for countries, especially for most low-income countries, are far from accurate, and even for countries where they are reliable they conceal the heterogeneity of the

357

education that is acquired within what is classified as primary, secondary, and higher education. In the United States, for example, the quality of elementary and secondary schooling in most of our large cities has been declining for years. National achievement tests show that the test scores of the children in these large cities are far below those of suburban children and somewhat below those of rural children who have been benefitting from improvements in the quality of the schooling they receive. The federal, state, and local politics that shape the performance of our public schools in these large cities are models of economic inefficiency, with very serious adverse welfare implications. Psacharopoulos's Tables 8–1 and 8–2 give us clues to the issues at hand and the puzzles that are to be resolved.

I find the section entitled "An Enlargement" even more rewarding. Seventeen issues are presented with comments that are succinct and to the point. Most of them, however—as is implied—are in substantial part unsolved issues.

I contend that the economics of the acquired abilities of people as economic agents is, as yet, dimly perceived and understood. Education is one of the important acquired properties of human beings; improvements in health also contribute to the quality of human capital. Education and health have various complementary relationships. The stock of knowledge is also a form of capital. Engineers who graduate today have learned many things in their field of specialization that were not known and therefore not taught to engineers who graduated during my college years. Ask the new breed of young economists what they think of those old-fashioned economists who have tenure!

In discussing increased ability of people as economic agents for the purposes at hand, I shall not deal with differences in the genetic endowments because as far as we know, the distribution of genes within most populations are about the same. Thus, for example, there is no appreciable difference in the level and distribution in the genetic endowment of the people of China and that of the U.S. population. The vast difference in the level of skills between them is a consequence of the differences in acquired abilities. The per capita human capital is small in China and very large in the United States.

We know that in the United States the real earnings of labor per hour of work in manufacturing industries between 1900 and 1975 increased well over fivefold. I contend that increases in the quality of the labor force and the changes in the supply and demand for this acquired quality are only vaguely understood. Although labor economics is being much enriched by the use of the concept of human capital, the analytical refined tuning, good as it is, does not tell us anything about the long-term dynamics that account for increases in labor quality since, say, 1900.

When the production of an economy increases, the marginal conditions of theory are seldom satisfied because growth as noted is beset with disequilibria. In large part it is up to entrepreneurs, who are the forgotten economic agents in the prevailing art of economics, to rectify these disequilibria. Education enhances their ability to deal with disequilibria (Schultz 1980). This important contribution of education is not generally reckoned on, as Psacharopoulos points out. The omission of the value of on-the-job training casts considerable doubt on the estimates of the returns to education. Here, too, Psacharopoulos is correct in alerting us to the fact that two decades have elasped since Mincer's findings were published showing that on-the-job training of males in the United States was as important as their formal education.

The remarkable increases in life span in many low-income countries since World War II have made primary education much more worthwhile than it was when life expectancy at birth was forty years and less. The implied improvements in health have strongly enhanced the incentives to invest in schooling. In high-income countries, the large increases in expenditures to maintain health over the last two decades of life are contributing much to the continuing productivity and welfare of these older people. Education is being credited, however, with what belongs to expenditures on health. Also, a part of the observed decline in fertility that is attributed to increases in education is a consequence of the improvements in health that account for the increases in life span.

Most of the points that I have made are extensions of matters on Psacharopoulos's agenda. He has written with authority on them. In closing I shall list four untidy issues:

1. The low rate of private returns to education as revealed to youth since the late 1970s is not proof that Americans are overeducated. What it proves, which is obvious, is that the economy has been performing badly and that as a consequence the returns to both physical and human capital have been low. Education is a long-term investment.

2. Public schools have long been an established institution. Presently in most of our large cities, public schools are performing badly. In terms of national test scores, the children who attend public schools in these large cities have test scores far below the national norms. Efficiency in instruction has been impaired by nationally mandated social reforms. Politics is to blame. Unfettered competition between public and private schools is an essential part of the solution.

3. I contend that if half or more of U.S. foreign aid were devoted to assist low-income countries in enhancing the amount and quality of their primary schooling, long-term productivity and welfare of poor people would increase very substantially compared with the present foreign aid,

which features primarily physical capital. Other international donors are making the same mistake.

4. While there are many more untidy issues, my last for now deals with research in our universities, which is in large measure dependent on federal funds. Briefly, what began during the 1970s and continues is an increasing array of interventions by the federal government. Those who do the research in our universities become ever more beholden to the regulations of government agencies (Schultz 1980). The most recent episode is the report from the White House Office of Science and Technology Policy demanding that agricultural research be shaken up and be made to shape up, which *Science* featured under the heading, "White House Plows into Agricultural Research" (1982). We are far along on the Soviet road of centralizing the management of our university research. What may be good enough for the military establishment of the Soviet Union is inconsistent with the traditional decentralized and successful freedom of inquiry in the basic sciences and in agriculture. While Denison is far too young to join me, I can with good grace express my pleasure in having the research baton carried by the younger generation of economists.

REFERENCES

Schultz, Theodore, W. 1980. "Investment in Entrepreneurial Ability." *The Scandinavian Journal of Economics* 8 (December): 437–48.
_____. 1981. "The Politics and Economics of Research." *Minerva* 19, no. 3 (autumn): 644–51.
"White House Plows into Agricultural Research." 1982. *Science* 217 (September): 1227–28.

9 U.S. AND EUROPEAN APPROACHES TO IMPROVING LABOR PRODUCTIVITY AND THE QUALITY OF WORK LIFE

Ted Mills

For reasons not yet historically clear, in the 1970s a succession of political and industrial events relating to the nature, rights, and functions of employees in work organizations began to occur simultaneously in Europe and North America. By the end of that decade, on both sides of the Atlantic, what some have characterized as an explosion of new concern, new work-related theories, new strong regulatory work-place laws (in Europe only), new government agencies, new industrial experimentation, and both minor and major new organizational restructuring in private sector firms had occurred in almost every industrialized nation in the West.

In the United States, as detailed in this paper, what began some ten years ago continued to grow and spread into the 1980s with no signs of abatement. The U.S. experience was characterized by *Fortune* magazine in 1981 as a potential "cultural revolution" (Editors of *Fortune* 1982). In Europe, a professor at the European Institute for Advanced Studies in Management characterized what was happening in Europe as "the third industrial revolution" (Cooper and Mumford 1979). Trend analysts in both the United States and Europe noted a clear causal relationship between the emergence of this growing focus on people at work and what U.S. sociologist Daniel Yankelovich (1981) called "an irrevocable watershed" of changed Western social values, or "value shift"—a prominent characteristic of which (among many) was a growing intolerance of and hostility to authority, at work and at home.

What is historically remarkable is that this outpouring of new interest and activity in the performance of work by human beings occurred con-

361

currently, in a single decade of the late twentieth century, in ten European countries and across the Atlantic in two North American countries, the United States and Canada. It is worth noting that no comparable interest or activity developed in Japan or Latin America or elsewhere in the world, except, perhaps, in a very limited sense, in Australia.

As will be examined in the following pages, what occurred in Europe in varying degress of intensity in various countries differed considerably in nature, form, and substance from the American and Canadian experiences, which closely resembled each other. On both sides of the Atlantic, however, so widespread and profound was the sudden eruption of activities and events that what occurred could accurately be considered a Western social phenomenon (Robow and Zager 1982).

The phenomenon has been given many names in many countries. So have each of its contributing notions and activities. Many of these have a distinct ideological and political character; many have an engineering and industrial design character; many are behavioral in origin. Some of the many names, or "aliases," for what occurred with such a rush in that decade are examined in "The European Approach" below. Perhaps as inclusive a term as any to identify the totality of the phenomenon is the value-free term "work restructuring," which these pages will use to identify the general contours of what has occurred in Europe and North America. For no matter what political, ideological, philosophical, or engineering form the various visible manifests of the explosion of activity took in any country, almost all focused on the restructuring of work tasks, work performance, work environments, work systems, work cultures, and work organizations, including restructuring of management.

NOT AN ECONOMIC PHENOMENON

All these activities occurred, with increasing momentum across the 1970s, *within* organizations producing work in Europe and North America, or economic institutions. It would seem plausible, therefore, to view them collectively as a phenomenon with actual or potential economic impact. This has yet, however, to be reliably demonstrated. In Europe, where the intrusion of legally mandated work reform has in several countries been profound, one might expect to discover significant positive or negative change in national economic performance, and thus a matter for economic inquiry.

From still-sparse data currently available, however, this does not seem to be the case on either side of the Atlantic. Certainly, a social, political, and cultural phenomenon has occurred here and abroad in the 1970s and—particularly here—continues to grow in scope and breadth; it does not seem, from its continuing vigor, to be a "passing fad" that erupted and will subside.[1] Yet the positive or negative impact of the phenomenon on economic performance in any affected nation has simply not been satisfactorily demonstrated. It is wholly possible that what has occurred, with major social impact, will prove to have been without assessable economic consequences.

There are perhaps three general reasons why, as of this writing. First is the economically elusive, bewildering multiplicity and complexity of the terms used by the work-restructure activists for their areas of advocacy. An intensive search conducted for the preparation of this paper, here and abroad, for data revealing demonstrable economic impact of work restructure events in any country proved barren. Of the 577 domestic and foreign titles under "labor productivity" in the U.S. Library of Congress, not one addressed the post-1970 economic impact of "work restructure" (not an indexed term), or "industrial democracy" (indexed but not economically addressed), or "quality of work life" (indexed but not economically addressed), or "co-determination" (indexed but not economically addressed), or "participation" (indexed but not economically addressed), or "organizational change" (indexed but exclusively behaviorally addressed). The same absence of correlation was evident in material available from the OECD and ILO. The bewildering array of work-restructure terms cited in "The European Approach" below apparently has precluded focused economic inquiry. The phenomenon seems to have no economically acceptable name, for it is not a phenomenon of discernible macroeconomic impact.

A second reason for difficulty in reliably valid analyses of economic correlation becomes evident on examination of the sparse but available microeconomic or company-level data here and abroad. At this level there is some data. But it is so random, so mixed, so imprecise and inconclusive in clear economic impact terms that to draw, or seek to draw, valid economic-impact assumptions would be at best presumptive and at worst fallacious.

An excellent example of this difficulty lies in the much publicized)in Europe) Biedenkopf Report, released in 1973 in West Germany. It was a massive study that sought to analyze and assess social and economic outcomes of twenty years of "co-determination" (see below) or workers-on-boards, which the occupying powers had imposed on the entire West German coal and steel industries in 1952 for anti-Nazi reasons. The report found economic impact so mixed in both industries (both of which had boomed in the period analyzed) that valid conclusions as to economic effect of co-determination were impossible to draw.

Another example of microeconomic research with inconclusive results was a major, two-year, $5 million study performed under a combined grant from West Germany's Ministries of Labor and Technology (part of a $30 million annual experimental program studying German work restructuring outcomes) at Volkswagen's large Satzigger location. Three varying kinds of work restructure approaches were instituted. Performance data was meticulously gathered during the study period. At the end, deductions found "advanced" work structures "insignificantly" more, or less, effective in economic terms, than traditional structures (despite highly significant positive and negative impact on morale and union relations). Similarly, in the United States and Canada where privacy of work restructure impact data tends unfortunately to be standard, there are sporadic claims by firms and unions here and there of important improvement of product or service quality resulting from employee involvement efforts, of productivity improvement, of reduced downtime, error or scrap rate, and other downturns in counterproductive human behavior indices. Most such announcements are PR, in stockholder reports, not reliable published company performance data. There may be a reason why a $1 million grant by the Ford Foundation to the Institute for Social Research at the University of Michigan in 1974 specifically to develop and apply a viable economic and social assessment methodology for "quality of work life" efforts ended in failure; researchers and companies (Weyerhaueser, Nabisco, and others) found so many extrinsic economic variables impacting economic performance—significant new technology and/or capital acquisition, market fluctuation, union relations, and/or production system efficiency—that isolation of "QWL" impact performance was impossible to accurately determine. In both macroeconmic and microeconomic areas of inquiry, therefore, reliable and extensive economic data are so scant, or so skewed inside other bodies of data as to be largely irrelevant or useless to the economic researcher, here and abroad.

A third reason to consider the subject area of this paper as probably noneconomic in impact is the basic motivation of the perpetrators of the work restructure series of events, here and abroad. Despite a mounting purely economic concern for productivity improvement, on neither side of the Atlantic has desire for basically economic improvement been a direct causal force or primary objective behind the work restructure phenomenon, even by management. In Europe and North America equally, the motivating forces underlying work restructure events and activities have postulated uniquely cultural objectives, or social, ethical, and—in Europe, particularly—ideologically based political goals.

This motivational distinction becomes particularly important in distinguishing between the so-called work restructure movement of the 1970s and concurrent "productivity improvement" activities on both sides of the Atlantic. Often, particularly at shop-floor levels, such efforts and techniques (see "The European Approach" below) seem deceptively similar, if not identical—except in purpose and motivation. In the United States today, a great many work restructure efforts that are culturally and ethically motivated, including most "QC Circle" efforts (see "The American Approach" below), are labelled "productivity" efforts; in motivation or principal objectives, they are not. This subtle distinction was made clear in

Detroit by the industrial relations vice-president of General Motors, a company that has been a pioneering leader in the emerging U.S. "quality of work life" movement. In a widely disseminated 1978 GM document (Mills 1976) that vice-president wrote,

> When we began applying organizational development principles seven years ago, our focus was on improving organizational effectiveness. We saw improvement in performance and the work climate naturally flowing from such efforts. *We have now reversed those objectives.* Our primary objective now is solely to improve the quality of work life throughout the organization. We feel that . . . by wisely managing the systems that lead to *greater job satisfaction and feelings of self-worth,* improvements in the organization will follow.

The italics above are mine, to highlight the QWL focus on social and cultural objectives as primary motivators. In this view, improved productivity becomes a byproduct, not an end. Such objectives as "feelings of self-worth" are hardly an economically measurable phenomenon. It is noteworthy that to my knowledge, in no North American or European work restructure activity or written documents does the term "labor productivity" appear. To work restructure advocates and perpetrators it is a nonterm, irrelevant to their social and cultural goals.

A major contention of this paper is that we may be experiencing the emergence of a new participative work ethic, feasible in and/or for the much-changed nature and goals of contemporary Western society. If this contention proves true, measuring its economic impact on the future course of Western economies may prove as near-impossible as measuring the profound impact of Weber's Protestant work ethic on the explosive economic vigor and achievements of the industrial age.

For this reason as well as the three reasons previously cited, this paper henceforth eschews economic consideration from its investigation of the phenomenon of the 1970s. In very large macroeconomic terms, its impact may one day be eminently visible to economic historians and perhaps be profoundly influential. It would seem, from avaialable data, to be far too early to tell. To date, at least, what has occurred and is still gathering steam would seem primarily to be a perhaps wholly cultural phenomenon. What follows, therefore, seeks to limit its examination to the cultural context, and no more, on each side of the Atlantic, in the past decade.

FIVE BASIC CONTENTIONS

Within this cultural context, five basic contentions of this paper underlie what follows below:

1. The explosion of interest and activity in work restructure techniques, notions, ideologies, and practices in both North America and Europe since 1972 has been almost uniquely a social, ethical, and political phenomenon.

2. The same work restructure phenomenon that occurred simultaneously in Europe and North America was remarkably different on each side of the Atlantic. As we will see, what generally occurred in most of Europe was political in character, and left-of-center in ideology, with social justice as its goal. While perhaps few Europeans would accept the term "social justice" as accurate, the objective of what most European participative activists sought and have significantly achieved (notably in West Germany, Holland, Denmark, Sweden, Norway, and Austria) was some discrete, mandated form of "industrial democracy" (Mills 1979). By strong contrast, what has occurred in the United States and Canada with very similar ends has remained astonishingly apolitical in those same years, as will be explored in "The American Approach" below. The very absence of political ideology and resulting law in the North American version of the work restructure phenomenon is itself a striking and revealing political phenomenon, worth carefully noting.

3. Driving advocacy and acceptance in both Europe and North America has been an emerging new work ethic desirable to the changed Western societies of the so-called postindustrial age. Under many activist names, such as quality of work life (QWL), employee involvement, employee participation, or participative management, but more and more under the catchall name "participation," this ethic essentially seeks to provide to employees at every level (in North America) and to workers (in Europe) greater financial and social participation in the organizations where they work. It can, on both sides of the ocean, be accurately called the participative work ethic of the 1980s and thereafter. The work restructure phenomenon, in all its forms, on both sides of the Atlantic, is the visible manifest of a cultural change in what people want from, and give to the daily experience of work.

4. The work restructure phenomenon here and abroad during the 1970s had three distinct or basic thrusts, or "faces"; all derive from the participative ethic. One was called *work humanization*. The essential focus of its adherents and advocates was task-related; it sought to enrich or enlarge jobs and their performance for humanistic motives. Its domain was the shop floor. The second basic work restructure thrust, quite distinct in its goals and objectives, was most often called *quality of work life or QWL*. The essential focus of its advocates was social change in work organizations, again for humanistic motives. If work humanization sought to restructure individual jobs for the benefit of the employee, QWL sought to restructure work societies and how they functioned for the mutual benefit of the employee *and* the organization's effectiveness. The third basic thrust was unique to Europe and was also derived from the ethical soil of participation. It could be called the ideological left-of-center *social justice* thrust. This thrust has been conspicuously absent in North American work

restructure advocacy, perhaps, as explored in "The American Approach" below, because American unions have not been the principal advocates of participation, as they were in Europe.

The work humanization advocates, the QWL advocates, and the social justice advocates have tended to be separate groups of individuals. The work humanization groups, particularly in Europe, tended to comprise theorists who were engineers, industrial design experts, and the ergonomists, a human-factors discipline little known in North America. The QWL group tended to be theorists predominantly composed of behavioral scientists, most with degrees or special interest in organizational development. The social justice group in Europe tended to be ideologues and political theorists, activist intellectuals in Europe's labor confederations or political parties seeking political reform. The fact that all three groups emerged in a single decade, separately pursuing participative ends by different means, lends credence to the third contention above—the emergence of a nutrient social ethic propelling all simultaneously.

5. The first through fourth contentions above seek essentially to explicate developments of the 1970s on both sides of the Atlantic. The fifth, and most important, deals with the 1980s and beyond, and very probably solely in North America. As the 1980s began, in American work organizations a major new thrust began to be clearly discernible. The American head of Norway's highly regarded Work Institute summed it up with total accuracy: "What previously [in Europe] led us to more democratic forms of organizing work," Max Elden wrote in 1979 (Cooper and Mumford 1979), "may now be leading us [in North America] to more democratic forms of *organizational restructure.*" What had been sporadic activity in restructuring work at shop-floor levels, here and in Europe, suddenly in the 1980s in the United States moved upward in the organization to the highest levels of management as *corporate policy for entire organizations.*

By 1982, when the New York Stock Exchange issued its startling survey of participation (in all its forms) in the United States, they could project that already thousands of American companies had made a total-organizational commitment to the participative ethic of involving employees in decisionmaking. General Motors, with some fanfare, had announced that total commitment in the late 1970s. Ford, with even more public fanfare, had followed suit in 1981 with their EI (employee involvement) program. AT&T, Westinghouse, Atlantic Richfield, Dana Corporation, Hewlitt Packard, many jointly with their unions, jumped—as one CEO put it publicly—"on the QWL bandwagon" as corporate policy. In the "American Approach" below, we will examine a QWL-bred event of total-organizational dimensions as evidence of the maturation and upward thrust of the new ethic in the United States.

In North America, as the 1980s mounted, participation as a long-term objective has become a concern and preoccupation at the highest policy-making levels of enterprise—a new, accepted concern of the art, science, and practice of corporate governance. In Europe, with rare exceptions, this thrust to policy levels has not occurred; participation and its ethic are still perceived as involving workers and their rights. It could be said with some accuracy that with the exception of Sweden, the 1970s explosion of industrial democracy in Europe has levelled, peaked, and perhaps waned. The major contention of this paper is that in the United States and Canada, it has continued to grow and spread, particularly in its total-organizational aspects.

THE EUROPEAN APPROACH

To attempt to identify the "European" approach to the work-restructure phenomenon of the 1970s in any single all-embracing manner is neither wise nor possible. The major work restructure events in West Germany during the decade, for example, used different terms, had wholly different political and social goals and objectives, produced wholly different laws and enforcing mechanisms than those in France, where very little of any serious nature ocurred in a governmental environment that was significantly to the right of Germany's reigning Social Democrats. What occurred in Sweden was astonishing but again different totally from what happened in neighboring Denmark or Norway—or Germany.

In 1978, this writer published a book entitled *Industrial Democracy in Europe*. It devoted a full chapter to work restructure events and trends in each of ten European countries. To cover that material, and what has happened since, in a handful of pages is clearly not possible. (See Table 9–A1 for thumbnail views of each country.) As substitute, the next pages provide a glossary of the terms used in various European countries by the three groups of work restructure advocates noted above. It should provide some insight into the kinds of issues and concerns occupying European attention during the "participative decade." Many are confusing and arcane. Many are political. Some are academic. Many are petty yet were furiously debated and fought over in back rooms and legislature floors. It is hoped that from such a brief glossary the motivations, motivators, and general mise-en-scène of participation in Europe in the participative decade—and since—may emerge.

As quick preface to the glossary that follows, it may help to remember that during most of the 1970s decade, most Protestant countries in Europe were controlled by left-of-center Social Democratic governments; the three Catholic countries—Italy, France, and Belgium (Spain and Portugal are not included)—had right-of-center governments in that decade.[2] In the former, participation under one name or another was politically urged as a major issue; in the latter, it was urged as a minor one. The most stringent work restructure—or co-determination or industrial democracy—laws of the decade were passed in Holland with Sweden, Denmark, and West Germany close behind. (See Table 9-A1.)

Generally, the European advocates of social justice legislation in all countries were left-of-center ideologues, many of them intellectuals with advanced degrees who belonged either in high places in the union confederations of their country or in the government itself. And generally the political clout to get the laws passed came principally from the voters and from the unions exercising power in the reigning Social Democratic parties, which they tended to dominate politically. (See Table 9-A2.)

One key word not in the glossary below, for it is not technical, is "influence." Behind most of the laws passed or proposed in most countries was union confederation desire for more worker and union "influence" over general management comportment and economic decisions. Except for the "crazies" of the extreme Left (see *worker control* below), the unions generally did not seek or want veto-power authority, which would have in effect made them co-managers (see *co-management* below). They settled for "influence." The strong 1977 West German Works Constitution Act sought and won the right for the mandated works council in every plant to *see* management books if it desired; it was discretely silent on any "rights" beyond inspection.

The glossary uses alphabetic form. Those terms marked with a "K" are *key* European terms of the decade, translated into English from the language of the source. In parentheses are the terms in their original language.

asset-sharing—A German term (*vermögenbeteiligung*). Used to define union programs to institute a central union-administered fund. (See *economic democracy, financial participation.*)

autonomous work groups (K)—A work humanization approach developed originally at the Tavistock Institute of Human Relations in London, which proposes dividing the work force into small, usually unsupervised groups, each of which collectively carries a major share of self-management. This term has also been associated with projects in Norway, where foremen were sometimes eliminated, as well as in a number of work humanization experiments in the United States. For a time, autonomous groups were seen by many work humanization theorists as a key to a complete transformation of the industrial system; the concept attracted strong emotional attention among radical groups in Italy and Yugoslavia. In Sweden, the term came to have such explosive connotations that an effort has been made to substitute the more neutral term, "productive groups." (See *shop-floor participation, sociotechnical systems.*).

co-determination (K)—A widely used term with a dozen meanings in as many languages; it is generally used to identify the notion of worker representatives serving on senior management boards. Legislation mandating it: Germany (1977, 50 percent in all companies with more than 2,000 employees); Sweden (1973, two per board); Denmark (1974, two per board); Norway (1973, 33 percent); Holland (1973, percent varies with size); Austria (1973, 33 percent). Workers-on-boards legislation was sought and lost in Belgium (1977) and in the United Kingdom (1977), with strong possibility of such legislation passing in France under the Mitterrand government. Its advocates argue variously that it (1) gives workers important power in determining management policy, (2) significantly improves manager/worker communications, (3) is a first evolutionary step toward eventual worker management, (4) provides employees limited influence in major decisions, and (5) provides a structure for bringing industrial democracy into the economic sphere. Its opponents argue that it is a union-pushed notion to provide unions greater power, that it is at best cosmetic, and that it is essentially without impact. There are few European instances of voluntary management appointments of workers on boards (viz., Chrysler in the United States), a practice strongly opposed by all employer confederations in all countries of Europe.

co-management—A predominantly French term (*co-gestion*). Sometimes used by the French to describe co-determination. Advocated principally in 1975, with no resultant legislation, co-management was devised to carefully set the proposed French system apart from the German system, which had been much criticized in France both by employers and unions because it gave too little power to unions. Since 1975 until the Socialist election in 1981, co-management remained without ardent advocates anywhere in the French political spectrum, except the extreme left.

company democracy—A term used in Sweden (*foretags-demokrati*) as a synonym for industrial democracy. (See *industrial democracy*).

democracy at work—Popular name given in Sweden to the 1976 "co-determination" legislation considered by many to be the most advanced industrial democracy legislation in Europe to date. Under that act, Swedish unions, beginning in 1977, were permitted to strike at local as well as national levels, for any reason they wished, including displeasure with any management decision, hiring and firing policies, and new product introduction.

economic democracy—A Danish term (*økonomisk Demokrati*) Used to describe union plans for a central, union-administered fund. (See *asset sharing, financial participation*).

ergonomics—A term (and discipline)—more prevalent and respected in Europe than the United States—used to define the "scientific" study of the human body at work (sometimes also called "human factors engineering"). When applied (particularly in West Germany) to psychological aspects of human beings at work, ergonomics studies with Skinnerian conditioned-reflex notions regarding how to engineer more work out of human bodies and how to implement manipulative psychological techniques.

financial participation—Any of several sorts of plans for granting employees some share of company results through governmental legislation. Unlike North American voluntary, company-level employee stock ownership plans, the various far more elaborate European plans proposed in the 1970s generally called for national profitsharing, with the unions as custodians of funds accreted for distribution, at the union's discretion, to union members. Strongly pushed in West Germany and Sweden in the mid-1970s, opposition was so intense that no legislation passed.

Perhaps the most revolutionary of all European participative notions, it was passed by no legislature; many attributed Sweden's Social Democrat-and-union-pushed "Meidner Plan" for financial participation as a primary cause of Social Democratic fall from power in 1977. As noted in note 1, however, the Social Democrats again used it as a key political issue in the September 1982 elections, which brought Palme's Social Democrats back to power. Now modified and called the "wage earner fund," the Social Democrats (with an absolute majority in the legislature) will propose legislation calling for a company-paid 1 percent levy on wages and a 20 percent levy on all corporate profits. Both sums, estimated at $1 billion annually, will be paid into a fund that will buy shares in Swedish industry, breaking the "monopolistic" control of industry by Swedish "capitalists" and permitting workers, through their unions, distantly to have greater influence over industrial conduct. Business claims it will eventually give unions control of the private sector; Social Democrats and the Labor confederations TO and LO claim it both gives workers greater voice in private industry and provides capital for new investment.

humanization of work (K)—A term used in all European countries (and in Germany particularly) to focus public awareness of human needs at work in industrialized society. The name was given to the government-sponsored "Humanization of Work Program" in Germany, which used a $50 million *annual* grant for "humanization" experiments in Bosch, Siemens, Telefunken, and Volkswagen (with inconclusive outcomes). The term also was used by the German metal worker union in its historic 1974 strike for more company attention to safety, noise abatement, and psychological aspects of working. (See *quality of working life, shop-floor democracies, work restructure*).

industrial democracy (K)—Used in widely different ways in all languages to subsume the various kinds of employee influence and involvement in the work place, and often used as an umbrella term to describe all work restructure efforts. In Britain, the term generally means *only* codetermination, or worker board representation, a connotation unknown in North American users of the English language. In French and Italian, the term is rarely, if ever used.

job enrichment (K); *job redesign*—A key term used by the "work humanizers" on both sides of the Atlantic in the early 1970s but gradually waning in importance and consideration on this side. Originally, it was a set of principles developed by U.S. psychologist Frederick Herzberg (probably better known and more influential in Europe than in the United States). To many QWL advocates who believe that workers should participate in deciding how their working lives should be "enriched," job enrichment is sometimes viewed as elitist and imposed by management-hired experts rather than participatively coming from employees themselves. Throughout Europe, many unions and workers look with hostility at job enrichment as a union-weakening "trick." Also on both sides of the Atlantic, the term is widely, loosely, and usually wrongly used to identify *all* general efforts for work restructure and participation, *including* that which is participatively arrived at.

parity—Ostensibly, an European concept referring to supervisory boards consisting of 50 percent workers and 50 percent managers. Actually, "real" parity (to unionists) also means equality in opportunity to elect the board chairman, who carries the deciding vote. The unions were unhappy with the parity provisions of the 1976 German *Mitbestimmung* law, which in effect gave the tie-breaker vote to management.

participation (K)—A term with widely and often differing significance in various languages. In Britain, it is usually used to identify any kind of worker involvement in shop-floor decisionmaking or to describe any of the governmentally mandated participative structures appearing in Europe. In France, where it means one thing to management and another to unions, the term is most often used to define either the French statutory *financial participation* measures or the vaguely defined participation ideas of De Gaulle in the 1950s (when the term was used in France as an unspecific cure for the "alientation of man in modern society"). It is not widely used in Germany or Scandinavia, which prefer the term "quality of working life" to describe participative activities. (See *shop-floor democracy, sociotechnical systems, quality of worklife, work restructure*).

quality of working life (QWL)—A term rapidly gaining in usage on both sides of the Atlantic and in most languages (including Hindi in India) to refer either to (1) shop-floor worker participation or (2) the entire socioeconomic area of concern the term identifies (i.e., the whole mix of notions, theories, and proposed humanist behavioral science engineering and ergonomic solutions for making industrialized work life less stultifying, safer, healthier, and more psychologically rewarding to those who perform it, thereby making organizations of people and machines more effective and contemporary). In both Europe and North America, even more than "industrial democracy," the term has come to subsume the whole range of participative activity of every kind. "Employee involvement," "productivity gain-sharing," and "work humanization" activities all tend to be considered as variants of "QWL." The term was adopted by the European Economic Community headquartered in Brussels to define the whole area of worker liberation from the dehumanization of much industrial work. The precise meaning of the term in Europe varies dizzily from one country to another and from one theoretician to another. (See *shop-floor democracy, work restructure*).

self-management—Usually used to describe the specific socialistic/communist system of worker management prevalent in Yugoslavia in which workers elect members of a works council, which then functions much like a capitalist board of directors, appointing all management and approving all major decisions. It is axiomatic that true self-management can exist only under socialism. Thus, work reorganization notions proposing improved quality of working life are rejected by the Marxist self-management proponents as of being no possible value to society, since they work to preserve—not to destroy—a capitalist system. (See *worker control, worker management*).

shop-floor democracy (K)—A term extremely widely, if loosely, used in every European country, essentially as a synonym for "quality of work life." Importantly, however, the term focuses solely on the worker and the workplace; organizational restructure is not included within its focus.

sociotechnical systems (K)—A term used to identify a method of analyzing the separate social and technical systems of industrial organizations and synthesizing both systems into a sociotechnical system, primarily in engineering design of new plants and offices. While frequently misused as a synonym for work-team or work-group structuring, it means neither. (See *work restructure, autonomous work group.*)

supervisory board—Under German company law, and in the Common Market "Fifth Directive" (1977), the supreme or senior governing body of a private company (*Aufsichtsrat*). It is similar to the U.S.-style board of directors except that it does not concern itself with day-to-day management practices. In countries with co-determination laws, it is the board to which workers are elected in varying percentages. German and Dutch co-determination advocates say placing workers at this level gives them the influence they seek at the top corporate level but bars them from intervening directly in management policies and decisionmaking. Under German law the supervisory board is the senior body of a two-tier management structure, the lower of which is composed of managers only but follows the policies of the supervisory board.

work restructure; work reorganization; work reform (K)—Terms used interchangebly in most languages essentially to suggest approaches to shop-floor democracy (Q.U. or QWL). It is viewed suspiciously by many European unionists as a term suggesting job enrichment without accompanying participative or democratic employee involvement.

worker control—A set of ideological principles developed by extreme far left theoreticians and unionists regarding the desired role of workers vis-à-vis management *in a capitalist system.* According to the doctrine, workers should have the right to be informed of all management actions and decisions and should be provided sufficient legal power to modify these decisions under certain circumstances, but should not participate in any way in the decisionmaking process nor share responsibilities for the consequences of the decisions thus made. The term is, confusingly, misused as a generic equivalent of worker management, industrial democracy, or participation. It is none of these things.

worker management (K)—A term widely misused in Europe to describe participative and increased worker-influence notions that are not worker management at all. It is worth stressing that not even the most extreme European advocates of various participative techniques ever propose or advocate actual management of enterprise by workers, Yugoslav-style, either through collective bargaining or legislation. Ideologically, the conspicuous absence of advocacy for real worker management—and responsibility therefor—may be the single most significant common characteristic of industrial democracy in Europe. (See *self-management, worker control*).

works councils (K)—An official European structure resident in plants and offices composed either of all workers or workers with one supervisor, formed through legislation with various rights and authorities under law. It is virtually unknown and unused in North America. In France it is called "enterprise committee"; in Denmark "cooperation committee"; in Sweden "company council." Council members in the various countries are generally elected by workers, not appointed by the union. Council rights vary according to national legislation: clearly cosmetic in France; extremely powerful with authority to review management decisions and books in Holland and West Germany; generally weak and unimportant in most Scandinavian countries. Some European companies have set up works councils voluntarily. Some European managements consider the works council an excellent vehicle to communicate day-to-day operating problems with employees and consider them extremely useful.

From this bewildering maze of terms and counterterms, of ideas and notions and structures and laws erupting all over Europe in the "participative decade," a few clear deductions can be drawn about participation, European style. First, most European advocates of some kind of work reform— what this paper has called work restructure—have derived their energies, advocacies, and actions from a profound, lingering sense of class; like an unscourable bathtub ring, class struggle is a basic reality of political life that has profoundly pervaded all European work restructure activities. Thus, European work reform has focused on "the worker"—not as an individual but as a class, as a collective social entity. Nothing illustrates this better than the "wage-earner plan" of the victorious Socialists in Sweden in late 1982. If they succeed in passing the legislation they propose, described under *financial participation* above, the huge sums generated will, in a collective sense, create a redistribution of wealth from which the individual worker will benefit only in a symbolic national sense. Compared to the North American approach described in the following section, the European approach and its collective social justice bias seems curiously devoid of *individual* participation, which is the "bigger piece of the action" goal of North American employee involvement activities. The European participative experience could be described as an orthodoxy of the left in which the individual is conspicuously absent.

Moreover, behind what has happened in Europe and in North America in the past decade lies an emerging Western participative ethic, cited above as a causal value-based force. It is my judgment that in Europe, lingering class struggle may have perverted that ethic into largely cosmetic pro-forma structures, most of which provide precious little individual employee participation at all. For all the political brouhaha that has occurred in Europe to provide the worker with a greater voice and influence, the real success toward that end began to occur on this side of the ocean in the same time period.

THE AMERICAN APPROACH

In June 1980, William Batten, chairman of the board of the New York Stock Exchange (and former chairman of J.C. Penney), made a major address to some two hundred leaders of American industry. His subject was corporate governance for the 1980s. In his talk, he noted that "a management style encouraging employee involvement and participation has become an accepted responsibility of U.S. management leadership."

In that same month, Charles Brown, chairman of the board of AT&T, wrote and sent a clearly unequivocal letter to the presidents of all then-twenty-three Bell System Operating Companies, urging them to "seriously consider" a new, more participative "management style" which he called "QWL."

Again in that same month, four major industrial unions, three of which were to become leading institutional players in the American work restructure movement—the United Steel Workers of America, the International Brotherhood of Electrical Workers, the Telecommunications International Union, and the Communications Workers of America (whose combined memberships exceeded two million American workers)—all signed formal collective bargaining agreements calling for immediate establishment of joint union/management "QWL" activities. The CWA's Glenn Watts, the TIU's John Shaughnessy, and the USWA's Lynn Williams formally joined the UAW's Irving Bluestone and Donald Ephlin as leading U.S. labor voices urging active union support of participative goals.

These random occurrences, with a simultaneity that in itself tells a great deal, all happened in a single month of 1980. Each is fragmentary; none is directly connected to the other. Yet viewed together, they indicate how far, how high, how deeply, and how powerfully the notions of the participative ethic had penetrated the vision and concern of major makers and shapers of U.S. corporate and union policy by midsummer 1980.

Behind Mr. Batten's and Mr. Brown's remarkable statements in mid-1980 was an unambiguous acceptance of an ethic even more foreign to North American management culture than to European management: giving employees a greater voice and active influence in the day-to-day operation of work organizations. Any of thousands of comparable statements by American business leaders could be substituted. What had exploded in Europe in political and legislative furor in the preceding decade had exploded here in almost equal measure. But beyond nearly identical new ethical *objectives*, there was a massive difference in approach on this side of the Atlantic. North American terms, structures, locus, and implementation techniques were completely different. North American advocates were different. The participative language was especially different. In a deceptively invisible way, the participative phenomenon in North America was far more profound than its European cousin, for reasons we shall explore. It didn't seem to be; it had almost no attention from the U.S. press until 1980 and later. But quietly, and often even secretly (as in Procter and Gamble), Americans had moved far and fast and widely toward the kind of acceptance symbolized in the Batten and Brown statements.

What had occurred here by 1980 was the cumulative outcome of some eight years of experimentation with new primarily American participative notions, most of them in the private sector, and most either in some form of productivity gain-sharing plan or some form of QWL (under one alias or another). In America, most experimenters relied heavily, some totally, on leadership by the behavioral science fraternity in participative innovation; in Europe, as we have seen, the behaviorists were conspicuously absent, their places largely taken by the political ideologues seeking social justice for alienated workers.

As the 1980s began, there was already a multitude of differences—nominal, structural, cultural, and causal—between emergent participation, American-style, and its European counterpart. Five salient characteristics of the full American experience—*all* of them largely unknown to and unpracticed in Europe in the same years—stand out clearly. For reasons of space, we will examine only those five. Yet in so doing, most of the rest are in effect summarized.

Certainly the first and most striking quality of the North American approach to participation was the absence, everywhere, of *political ideology* as a driving force—an intriguing and telltale commentary on basic cultural and societal dissimilarities. In neither the United States nor Canada has any kind of regulatory participative legislation been either sought or passed. Workers-on-boards, co-determination, national-level financial participation, so-called shop-floor democracy have been such nonissues that even the terms are largely unknown to the majority of our legislators.

A major contributor to the remarkably apolitical character of participation in America has been what Europeans call the "rightist" U.S. labor confederation, the AFL-CIO. In strong contrast to its European labor brethren, it has raised no clamor whatsoever for greater influence or participation of its worker members with American managements. It has rather more nearly opposed such developments as an ideological position. The 1980 appointment of the UAW's Douglas Fraser to Chrysler's board of directors remains unique in the United States and Canada; it was clearly not the beginning of a trend.

The second—and perhaps even more profound—uniquely American thrust toward participation at work has been the emergence, on this side of the Atlantic only, of the notion of *voluntarism*, as key to any kind of participative activity. The tens of thousands of North American companies that have entered into some kind of participative activity have done so independently, in private company-by-company decisions, solely because *they* felt it wise or desirable or, in some instances, necessary; none were involuntary or required by government.

The total voluntarism of North American participation conceptually startles its European advocates. Even more startling to Europeans is how uniquely voluntary American participation has become *in practice*. Almost all U.S. and Canadian QWL or gain-sharing efforts insist that voluntarism be both top down and bottom up. Top down, this has meant that employee participation is never imposed by fiat from on high. Doing so would be a contradiction of values. Bottom up, this has meant that only those employees gain-sharing activities; anyone can freely opt in or out as he or she sees fit. Many companies carry voluntarism still further and even leave it wholly up to participative bodies to decide what their activities should be.

The democratic ethic of such American voluntary freedom to participate, or even to define what participation means, in each small work universe, cannot be overstressed. There are two reasons why. (1) First, it provides a freedom of choice virtually unknown in even the most participative countries in Europe, where participation has become political, legalized orthodoxy and thus is not truly free.

Second, as we will see, voluntarism has permitted the evolution of a new voluntary culture inside each work organization—or what some call the participative "parallel organization," which exists interdependently with the formal organization. In many companies, this parallel organization has become a joint union/management culture; in which all union and management titles and labels are parked outside the door while participating in it. It is wholly possible, if not probable, that the uniquely American invention of voluntarism as *the* key to feasible participative efforts in organizations may prove to be the most significant cultural breakthrough of this quarter century in U.S. work organizations.

The third salient thrust of made-in-USA participation, which has significantly shaped its nature on these shores, has been its pragmatism. Certainly, notions of social justice and work humanization have played contributing roles in much if not all of the North American developments, but they have been more nearly minor propelling forces in the eyes of the participants. The major driving force in American participative efforts, expressed over and over again by participants in company after company, has been seeking or inventing pragmatic new ways and means to increase organizational effectiveness or to improve product or service quality, or operational productivity, or all three.

An excellent example of participative pragmatism, American style, is the so-called quality circle "QC" structure, which has exploded by scores of thousands in American and Canadian industry since the late 1970s and is continuing to spread. A large plant may have thirty or forty such structures operating concurrently, under many pseudonyms, such as "systems retirement team" or "employee participation team." A notion originally imported from Japan and Americanized, it is the epitome of the participative ethos. Yet each circle, always at its sole discretion, is the epitome of pragmatism. It neither has nor seeks organizational power beyond the power of its collective "doing" insights and problem-solving abilities. Its ten or twelve members are always volunteers. It usually operates at shop-floor levels, sometimes with and sometimes without management members. It meets perhaps an hour or two a week or month. It creates its own rules. But it always operates by the participative principle of consensual decision-making on all matters it may opt to consider. It is a "parallel" structure; its authority is usually limited to making recommendations to management. Yet although structurally wholly participative and democratic in ethical terms its sole perceived function is *operational improvement:* total pragmatism. Most circles call themselves problem-solving bodies. But the problems they, at their discretion, opt to solve are invariably pragmatic: how to improve a tool, a weld, a communications problem, a machine operation, a work process, or some aspect of the quality of a product or service. Using the ethical juices and democratic forms of participation as propellant, the employee participation team structure has become an ever-more-popular American instrument of hard-nosed operating pragmatism.

Some have argued that today's mandatory German and Dutch works councils and comparable worker-only bodies in Scandinavia are equally participative and equally pragmatic in focus as the American (and Japanese) circles. The point is moot, except in the profound difference that the U.S. structure is not mandated by law, or even by management, where and when it operates.

It is worth noting, particularly to pragmatic economists, that an impressively large percentage of American *productivity improvement* efforts in the United States and Canada have, in implementive techniques used, been participative in nature, form, and objective. Notable among these have been the thousands of participative productivity-gain-sharing plans that have been inaugurated in the past decade with excellent outcomes. Further evidence pointing to the role of participation in productivity improvements was the 1982 reorganization of the powerful American Productivity Center in Houston. In the reshuffle, the QWL arm of that institution was significantly strengthened, including the acquisition of a crack QWL consulting staff, new autonomy, and the appointment of a new senior vice-president for QWL affairs, notably in the steel industry. It is not inaccurate to state that some form of participative effort, operating under one of its many aliases, has underlaid a significant portion of *all* U.S. productivity improvement activities. In this writer's judgment, there has been perhaps too much focus on *shop-floor-level* QWL or similar remedial efforts in the name of so-called productivity improvement, and too little remedial work done on the productivity of overstaffed, short-sighted, fearful U.S. *management,* which—as U.S. Commerce Secretary Malcolm Baldrige noted pungently—is often less productive than the employees it seeks to manage.

There is another uniquely American pragmatic aspect to all participative structures and activities in the United States, which is worth stressing. In it lies the fourth salient thrust of participation American style. Whereas in Europe the major driving force behind the participative political explosion of the 1970s was the various labor confederations, in North America the major driving force has been management.

The experiments of the 1970s and the increasing participative activity of the 1980s have been devised and implemented by managements for pragmatic reasons of performance and survival. Those managements that have led the participative explosion in the United States and Canada have had vision and courage; they had to. As AT&T's Chairman Brown put it, it involves a resolute revision of "management style,"—an awareness that our society has left the "industrial age" and entered a very different, turbulent new one, which has to be coped with surefootedly. It involved pragmatic management recognition that work performance by human beings in the 1980s and thereafter—in the new age already here—can no longer be successfully demanded or ordered; it must be sought. It involved inventing feasible new ways to *win*—not demand—excellence in performance from an increasingly restive, anti-authority work force (including managers). In a 180-degree switch from the long-prevalent mechanistic notions of Taylorean scientific management which postulated people as potential machines, it meant a new humanistic view of people as people, and in the process, new sharing of decisionmaking power with subordinates to elicit and keep their allegiance and productivity.

It involved getting by giving—a new ethical notion in U.S. management. And at base was American pragmatism: Moving slowly in the direction of the participative ethic was simply good "doing" business management. As one company deeply committed to participation said of their QWL activities, "it's part sound management, part union-management cooperation, part employee awareness, part communications, but basically just good business."

According to The New York Stock Exchange survey of 1982, many large, medium, and small U.S. companies have begun to make the move—most in cautious steps, one at a time. Most have begun at shop-floor levels first, with structures such as QC circles. Hundreds have written and circulated 1980s-based new "management philosophy" statements accepting the new participative ethic as a firm covenant of management commitment as policy.

The fifth uniquely American participative thrust, which startles most European managers and unionists equally, was the 1970s emergence in the United States and Canada of what most call "joint union/management cooperation," under one or another work restructure alias. Despite AFL/CIO reluctance to advocate or endorse it, such cooperation (unlike traditional adversarial we/they labor relations) began to be sought by some of the most powerful individual American and Canadian unions and many of their bargaining partners, as noted at the beginning of this section. Most of the new joint QWL or employee involvement activities originated in collectively bargained agreements, usually calling for new parallel QWL structures in which union and management members jointly and equally participated in improving the "quality of work life" for all.

An extraordinary story of union/management cooperation at work was the Ford/UAW Mutual Growth Program negotiated and signed in early 1982. Both in the remarkable way in which this contract was negotiated and in its even more remarkable outcomes, it is a stunning—many have called it historic—proof of how participatively driven cooperation can work near-miracles of productive joint achievement in which everybody wins. It represents one of the finest examples to date of the American experience with participation in any of its many forms. It is worth inspecting in some detail, as symbolic of what participation, American-style, can achieve if properly and wisely undertaken.

In 1979, in formal letters of agreement, Ford and the UAW had begun a "worklife" process they agreed to call "EI" or "employee involvement"— the Ford/UAW alias for participation and QWL. By late 1981, through the strong urging of Ford's industrial relations vice-president, Peter J. Pestillo, and the UAW's vice-president, Donald F. Ephlin, UAW/Ford joint EI programs had been launched in over sixty-five major Ford plants and locations, involving over 10,000 Ford employees, most of them "hourly."

In each, a joint, plantwide EI steering committee had been formed, consisting usually of ten management and ten union members. Often the plant manager was a member of these "parallel" structure committees. All members of the committee received "EI orientation" training in participative techniques and principles. The steering committee, a diagnostic and problemsolving body whose focus was the whole plant or location, conducted what is called an "organizational diagnosis"—identifying specific supervisory or employee practices, performance practices, task and role characteristics, employee needs and wants, employee identification with their job, working relationships, and so forth—that might be improved. From these, it established "projects" or improvement goals and formed problemsolving teams (elsewhere called "circles") to accomplish an assigned project task. As one Ford plant manager said after EI began, "it allows those most intimately involved in the process on a daily basis to contribute to improving quality through a group problem-solving mechanism."

Despite the disaster that hit American automakers in 1979–82, the closing of many Ford plants, the resultant loss of 46 percent of Ford's union jobs, and a more than $2 billion loss to Ford in those years, EI thrived and grew. But by late 1981, both company and union knew something drastic and major had to be done, particularly about labor costs.

In January 1982, with no threat of deadline or strike, Ford and UAW representatives sat down to jointly face catastrophe, six months before traditional triennial negotiations were due to commence. Ernest J. Savoie (1982), Ford's director of labor relations planning, and vice-chairman of the Ford national negotiating committee, wrote an account of what happened. Speaking of the precedent-setting Ford/UAW employee involvement effort, he said,

> These cooperative experiences were laying a foundation—sometimes without the parties being aware of it—for a massive exercise in collective trust and mutual support. Many of the people who negotiated the new Agreement—on both sides—came to the bargaining table with extensive first-hand experience in the EI process. They had already extended their relationships, including increased information-sharing, joint problem-solving, expanded communications. Some had visited numerous . . . local EI activities; some had visited Japan to study differences between U.S. and Japanese approaches. . . . They thus came to the 1982 table in a problem-resolution mode . . . without the posturing that is sometimes part of more traditional bargaining. The spirit manifested itself [both] in the day-to-day conduct of the talks [and] in much of the final Agreement language.

EI (elsewhere QWL) had culturally affected the nature of the economic bargaining. It profoundly affected the historic outcomes, never before appearing in any union/management contract negotiated anywhere in the world. Mr. Savoie wrote,

> The national negotiators are convinced—and such conviction is the final test of any operable belief . . . that the experience of trust which they learned from EI helped them fashion an innovative, human-centered Agreement that starts with cooperation to promote competitiveness, progresses through job security and equality of contribution, and closes with profit sharing and future human growth through new modes of participation.

Note the following as clear evidence of an ethical principle at work in the negotiations. Mr. Savoie went on to observe,

> The contract recognizes, more explicitly than ever before, that a work unit is a social organism, with diverse inner and outer forces, and with differing sensitivities to rates of change and to persuasion. It also recognizes that a modern work unit will not, in the long run, be productive if it is run on a purely mechanistic basis.

The UAW's Ephlin said of the agreement that it "builds on the EI experience to create a complete framework within which we [the union and the company, jointly] can further address and discover common concerns."

Its many first-of-a-kind provisions—a guaranteed income stream, a profit-sharing plan, seniority recall rights, a preferential placement opportunity provision, and particularly its startling invention of what it calls a mutual growth forum to monitor human development across the years—individually and severally reflect the "spirit" Mr. Savoie referred to.

Both Ford and the UAW have wisely stressed the fragility of their joint "getting by giving" achievement. Both are aware, and say so, that the cultural shock of the agreement will for many years be troubling, as the new participative culture gradually erodes and replaces traditional we/they orthodoxies in more and more nooks and crannies of the vast company.

The UAW/Ford mutual growth agreement serves as an impressive close to this paper. It is a landmark breakthrough of American participation, with immeasurably huge potential cultural and economic impact on the future of an American company with enormous economic outreach. As noted earlier, no sound objective economic assessment methodology exists to help predict how large the impact of the emerging new participative way of working together will be on economic performance, here and abroad. Yet some very wise pragmatists in U.S. management are betting on it. Their number mounts almost daily.

This paper set out to give an accounting to date of the European and American experience with "labor productivity" (an antiparticipative form) and "quality of work life" or QWL (a term that on both sides of the Atlantic subsumes all participative effort). It ends with a series of questions, which concludes its exploration with an unanswerable riddle. Could Ford, without the very American UAW as inseparable ally, export its apolitical, voluntary, pragmatic, cooperative "cultural revolution" to its vast European operations? Would European legislation permit it? Could European unions (very different in Germany, France, Scandinavia, Italy, Holland, Britain) understand the cooperative, egalitarian, individualistic democratic "spirit" Mr. Savoie described? If they could, would they? Or is participation, American style, culturally unexportable? And finally, if it *is* unexportable—uniquely ours—is it the beginning of the beginning of a vigorous new contemporary American work ethic that, like its Protestant work ethic predecessor, might lead us to world leadership again?

APPENDIX TABLES

Table 9-A1.   Industrial Democracy in Europe: Analysis by Country.

Country	Co-Determination	Works Councils	Shop-floor Participation	Collective Bargaining	Financial Participation
Austria	1973 law provides that one-third of board represents employees.	First established in 1919, abolished in 1934; reestablished works councils strengthened by 1973 law.	Few experiments; some successes in steel industry.	Nongovernmental Austrian Parity Commission rulings normally determine bargaining results harmoniously.	OCP presented union plan in 1975: union fund managed by workers and management.
Belgium	Little interest but will probably accept EEC proposals.	1948 law made mandatory, with management representation; 1973 decree provides that employers must share information with councils.	Lagged behind other countries, but some union and government interest and experiments.	CSC bargains for shop-floor democracy. FGTR wants only information, not decision making responsibility.	Little interest.
Denmark	1973 law provides for two employees on board.	"Cooperation councils" established under agreement between LO and employer association; elected by all employees, with shop stewards ex-officio.	1976 law on work environments gave workers more control.	Main Agreement of 1960 regulates relations between LO and employers confederation, with centralized bargaining and few strikes.	LO pushes plan for investment fund managed by unions and government, thus far without success.

France	Government's Sudreau Report included co-determination, but union and management opposition fore-stalled action.	Comitise d'enterprise instituted in 1945; generally insignificant.	Sudreau Raport recommended increased shop-floor democracy; many voluntary projects, often with government support.	Low unionization and ideological unions lead to little successful bargaining.	1967 law established mandatory fund with limited individual withdrawal rights after five years; few workers benefit significantly.
Italy	Little interest, except as analogy to rights gained through bargaining.	1969 labor disturbances led to spontaneous "factory councils" to replace old and ineffective "internal commissions"; recognized by employers in 1972.	Innovative agreements reached through bargaining, including plant design and elimination of fixed-speed assembly lines in some plants.	Almost all industrial democracy achieved through bargaining.	No interest in legislation.
The Netherlands	1973 law made supervisory board mandatory, with members "coopted" by board from nominees of shareholders and employees.	Established in 1950, strengthened in 1971, 1976; consulted on major changes, co-decision rights on some employment matters; second only to German councils in strength.	Among leaders in voluntary action, with projects sponsored by employers, unions, government.	Unions moving to left, abandoning postwar cooperative attitude.	Unions propose profit-sharing fund from "excess profits" managed by unions; limited withdrawal rights by individuals after seven to ten years.

Table 9-A1 (continued).

Country	Co-Determination	Works Councils	Shop-floor Participation	Collective Bargaining	Financial Participation
Norway	Union plan in early 1960s dropped, resurrected in 1971, statute providing one-third of board members (minimum of two) be worker representatives; also a "company assembly" with one-third workers to approve major employment decisions.	1945 agreement created works councils as essentially consultative forums.	Decade of experimentation led to 1976 law on work environments requiring maximum job variety, interest, safety, and worker contact.	Highly centralized unions cooperate in shop-floor projects, favor industrial democracy, but not devoted to parity codetermination by statute or agreement; amazingly peaceful, harmonious.	Not high legislative priority.
Sweden	1972, 1976 statutes provide two employee places on board; no significant drive for parity; used predominantly for communication.	1946 agreement created works councils, strengthened in in 1966 but seldom strong; importance depends on management attitude not legislation.	Innumerable experiments, projects, styles; leader in field; government, managements, unions cooperate.	1976 Democracy at Work Act expands (and does not limit) areas subject to bargaining; all industrial democracy subjects now can be bargained about.	1975 LO plan (Meidner Plan) takes some profits for fund to buy stock, support union projects and activities; stirred up great opposition.

United Kingdom	Government's Bullock Committee reported in 1977 recommendation of unitary board with equal number shareholder and employee representatives, with coopted third group; employers oppose, mixed reactions from labor.	No mandatory councils; shop stewards fill many of their normal functions.	Various projects springing up voluntarily, some with government support; Tavistock theories not applied as broadly as elsewhere.	Nonlegislated system of bargaining by unions (not TUC) occasionally leads to major disruptions in certain industries; more than 100 unions.	Not high legislative priority.
West Germany	1947 agreement in coal and steel for parity co-determination, made permanent by 1951 legislation; 1976 law for all industries (except coal and steel) provides equal numbers of members from employees (including middle management).	1952, 1971 Works Constitution Acts produced strongest councils in Europe; arbitration or judicial action available if recommendations ignored; wide-ranging powers.	1974 government humanization of work program responded to strikes, emphasis by workers; $30 million annually, covering work structure, safety, noise, ergonomics.	Highly organized DGB coordinates national bargaining strategies; only sixteen sector unions.	Decade-long DGB push for participation in form of union-administered fund with limited individual withdrawal rights after seven to twelve years; no immediate passage likely.

Table 9-A2. Selected Data on Labor in Europe: Analysis by Country.

Country	Population	Economically Active Population	Industrial Disputes, 1975	Union Confederations	Unionization (percentage)
Austria	7,456,403	3,097,986 (41.5%)	3,783 workers 5,512 days	OGB, highly centralized, powerful, represented on Austrian Parity Commission	60
Belgium	9,813,152	4,003,134 (40.8%)	85,801 workers 610,186 days	CSC (Christian), 17 unions; FGTR (socialist), 14 unions	70 (85% blue-collar, 40% white-collar)
Denmark	5,053,803	2,478,619 (49.0%)	59,128 workers 100,100 days	LO, 900,000 members, 40+ unions; FTF, 150,000 members	70 (90% industrial)
France	52,841,746	22,133,600 (41.9%)	1,827,142 workers 3,868,926 days	CGT (Communist), 2,000,000 members; CFDT (socialist), 700,000 members; FO (moderate, independent) 600,000 members	20
Italy	55,274,000	19,615,000 (35.5%)	10,717,000 workers 22,625,000 days	CGIL (Communist), 3,500,000 members; CISL (Catholic), 1,500,000 members; UIL (socialist), 500,000 members	45
The Netherlands	13,060,115	4,788,855 (36.7%)	268 workers 480 days	NVV (socialist), 620,000 members (FNV); NKV (Catholic), 420,000 members (FNV); CNV (Calvinist), 240,000 members	40
Norway	3,874,133	1,462,159 (37.7%)	3,282 workers 12,473 days	LO, highly centralized and peaceful	50
Sweden	8,173,200	4,061,900 (49.7%)	23,631 workers 365,507 days	LO, centralized bargaining, end to postwar harmony	80 (90% blue-collar, 70% white-collar)
United Kingdom	55,514,600	25,715,156 (46.3%)	808,900 workers 6,012,000 days	TUC, weak coalition, 10,000,000 members, over 100 unions	45
West Germany	61,886,000	26,878,000 (43.4%)	235,814 workers 1,068,680 days	DGB, 8,000,000 members, 16 unions, centralized; DBB (independent), 700,000 members; DAG (white-collar), 500,000 members; CGB (Christian), 200,000 members	35

NOTES

1. In the Swedish elections of September 19, 1982, the Social Democratic Party and its leader Olaf Palme were overwhelmingly reelected after a seven-year period out of office. A key plank in the winning Social Democratic 1982 platform was financial participation of workers in corporate ownership, explored in the preceding chapter; participation was clearly still a major Scandinavian issue in late 1982.

2. This was true until the fall of the Giscard d'Estang government in France, and the assumption of power by the Socialists under Francois Mitterand in 1981. There may be a policy change in 1983 reversing French avoidance of more than cosmetic participative legislation.

REFERENCES

Cooper, Gary L., and Enid Mumford. 1979. *The Quality of Working Life in Western and Eastern Europe.* Westport, Conn.: Greenwood Press.

Editors of Fortune. 1982. *Working Smarter.* New York: Viking Press.

Mills, Ted. 1976. *Quality of Work Life: What's in a Name?* Detroit, Mich.: General Motors Corporation.

_____. 1979. "Industrial Democracy in Europe: An American Response." *Harvard Business Review* (November/December).

Rosow, Jerome M., and Robert Zager. 1982. *Productivity through Work Innovation.* New York: Pergamon.

Savoie, Ernest J. 1982. "The New Ford-UAW Agreement: Its Worklife Aspects," *The Work Life Review* 1, no. 2, Michigan Quality of Work Life Council (June).

Yankelovitch, Daniel P. 1981. *A World Turned Upside Down.* New York: Simon & Schuster.

COMMENTS

Joji Arai

Japan has learned a great deal from North American and European experiences. As a matter of fact, we started our productivity program patterned pretty much after the program the United States had developed for reconstructing the European economy after the war. This opportunity to discuss Ted Mills's paper, which deals with the North American and European experiences in the area of quality of worklife, makes me feel like a student in the position of criticizing a teacher's paper.

I recall that when Japan was struggling for survival back in the 1950s, groups of American economists, businessmen, and business management consultants came to Japan to analyze Japan's potential at that time. The consensus of the American experts then, after studying and analyzing the situation in Japan, was that Japan could not possibly make progress due primarily to:

1. The lifetime employment system, which would constitute a retardant to the effective employment of highly talented people;
2. The promotional system based upon seniority, which prevents the effective use of talented people and therefore discourages those who do not get appropriate compensation and prevents them from making a contribution to the progress of the company or the country; and
3. The Japanese tendency to arrive at a decision based upon consensus, which is time consuming and sometimes impossible.

Twenty years later Daniel Bell and George Lodge published books saying that America was experiencing changes in the value system. Participation

393

and cooperation were rapidly becoming key factors in making progress in this society. If I may borrow from George Lodge, America made the shift from the conventional society to a communitarian society. The participatory, cooperative sense of the members of this society will enable America to make progress. Daniel Bell said it in a different way: Most of European and American societies experienced for a relatively long period of time what he calls the second stage of historical development—that is, struggle between men. The final stage of the historical development will produce the society of participation and cooperation, as he terms it. Japan, because of its lack of natural resources and its large population living in a confined area, developed into this particular stage faster than most other countries. The Japanese system, which at that time was considered to be highly ineffective, is twenty years later praised by those who once criticized the system.

I suppose that North America and Europe have to pass through that societal transition now because of this historical sequence. In the case of Japan, because of an historical accident we reached that stage very early without knowing that we had developed some of the systems that at the moment are fortunately working well. By no means do we claim a cooperative monopoly on those systems (i.e., the participatory management cooperative relations among government, management, labor, and others).

If we trace the origin, we will discover that even the famous quality circle program that is becoming popular in this country as well as in Canada and Europe is nothing more than a combination of the basic statistical principle advanced by Juran and Shewhart and a group dynamic theory advanced by Cartwright and Saunders, all Americans. In the Japanese situation, the combination of what those researchers were saying at that time (which was not popularly practiced in the United States) worked quite well because of the acute need to improve the quality of our products.

Again, that was a historical accident, and we do not claim that the system was devised by Japanese. Mills stated that a major difference between the U.S. and European experiences in the quality of worklife problems is the apolitical nature of the U.S. system—there is no government interest in installing such a system in the United States. This is exactly what we thought U.S. economists were advising us twenty years ago: Both the absence of political interest in the labor movement and a policy of rapid economic growth were essential to our success. As a matter of fact, the Japan Productivity Center was created at that time to remove the political characteristics from the labor movement.

The labor movement in the 1950s reflected the influence of the European class struggle principle. I have an observation regarding the usage of certain words that appeared in Mills's glossary. For instance, I found the British system called the "autonomous work group." We have effectively utilized that system; the difference again is the absence of political characteristics. We, of course, changed the name. We call it autonomous management. It is an advanced version of the quality circle program that is becoming popular in this country, in that the participants in the program are given higher-level skills, not just problemsolving techniques that are utilized by shop-floor people. Those who participate in an autonomous management group sometimes tackle purely management issues, and management actually encourages people to do this. In some companies they go to the extreme of having employees participate in the formulation of corporate strategic policies. This of course is the extreme form, but we found it useful in facilitating the understanding of all employees as to corporate goals.

We also used the term "labor management/quality of worklife." The term as defined by Mills carries the connotation that the quality of worklife is related only to the new relationship that emerges between labor and management. When we use the term "quality of worklife" it encompasses the total quality concept of a corporation, equivalent to the European system of corporate-wide quality control. Changed to the Japanese way, the system covers the relationships among senior managers, middle managers, shop-floor workers, and white-collar staff. The total quality control program is nothing more than organizing a company so that members of the corporate community are in constant communication irrespective of their positions. Therefore, we seldom use the term "labor management" in connection with quality of worklife. I find the term interesting because defining the quality of worklife program in such a fashion gives me the impression that perhaps in the United States many executives consider the quality of worklife rather than the generation of profits—to be the corporate goal.

Surprisingly, many Japanese executives feel that the profit goal is more important because you cannot offer high-quality worklife unless a company is stable and healthy and has the potential to grow. Yielding the highest profit in business is important because profit means necessary expenditures for tomorrow, as defined by Peter Drucker. I note a contrary trend now emerging among European, American, and Japanese business philosophies. In closing his paper, Mills commented that perhaps the American-type quality of worklife can be exported to Europe and that legislators and politicians in European countries might accept such a program as a political solution to the current labor/management problems they face.

We saw tremendous expansion of the economy in the 1950s and 1960s, due primarily to the effective application of mass production techniques. However, beginning with the slow growth era of economy starting in 1973, we have found that mass production will not be able to cope with a rapid change in the marketplace. We must develop a system that will enable us to produce the smallest number of products in the largest variety to satisfy the emerging needs of the marketplace. In order to cope with that type of demand, we must develop flexible manufacturing systems—which include robotic systems, numerically controlled machinery, machining centers, manipulators, and so forth.

A single robot replaces a single man no matter how intelligent the robot. The combination of these automated devices however, produces fantastic results. We discovered through the prototype operations of many companies using FMS that in the machining operations a company can maintain the same level of output with one-tenth of the human input. Assuming that in the United States as well as European countries and Japan, between 25 to 28 percent of the people work in the manufacturing sector, and further that one-third of this work is in machine operations, a substantial number of people will have to be replaced. If a company has the quality of worklife in which management wants people to enthusiastically participate, it cannot lay off people. If the assumption is that if people have to be laid off at one time or another to adjust to a demand change in the marketplace, most likely they will not participate in the program. Our experience showed that the most fruitful or most highly valued input that comes from a participatory program is the very suggestion to eliminate one's own job. If that happened in a situation in which there is a possibility that 90 percent of the people have to be replaced, would the employees enthusiastically participate in such a program?

Another question relates to the very nature of the U.S. unions that have a craft orientation. We are finding out in this high technology era that the conventional skills disappear quickly. A union organized in a craft with rigidly defined scopes of jobs for members will not be able to adjust to changes that will be made by business. This means that the unions have a self-destructive element in coping with emerging change. Mills stated that the quality/ of worklife essentially has to be based on cooperative labor/ management relations. Will labor that has this self-destructive characteristic be able to cooperate with management in phasing out the very skill on which its organization is based?

The lifetime employment system is considered to be the most important factor in enabling us to install the quality of worklife program because the ultimate participation on the part of employees is a suggestion that eliminates his job. The ideal QWL system can be maintained only when a company guarantees lifetime employment. The company must be responsible for training and retraining people so that within the framework of cooperation workers may change their skills. There is a highly mobile labor force in the United States. With the current quality of worklife program, would a new system that disregards the skill boundary be compatible with the U.S. labor movement? We are very interested in seeing the U.S. responses to these questions because we still consider the United States to be a great teacher.

10 WHERE ARE WE IN THE DISCUSSION? RETROSPECT AND PROSPECT

Richard R. Nelson

This conference proposed to review what is known—and what is still mysterious—about the sluggish productivity growth of the American economy over the past decade. The strategy was to illuminate the American experience by considering what has been happening in other countries. To the extent that the experience of other countries has been similar to ours, presumably we should look at factors that have influenced those countries as well as our own. Where the U.S. experience has been sharply different, the hunt ought to be for factors that are special to the United States. My task is to review the discussion, evaluate it in broad terms, and to suggest some new ways that the problem might be addressed.

REVIEW OF THE CONFERENCE

The conference first examined the productivity growth experience from a macroeconomic perspective. Many of the themes, ideas, controversies, and intellectual tensions that marked the entire conference were present in papers by Edward Denison and Angus Maddison.

The Denison paper was archetypal Denison. Within the growth accounting framework drawn from the new classical theory of production (which he has elaborated and fine-tuned over the years), he considered a number of factors that arguably are related to a country's output, attempted to assess how these factors differed recently from what they had been during the period of more rapid growth, and estimated the impact of these changes

397

on the growth rate. The factors considered ranged from those that almost always are considered in analyses of the determinants of output, like the quantity and quality of labor and capital; to those that often are neglected, at least in elementary treatments, like the force of regulation; to those whose effect on productivity are seldom treated by other scholars, like the quantity of crime. Denison's analysis of the impact of some of these factors on productivity was well-grounded in the standard theory of production; for other factors, his estimates were somewhat less convincing. The size and effect of changes in each of these variables were analyzed separately, the total effect examined, and a "residual" identified. The residual was then associated with advances in total factor productivity resulting from the growth of knowledge and other miscellaneous variables that were not or could not be analyzed directly.

Denison's paper identified the major intellectual puzzle discussed throughout the conference: In Denison's analysis, the major culprit behind the productivity growth slowdown has been the residual. During the heyday of rapid growth, the residual—labelled as largely the contribution of the growth of knowledge to economic productivity—was positive and large. During recent years, it has been negative. The difference accounts for most of the productivity growth slowdown. What is going on?

Angus Maddison's paper was broader in geographical scope and less formal in methodology. He provided data on the productivity growth trends in the major capitalist industrial countries, and his principal message was that all of them, not just the United States, have experienced significant slowdowns. In contrast with Denison, who presented his analyses of factors one by one, Maddison grouped his candidates for the major underlying causes. One group he called "conjunctural," and he included here the slowdown in the growth of capital stock experienced in most of the countries, the simultaneous presence of high unemployment and inflation rates, the economic slack and inefficiencies associated with these conditions, and microeconomic adjustments to the two energy price shocks. By "conjunctural" Maddison meant that these macroeconomic and microeconomic developments needed to be considered together, since they have the same root causes. While he did not discuss this in any detail in the present paper, his earlier papers indicate that he sees causation as flowing from the energy price hikes to restrictive macroeconomic policies to economic slack and slow capital growth. Maddison also noted a cluster of other factors that have slowed technical progress. He noted that Europe and Japan have come progressively closer to the United States in productivity levels and therefore have less room to advance simply by adopting American techniques. This, of course, does not explain the American slowdown. In general, the looser theoretical leash on Maddison's analysis gave him room to examine connections and interactions that are not treated easily within Denison's tidier framework.

The paper by Irving Kravis and Robert Lipsey extended the horizons even further by presenting data on what has been happening to per capita income in the less developed countries, the socialist ones, and the advanced capitalist economies. Their data show that productivity growth decline has occurred in these other groups as well. There was an interesting exchange in the discussion of this paper. Laurits Christensen, the discussant of the paper, proposed to the authors that they ought to use a different index number than the one they had used. He called his proposed index "superlative" and stated that it was the "right" one to use. When asked by William Fellner to explain, he replied that it was the index number to use if one has in mind the standard neoclassical theoretical model of production and technological change. However, one can question whether there is any unique and correct theoretical perspective from which to view the productivity growth slowdown. The existing orthodox theory of production and technical change does provide a way of identifying possible important variables, and does suggest certain methodological approaches to estimating their effects. The framework, however, is not the only thinkable one. Ought analysis really be bound by it?

The paper by Geoffrey Moore and John Cullity was motivated by a quite different theoretical perspective. Many years ago Wesley Clair Mitchell proposed that a business downturn tended to occur when costs encroached on profits and dampened incentives for investment and that recovery occurred when costs had fallen enough so that investment was profitable again. The Moore and Cullity paper reviewed postwar experience in the United States during business cycles and in particular the performance of productivity during the upturns and the downturns. The paper also considered trends in productivity. The paper itself, and the discussion about it, underscored an important question flagged by Maddison: Are cycles simply to be considered noise in data that need to be purged so that one can see what is happening to the long-term trends in productivity growth, or are the connections between cycle and trend more complex than that?

The conference next turned to several papers that focused on possible determinants or causes of the productivity growth slowdown. The paper by George Tolley and William Shear discussed how the tax systems in several advanced countries affect private returns to capital and labor, with particular attention paid to capital. One of their key findings is that capital earnings are taxed much more heavily in the United States than in Germany, Britain, and France and that in Japan the tax on capital earnings is significantly lower than in any of these other countries. This is interesting news. The authors then went on to estimate the effect that these tax rate differences might have had on savings and capital formation and growth rates. They concluded that the differential impacts could not have been very large. The discussion of this conclusion turned partly on what they had assumed about the response of savings to the returns to capital and partly on the

presumed impact on productivity growth of a faster rate of capital formation. It was noted that within orthodox models of production and technical
change it takes a very large increase in the rate of growth of capital to have
more than a modest effect on the rate of growth of labor productivity.
Some participants wondered if this actually were the case.

Rolf Piekarz, and his colleagues at the National Science Foundation,
presented a paper that contained important information about the similarities and differences among the major capitalist nations in total R&D spending, R&D spending patterns, and government policies toward R&D. They
pointed out that with the exception of the United States and France there
had been no significant decline in the rate, or the rate of growth, or R&D
spending that could have foreshadowed the deceleration of productivity
growth rates, and that in these two countries the early decline in R&D was
on military spending. They expressed doubt, therefore, that a decline in
R&D spending was a cause of the productivity growth slump. A discussion
about the relationships between R&D and technological advance followed,
and it was stressed that the connections were relatively loose and that many
other forms on investment also were required if new technology was to be
created and introduced. A question was asked: In theoretical and empirical
analysis of the effects of R&D on productivity growth, should the righthand
side variable be total R&D spending, or R&D spending divided by sales, or
GNP? Most empirical analyses use R&D spending deflated by some measure of size. It was noted that Denison some time ago had questioned why
the fact that output is large means that it takes more R&D to enhance productivity by a given amount than would be the case were output smaller. To
anticipate some remarks I will make later, an answer might be that the
larger output involves a wider product mix or is produced by a larger
number of independent firms. Analysis based on the standard theory of
production tends to be blind to issues of these kinds.

In his paper on the role of the energy crisis shocks on productivity
growth, Dale Jorgenson advanced his thesis that the causal chain worked
in the following manner: In most industries technical advance is energy using
and a rise in energy prices reduces the cost-saving advantages of new technologies; presumably, then, the incentives to engage in R&D are dampened.
This line of reasoning would explain the slowdown of growth of total factor
productivity, which his analysis as well as Denison's identifies as the culprit—it would, that is, if growth of total factor productivity could be interpreted as a decline in the rate of technical advance. Jorgenson admitted
that, given this logic, it was something of a puzzle that industrial R&D spending did not fall off significantly after the energy price shocks. Ernst Berndt,
the discussant of Jorgenson's paper, remarked that the theory behind the
current analysis represents Jorgenson's second or third attempt at understanding the effects of the energy price hike on economic growth. In earlier

studies, Jorgenson had proposed that capital and energy were strongly complementary and hence that the energy price hike had reduced the returns to investment. Berndt also noted Martin Baily's recent argument that the energy price hike had obsoleted a considerable portion of America's capital stock and drew considerable discussion about what that might mean.

George Psacharopoulos presented a broad analysis arguing that most economists tended to underestimate the importance of rising educational attainments for productivity growth. While his particular focus was on the less developed countries, some, but not all, of his arguments also carry over to high-income countries. His argument was partly about complementarities: He proposed that higher education enabled farmers to take better advantage of new technologies. Part was about other kinds of interaction: Thus, a well-educated farmer or worker is likely to be more willing and able to migrate to find a better job. These kinds of relationships are not likely to show up in the standard growth accounting exercises as contributions made by higher educational attainments.

Finally, Ted Mills discussed recent developments in labor management relations in the United States and Europe, noting similarities and differences. In particular, he proposed that developments in the United States were apolitical and represented major steps toward a U.S. management style that treats workers as long-run members of a firm rather than simply as employees. This is very much the Japanese pattern. Several scholars have proposed that because workers in Japan feel themselves as long-term members of a firm, technical advance and efficiency enhancement proceed with less obstruction in Japan than in other countries. It should be noted that the view of the firm, and of the determinants of productivity, contained in Mills's paper diverge greatly from those implicit in the standard economic theory of productivity.

AN EVALUATION OF THE DISCUSSION

This was a good conference: A bit more light has been shed on the puzzle. However, no major new insights or evidence was presented. Perhaps this is inevitable, if one continues to look at the problem through orthodox lenses. Denison, Jorgenson, and virtually every other scholar who has applied an orthodox model to analyze the productivity problem have concluded that not much can be explained on the basis of changes in the rate of growth of traditional factors of production, at least if their impact on productivity is measured in ways suggested by the standard production function idea. Under the classical interpretation of the data, it is the residual, or total factor productivity growth, that has fallen off. But the orthodox theory of production was not designed to illuminate the process of total factor productivity growth, which is why it is estimated as a residual. If the objective is to see more clearly something that cannot be viewed with the aid of orthodox spectacles, perhaps we need another set of glasses. At least we should think carefully about what is built into the standard theoretical perspective.

The standard formal framework used to analyze productivity growth is analytically rooted in the neoclassical theory of production by business firms. Firms are assumed to have production functions that reflect their technological knowledge. They choose outputs and inputs so as to maximize profits, subject to that production function constraint. Technological knowledge generally is assumed to be public; thus, all firms have the same production function. Generally, product factor markets are presumed to be perfectly competitive and in equilibrium, although there can be some adjustments for noncompetitive elements. In the theory behind growth accounting and standard growth econometrics, technical change is admitted to the picture as a "shift" in the production function, and factors of production are allowed to change in quantity over time. Factor prices also may change, and these changes measure changes in marginal products.

It is apparent that this basic intellectual starting point leads to analyses with the following characteristics:

1.   The time series of observed outputs, inputs, and prices are presumed to have been generated by a moving competitive equilibrium. This follows naturally from the basic theoretical setup. On occasions, the analyst can get outside of that framework and consider certain disequilibrium aspects explicitly, but to do this involves a conscious pulling back from the theoretical logic.

2.   The effects of various variables on output growth are treated separately. While there is nothing inevitable about this, a growth "accounting" framework follows rather naturally if one differentiates the production function with respect to time. Perhaps as important, there is nothing in the underlying theory that would lead anybody to look for strong interactions, or packages, of elements.

3.   Institutional complexity is ignored. The theoretical economic universe consists of perfectly competitive firms, workers, and resource owners, and consumers. As stated, it is possible to build into this structure a few market imperfections, but there is not much room here for serious analysis of the effect of oligopolistic rivalry, patents and industrial secrecy, labor unions that generate strikes, government agencies, or even universities.

4.   Short-run fluctuations in the degree of capacity utilization and unemployment are treated as phenomena calling for adjustment of the data, so that cycle and trend need not be confounded. Partly this reflects that the background theoretical framework is committed to equilibrium and full employment and that deviations from these conditions

are an intellectual bother. More important, the particular productivity growth models that have been built with neoclassical intellectual building blocks do not have anything in them suggesting that the short-run and the long-run interact in complicated and perhaps durable ways.

I am not arguing here that all the papers presented at this conference analyzed the productivity growth slowdown by using an orthodox model, although some of them did. As noted in the foregoing conference resumé, several of the papers explicitly diverged from the canonical viewpoint. Several proposed that sources of the slowdown needed to be studied as clusters or that there were important interactions. A number of participants clearly recognized institutional complexity and wondered how that affected the analysis. Several exchanges questioned whether cycles and trends could be neatly separated. For the most part, however, the authors of the papers with divergent views tended to recognize their divergence as being atheoretical or as not being well-justified by a theoretical backing. I share with these authors the belief that in order to understand the economic slowdown, it might be useful to look at the problem from somewhat different angles.

SOME DIFFERENT PERSPECTIVES

I will explore here four propositions. I will not argue that they are always valid or that analyses of the productivity slump that do not recognize them are beside the point. Rather, my argument is that these propositions help clarify part of the problem that we have not been able to analyze very well from an orthodox perspective.

Interaction among factors is important. Several different kinds of interactions were discussed at the conference. Psacharopoulos argued that education interacts strongly with technical advance and other variables that in most conventional treatments are considered separately. In farming and probably in a number of other activities, an important return to education is the ability to screen, and where appropriate implement, new methods. Moreover, highly educated people are the key actors in the processes that create new technologies. These strong interactions suggest that something important may be missed if the variables are treated separately.

It is interesting to note that higher education and science often are practiced at the same place—universities. Universities themselves need to be understood within the larger education system. Primary and secondary education influences what students know when they get to the university and determines to a considerable degree their interests in higher education.

Undergraduate science and engineering graduates enter the world of business and refresh the applied research and development capabilities of the nation. Some also return to the primary and secondary education system to teach. Some do graduate work, and of these a good portion are retained as university faculty.

What I have been describing is a complicated system that influences a nation's long-run capability to do research and development and to screen and implement effectively the new technologies that are developed. Analysis of the long-run determinants of a nation's productivity growth might profit from a study of this education/science system and how it has been working. I doubt that much of the U.S. productivity growth decline since the late 1960s can be ascribed to worsened functioning of the system, but many observers have noted that the system seems to be in trouble, and that bodes ill for the long run. If the question is, Why did Britain fall back relative to Germany and the United States at the turn of the century, or why has Japan been doing so well recently?, it seems plausible that part of the answer lies in the education/science system. Study of the system is not a substitute for more standard analyses but might enrichen and deepen the discussion.

There also are strong interactions among capital formation and technical advance that might fruitfully be studied in more detail. It is not simply that new capital is required to carry new technology into practice; this can be caught, readily enough, in standard growth accounting. In many industries and technologies, however, the new plant embodying the new technology is an important arena for learning the strengths and weaknesses of that technology. Some of the learning, and fixing, goes on in the plant, and operating experience with new technologies guides research and development allocation. Notice that in industries and technologies where this type of interaction is important, a slowdown in capital formation leads not only to a reduction in the pace at which average practice tracks best practice. It also may lead to a slowdown of the rate of advance at the frontier. Again, we have here a complex system of interaction that is worthy of study in its own right.

As my last example, I refer to the web of interactions among energy prices, physical capital formation, and technological advance. Jorgenson himself has pointed to several different possible kinds of connections, as has Martin Baily. It is a fact that the sharp jumps in energy prices induced a significant reorientation both of business investment plans and their R&D allocations. With the sharp increase in energy prices, investment projects that cut back on energy use became much more attractive than projects whose primary purpose was to enhance labor productivity. Similarly, R&D was reoriented toward projects that were likely to conserve energy and therefore away from projects whose principal contribution would have been to save on labor. But whether there has been a strong interaction of the sort just described, or of the sorts described by Jorgenson and Baily, the system of interaction must be explored and understood. This requires much more than simply studying the various factors, one by one.

It has been suggested that consideration of interaction can be incorporated relatively easily into the standard accounting and regression frame work by introducing some second-order terms to the implicit Taylor expansion and some interaction terms to the regression equations. My point goes well beyond that, however. I am proposing that certain sources of growth that conventionally are considered separately ought to be considered as clusters and that the nature of their interaction is an important part of the story. It is one thing to say that by the turn of the century the United States was providing many more years of schooling to its new entrants to the work force than was Britain. It is something else to note that the United States and Germany were producing many more people with technical training and to go on to consider the impact of this on the technological progressiveness of the nations. It is still something else to observe that the U.S. and German school systems had oriented themselves to technical education much more effectively than had the British.

Complex institutional structures influence the connection between the sources of growth and the growth actually experienced. Consider, just as one example, the question of whether it is total R&D expenditure, or R&D expenditure deflated by some measure of industry size, that drives total factor productivity growth. The answers depend on the nature of the technology, the various kinds of R&D that advance it, the people doing the R&D, and the institutional structure in general.

Think about research relevant to corn seed in the northern midwest. Here there are at least two kinds of R&D that might be distinguished. There is research done with public monies mainly at the land grant colleges. In recent years, this research has not created new seed varieties of use to farmers but has provided general knowledge and certain pure seed varieties that can be used by private seed companies that are in the business of developing and selling hybrid seed to farmers. The private seed companies have been the principal source of R&D on new seed varieties used by farmers. If farmers' sales increased in the region, would a given total and distribution of R&D expenditures on seeds yield a lower expected productivity gain? Probably not. One might get a different answer, however, if the output of the farmers in the region was expanded because some new farmers started operations in the lands to the north of the currently cultivated areas. To farm effectively in these new climates, new seed varieties might be required. The effect of given R&D investment on average productivity growth then would be diminished in the now enlarged region selling more output. For productivity growth in the new region to match that in the old might require new kinds of public research and new kinds of private R&D aimed at tailoring seeds to the different conditions.

Alternatively, consider R&D relating to pharmaceuticals. Some of this R&D, as some relating to seed varieties, is publicly financed and in effect creates public knowledge. But most new pharmaceuticals are developed by private companies. In the pharmaceutical industry, companies are quite fierce about protecting their proprietary rights on the new drugs they develop. The R&D spent by a particular company to create a particular new drug creates new knowledge (the chemical composition of a drug that has certain desirable effects) that it alone can exploit directly. Thus it is not meaningful, in this case, to think of an R&D capital stock for the drug industry as a whole. But neither is it meaningful to think of a set of strictly private capital stocks. Publicly financed research yields industry wide knowledge, and surely there are some spillovers from a successful R&D effort by one company to other companies. In particular, these other companies may, as a result of their competitor's successful development of a particular drug, try to develop something similar but outside the range of patent protection. The appropriate modeling is clearly quite subtle.

What does increasing the sales of the industry do to the likely effects of a given size and allocation of R&D on average industry productivity growth? If sales increased because people bought more of existing drug types from existing firms, one would not expect any dilution of the productivity-enhancing effects of the existing portfolio. But what if the increase in sales was associated with new firms entering the industry? Then the matter, certainly, would be more complicated.

Finally, consider the case of the semiconductor industry. Here, unlike in pharmaceuticals, patent protection is not strong, and the advances created by one company's R&D can be imitated, relatively quickly, by another company. It is the lag, and the associated ability to run down the learning curve, that is the source of profit for the firm that gets in first. Here, perhaps, it does make sense to think of all R&D as ultimately providing knowledge available to all. However, different firms gain access to that knowledge at different times.

I am not proposing that in order to do growth analyses at an economy-wide level—or to do cross-industry analyses of the sort described in several of the conference papers—it is necessary to model in fine detail the institutional structures of the different industries. What I am saying is that these structures do tend to be complex and that they differ significantly from industry to industry. The analyst should be aware of this complexity when deciding how to model the connection between R&D and other variables and measured technical change, and how to look at certain things when the regression results turn out to be puzzling.

The connection between short-run and long-run events may be quite complex. Recessions clearly interfere with productivity growth in the short run. Okun's law (and more up-to-date like formulations) provides a way to estimate the impact of recession on productivity in the short run and thus provides a way of purging the long-run productivity series of cyclical influences. This purging, however, implicitly presumes that the effect of recession on productivity is short run. Is it possible that recessions, and particularly a prolonged recessionary condition, have long-lasting effects on productivity growth? Several of the conference participants thought that this might be the case. There are a number of mechanisms through which long-lasting depressed conditions and stop-and-start economic policies of the sort we have experienced over the last decade might have a long-lasting, perhaps permanent, effect on productivity growth. These ought to be studied more carefully.

In the first place, recessions dampen capital expansion. This slows down the rate of growth of capital stock at least temporarily, reduces the rate at which best practice technology is implemented, and decreases opportunities to learn about the new technologies in actual practice. What happens when the economy recovers? Is the investment loss during the recession ever made up? Different theories of savings and investment give various answers to this question. Is the learning ever made up or is the level of knowledge always somewhere behind where it would have been, had there been greater opportunities to learn? Again, the answer is not clear, but the question is important.

This particular period of recession has depressed various forms of public, as well as private, spending. In many instances, state and local governments have cut back their funding of elementary and secondary education; many universities have been hard pressed financially. How has this affected the education that has been imparted to young people? Arguably, they would have received a better education had times been better. Will the effect of this ever be made up? Or will we have a wave in the population, like the demographic waves set off by deaths during World War II?

The system of international trade has stood up surprisingly well under the battering of hard times—much better than during the 1930s. However, it is evident that within the United States and other advanced industrial countries, workers now are much less confident than they were that if they lose their jobs they can easily find new ones. Pressure to enact public laws and policies and to write private contracts to protect jobs, firms, and industries have been heightened by the recession. Once in place these restrictions will be difficult to remove. In this way, too, short-run events may have long-lasting effects on long-run prospects.

Seeing growth as a disequilibrium process produces a different model of growth mechanisms than seeing it as an equilibrium process. Instead of the neoclassical model of output growth, entertain the following hypothesis. At any given time within the economy (or within any particular industry), there are a number of different firms. In general all these firms will not be employing the same technique of production. Different firms, using different techniques, will be characterized by different input coefficients. Aggregate variables, like output per unit of labor and the capital/labor ratio, then must be understood as being the weighted average of the diverse coefficients of individual firms. Given prevailing product and factor prices, firms with different techniques will not have the same profit rate.

Regarding physical investment, assume the following. Profitable firms expand, and unprofitable ones contract. Also, firms with unprofitable or barely profitable techniques with some finite probability learn about, and are able to imitate, the techniques of more profitable firms. Both of these mechanisms will tend to move the industry as a whole toward an equilibrium in which all surviving firms use the same technique.

However, in this model, tendencies toward equilibrium are always being offset by the introduction of new and superior techniques by some firms. The firms in the industry might differ in their level of R&D spending, and the probability that a firm makes an innovation might be proportional to its R&D spending. In any case, a flow of new innovations into the industry, like mutations in a biological evolutionary system, means that at any one time the system as a whole may be far away from equilibrium and that there may be no tendency for it ever to converge to an equilibrium.

Within such a model one can record the time path of output per unit of labor, capital per unit of labor, and other variables that are important in more conventional growth analyses. For a given specification of the labor market, the model will generate a time series of the wage rate and of labor and capital shares in total income. One can, therefore, "do" growth accounting. Employing conventional methods one can attribute a certain amount of growth of output per worker to growth of capital per worker, and a certain amount, therefore, to a "residual," which could be interpreted as "technical advance." But given this model, the rationale for this particular way of attributing growth is quite unclear. In this model capital's share is not readily interpreted as the elasticity of output with respect to capital. Also, in this model there is no well-defined distinction between moving along a production function and having the production function shift. Indeed, there really is no industrywide production function. Variations in the rate of growth of total factor productivity, conventionally measured, have no particular meaning. In particular, "growth of total factor productivity" is not a meaningful measure, within this model, of the effects of "advances in knowledge" (although there are some complicated and subtle connections).

Thus, what is a particular and bothersome puzzle about the productivity growth slowdown, interpreted within the framework of orthodox analysis, does not pose any special puzzle if one has in mind something like the model discussed above. In order to analyze the sources of productivity growth within this kind of a model, one would have to scrutinize what was happening, and what had changed, at a quite microeconomic level. One would have to explore what had been happening to the stream of innovation, to the rate at which firms with inferior technologies were imitating firms with superior ones, to differential growth rates of high productivity firms and low productivity ones, and so forth. All of these probably would be related to macroeconomic variables, like the rate of growth of the capital stock, of the labor force, and of total R&D spending. But the connections would be complicated, and a conventional growth accounting would not provide much illumination regarding what was going on.

I am not saying that the standard analyses of the productivity growth slowdown are wrong-headed or that they don't provide some insight into what has been happening. I am saying that how the results of growth accounting, or a growth regression analysis, are interpreted depends very much on the model of growth one has in mind. The falloff in the "residual" is interpreted, within an orthodox framework, as signifying a decline in the rate of technical change; indeed what has especially puzzled several of the authors of the papers presented at this conference is that the residual recently has been negative and this seems to imply technology has been retrogressing. However, this particular interpretation comes from the particular theory being assumed. There are reasons not to accept, more or less automatically, that that theory provides an adequate account of all the forces behind productivity growth.

INDEX

Ability adjustment, 343–344
Abramovitz, Moses, 326
AFL-CIO, 377, 381
African countries, 129, 130, 134–135, 337, 338
Age/sex composition, 19, 51, 77–79
Agricultural productivity, 99; and education, 340–342, 343, 344, 351
Agricultural R&D, 238, 260, 264, 276, 360, 405–406
Aircraft industry R&D, 257, 264, 278
Alterman, Jack, 31
American Productivity Center (Houston), 379
Applied research, defined, 237
Argentina, 126, 337
Aryee, G.A., 348
Asian countries, 337
Asset-sharing, defined, 369
AT&T, 367, 376, 380
Atlantic Richfield, 367
Australia, 103, 115, 362
Austria, 103, 366, 370
Automation, 396
Automobile industry, 257. *See also* Chrysler; Ford; General Motors
Autonomous work groups, 394; defined, 369–370

Bacon, R., and W. Eltis, 76
Baily, Martin N., 13–14, 28, 59–60, 64–65, 66, 331, 404, 405
Baldrige, Malcolm, 380
Barro, Robert J., 221
Basic research, 255; defined, 237
Batten, William, 376
Behavioral science, 371, 372, 373, 377
Belgium, 103, 337; R&D, 244, 261; work restructure, 368–369, 370
Bell, Daniel, 393, 394
Berndt, Ernst R., 31, 328
Bernstein, Paul, 28
Blades, Derek, 76
Blaug, M., C.R.S. Dougherty, and G. Psacharopoulos, 347
Bluestone, Irving, 376
Bosch, 371
Bowman, M.J., 340, 344
Brown, Charles, 376, 380
Business cycles, 159–160, 399
Business-funded R&D, 248–253 *passim*, 257–260 *passim*, 277

Cain, G., 351
Canada, 116, 193, 337; R&D, 251, 261, 264; work restructure, 362, 364, 366, 368, 376–383 *passim*, 394

411

Capital earnings, effect of tax rates on, 199–201, 204–215 *passim*
Capital flows, international, 222
Capital gains taxation, 200, 206, 208, 212, 214, 267
Capital input, 8–17, 49–61, 54, 64–66, 81, 120–121
Capital stock and neoclassical growth model, 220–221
Capital stock effect of energy crisis, 331–333
Capital utilization, 15
Carter administration, 233
Cartwright and Saunders, 394
Catholic countries, 368
Centrally planned economies, 111
Chemicals and drugs industry, 257–260, 406
China, 358
Chrysler, 370, 377
Civil service salaries, 342
Clark, Peter K., 30, 32–34
Class struggle principle, 375, 394
Cochrane, S.H., 344, 346
Cochrane, S.H., J. Leslie, and D.J. O'Hara, 347
Co-determination, 363, 374; defined, 370
Collective bargaining agreements, 376
Collins, Eileen, 265
Co-management, defined, 370
Common Market Fifth Directive (1977), 374
Communications Workers of America (CWA), 376
Company democracy, defined, 370
Competition, 30–31
Conjunctural forces, 62–68, 398
Consensus decision-making (Japan), 393
Consumer durables, 15
Consumer price index (CPI), 188, 193
Consumption taxes, 199
Cooper, Gary L., and Enid Mumford, 361, 367
Corporate income taxation, 200, 206, 207, 208, 209–210, 211, 212, 213
Corporate tax incentives for R&D, 265–268, 278
CPI-X, 188
Cyclical movements, 159–176, 399

Dana Corporation, 367
Defense and space R&D, 100, 238, 244, 250, 260, 261, 263, 276, 277
De Gaulle, Charles, 372
Democracy at work, defined, 370
Denison, Edward F., 66, 67, 68, 77, 79–81, 120, 198, 243, 326, 335, 336
Denison, Edward F., and William K. Chung, 198
Denmark, 261; work restructure, 366, 368, 369, 370, 371, 375
Depreciation allowances, 266
Developing countries and education, 338–351 *passim*, 359
Developing market economies, 111
Development, defined, 237
Dividend income, taxable, 200, 205, 206, 207–208, 210, 211–212, 213
Drucker, Peter, 395
Duality hypothesis (Gordon), 351

Easterlin, R., 335, 350
Econometric models of sectoral productivity, 283–305, 309–321; concavity, 312–315; estimation, 319–321; homogeneity and symmetry, 310–312; index numbers, 315–316; stochastic specifications, 316–319
Economic democracy, defined, 371
Economic historians, 350
Economic Recovery Tax Act of 1981 (ERTA), 267, 268
Education, 20–21, 51, 79, 99, 201–204, 335–360, 401, 403–404; and ability adjustment, 343–344; and farm labor productivity, 340–342, 343, 344, 351; and fertility, 346, 359; and health, 358, 359; and household production, 347–348; and income distribution, 347; and infant/child mortality, 347; and labor migration, 345; and life expectancy, 344–345, 359; and literacy, 338, 344, 345–346; on-the-job training, 204, 344, 359; and personal income, 338, 339; quality of, 349–350; and recession, 407; social welfare function of, 346–348
Educational maintenance component, 340
Eisner, R., and D. Nebhut, 103

Elasticities, 15–17
Elden, Max, 367
Electric and electronic equipment industry, 257, 260, 406
Electricity, utilization of, 279–280, 305–307
Employee involvement (EI) program. *See* Ford
Employment, 36, 96
Employment Cost Index (ECI), 193
Energy, 31, 67–69, 279–334, 400–401; capital stock effect, 331–331; electrical, 279–280, 305–307; nonelectrical, 307–308; R&D, 264, 404–405; substitution (share elasticities), 281, 300–301; and technical change, 301–305
Energy-capital complementarity hypothesis, 328–329
"Entry fee" (R&D), 277
Environment, legal and human, 17–18, 52, 76–77, 102–103
Ephlin, Donald F., 376, 381, 382
Ergonomics, 367; defined, 371
European Economic Community, 373
Excise taxes, 199, 207

Fabricant, Solomon, 326
Fallon, R.P., and R. Layard, 339
Farm labor, 7–8, 18, 51, 99; and education, 340–342, 343, 344, 351
Feige, Edgar L., 34, 75–76
Feldstein, Martin S., 221
Feldstein, M.S., and Charles Horioka, 222
Feldstein, M.S., Joel Slemrod, and S. Yitzhaki, 26
Feldstein, M.S., and Lawrence Summers, 201
Fertility and education, 346, 359
Filer, Randall K., 27
Financial participation, 372, 375; defined, 371
Financing, debt/equity, 230
Fisher, W. Halder, 238
Fisher's Ideal Index, 154, 399
FMS, 396
Ford, 367, 381–383
Ford Foundation, 364
Fortune, 361
France, 75, 77, 103, 116, 193, 232; R&D, 244, 245, 246, 248, 249, 250,

255, 257, 261, 263, 266, 267; effect of tax rates on labor and capital earnings, 198, 199, 200, 208–210; work restructure, 368–369, 370, 372–373, 375
Fraser, Douglas, 377
Fuller, W.P., 348

General Motors (GM), 365, 367
Germany, 75, 77, 100, 103, 116, 161–165, 176, 192, 193, 232, 404, 405; Biedenkopf Report (1973), 363; *Mitbestimmung* law (1976), 372; R&D, 244, 245, 246, 255, 257, 261, 264, 265; effect of tax rates on labor and capital earnings, 198, 199, 200, 210–212, 223; work restructure, 363–364, 366, 368, 369, 370, 371–372, 373, 374, 375; Works Constitution Act, 369
Ghana, 348
Goods and services taxes, 199, 205, 206, 207, 209, 210, 211, 212, 213, 214
Gordon, E., 351
Government-funded R&D, 248–253 *passim*, 257–260 *passim*, 360; agriculture, 238, 260, 264, 276, 360; industry, 264–265; social objectives, 260–264, 277–278
Government regulation, 12, 25–26, 52, 76–77, 102–103, 360
Government sector, 53, 74–77, 103
Greece, 103
Greenwood, M.J., 345
Gregory, Paul P., 31
Griliches, Z., 339, 341, 344
Gross domestic product (GDP), 61, 67, 75–76; "real" per capita, 109–110, 112–116, 122–132, 399
Gross national product (GNP), 12–13, 52–53; and life expectancy, 344–345; and R&D, 243–245
Growth accounting and education effects, 340–350 *passim*
Gutmann, Peter M., 34

Hammer, Richard, 265
Hansen, W. Lee, 201
Harberger, Arnold C., 222
Harbison, F., and C.A. Myers, 345
Hausman, Jerry A., 222

Hayami, Y., and V.W. Ruttan, 341
Health: and education, 358, 359; R&D, 100
Herzberg, Frederick, 372
Hewlitt Packard, 367
Heyneman, S., and W. Loxley, 350
Hicks, N., 335, 338, 344
Home mortgage interest, 232
Homes and automobiles, demand for, 230
Household production and education, 347-348
Housing services, 53
Hudson, Edward, 328
Hudson, E.A., and W. Jorgenson, 68, 328-329
Hulten, Charles R., 331
Human capital, 335, 358; and physical capital, 339-340. See also Education
Human capital earnings, effect of tax rates on, 201-204, 206, 208, 210, 212, 214
Human capital formation, 98-100
Human factors engineering, 371
Humanization of work, 366, 367, 373, 378; defined, 371-372

ICAM programs, 278
IMF, 136, 137-138
Imputation system (U.K.), 207-208, 209-210, 211, 212
Income, personal, and education, 338, 339
Income distribution and education, 347
Income tax, personal, 199-200, 205, 207, 208, 209, 210, 211, 212, 213, 214
Indexes, 173-176
India, 129, 348, 373
Industrial countries, 110
Industrial democracy, 363, 366, 368, 370; defined, 372
Industrial R&D, 257-260, 263, 277, 278
Infant/child mortality and education, 347
Inflation, 29-30, 32-34; and effect of tax rates on capital earnings, 201, 232
Inflation shelters, 229
Information hypothesis, 345

"Intensity of demand," 19-20
Interest taxation, 205-206, 208, 210, 212, 213; elimination of, 229-231
Interindustry Transaction Accounts, 287
International Brotherhood of Electrical Workers, 376
Investment companies, 267
Investment tax incentives, 266
Irregular factors, 19-20
Israel, 98
Italy, 176, 193; R&D, 243, 244, 255, 257-260, 261, 264; work restructure, 368-369

Jamison, D.T., and L. Lau, 341, 351
Jamison, D.T., B. Searle, and K. Galda, 350
Japan, 66, 78, 98-99, 100, 103, 115, 116, 161-165, 176, 192, 193, 232, 332, 333; education, 337, 350; R&D, 237, 243, 244, 245, 246, 248, 251, 254, 255, 257-260, 261, 264, 265-267, 276, 277; effect of tax rates on labor and capital earnings, 198, 200, 212-214, 223; work restructure, 362, 379, 393, 394, 395, 396, 401
Jarrett, J. Peter, and Jack G. Selody, 30
Job competition model (Thurow), 351
Job enrichment/job redesign, defined, 372
Job protection, 66-67
Jorgenson, Dale W., 72
Jorgenson, D.W., and Barbara Fraumeni, 329
Juran and Shewhart, 394

Kahn, Herman, 72
Kay, J.A., and M.A. King, 208
Kendrick, John, 16, 67, 68, 72, 77, 79-81, 103, 176, 326, 339
Kenya, 343
Knowledge, advances in, 21-22, 261-263
Kopcke, Richard W., 15
Krueger, A.O., 335, 339
Kuznets, S., 70-72, 109, 115, 123, 127, 136

Labor earnings, effect of tax rates on, 198-199, 204-215 passim, 222-223

Labor force: age/sex composition of, 19, 51, 77–79; educational maintenance component of, 340
Labor force participation rates, 117–119
Labor hoarding, 66–67
Labor-management relations, 361–396, 401
Labor market segmentation, 351
Labor markets, nonclearing/competitive, 351
Labor migration, 345
Labor productivity, 361–396, 401; and energy crisis, 332, 333
Labor quality, 79,120
Labor strikes, 370, 372
Labor substitution, 281, 300–301
Labor unions, 369, 370, 371, 372, 374, 376, 380, 381, 383, 396
Land, 19
Landes, W.M., and L.C. Solmon, 350
Latin America, 337, 362
Leibenstein, Harvey, 28
Leijonhufvud, A., 29
Leveson, Irving, 31–32
Lewis, Jordan, 240
Libya, 137
Life expectancy and education, 344–345, 359
Lifetime employment system (Japan), 393, 396
Ling, Robert R., 23
Literacy, 338, 344, 345–346
Lodge, George, 393, 394
Long-term trends, 176–189, 193
Los Angeles Times, The, 37
Low-income countries, 111

MacAvoy, Paul W., 34
Machinery industry, 257
Management, 380; union-management cooperation, 381
Manne, Alan, and William Hogan, 327–328
Mansfield, Edwin, 237
Manufacturing sector, 257, 286
Marin, A., and G. Psacharapoulos, 347
Marris, R., 335, 339, 340
Mensch, Gerhard, 72
Mexico, 112, 347

Michael, R.T., 348
Middle-income countries, 111
Migration, rural-urban/rural-rural, 345
Mills, Ted, 365, 366
Minarik, Joseph J., 27
Mincer, J., 344, 359
Mitchell, Wesley C., 159–167, 399
Mitterrand, François, 370
Moock, P., 343
Mutual funds, 267

Nadiri, M.I., 335
National Aeronautics and Space Agency (NASA), 264, 278
National income, effect of tax rates on, 197–233
National income and product accounts (NIPAs), 2, 287
National income per person employed (NIPPE), 2–3, 11–12, 47–49
National Science Foundation (NSF), 237, 265; industry/university programs, 240, 269
Natural resources, 74, 120
Nelson, R., 340
Neoclassical growth model, 215–223
Nepal, 344
Net national product (NNP), 198
Net stock, 10
Netherlands, 66, 75; R&D, 244, 251, 261, 264; work restructure, 366, 369, 370, 374, 375
New York Stock Exchange, 367, 376, 380
Nordhaus, William D., 30
Norsworthy, J.R., 326, 328
Norsworthy, J.R., M.J. Harper, and K. Kunze, 66
Norway: R&D, 243, 245, 261, 264; Work Institute, 367; work restructure, 366, 367, 368, 369, 370

Oil crisis, 280, 281, 330–333
Oil exporting countries, 111. See also OPEC
On-the-job training (OJT), 204, 344, 359
OPEC, 330–333
Organization for Economic Cooperation and Development (OECD), 136; R&D data, 241–242

Organizational change, 363
Ott, Mac, 35

Palme, Olof, 371
"Parallel organization," 378, 381
Parity, defined, 372
Parker, Robert, 35
Participation, 363; defined, 372–373
Participative management, 366
Patent sales, 267
Peck, Merton J., and Akira Goto, 238
Pension fund taxation, 200–201, 206, 208, 212
Perry, George L., 327
Pestillo, Peter J., 381
Physical capital and human capital, 339–340
Political ideology, 377
Pollution abatement programs, 17–18, 52, 266
Population growth, 127, 340
Portugal, 103, 368
Pragmatism, 378–380
Price deflators, 188–189, 194, 243
Procter and Gamble, 377
Productivity gain-sharing, 373, 377
Productivity growth models, 408–409
Productivity improvement, 364, 379–380
Profitsharing plans, 371
Property taxes on housing and real estate, 199, 205, 206, 207, 208, 209, 210, 211, 212, 213
Proprietors and rental income, 199–200, 206, 208, 210, 212, 213
Protectionism, 407
Protestant countries, 368
Protestant work ethic, 365, 383
Psacharopoulos, George, 102, 339, 344, 351
Psacharopoulos, G., and B. Sanyal, 351
Psacharopoulos, G., and J. Tinbergen, 351
Public sector, 76, 342
Puerto Rico, 342–343

Quality circle (QC) programs, 364, 378–379, 394, 395
Quality of work life (QWL), 361–396; defined, 373

Rasche, Robert H., and John A. Tatom, 31, 68, 328
Recession, 407
[Recession] recovery patterns, 167–173, 192–193
Rees, Albert, 33
Regional development, 266
Relatively industrialized countries, 111
Research and development (R&D), 24, 56, 100–102, 235–278, 400, 405–406; agriculture, 238, 260, 264, 276, 360, 405–406; aircraft industry, 257, 264; defense and space, 100, 238, 244, 250, 260, 261, 263, 276, 277, 278; defined, 237; energy, 264, 404–405; funding, 238, 248–253, 257–265, 276, 277–278, 360; independent research and development (IR&D), 264; industry, 257–260, 277, 278; social objectives, 260–264, 277–278; tax incentives, 265–268; effect of tax rates on R&D capital earnings, 204, 206, 208, 210, 212, 214; time lag, 277, 278; and universities/advancement of knowledge, 240, 255, 261–263, 269
Residential sector, 53
Residual, 22–37, 54–56, 398
Resource allocation, 7–8, 51–52, 55, 66–67, 81
Revenue Acts (1969, 1978), 26–27
Rizzuto, R., and P. Wachtel, 350
Robotic systems, 396
Robow, Jerome M., and Robert Zager, 362
Rosenberg, Nathan, 96, 280, 282, 284, 285, 306–307, 309
Royalty payments, 267
Rutgers Center for International Business Cycle Research (NBER), 161

Sadler, George, 31
Sales taxes, 199
Savings taxes, 199
Savoie, Ernest J., 382, 383
Saxonhouse, G.R., 350
Scale economies, 20, 52, 67
Scandinavia, 373, 375
Schools, 358, 359. See also Education
Schultz, T.W., 335, 336, 341, 347, 359, 360

Schumpeter, Joseph, 172–173
Schurr, Sam, 279, 280, 281, 282, 285, 306, 308, 309
Schwartz, A., 345
Science, 360
Science and technology, 239–240
Scientific management (Taylor), 380
Scientific organizations, nonprofit, 267
Scientific research institutions, 255
Screening hypothesis (Taubman and Wales), 351
Sectoral shifts, 31–32, 55–56, 72–74, 79
Seed companies, 405–406
Self-employment, 351
Self-management, defined, 373
Selowsky, M., 340, 347
Seniority-based promotion system (Japan), 393
Service life, 13–14
Service sector, 31–32, 53, 72–74, 76, 79
Shaughnessy, John, 376
Shop-floor democracy, 374; defined, 373
Sickness benefits, 75
Siemens, 371
Simon, Carl P., and Ann D. Witte, 35
Skinner, B.F., 371
Social Democrats, 368, 369, 371
Social justice, 366–367, 369, 375, 377, 378
Social security and payroll taxes, 199, 205, 207, 209, 211, 213, 221–222
Social welfare function of education, 346–348
Socialists, 370, 375
Sociotechnical systems, 373–374
Solmon, L., 350
Solow, Robert M., 30
South Korea, 155–156
Southeast Asia, 130
Soviet Union, 360
Spain, 103, 368
Steel industry, 276
Stone, Richard, 37
Structural model, 94–95, 104–106
Supervisory board, defined, 374
Sweden, 115; labor confederations TO and LO, 371; Meidner Plan, 371; R&D, 243, 245, 251, 254, 255, 261, 263; work restructure, 366, 368, 369, 370, 371, 375
Switzerland R&D, 248, 261, 277

Taubman, P.F., and T. Wales, 351
Tavistock Institute of Human Relations (London), 369
Tax credits for R&D, 266–267
Tax expenditures, 77
Tax incentives for R&D, 265–268
Tax rates, 26–27, 197–233, 399–400; effect on capital earnings, 199–201; effect on human capital earnings, 201–204; effect on labor earnings, 198–199, 222–223; and R&D, 204, 265–266; France, 208–210; Germany, 210–212; Japan, 212–214; U.K., 206–208; U.S., 204–206
Tax shelters, 229
Technology, 24–25, 70–74, 404; "advantages of backwardness," 96–98; and energy, 301–305; sale or license of, 267; and science, 239–240
Technology transfer, 237–238, 276, 278
Telecommunications International Union (TIU), 376
Telefunken, 371–372
Thailand, 341–342
Thurow, L., 351
Time lag (R&D), 277, 278

Underground economy, 34–37, 75–76
Under-utilization of human and physical capital), 95–96
Unemployment, 96, 351
United Auto Workers (UAW), 376, 377, 381–383
United Kingdom, 66, 75, 76, 161–165, 176, 192, 193, 232; education, 347, 404, 405; R&D, 243, 244, 245, 246, 254, 255, 257, 261, 263, 278; effect of tax rates on labor and capital earnings, 198, 199–200, 206–208; work restructure, 370, 372
United Nations, 136, 137, 318
United Nations Conference on Trade and Development (UNCTAD), 136, 138
United Nations International Comparison Project (ICP), 109–112, 153–155
United States: education, 337, 358, 404, 405; foreign aid, 359–360; R&D, 237–238, 243, 244, 245, 246, 248, 249–250, 251, 252, 253, 254,

United States *(continued).*
255, 257, 260, 261, 262, 263, 266, 267, 277–278; effect of tax rates on labor and capital earnings, 198, 199, 200, 204–206, 399; work restructure, 362, 364, 366, 368, 369, 376–383, 393, 394, 395, 396, 401
U.S. Bureau of Labor Statistics (BLS), 159, 188, 193
U.S. Defense Department, 238, 264, 278
U.S. Office of Science and Technology, 360
United Steel Workers of America (USWA), 376
Universities R&D, 240, 255, 261–263, 269, 360, 403–404
University of Michigan Institute for Social Research, 364
Upper Volta, 115
Uri, M. Pierre, 232–233
User fees, 199

Value added taxes, 199, 207, 209, 210, 211, 212
Venture capital investments, 267
Vernon, Raymond, 236
Vintage model, 10–11
Volkswagen, 363–364, 372
Voluntarism, 377–378

Wachtel, P., 350
Wage differentials and education, 342–344
Wage-earner funds, 371
Wage-earner plans, 375
Wages, 176–189, 193
Wall Street Journal, The, 26
Watts, Glenn, 376
Wealth redistribution, 375
Weber, Max, 365
Welch, F., 341
Westinghouse, 367
Wheeler, D., 335, 338
Williams, Lynn, 376
Wolf's Law, 70–74
Women and education, 342–343
Wood, David O., 328
Work effort, 27–29, 75
Work ethic, 365, 366, 376, 380, 383
Work hours, 18–19, 51, 79
Work humanization, 366, 367, 371–372, 373, 378
Work restructuring, 361–396; defined, 374
Worker control, defined, 374
Worker management, 370; defined, 374
Workers-on-boards, 363, 370
Works councils, 373, 379; defined, 375
World Bank, 136–137, 138

Yamada, S., and V.W. Ruttan, 99
Yankelovich, Daniel P., 361
Yugoslavia work restructure, 369, 373

ABOUT THE
CONTRIBUTORS

Joji Arai has been in charge of the United States Office of the Japan Productivity Center since 1971. Prior to joining the Center as Assistant Manager in 1965, he worked as an escort/interpreter for the Agency for International Development in Washington, D.C. Arai has conducted seminars throughout the United States and has appeared on network television, including the NBC White Paper, "If Japan Can—Why Can't We," and "Economic Strategies for the 1980s" for CBS. He has contributed numerous articles to professional and technical journals.

Ernst R. Berndt is an applied microeconomist who specializes in the economic theory of cost and production, productivity, energy demand modelling, and empirical econometrics. In addition to holding the position of Professor of Applied Economics at the MIT Sloan School of Management, Berndt is a research associate at the National Bureau of Economic Research. He also serves as Associate Editor of *Resources and Energy*, the *Energy Journal*, the *Journal of Business Administration*, and the *Journal of Econometrics*.

Laurits R. Christensen is Professor of Economics at the University of Wisconsin–Madison. He has been at Wisconsin since 1967, after having received his Ph.D. at the University of California at Berkeley. From 1971 to 1973 Christensen served as a full-time consultant to the U.S. Treasury and the U.S. Bureau of Labor Statistics. Since 1976 he has split his time between the University of Wisconsin and Christensen Associates, a Madison-based

419

economic consulting firm of which he is President. Christensen has written extensively on issues related to measuring and modeling the structure of cost and production in the private sector of the economy—including numerous comparisons of productivity over time and across firms, industries, and nations. Recent studies in this genre have appeared in the *European Economic Review* and the *Quarterly Journal of Economics*.

John P. Cullity is Professor of Economics at the College of Arts and Sciences and the Graduate Faculty at Rutgers—the State University, Newark. He is also a research associate at the Center for International Business Cycle Research at the Graduate School of Business, Columbia University. He was formerly Director of the Graduate Program in Economics and Chairman of the Economics Department at Rutgers in Newark. He received his graduate training and degrees at Columbia. He has published articles and reviews, mainly in the area of economic growth and cycles, in numerous professional and business journals including the *Zeitschrift fuer die Gesamte Staatswissenschaft, The Journal of Human Resources, The Financial Analysts Journal*, and *Business Economics*.

Edward F. Denison is Senior Fellow Emeritus in the Division of Economic Studies of The Brookings Institution. He graduated from Oberlin College in 1936 and received his Ph.D. from Brown University in 1941. Denison's national income research was mainly performed from 1941 to 1956 and from 1979 through 1981 at the Bureau of Economic Analysis of the U.S. Department of Commerce, where he served as economist, Acting Chief of the National Income Division, and Associate Director. His investigations of economic growth were conducted from 1956 to 1962 at the Committee for Economic Development, where he was Associate Director of Research, and at Brookings, with which he has been associated since 1962.

Among Denison's books are *The Sources of Economic Growth in the United States and the Alternatives Before Us, Why Growth Rates Differ*, and *How Japan's Economy Grew So Fast* (with William K. Chung). The present article is an extension of Denison's *Accounting for Slower Economic Growth*.

Charles S. Friedman received his MA and Ph.D. degrees from Columbia University. He has taught at Ithaca College, Cooper Union, and Columbia University. Dr. Friedman currently works in the International Trade Administration in the Department of Commerce, and was formerly employed in the Bureau of Economic Analysis.

Donna Jennings is on the Science and Innovation Policy Staff in the Division of Policy Research and Analysis at the National Science Foundation.

She has collaborated on a number of projects in the R&D and tax areas, including "Industrial Trends in R&D and Basic Research," and "The Economic Recovery Tax Act of 1981: A Bibliography about Effects of the Capital Cost Recovery System on Investment in Different Sectors."

Dale W. Jorgenson is currently Frederic Eaton Abbe Professor of Economics at Harvard University, where he has taught since 1969. He taught at the University of California, Berkeley, from 1959 to 1969 and has been Visiting Professor at Stanford University, the Hebrew University of Jerusalem, and Oxford University. He has also served as Ford Foundation Research Professor of Economics at the University of Chicago. Professor Jorgenson is a member of the National Academy of Sciences, the American Academy of Arts and Sciences, and the American Association for the Advancement of Science. He received the John Bates Clark Medal of the American Economic Association in 1971.

Irving B. Kravis is University Professor of Economics at the University of Pennsylvania and a research associate of the National Bureau of Economic Research. He was a contributing author of several volumes on the United Nations International Comparison Project, the latest of which was *World Product and Income: International Comparisons of Real Gross Product* (1982). Professor Kravis has previously collaborated with Robert Lipsey on publications on international trade, including *Toward an Explanation of National Price Levels* (1983).

Robert E. Lipsey is Professor of Economics at Queens College and the Graduate Center, City University of New York, and New York Director of the National Bureau of Economic Research. He is the coauthor of *Studies in the National Balance Sheet of the United States, The Financial Effects of Inflation*, and, with Irving Kravis, *Price Competitiveness in World Trade*.

Angus Maddison is Professor of Economics at the University of Groningen, Netherlands. His degrees are from Cambridge University (B.A. 1947 and M.A. 1951). He has served as a consultant to a number of governments, and was Research Director for the Twentieth Century Fund Project on Economic Policy, 1966–69. He has been Visiting Professor at Harvard University and formerly headed the OECD Central Analysis Division. Professor Maddison has written many articles and books, including *Economic Growth in the West, Economic Progress and Policy in Developing Countries*, and *Phases of Capitalist Development*.

Walter W. McMahon is Professor of Economics at the University of Illinois at Urbana–Champaign, where he specializes in macroeconomic analysis and in human capital. He did his graduate work at the London School of Economics and the University of Iowa. He has had visiting appointments at various times at the Brookings Institution, the London School of Economics, INSEE in Paris, and the Institute of Economic and Social Research in Stockholm. He has served on National Academy of Sciences missions to Indonesia, Singapore, and Thailand, concerned with the education and manpower planning for transfer of science and technology for economic development. His most recent book is *Financing Education: Overcoming Inefficiency and Inequity*. Recent articles include "Expected Returns to Investment in Higher Education," *Journal of Human Resources*, and "Why Families Invest in Education" in Seymour Sudman, ed., *The Collection and Analysis of Economic and Consumer Behavior Data*.

Ted Mills is Chairman of the Board of the Washington-based American Center for the Quality of Work Life, a nonprofit organization devoted to the advocacy and creation of QWL action projects in unionized organizations which he founded in 1973. From 1971 to 1973, Mr. Mills was Special Assistant for Productivity to Dr. C. Jackson Grayson, Jr., Chairman of the Price Commission. He is formerly president of Ted Mills Associates and Information Management International and Executive Producer for NBC Television. Among his published works are: "Quality of Work Life: A Clear and Present Danger," *Planning Review*; "Industrial Democracy in Europe: An American Response," *Harvard Business Review*, and *Industrial Democracy*.

Geoffrey H. Moore is Director of the Center for International Business Cycle Research, Graduate School of Business, Columbia Univerity. He is Director-at-Large of the National Bureau of Economic Research and was on the staff of the National Bureau from 1939 to 1979. He served as Commissioner of Labor Statistics, U.S. Department of Labor, from 1969 to 1973. In addition, he has taught at New York University and Columbia University, was a Senior Research Fellow at Stanford University's Hoover Institution and is presently an Adjunct Scholar at the American Enterprise Institute. Mr. Moore is the author of numerous articles and several books. The second edition of his *Business Cycles, Inflation and Forecasting* appeared in 1983.

Richard Nelson received his B.A. from Oberlin College, and his Ph.D. in Economics from Yale University. After his classwork at Yale he spent a year as a postdoctoral fellow at MIT studying engineering. For many years he was with the RAND Corporation, where he conducted research in the fields of technical change, economic development, and a variety of other public policy issues. Professor Nelson has taught at Oberlin College, Carnegie Institute of Technology, and since 1968, at Yale University. He is presently Professor of Economics, and Director of the Institution for Social and Policy Studies at Yale. His most recent publications include (with Sidney Winter) *An Evolutionary Theory of Economic Change*, and (as editor) *Government and Technical Progress: A Cross Industry Analysis*.

Rolf Piekarz is on the Science and Innovation Policy Staff in the Division of Policy Research and Analysis at the National Science Foundation. He is a political economist and received his doctorate from the Johns Hopkins University. Dr. Piekarz has published papers and edited studies in science and technology policy and in international economic policy. His recent publications include *Technology, International Economics, and Public Policy*, and *International Economic Policy Research*.

George Psacharopoulos is Head of the Education Research Unit at the World Bank. He holds a Ph.D. in economics from the University of Chicago. Most of his professional career has been spent at the London School of Economics, where he taught between 1969 and 1981, and he has served as a consultant to many governments and international organizations on matters of economics of education, manpower planning, employment, and income distribution. He is best known for his books *Returns to Education: An International Comparison*, and *Earnings and Education in OECD Countries*.

Theodore W. Schultz is currently Charles L. Hutchinson Distinguished Service Professor at the University of Chicago, where he has been Professor of Economics since 1943. Before coming to Chicago, he taught at Iowa State College and served as the head of the Department of Economics and Sociology. Among his many honors, Schultz is a Nobel prize winner in Economic Science (1979), a distinguished fellow of the American Economic Association since 1965, a founding member of the National Academy of Education (1965) and an Honorary Member for Life, Phi Kappa Phi (1981). Dr. Schultz has held numerous offices in non-academic organizations such as the Institute of Current World Affairs (Trustee, 1935–58) and the National Bureau of Economic Research. His most recent book is *Investing in People: The Economics of Population Quality*.

William B. Shear is a senior economist in the Resources, Community and Economic Development Division at the U.S. General Accounting Office. He received his Ph.D. in economics from the University of Chicago. His

Ph.D. dissertation, "The Urban Housing Rehabilitation Decision," won third prize honors in the 1981 Dissertation Award Competition sponsored by the American Real Estate and Urban Economics Association. He is formerly an assistant professor of economics at the George Mason University.

Eleanor Thomas is on the Science and Innovation Policy Staff in the Division of Policy Research and Analysis at the National Science Foundation. She is a biostatistician and received her doctorate from Johns Hopkins University. Dr. Thomas has authored a number of papers on the economics of R&D, including "Recent Research on R&D and Productivity Growth: A Changing Relationship Between Input and Impact Indicators," OECD Conference on Science and Technology Indicators, September 1980; and International Comparison of Enterprise Funded Research and Development in Manufacturing," in *Proceedings of a Conference on Engineering and Science Research for Industrial Development*, sponsored by the Engineering Foundation, 1977.

John K.L. Thompson is President of Lumley Associates, consultants on technology transfer. After serving in the British army, he obtained an honours degree in Physics at Durham University. In 1948, he began his career with the government, ending as Counsellor for Science and Technology at the British Embassy in Washington, 1978–83. He is a fellow of the British Institute of Management, and has received a number of awards, including Companion of the Order of St. Michael and St. George, awarded in 1982 by Her Majesty the Queen. He has lectured extensively and published a number of articles on the subjects of science and technology.

George S. Tolley is Professor of Economics at the University of Chicago. He was Deputy Assistant Secretary for Tax Policy and Director of the Office of Tax Analysis in 1974 and 1975. He is also Cochairman of the Program on Resources of the Committee on Public Policy and Director of the Center for Urban Studies at the university. He is coeditor of the journal *Resources and Energy*. Dr. Tolley has been on the faculty of North Carolina State University and Visiting Professor at the University of California and Purdue University. Prior to joining the Chicago faculty in 1966, he held an executive position in the U.S. Department of Agriculture concerned with economic development. His activities include serving on the National Academy of Sciences Committee on Water, the National Academy of Sciences Committee on Automotive Pollution, and the President's Task Force on Urban Renewal. He has served as consultant to the Ministers of Planning of Venezuela and Panama, the Ministry of Agriculture of South Korea and the International Bank.

William H. Waldorf is Chief of the Division of Productivity Research, Bureau of Labor Statistics, U.S. Department of Labor, and Professor of Economics, SUNY-Binghamton. Dr. Waldorf received his doctoral degree in Economics from the University of Chicago. He is formerly Research Head at the Economic Research Service, U.S. Department of Commerce and an econometrician at the Bureau of Economic Analysis, U.S. Department of Commerce. He has also served on a number of overseas missions in developing countries for the United Nations and the World Bank.

Edward Wolff is currently Associate Professor of Economics at New York University. He received economics degrees from Harvard College and Yale University. He has been teaching at New York University since 1974 and also worked as a research associate at the National Bureau of Economic Research from 1974 to 1977. His current research interests include the analysis of productivity growth trends in the United States, with special focus on the role of R&D and compositional effects. Professor Wolff has recently published work in the *Review of Income and Wealth* and the *Scandinavian Journal of Economics*.

ABOUT THE EDITOR

John W. Kendrick is Professor of Economics at The George Washington University and an Adjunct Scholar of the American Enterprise Institute. He has served as an economic consultant to industry and government and on advisory committees to the Department of Commerce, Office of Management and Budget, and the National Science Foundation, and was Chief Economist for the Department of Commerce in 1976–77. Kendrick received his B.A. and M.A. degrees from the University of North Carolina, and a Ph.D. at The George Washington University. His books include *Productivity Trends in the United States, Economic Accounts and Their Uses*, and *Understanding Productivity.*